author of
the word on **the street**

the liberator

rob lacey

ZONDERVAN™

GRAND RAPIDS, MICHIGAN 49530 USA

ZONDERVAN.COM/
AUTHOR**TRACKER**

ZONDERVAN™

The Liberator
Copyright © 2006 by Rob Lacey

Requests for information should be addressed to:
Zondervan, *Grand Rapids, Michigan 49530*

Library of Congress Control Number: 2005934466

ISBN-10: 0-310-25817-0
ISBN-13: 978-0-310-25817-9

This edition printed on acid-free paper.

As of the date of publication, the websites listed in the main text of this book were fictitious. Although some of the site names used in this book have been registered, at the time the book was written there were no live sites at these addresses.

The copyright holder's permission need not be sought for public reading/performance of this material when done on an amateur basis. For permission to read/perform the material on a professional basis, please contact Rob Lacey, Mail Box No. 238, 61 Wellfield Road, Roath, Cardiff, CF24 3DG, Wales, UK or visit www.thewordonthestreet.co.uk for more information.

All recording, radio, television and film rights are reserved.

Interior design by Rob Monacelli

Printed in the United States of America

06 07 08 09 10 11 • 18 17 16 15 14 13 12 11 10 9 8 7 6 5 4 3 2 1

Contents

Part **Three**
(Com)passion Week

Foreword

Okay, now stop. Go and get yourself a deck of those little stickies. 'Cuz this is not one of those books you're going to read and then be done with. You're going to want to mark passages, lots of passages, for revisiting, rereading and reading aloud.

Also, if you're reading this in a library or on a train or in a doctor's crowded waiting room – forget it. Read something else. With this book, you'll grin, you'll laugh and generally look foolish to strangers nearby.

Oh, and one more thing. This isn't your only copy, is it? I'm asking because once you start reading, you'll want to do two things at once: (1) read the next bit and (2) make someone else read the bit you've just marked with those stickies you went for. You're going to give this book away – more than once – better stock up from the get-go.

Translators have a phrase – "dynamic equivalent" – for when a translation is really humming. I've gotta say, Rob definitely leans toward the dynamic. As in dynamo. As in dynamite. I don't know where the guy gets his energy. Oh, wait. Yes I do. That's what this book is about.

Dr Conrad Gempf, London School of Theology

Rob Answers Some Frequently Asked Questions

So how do I use this book?

Some might say as a door stopper, but I'd like to think it will get you into the story and maybe even get some of the story into you. There are loads of ways to use it, depending on where you're coming from. Pick and mix from these four options ... and, hey, add your own!

1) Novel approach: Read the paraphrase passages right through like a novel and get a sense of the entire story – the Big Picture. Realise where Jesus was when he said some famous line you've heard before; connect with what just happened and how that influences the bit you're into now; imagine you didn't know the ending! All too often we slice it up into bite-size pieces, but we also need to get the full feast.

2) Individual study: This whole *the word on the street* project began back in 1999 when I admitted to myself that my daily Bible study had gone a bit stale on me. My hope is that this new treatment of the Jesus story will put some spark back into your time with the Bible – especially if you have a proper translation open at the same time! But not everyone has spent years buried

under Bibles, so this is also for those intrigued by the Christian faith who want to dip in and those who've newly signed up for service and are still wondering what it's all about.

3) Group discussion: Use the running commentary bits at the bottom of each page to kick-start discussion. Check out what a proper translation says and then allow these questions to encourage people to express their take on who Jesus was and what he was saying. Understand that the role of this section is to get you inside the story: provocative questions can often be mistaken for a fixed position, but my role in these sections is not all-knowing teacher, but fellow seeker. Thrash it out late into the night, but don't sue me for sleep deprivation!

4) Public readings/performance: Get the words off the page and onto the stage! Flesh them out with voice and body! Eternal truths in black and white are fine, but flesh-coloured is even better. Read a bit as part of your sermon, recite something during worship, perform the stories in public spaces – this is how the stories of antiquity became memorized before they were ever written up. Use the comments as director's notes to get you inside the head of the character you're portraying – even if it's just part of a sermon!

Another idea would be to focus in on one of the "interviews" and get inside the head of one of the people who encountered Jesus. Maybe role-play other characters in the same story or other stories. Liberate these first century people from the restrictions of the page and allow them to discuss, argue and agree or disagree about what it all means. Take characters I've not interviewed and chew over what they might have said. Be honest about your reaction and let the story intertwine with *your* story.

And perhaps organise a 24-hour Liberator recital: set up a sponsored reading to raise money for people who need it while throwing the words out. Pray they land on "good soil"! And why not go public?! On the street – not on a plush church carpet – the acoustics are more alive!

Please note, if you're doing this on an amateur basis, you don't need to get my permission; just go for it! If you're a professional, then get in

touch about performance rights, etc. by contacting roblacey@theword
onthestreet.co.uk. Either way, let's get it off the page! And don't keep
it to yourself, e-mail me and let me know how it's gone/what happened/
what you're planning next!

Who's it for?

Like with *the word on the street* – my retelling of the whole story of the
Bible in today's language – this story of Jesus is for those who've never
read the Bible and those who've read it "too much".

On the one hand, it's got to make sense and be a page-turner for those
who'd not call themselves religious. But on the other hand, plenty
of Christians struggle to read the Bible too, so it should help bring a
fresh angle for those who would say it's gone a bit dead on them. Of
course, if people find that a more formal translation makes more sense
to them, then great! But if people find, as I did, that the more formal
text has lost its power, then my approach may have a role to play.

The great thing about story is that people take from it what they will.
My job description isn't about telling anyone what to think, it's to
bring the story alive by using today's language. I've tried to fill in the
gaps behind what it would've meant back then while having a bit of
fun with applying it to today's culture.

So there should be something for everyone!

What age group d'you have in mind?

Anyone who likes a good story! This is not to be limited to use as
a youth resource or to the confines of a trendy, young adult ghetto.
Experience with this book's predecessor, *the word on the street,* is that
kids as young as 6 years old have loved having it read to them and
older people in nursing homes are ordering extra copies to give to their
mates! I've realised that what I'm doing is treating kids as adults and
treating adults as big kids! What I mean by this is, for kids, I'm not
dumbing down the vocabulary, so there's no question of them being
patronised; then for the older generations, I'm allowing myself some
creative play so that the over-earnest adult can get some chuckle
therapy.

By the time this book comes out, I'll be 43 – that's 25 years of being an adult! What I'm realising is that, despite the pressure to be "mature", it's really crucial to stay playful since this is often the door to creative expression. What does "being made in God's image" mean if we're not free to be creative? How does Jesus' talk of being childlike fit with our oh-so-sombre expression of faith? Is our joy so deep you can't even see it, or did it escape years back without us noticing?

Basically, I'm just writing what works for me and hoping that it connects across the spectrum of ages.

So, d'you see this as the proper Gospels?

Nope. Never said it was. Again, like with *the word on the street,* the same "purist alert" applies: "This is not the Bible, but it might just get you reaching for one". The paraphrased gospel passages are intended to communicate the meaning of the Scriptures to a twenty-first century reader in an engaging and entertaining way. If people are intrigued with this version of the story, I hope they'll then check it out in a proper Bible. Thus I'm probably one of the few authors who is not satisfied when people have read only his book!

So what's wrong with the King James Version?

Nothing – if you speak that language. I was brought up with the Authorised Version and I love it because I know what those archaic words mean, and I appreciate their beauty and depth. But why should we expect people to learn what is virtually a second language from way back in Shakespeare's day if they want to get into God stuff? Of course, my contemporary vocabulary can't match the richness of some words found in the good ol' KJV, but if no one's able to follow it, then they're not getting the message anyway. Again, my aim is to produce a stepping-stone to a proper Bible. No point in the Bible being the most published book in the world if it's not also the most read.

Why combine three different gospels as one story?

The gospels of Matthew, Mark and Luke are quite similar in the accounts of Jesus' life that they cover. The technical term is "the synoptic Gospels" – literally "the similar optical view Gospels" because, as the Concise Oxford Dictionary says, they "describe events from a similar point of view". This makes a harmonisation of their narratives a relatively easy process and one which provides as full a version of the story as possible. It seems likely that the three biographers used similar source material and their differences lie partly in that they were just trying to connect with different audiences:

- Matthew was writing with a strong Jewish accent for the readers in Judah who would've known all the Old Testament references he quotes throughout;
- Mark's approach was to produce a quicker-pace account – like a populist blockbuster – for the dominant world culture of Roman readers; and
- Dr Luke intended to address the well-to-do individual, Theophilus, who was probably going to publish it more widely. Luke's approach was more cosmopolitan and academic: logic and order are key words for him and for his readers – all very Greek of him.

By combining the three, I'm hoping to gain the best of all the cultures – Jewish, Roman and Greek – to produce a page-turner for a society influenced by all three ... yes, ours!

Why not John too?

I love John's gospel; it's probably my personal favourite. But since it is so distinctive from the other three accounts, to build it in inevitably takes away from the flow of the story Matthew, Mark and Luke develop. John's gospel was probably written later and takes a more poetic approach to the story (probably why I love it!), but academics agree it stands apart from the other three. John's take on things is so unique, it's best dealt with separately. Who knows, maybe one day I'll get a chance to write something based on John's gospel!

Which bits are paraphrase and which bits are made up?

It's crucial that you know how to handle the different parts of the book. The verse-for-verse paraphrase is my take on what the gospel writers were getting at – technically a "meaning translation" of Scripture. My theological advisers and editors have kept me from getting carried away with adding in too many bits that aren't in the original; they've challenged my version of the text; they've chipped in their wealth of knowledge, and hopefully together we've created a responsible and meaningful paraphrase of the gospel passages.

Then there's the other stuff: All the peripheral material (the commentary, the interviews, the satirical asides), which are my creative response to the gospel stories. So, they're not meant to be relied on in the same way...

Sorry, what? You've been creative with the Scriptures?!

It's not a new thing. The approach taken in the commentary sections and the interviews with characters who encountered Jesus are inspired by the spiritual exercises of St Ignatius of Loyola from back in the sixteenth century. His big thing was to encourage people to contemplate on the stories of the Gospels and to imagine themselves in the scene and reflect on their reactions. My fictional interviews with the people who met Jesus are merely a combination of this approach with me recording my reaction in the voice of the character being interviewed. My hope is that by using my imagination to get inside the skin of the story, the actual Gospel material will spring off the page and start living. But, obviously – for the record – there were no recorded press interviews with these people; there was no publication called *Jews News*. This is simply me asking one of the best questions ever ... "what if?"

And what's with the "Don't Like This?" features?

Best not go there if you've had a humour-ectomy! From more than 20 years worth of experience acting on stage, I'm convinced that one of the best ways to challenge and provoke change is to be able to laugh at ourselves – and I do mean "*our*selves". Most of what I'm satirising here is my own reaction to the more challenging aspects of Jesus and his story. Let's face it, we all find ways of wriggling out of applying what

Jesus teaches. So please read these bits while imagining a glint in the
eye of the guy writing it!

How did you decide which bits to tackle?

You might think I've just picked the bits I like and pasted them
together in an order which suits me. But no, I've left those choices to
fully qualified academics, basing the chronology on Robert L. Thomas
and Stanley N. Gundry's book, *The NIV Harmony of the Gospels* (Harper-
Collins, 1988), which is a reworking of an older book by John A
Broadus and AT Robertson. Of course, no one knows exactly where
and when all this stuff happened; Matthew, Mark and Luke are each
standing in different places and speaking to different audiences, so
there's bound to be some differences in their accounts. When it came
to an event that more than one, or possibly all three biographers tack-
led, then I simply chose the fullest version available.

One example is the Sermon on the Mount. Matthew places this talk
on a mountainside, while Luke writes up very similar lines but sets the
location on a "level place". What's up with that – contradiction? Probably not. It's more likely that either Jesus gave the same talk in two
different places or there was a level plateau halfway up the mountain.
So both Matthew and Luke were right. In Chapter 5 you'll see me cut
back and fore between the two so as to provide the most well-rounded
account of Jesus' famous talk. Check out the index of passages at the
back of the book if you want to look up where I dealt with the bit
you're looking for or which equivalent bit I did instead.

What theological backup did you have?

Apart from two excellent Zondervan editors, Amy Boucher Pye and
Ben Irwin, we also constructed the theological safety net of two
professional academics – Dr David Trobisch from Bangor Theological
Seminary, Maine, USA and Dr Conrad Gempf of the London School of
Theology, UK. These "academic antagonists" ensured that my creative
approach to Scripture was never allowed to fly off unchallenged into
the territory of the right brain. The aim throughout has been to com-
bine left and right brain approaches to emulate the central character
of the gospel stories – Jesus himself – and find an accessible and non-

elitist form of communication which engages people of all levels of intellect and education.

I'm told that the Greek of the New Testament is often called *koine* or "common" Greek. It wasn't the polished language used by the educated elite. So, when it was first published, those fluent in the intellectual Greek of ancient philosophy looked down their noses at it. But the writers were determined that it would be grasped by normal people, not just those privileged enough to understand the language of the universities. Again, I've attempted to speak my natural language – the language of normal people – in producing an accessible version of Matthew, Mark and Luke's gospels. My hope is that it'll inspire you to answer the question, "what have we made of Jesus?" and perhaps even, "what have *you* made of Jesus?"

When you wrote *the word on the street* you were ill with cancer, how are you doing now?

As we go to press it has been more than three years since getting the all clear from the bladder cancer which had spread into the lymph nodes and into the bones. But, after three years clear, I'm told the cancer's back in the bladder and a couple of lymph nodes. The medics held their hands up last time admitting that it wasn't their treatment which got me back up and performing/swimming/working/playing, so we're looking to download some of The Liberator's healing this time around. As ever, marinating myself in Scripture when facing tests and juggling pain control pills has been a lifeline to health – if not in body, then certainly in mind and spirit.

The Story So Far...

First off, nothing ... but God.

Second off, God says the word and WHAP!

Stuff everywhere!

God loves it. "Fantastic! Heaven on Earth!"

But the snake does some word twisting.

Adam and Eve fall for it, and God kicks them out of their messed up world.

Death strolls in, and top of the human wish list is liberation...

But when?

How?

Who?

They make babies and world population stats increase.

As does the mess.

So God shouts, "Water world!"

And only Noah and company survive the flood.

Press Restart.

More babies.

Then the first Jew: Abraham...

and his boys Isaac, Jacob and Joseph.

Joseph "Dreamboy" Jacobson gets carted off to Egypt mid-famine

and saves the Jewish Nation from a strict starvation diet.

Four hundred years on, the Jews are just slave labour for Pharaoh

till God waves them out of Egypt via ten plagues.

Moses downloads the Big Ten Rules ... they mess up on all ten.

Grumbling round the desert for 40 years.

Joshua gets them into a land with milk and honey on draught.

Occupied by "absolute Philistines"

who pick 'n' mix their idols as suits the mood.

"These days, with no King to call the shots, everyone does their own thing."

"If it feels good, just do it!"

What a mess!

Enter King David:

Famous for flooring the giant Goliath

in between recording his "greatest hits" compilation.

His boy Solomon downloads some cracking, wise one-liners direct from God:

"Train children to click on what's right when they're young;

they'll be downloading it long after you're gone."

But he doesn't.

His pure romantic side warps,

and he ends up totally depressed – a sad, messed up old man.

Loads of history – lists of naff King after naff King messing up the people.

Elijah gives the Jews an ultimatum on Mount Carmel:

"God versus Baal: Who you going to lean on?"

They're not sure!

MESS!

Elisha can't stop the rot,

More MESS.

Amos tells them God hates their religion:

"Oh, your songs! Shut it!

What I want to hear is the roaring river of justice

sweeping through your towns."

God's patience with Israel finally runs out.

The new world superpower Babylon trashes their capital Jerusalem.

They're carted off as refugees.

Enter Daniel – defying the authorities and playing "sleepy lions".

God's telling Jeremiah, "Their names are tattooed on my palms.

I've still got plans to do them good – open, on my desk, permanent."

And God proves it by tipping off Esther,

who stops a Persian plot for a holocaust of the Jews.

Loads of Jews trek back home to Jerusalem for construction work.

But more "idol" promises wind God up.

Haggai tells them, "Stop just looking after no. 1. Sort it!"

Malachi's going, "Halve your double standards!"

But they're still giving God the butt-end of their lives.

So God stops talking to them for 400 years.

Dot

Dot

Dot

The Greeks muscle in.

Dot

Dot

Dot

Then the Romans.

Same old story: occupied territory.

Where's The Liberator?

WHERE?

Prologue

John 1:1 - 18

1-2

Nothing. No light, no time, no substance, no matter – the Voice was there.

Before anything moved, mutated or mated, Jesus, "God's Voice", was there with God from the kickoff.

How come?

'Cos Jesus, "God's Voice", is God. Before anything began, they had always been. Before there was even anywhere to be, they were there.

3-5

Jesus got the name "God's Voice" because he just spoke and stuff started. From nothing to everything, sparked only by the Voice. There's nothing that doesn't have the phrase "made by Jesus" stamped on it somewhere. His words were life itself, and they lit up people's lives. His light could blast its way into the dingiest corner, and yet the people who preferred darkness still missed it.

6-9

So God sends John Baptizer to raise Jesus' profile: to lift up the light. His job spec doesn't exactly fill a page, it just reads: "Help people take it in and take it on". Obviously, John's not the light; he's just there to build expectation and commentate when the genuine article makes his entrance and starts lighting things up.

10-13

And when he does? Bizarre! No one recognizes him! He speaks them into existence, but they don't recognize him or his voice. He arrives at the front door of his people, and most don't even peek out of the spy hole to check. The few who take the risk realize who he is, open up and knock a meal together. To these guys he starts doling out adoption papers to sign them up as God's children. Conceived by *human* passion? No, by *God's* passion!

14

So God's Voice gets flesh and blood, skin and bone. He spends time with us; we hang around with him, get to know him, see what he's like. And? As magnificent, as superb as you'd expect God's only Son to be ... and heaps more! God's over-the-top gifts oozing from every pore. Everything he does and says rings true.

15-18

Like John Baptizer says, "Yeah, I hit the headlines first, but *he's* the one you should get excited about. He was around well before me." And because he was so stuffed full of good stuff, we've benefited – big time. Okay, Moses gave us the Contract, but Jesus The Liberator gave us God's gifts and God's truth – loads better. Who's seen God? No one. But we've seen his only Son, Jesus, and you don't get closer than that.

Part 1

Who Is He?

Chapter One

And Finally...

Exclusive? Luke 1:1-4

1-2

Okay, so I'm not slapping the word "EXCLUSIVE" all over the front cover – I'm not the first! There's plenty of other bios (authorised and unauthorised) flying up the bestseller lists. Other authors have published their take on how ancient predictions have come to life in the Here and Now with us – most of them reliable transcriptions from eyewitnesses and accredited storytellers who can say, hand on heart, looking you straight in the eye, "I was there."

[Luke 1:1] "Authorised" would be Dr Luke's version, Matt's account, Mark's take on Pete's story and then, much later, John's account. "Unauthorised" would be more dodgy versions supposedly from Thomas, Mary Mag, and plenty of other sensationalised, semi-fictional accounts of what might've possibly happened; some of them should be called the Jostick-Gnostic Gospels. Not that anyone would mess with the text today, surely!

[Luke 1:1 – 2] Where do we get the word "authorised" from – if it's written by an author, then it's ... erm ... "authorised", no?

[1] **God Reps = Priests.** The "go between" for God and his people – not to be mistaken for the "get-in-between". Years back, this guy named Aaron was the very first God Rep, and since then only his family line was eligible for the post.

[2] **Religious HQ = Temple.** Jerusalem's focal point of the Jewish Religion. Literally a house for God. Question is, how much does God get let out?

[3] **Purest Place = The Holy of Holies.** The heart of the Religious HQ complex: the inner sanctum. Off-limits for all but the most devoted and then only once a year on a rota basis!

3 – 4

So since I'm well into this and have read around the subject, soaking myself in research, it rings true for me to lay down for you a definitive bio for you great Godloving readers: the What, Where, When, How and Why of the whole story. So you'll be convinced that the stuff you've been taught is watertight.

Here goes...

Expecting Luke 1:5 – 25

5 – 7

Old man Zechariah is standing beside one of a series of huge billboards with the giant-sized image of Herod the Great keeping Judea's throne warm.

Quick Bio on Zechariah: One of the God Reps[1] – part of Aaron's family tree, on the branch of the Abijah family. His missus, Elizabeth, could also claim an Aaron family surname. Both of them genuinely good people in God's eyes, living in line with the Maker's Instruction Manuals. The bad news? Their branch of the family tree is about to get lopped off; Elizabeth can't conceive. Plus, they're both clocking up the years.

8 – 10

It's Zechariah's 15 minutes of fame, the Mount Everest moment of his God Rep career.

It's his group's shift at the Religious HQ[2] and the old God Rep dice have landed on his name – he's "randomly" picked out to do the incense-burning honours in God's Purest Place[3].

[Luke 1:3 – 4] The dignitary Dr Luke was writing to was a Greek name: "Theophilus." Literally, Mr God Lover.

[Luke 1:7] In first century Near East, pre-PC days, couples who can't moan about the stress of the school run are treated like they're virtually disabled. The standard knee-jerk reaction was, "No Kids = No Values". Back then, they were convinced it was God's way of saying, "Not best pleased with you!" Course we know that God's not like that, don't we?!

His colleagues, the public, everyone – they're all outside, in deep conversation with God.

It's now! His big moment. He moves into the Purest Place to burn the incense to God.

11-13

Old Zech's doing the stuff when God's top angel is standing there to the right of the Incense Altar. Zechariah's freaked! He's frozen with fear, but the angel gives it, "Whoa! Don't panic, Zechariah. The top item on your wish list to God has been stamped with the word 'ACTION' and signed off by God. Your wife, Elizabeth, is going to have your baby boy. His name? John.

14-15

"He'll be a joy-factory for you and his birthday will be party time for so many. God'll look at him and always see the caption "Great" large in the frame. He'll be teetotal – no beer, wine or spirits. He'll be crammed full of the Holy Spirit. From manhood? No. From childhood? No. From birth? No. Get this: from conception!

16-17

"He'll round up so many Jews and bring them back to God their Boss. He'll clear the way for God; it'll be an action-replay of old Elijah, turning dads' hearts back to their kids, turning rebels' ears back to the wise words of their right-living advisors. He'll get people ready for God the Boss to show."

[Luke 1:11] Question is . . . does Zechariah dare to wonder if God's speaking to them again?

God's voice has been on mute for 400 years! No couriers, no memos, no nothing. Check out God's last words of the Old Testament in a proper Bible. The last memo before God pressed pause was Malachi 4:5 – 6.

So what's the message now? Is it a mobilisation order for the underground insurgents to rise up and overthrow their Roman Oppressors? Is it the rallying call for the people's revolution? Nope, it's that Zech's going to be a dad!

18

But Zechariah comes back at Gabriel and asks, "And you can prove this? Face it, I'm not exactly just out of college, and my missus is no teenager either!"

19-20

The angel lays into him. "Have you any idea who I am?! Gabriel's the name. I've got an all-access pass to God's heaven! I'm delivering this message to you personally! And you have the nerve to interrogate me? You won't say one more word until all this has played out its natural course and the baby's gurgling away."

21-22

Shift scenes to God's Religious HQ, just outside the Purest Place. The crowd are nudging each other, raising their eyebrows, palms, shoulders asking, "What's keeping him?"

He steps out, and all he can do is mime. They realise, "It's some sort of visitation." "He's had a vision!"

23-25

Zechariah ties up the loose ends and clocks off duty. He goes home. Then Elizabeth gets pregnant, but keeps it on the quiet for five months. But she's convinced, "God's done this for me. He's proved he's for me by operating his shame-ectomy procedure and giving me my baby. From now on no one will look down at 'Old-Mrs-No-Kids'."

Luke 1:26-38

26-28

Second time in six months, God sends his top angel on an "overseas" trip: Gabriel picks up his work order for the day. It reads, "Destination:

[Luke 1:23 – 25] Would Elizabeth's Psalm 23:1 read, "The Lord is my Gynaecologist … he leads me besides broken waters…"!?

[Luke 1:24] So why does she keep it to herself? She must've been bursting to tell her neighbours, family, anyone – she's pregnant! At her age!

[Luke 1:26 – 28] Does God have "bad books"?

Nazareth, Galilee County. Contact: Mary, fiancée to Joseph Davidson. Special note: she's a virgin."

Gabriel wings it up to Nazareth and hits Mary with the line, "Hi! D'you know what? You're in God's good books! God's with you."

29 – 33

Mary's emotions are churned up, thoughts flying round her brain trying to get a grip on what's going on. But Gabriel cuts across her short circuiting thoughts with, "Whoa! Don't panic! Like I say, you're in God's good books. Here's the plotline: you'll get pregnant, have a baby boy, call him Jesus, he'll be Great! Like, Son-of-God Great. Like, Invited-To-Sit-On-David's-Throne-By-God-Himself-Great. Like, Running-Jacob's-Whole-Family-Line-Of-Jews Great. Like, No-'Best Before'-Date-On-His-New-Nation Great. We're talking Divine God level of Great. We're talking none other than The Liberator."

34

Mary comes back asking, "Uh ... er ... um ... exactly ... uh ... how am I to have a baby? You know I'm a virgin, yeah?"

35 – 37

Gabriel tells her, "It'll all be down to God's Holy Spirit: you'll conceive under his shadow. The Pure Child you'll give birth to will go by the title 'God's Divine Son'.

[Luke 1:28] How does Gabriel manage to relate to both ends of the generational spectrum? Mary could've been as young as 13. Bit of a gap from his last official visit to Old Man Zech. Does he change his approach? Or just tell it like it is?

[Luke 1:29] Were Isaiah's words on the tip of her tongue? Didn't every Jew know the classic line predicting The Liberator? (Isaiah 7:14 in a proper Bible): "Therefore none other than God Himself will give you the stomping great big clue: A virgin will get pregnant, she'll give birth to a son, and she'll call him God-With-Us."

[Luke 1.29 – 33] Was Gabriel wishing he'd brought his lead trumpet from the band for this announcement? Or did he deliberately choose to underplay the Big News?

[Luke 1:34] So how come Old Zech got "muted" for answering back to an angel and Mary gets off scot-free? Or does Gabriel pick up a difference in tone, gesture or body language? Or is it 'cos she's only about 13?

The Jews News Interviews

Local girl in miracle baby claim!

The locals up in Nowheresville Nazareth are up in arms over a teenage pregnancy with a difference. The mum-to-be, Mary Davidson, is making the controversial claim of what some are calling Divine Insemination. Outraged neighbours are calling for Ms Davidson to be stoned, but others think there might be something to her "miracle baby" story. We talked to the girl at the centre of the controversy.

JN — Mary, thanks for giving us this exclusive. Well! What's it feel like?

MD — Weird! Wonderful! Both … somehow at the same time. I mean, what Jewish girl hasn't brushed her hair while dreaming of being pregnant with The Liberator? I mean, most pregnant women wonder what their child will be. Boy or girl? Rich? Famous? But it's weird actually *knowing*! It's a boy and he's the one to liberate us.

JN — From the Roman Occupying Forces, right?

MD — If that's the big thing we need liberating from then, yes, I guess that's top of God's list.

JN — So are you ready for all the celebrity? Your life's not going to be the same. You know that don't you?

MD — No, I suppose not. It's not really sunk in yet.

JN — And it won't all be "congrats, Mary". Are you aware of the gossip flying round which, shall we say, questions the parentage of your little baby?

MD—Yes, it hurts, but I can't stop it. I'm not exactly going to make this up, am I? Not when it's just asking to be labelled a ... well, you know what. Not when they're going to call my boy a, uh ... all sorts of names!

JN—And, we hear it's all the rage in your family, this "miracle baby" thing?

MD—Yes, my cousin Elizabeth's also expecting, also a boy! She's, like, oh, fifty or sixty years older than me – I've never asked – so hers is just a bit amazing as well. I just hope she's not feeling as sick in the mornings as I am! Not at her age! Something's really going on.

JN—Yes, but *she's* married. And her hubby's not exactly a toy boy either! How's it been with the hardliners campaigning to have you, uh, dealt with by The Good Book?

MD—Well, I switch: sometimes I'm scared stupid; sometimes I get this image of stones flying at my skull and they've got my name on each one. But I've got to try and pull the plug on that. Most times I just think if God's got plans for the boy, then who's going to damage the mum? Then the stones seem to curve past me, like I've got some sort of force field or there are angel bodyguards throwing themselves in front of me and taking the fire.

JN—You're a brave girl. And how d'you see the nipper dealing with the inevitable playground rumours and nicknames?

MD—I have thought of that. Nothing's private in a village this small. And kids are cruel, but he'll know he's special. And maybe the bullying will be the making of him: help him get inside the head of picked on people. Maybe it's all part of the plan, if he's going to liberate us from the Roman bullies.

Don't Like This? [Matthew 1:1 – 17] Just skip it. Most do. Say, "Who needs family history? Just give me action."

"What about your cousin Elizabeth?" Gabriel asks. "And how old is she? Yes, Elizabeth, who's had to carry the label 'Old-Mrs-No-Kids' – now six months and showing! Proof that God's vocab. doesn't include the word 'impossible'."

38

"I'm at God's service!" Mary says to him. "Bring it on, bring it all on! Just like you said."

Gabriel leaves, mission accomplished.

"Family Tree" Matthew 1:1-17

1

For the record: "The Family Tree of Jesus 'Liberator' Davidson. True Jew. Abraham's Boy."

2-6

Abraham Terahson is Isaac Abrahamson's dad, who is Jacob Isaacson's old man, who is called "Papa" by Judah Jacobson and his 11 brothers. Judah marries foxy Ms Tamar and they become ma and pa to the Judahson boys, Perez and Zerah. Perez calls his nipper Hezron, who calls his lad Ram, who goes for the name Amminadab when he has kids. Amminadab Ramson lands on the name Nahshon, who grows up to have Salmon, who gets together with that (in)famous lady

[Luke 1:36] Did Mary not know Elizabeth was pregnant till Gabriel spilt the beans? Did this miracle turbo drive her conviction levels?

[Matthew 1:1 – 6] Anyone with a Jewish head would be replaying great stories of most of these characters. They're more than names; they're bedtime stories; they're playground role plays; they're Saturday School tales told by their favourite class teacher. It's like the Jewish mind has a whole series of drop-down menus from which they can select scores of great stories (blockbusters, soaps, epics) and song lyrics from their proud national heritage. Surnames are important these days.

[Matthew 1:5] Hey, how come there are women in this family tree? Isn't that a bit PC for these times? Maybe in Greco-Roman culture, but not in their culture! And what women?! Iffy or what? Tamar was a Canaanite, Rahab was a prostitute, Ruth was also a non-Jew and Uriah's widow Bathsheba was involved in an extra-marital affair with King David. What sort of God uses such dodgy people to produce a New United Nation of Israel?

[4] **Eviction** = **Exile**. Posh word for "kicked out" from the Hebrew verb "to uncover" or "to remove" into captivity. "Home" was a big word back then too.

Rahab to produce Boaz. And it's foreign girl Ruth who lands Boaz and they call their lad Obed. This is the Obed who grows up to have a nipper called Jesse who is granddad to King David's children when the famous King marries Uriah's widow and has Solomon Davidson with her.

7 – 11

Solomon is paternal unit to Rehoboam, who's daddy to Abijah, who likes the name Asa for his baby boy, who goes for the longer name of Jehoshaphat for his offspring (which can be shortened to Jeho if the boy thinks it suits him better). Jeho (shaphat) gives his boy the option of having the same shortened name as his dad by calling him Jehoram, who obviously doesn't like it 'cos he calls his little one Uzziah. Uzziah has a tot and calls him Jotham, Jotham has an Ahaz, Ahaz has a Hezekiah, who brings up Manasseh, who raises Amon, who does his bit to make Josiah, who produces Jeconiah and all his brothers. Quick time check? We've arrived at the Babylon Eviction[4] (around 600 BC). Fast forward 70 years...

12 – 16

Once they're back home we pick it up with Jeconiah having baby Shealtiel, who grows up to have Zerubbabel, who fathers an Abiud, who sires an Eliakim, who produces Azor, who creates a Zadok, who makes an Akim, who names his ankle biter Eliud, who's always liked the name Eleazar, who chose Matthan for his crumb-crusher, who went retro with the name Jacob for his kid, who followed suit with the name Joseph for his little man, who got engaged to Mary who gave birth to Jesus Josephson ... aka Jesus Davidson ... aka The Liberator.

[Matthew 1:7 – 11] But it's all sliding downhill from here: Again the Jewish mind throws out graphic images of this era ending with Jewish slaves being carted off to Babylon City. Horrific scenes of the history-changing national disaster – which you'd not want to maximise to full screen – sending a shiver down any Jewish spine. Not the most visited part of the Heritage Programme, but a vital time in their history.

[Matthew 1:12 – 16] The Jewish mind gets to feel more positive with these roll calls: King Cyrus of Persia "liberating" the Jews and letting the people buy a single ticket back to Jerusalem. With Zerubbabel rebuilding the rubble of Jerusalem and the Nation getting back to something approaching Solomon's "good ol' days".

Don't Like This? [Luke 1:39-41] All this baby leaping malarkey! Call it coincidence or old/young wives' tales! Work out the statistical chances of this happening and then snort in a derisory fashion. Build in favourable assumptions about baby John being an active baby in the womb, which would increase the random chance of him leaping on Mary's entrance. That should just about scupper the spooky inference that the foetal John "sensed" Jesus enter the room. Yeah, as if!

17

So, 14 generations of a family tree from Nowheresville with Father Abraham to the Great Kingdom of David. Then 14 generations diving back down from David to the ultimate low of the Babylon Eviction. Then 14 generations from the end of the Eviction up to The Liberator.

Mums united Luke 1:39-45

39-41

Mary packs her necessaries and heads south (70 miles/110 km) to Zechariah's house in the sleepy hill towns of Judea. She makes straight for her cousin and says, "Hey! Cuz!"

Elizabeth hears Mary's voice and inside her, pre-baby John nearly leaps through the wall of his mother's womb. Elizabeth's filled to spilling point with the Holy Spirit.

42-45

She's splurting out, volume cranked right up, "How happy are you?! Of all women, just how ecstatic must you be?! How special is this tiny baby inside you?! But whoa, how big is this? You come to me! The mother of my God comes round to my place? The second I heard your voice, baby John did cartwheels to kick off the party! You are so happy to be convinced of what God has said will happen."

Mary's big single Luke 1:46-55

46

Mary improvises and says, "My soul is a magnifying glass for God.

47-55

"My spirit is a joy-machine working overtime for God my Liberator.

It's like he's only thinking of me!

It's like he's only focused on me his worker, his menial task coworker.

From here on in, history will mark me down as the happy Mrs Happy of Happyville.

[Luke 1:41] Does baby John hear Mary's voice, or does he sense cousin Jesus is only yards away – just the other side of two sets of skin?!

For the Potent God has worked incredible things for me. He's purity itself. He's outstanding!

Ah ... the way he gives out the slack – for the young, the middle aged, the old, all the generations – all the nations for respecting him.

Ah ... the way he waves his hand and the draught blows the arrogant off the scene for neglecting him.

Ah ... the way he pulls thrones from under the rear ends of kings.

The way he escorts the modest into high profile things.

Ah ... the way he nourishes the poor, those wasting away, with food that gives life.

The way he shows the rich the door, how he waves the rich away from the buffet of life.

The way he's always been with Israel – giving out so much slack, from today right back to Abraham and his boys, right down to now, right down to ever, and farther.

The way he said he would, to our fathers.

The way he said he would, to our fathers."

56

Mary settles in at Elizabeth's for about three months.

Then she goes back up north, to home.

Don't Like This? [Luke 1:46-55] Just harden yourself to the emotive power of music. Write it off as manipulation through the overuse of the string section. Even better, conveniently forget that this is poetry and interpret everything literally, which makes it suitably unbelievable!

[Luke 1:47-55] No, Mary's not some 13-year-old singer/songwriter prodigy. Rather, she's adapting a song she'd have known well from Saturday School at the local religious HQ in Nazareth. She's improvising around some classic words of poetry from 1,000 years back by Hannah – like Elizabeth, another lady with infertility struggles in pre-IVF days. Hannah got her "miracle baby" – Samuel, kingmaker for David, 1,000 years before. And now Mary's expecting the ultimate "miracle baby" – The Liberator himself. So she's playing around with Hannah's words and injecting them with energy and exhilaration. For the original lyrics, check out 1 Samuel 2:1 – 11 in a proper Bible.

⁵ **Local Religious HQ=Synagogue.** Local meeting place for Religious Jews to worship their God. Central point of any Jewish community.

John's delivery Luke 1:57-66

57-58

Soon after Mary leaves, Elizabeth's baby's due. She has the boy, and it's party time! All the locals – extended family, neighbours, the whole community – are bubbling over with the way God's given Elizabeth a break. They're thrilled for her.

59-60

One week and one day later, they're at the circumcision ceremony in the local religious HQ⁵. The order of service is all written up with the family name "Zechariah Abijahson" written into the space for the "BABY'S NAME".

Elizabeth blurts out, "No! Wait. Sorry, um, his name's going to be ... well ... John, actually!"

61

"John?! John?!" they blurt out. "Who in the whole dynasty of Aaron has ever been called something as, well, sorry, but common as ... John?"

62-64

They make signs to the baby's dad to get his take on it. Zechariah's miming, "Notepad, bring NOTEPAD. Urgency!"

And with multiple chins hitting the HQ stone floor he writes, "H-i-s n-a-m-e i-s J-O-H-N."

On the final stroke of the letter "N" his mouth's in gear again, and he's spouting off about how brilliant God is.

[Luke 1:59 – 60] Babies have always been named after cultural heroes – it's just that there weren't so many Old Testament couriers called Britney or Justin back then.

[Luke 1:60] Outrageous! Okay, so she's a "woman of a certain age", but it's still out of line for a woman to speak out and name the child. But what's she to do, when her husband's tongue-tied?

[Luke 1:62] What's with the sign language? Was Zechariah deaf as well as mute? Seems that way.

[Luke 1:62 – 64] Wondering if Zechariah tried to mime the name "John" before he went for the notepad option. Particularly iffy for the North American reader!

[6] **God's Courier = Prophet.** Personal message delivery service direct from God. Think any package delivery corporation, but think "quick". Although, thinking about it, with their record, the depot for uncollected packages would've been pretty chocka by the end of the Old Testament.

65 – 66

The locals are blown away and the rumours bounce around the hill towns of Judea like billiard balls. Everyone who hears the news chews it over with the incisors of the heart: typical lines are variations on, "Who's this lad going to be?" 'Cos, no question, God's got his vision locked onto this boy – to do him good!

Zech's big release Luke 1:67 – 80

67

John's dad, Zechariah, is bursting out with Holy Spirit energy. He gushes,

68 – 69

"Celebrate God, Israel's God:

'Cos he's bought back his people from their liberty loss.

He's turned up and shown the people-stealers who's Boss.

He's bought back his people from the confidence shakers, the hostage takers.

He's gone to great lengths to erect a great symbol of strength.

Plastered it all over hoards of billboards around David's place.

A strong symbol of Liberation: blatant, strong and in-yer-face.

70

"(God's old couriers[6] hand them the mic; let them say what they like. They'll say, 'Hey, we told you, told you it'd be this way!')

[Luke 1:67] What might Zech have blurted out? Possibly, "Listen, all I did was ask a question!" Or "Right, now you listen to my side of the story." Or even, "I'm suing that Gabriel for defamation of character. Especially if this ever gets written up into a book!"

But no, only good things to say!

[Luke 1:68] Is Zech some stream-of-consciousness lyricist? Is he a creative genius who can write top song lyrics off the hoof? Maybe, but like with Mary's song, this could be him improvising around standard phrases – creating a remix version of previously released material from old time poets. Check out Isaiah 9:1 – 7 in a proper Bible for the sort of cracking lines that would've been a major musical influence on Zech the singer/ songwriter.

Don't Like This? [Luke 1:68-79] Easy to write off as over-the-top song lyrics. Even better, just get off on the tune and ignore the lyrics – they'll mostly bi-pass your brain. A slight risk of subliminal influence, but this is marginal.

71

"Liberation – from the nation that occupies, the nations that tyrannise.

Freedom – from the grabbing hands from foreign lands.

72 – 77

"All designed to remind us of promises, contracts with our history, with the forefathers of you and me.

The promises he made on oath with his main man Abraham.

Promises of respite, of civil liberties despite our enemies.

Promises of Religious freedom, of license to burn our incense in purity and integrity.

And here, baby John, you bundle of potential:

You'll move on to help people take it in and take it on;

You'll step up to become a League Number One courier of God.

You'll be the trailer, the compeer, the emcee to build expectancy, to get agnostics off the shelf, off the fence, before the main act – God himself makes it all make sense.

You'll be an educator, running crash courses in Liberty, workshops in Being Free.

You'll be an instigator, sorting out their mess by getting people saying yes to God.

78 – 79

"All this because the tenderness of God goes easy on our mess.

His scorching sun rises and compromises the shadow of death's dark cowl.

His rising sun warms away our cold, dark world with heaven's rays, and guides our wandering ways onto paths of peace.

Guides our wandering ways onto paths of pure release."

80

As the boy John notches up the inches on the doorframe, his height is only outgrown by his spiritual stature. He makes his HQ out in the wasteland until it ticks around to "going public time".

The Jews News Interviews

Old Man Zech breaks his silence

It's some people's secret wish—a Religious Leader with nothing to say! But in Zechariah Abijahson's case, it was an angel visitation which struck him dumb. Now the new dad's got his voice back, so we sent Ben Fischer to see what he had to say.

JN—So Rabbi, you were unable to speak for more than six months after a freak happening in the religious HQ! Tell us about it.

ZA—Well I won the toss to go into the HQ proper. I'm doing the stuff and, weird, I'm not alone. I look round and there's this—I don't know—guy: big shining, telling me Liz is going to be pregnant.

JN—And you said...?

ZA—Well, I made some wise crack and that was the last line for about six months.

JN—So, let's get this straight. You were in the hot spot of Religious HQ and you didn't expect God to talk to you.

ZA—Well, no I...

JN—And even when you saw a heavenly messenger you still weren't convinced?

ZA—No. It'd been over four hundred years since any one had heard anything so... I just didn't...

JN—And then baby John comes along and your lips unzip?

ZA—Yes. And I'm a different guy!

JN—So I suppose you're talking 24/7 now, yes?

ZA—Well, no, actually. It's not a bad discipline to be forced to shut up —it's like an extended silent retreat. Can't tell you the number of times in the last nine months where I would've given someone the benefits of my learning, only to think, later, what an intrusion it would've been. When you really think things through from every angle, you often take a totally different tack from your first knee-jerk ideas.

JN—So will you be going back to all your parishioners with some well-thought-through advice for them?

ZA—Some, but I won't be going to most of them, since actually all they wanted was someone to tell—get things off their chest, feel listened to. They've probably worked it out themselves by now.

JN—So you'd recommend this for all Religious Leaders then?

ZA—Well, I wouldn't advise anyone to talk back to an angel, especially not Gabriel himself! I think I got off lightly – could've been much worse. What *was* I thinking?

JN—Thanks for the tip.

Chapter Two

Christmas Presence

Two teenagers in love Matthew 1:18-25

18-19

So, how'd it happen? Baby Jesus. The Liberator? You ready for this?
I'll tell you: his mum, Mary, is engaged to Joe. They'd not had sex
yet – but – weird! She's pregnant. And it's courtesy of the Holy Spirit.

Pull focus onto Joe – a good guy, trying to do the right thing, and
he's desperate to keep this news off the grapevine channels. The locals
would come down so hard on her. He's working out how best to
deliver the "sorry, but it's off" speech – without the gossip grapevine
crashing from overload.

[Matthew 1:18] You sitting comfortably? You won't be soon: this is not the sugarcoated version of Christmas we've all come to love/hate/survive (delete as applicable). This is Christ-mas with no extra additives. Chew it over!

20 – 21

He's smashing the billiard balls of his best options around his brain, well into the early hours. Finally he drops off and God downloads a dream: An angel's saying:

"Joe Davidson, don't bottle out of making Mary your wife. I'll tell you why. 'Cos it's the Holy Spirit's baby. She'll have a boy, and you'll put the name Jesus down on the birth certificate. Why 'Jesus'? 'Cos it means Liberator, and that's what he's going to do for all his people … liberate them from all the mess they've gotten themselves into."

22 – 23

Look it up! It's exactly what God got his courier Isaiah to predict years back. And I quote:

"Step back! Get your head around this headline: 'Pregnant Virgin!!' Virgin girl will get herself a baby boy who'll answer to the name 'Immanuel', which everyone knows means 'God's with us'. "

24 – 25

Joe wakes up and, yes, realises it was all a dream. But he follows his Angel Orders to the letter and the wedding's back on! Joe and Mary still don't have sex till the boy's born. Joe makes sure the birth certificate reads, "First name: Jesus".

[Matthew 1:20] Why did an angel actually put in a personal appearance for Mary and Zech, but only had a walk-on part in one of Joe's dreams? Would it be harder, and therefore more impressive, if Joe acted on just a dream, not an actual angel sighting?

[Matthew 1:21] Joe would've known that Jesus is an ethnic Hebrew variation on Joshua – like David is Dai in Welsh, and John is Juan in Spanish or Jean in French. So was Joe getting flashbacks of stories of Joshua back 1400 years ago, finishing off what Moses had started?

[Matthew 1:24] Two names then? "Jesus" – a typical, normal, no fanfare, everyday name. And "Immanuel" – an outrageous, controversial, surprising, brand new, fresh out-of-the-box, no previous owner type of name. Which would he choose to go by in later life?

Delivery suite 38b Luke 2:1-7

1-3

Meanwhile, in the depths of the Roman Empire, he-who-must-be-obeyed, Augustus Caesar, announces the Big Count-up. Caesar the Big Cheeser wants accurate population stats across the Roman Empire at the time when Quirinius is in the Syrian governor's mansion. Everyone is expected to trek back to their hometown for registration.

4-7

So Joe Davidson sets off on the 80-mile (130 km) trip down the map from Nazareth, County Galilee in the north, crossing the border to Bethlehem (aka Davidstown), County Judah in the south. He takes his fiancée, Mary, who's pregnant and showing. Three, four, maybe five days later they arrive and realize someone else is about to cross a border and arrive – her waters break. Crisis! "No Vacancy" signs in every B&B window. Decision. Mary has a "home birth" in a livestock shed. She wraps strips of cloth round the baby and uses an animal feeding trough as a cot.

[Luke 2:1] Quick Bio. Augustus Caesar was the adopted son of Julius Caesar. He'd wiped out the A-list celebrity figure of Marc Antony in 31 BC (whose main publicist was William Shakespeare – only 1600 years late!). Now Augustus has created a personality cult, setting himself up as "World Liberator/Saviour". Anyone spot a power struggle in the making? Add to this the fact that he talked up his adoptive dad as divine and much of the press pumped out the line "Augustus, aka Son of God". Mmm, sparks could fly!

[Luke 2:4 – 7]

"Noisy night, chaotic night. All is alarm, all is fright.
Rounded virgin now mother to child. Wholly infant, so Other, so wild.
Awake at an unearthly hour." (x2) © Joe Davidson

[Luke 2:7] No vacancies? Why didn't he pull in some family favours – it's his hometown after all! Or were family ties a bit frosty with the rumours flying round? Was this "Do It Yourself" stable birth a result of the Davidson clan's collective cold shoulder? They're on their own and whatever Joe's "involvement" in the "women's work" of childbirth, can't help wondering if the words of Micah were ringing round his ears. Check out Micah 5:2 – 5a for this 700-year old prediction. (Don't check it out if you want to leave things as a surprise!)

The Jews News Interviews

Carpenter delivers!

Handyman Joe was used to making deliveries, but mostly household furniture from his Davidson Designs workshop. Here he tells Jews News how he delivered his own baby ... or was it someone else's?

JN—So, Joe, Caesar's population census couldn't have been timed worse for you?

JD—It wasn't ideal, but I was proud of being a Davidson and loved going down to Bethlehem. But, no, taking Mary at nine months' pregnant wasn't great timing!

JN—Bureaucracy, eh?! So you just rolled up your sleeves and got on with all that yucky stuff?

JD—What other options were there? Leave her to get on with it? Hope an angel gynaecologist turns up with his heavenly forceps?! I wasn't even the dad—we'd not had sex—but hey...

JN—So "stepdad" just had to step in! Did you expect a little more help from the locals?

JD—The irony was that I couldn't play the "Baby Immanuel" card. The angel told me, but what am I to do? Say, "I'd really appreciate en suite facilities since my wife's expecting God's predicted Liberator—I'm sure of it, 'cos an angel told me ... in a dream"? Like that's really going to open some doors! Not.

JN—So you really believe this little lad Jesus is going to be The Liberator?

JD—Hey, if you can't trust the girl you love, then who can you trust? Plus the angel dream backing up her story. If you're going to walk through your local shopping centre with your arm around the subject-of-all-gossip, you've got to be pretty convinced.

JN—Only "pretty convinced"?

JD—Well, 'course, I've lost sleep thinking, "What if the dreams were—you know—just too much cheese before bedtime?" But you've just got to take it on the chin. Besides, I know Mary! The Good Book says it's got to happen to someone, why not her?

JN—Why not exactly! Will you promise to come back and let us know how he's taking shape? Maybe he could write a regular column for us, when he's older.

JD—Maybe, yes. You can get me on www.davidsondesigns.bis.is.

JN—You're a brave man.

Abandon sheep Luke 2:8-20

8-12

Pull back to the fields outside the (overpacked) town, focus in on a local Sheep Security Team sitting through their night shift.

One of God's angels turns up, with brilliant supernatural special FX packing the fields with God's radiance. The guys are scared stupid!

The angel delivers his standard "Don't panic!" line, then hits them with, "I've got great news, great news to bring a smile to every shape of face on the planet. Mark the date in your diaries! Today over in Davidstown there's a new baby born. Not just any baby – *the* baby! The Boss, Liberator God himself, turning up for you in baby-shape. You'll know which baby – he'll be wrapped up snug and lying in a feeding trough caked with old animal grub."

13-14

Cued to make their entry on the last line of the breaking news, the whole angel choir turn up and blast out the song:

> "Celebrate his worth.
> Elevate the God of heaven's worth.
> And on planet Earth, serenity;
> In your earthly home, shalom[1];
> For all who have known God's smile.
> For all with a God-pleasing lifestyle."

15

Once the angel choir scoots back up to Heavenly HQ, the Sheep Security Team come out with, "Let's check it out." "Yeah, let's hit the

[1] **Shalom = Peace/Serenity.** Just one of the best words ever! Hebrew for peace and wholeness. Oh, and completeness. Throw in soundness and neighborliness, and you're nearly there. Just needs a bit of well-being and security and finish off by adding honest dealing and true justice. Not bad for a six-letter word (or, in Hebrew, a three-letter word plus optional assorted dots!).

[Luke 2:8] When the angel picked up his work order and read his speech, did he baulk at the bit marked "recipients of message"? Did he have the same prejudice as most well-to-do people back then – that shepherds were dodgy, unreliable characters? Did he question why he was to set up such lowlifes as key witnesses to the Big Event? Did he check the "animal feeding trough" line wasn't a typo? Or do angels never question orders?

[Luke 2:13 – 14] Question is, how long had the angel choir been rehearsing this track? Just recently when they went to the state of "high alert" in heaven? Or was it part of their repertoire since Adam and Eve's rather costly snack?

---

town." "Search the whole of Bethlehem for this baby." "God's putting us in the picture – let's go!"

16-20

They leg it and, sure enough, they track down Mary and Joe, then find the baby in his makeshift cot. The next days they fill the pubs with echoes of what they'd been told about this baby. The public pulse is breakneck pace as "Liberator Talk" bounces round the walls of the town. The reactions range from amazed to, well ... amazed!

And Mary's reaction? She's quietly storing all this away in a safe place in her heart, bringing memories out whenever she has some space to wonder.

The Sheep Security Team go back to work, talking up God for letting them in on the whole adventure which had played out just the way the angel had said when he got them ahead of the game.

Old people's eyesight Luke 2:21-38

21

Eight days on, the Davidson family sort out the Religious and legal side of things by getting Jesus circumcised. The baby's formally registered with the name the angel had given him before he was even a lump in her belly – the name Jesus.

22-24

On Jesus' 40th day "birthday", ie, when Mary was ritually "clean" again (in line with Moses' Instruction Manuals), Joe and Mary cuddle the baby up to Jerusalem (5 miles/8 km north

Don't Like This? [Luke 2:16-20] Not so convinced that the message gets priority delivery to people who probably couldn't even sign their name? If it helps, imagine that the sight of the baby inspired them all to take literacy classes and become upstanding characters who went off to college, graduated to more respectable jobs and became, well, nicely middle class. Happier now?

[Luke 2:22] Just how poor were this Davidson family? According to Moses' Instruction Manuals, they had options on what animal to offer up to God on Mary's first baby. Rich families were to sacrifice a lamb; poor families two doves or two young pigeons.

Is this our not-so-subtle clue as to why Jesus ended up always fighting in the corner of the poor?

[2] **The Good Book = Old Testament.** The bit of the Bible they had in first century Judah. Aka God's Instruction Manual.

Don't Like This? [Luke 2:33-35] Skip this. Focus on the image created by more recent PR teams – the "gentle Jesus, meek and mild" persona. Soon the "controversial, dangerous Jesus" will conveniently disappear off the character radar screen. Phew!

of Bethlehem) to present him back to God. (It's all in there in The Good Book[2], Exodus 13:2,12. "Every first male baby is to be set apart as God's.")

They also do things by the Book in the sacrifice department, by making the Religious offering of, quote, "either a pair of doves or a pair of young pigeons", unquote.

25 – 28

Now Simeon is one of Jerusalem's "silver citizens". He's a totally together and right-living guy and only interested in one thing: relief for Israel. God's Holy Spirit is close with Simeon. He'd already had a Holy Spirit communiqué that he'd not die till he'd seen God's Baby Liberator – so now the Holy Spirit is tipping him off to be there the same time as Jesus' dedication. Joe and Mary bring Jesus in for the legal business and the old codger cuddles the baby and calls out to God,

29 – 32

"Whoa! This is it God! I'm at your disposal and I'm ready to go peacefully. Bury me a happy old man! You said it – you've done it! I've seen your Liberator, an eye-opener for outsiders, the pride and joy of our nation. I'm happy. Take me now!"

33 – 35

The Davidsons are stunned. Simeon wishes ma and pa well, and he's got a PS for Mary: "This is going to impact everyone, one way or the other – pulling them up or knocking them down. I'm talking controversial. He'll expose people's thought bubbles; he'll uncover hidden attitudes. It'll be a sniper's bullet through the soul for you, mum."

[Luke 2:25] Want the full picture of what Simeon's up on his ageing toes for? Get hold of a proper Bible – flick to Isaiah 40:1 – 5 and verse 9. Oh, and Isaiah 49:6 is a cracker too!

Not connecting? Okay, what if you knew that Isaiah wrote around the time when the Jews were refugees in a strange culture? What if you imagine your homeland occupied by enemy forces, so you were a virtual refugee in your own hometown? Connecting now?

[Luke 2:33] Why? Why so stunned? Haven't they realised what's going on? Or are they still catching onto all this baby will grow up to do?

---

36 – 37

There's also a crinkly old woman courier for God, Anna Phanuelson, a true blue Jew of the Asher dynasty. Quick bio: back before most could remember, she'd been married, but her husband had pegged it after just seven years. Since then – and we're talking 84 years – she's been a permanent fixture at God's HQ in Jerusalem, often going without food so as to be 100 percent focused on talking up God and talking with God.

38

Old Anna makes a beeline for the Davidsons and gets vocal, thanking God for the baby, going off on superlatives for all those in the crowd who were looking forward to the days of God buying back Jerusalem from the enemy.

Eastern Astrologers Matthew 2:1-12

1 – 2

So, Jesus is delivered in Bethlehem, Judea while King Herod's keeping the throne warm.

Same time, a crack team of Eastern Astrologers – boffin types – turn up in the capital Jerusalem with questions.

"Where's the new royal nursery, and the baby-sized King? We clapped eyes on the star with his name on it; we did the calculations back in

Don't Like This? [Matthew 2:1-2] Not sure about a major plot development in the story being based on people reading things into the stars? Well, just write it off as Eastern New Ageism and you should be fine. Better still, just tell it to groups of little children and don't think about it too much.

[Luke 2:36] How old was she? Over 100? Depends which text you dig up. Some say she was 84. Others that she was a widow for 84 years plus 7 years married plus what, say, 16 years as a girl before getting married ... equals, urm, 107? Let's just say she was old: 1, 2, 3 ... "She was old."

[Matthew 2:1] How come Herod's on the Jewish throne? Being only a half-Jew and not being descended from King David makes him doubly not qualified. Did he have the constitution changed so he could progress in his career as Control-Freak-Tyrant-Type?

[Matthew 2:2] And what's with this astrology/onomy business? Was this a miraculous intervention from the God who set the stars spinning like a game of cosmic frisbee? Or was this a natural phenomenon? Astronomers have done their sums and they reckon Halley's Comet was around 12 BC-ish, which'd be too early. So was it a star getting all excited and going all supernova on them? Or maybe it's the conjunction of "the royal star" Jupiter and "the Jewish star" Saturn, which they reckon was around 7 BC? Whatever, they saw something and took it as a clue.

the Far East, and we've been foot-to-the-floor ever since to join the celebrations! Where is he, this Baby King?"

3-5

King Herod's thrown.

All Jerusalem's thrown at The Throne being thrown.

Herod calls an emergency meeting with his "Religious Expert Advisory Committee for Herod" (aka REACH), made up of Top God Reps[3] and Religious Law Enforcers[4]. One point on his agenda, the question, "Where's The Liberator supposed to arrive?"

The Religious Leaders know their stuff and fall over each other to quote him the 700-year-old line of God's courier[5] Micah:

6

"Okay, Bethlehem, I know you've got an inferiority complex. You may be a small noise in Judah, but the one who's going to run the Nation will be a Bethlehemite. He'll be a role model for Israel."

7-8

Herod calls the Astrologers back in for a private meeting, makes all enthusiastic, asking them for details on the first sightings, etc. before sending them down to

[3] **Top God Reps = High Priest.** The main man, the head honcho responsible for all the people's spiritual health. His job description states he's the middleman between God and the people; a "go between" for all negotiations … in both directions. No pressure then?!

[4] **Religious Law Enforcers = Teachers of the Law/Scribes.** Experts in Moses' law. Academics, who sadly, often became "academic" in the sense of "irrelevant".

[5] **God's Courier = Prophet.** Personal message delivery service direct from God. Think any package delivery corporation, but think "quick". Although, thinking about it, with their record, the depot for uncollected packages would've been pretty chocka by the end of the Old Testament.

[Matthew 2:3] Why? Well, Jerusalem's thrown knowing that when The Throne's thrown then tempers get thrown and principles get thrown out the window as people get thrown into graves.

[Matthew 2:5] See Micah 5:2 in a proper Bible.

[Matthew 2:6] So if the star stops over Bethlehem, how come the star-spotters go to Jerusalem? Was it that they were sooo convinced it was a royal planet they were tracking, that they assumed Jerusalem was the place? Did they not have a copy of Micah in their back pocket then?

[Matthew 2:7] Just how worried was Herod? Just vaguely twitchy or off-the-scale paranoid? Whatever, he's too polished a political animal to let the Astrologers spot any stress. But had they heard Herod's reputation for killing sprees? Did they know what they were dealing with here?

Bethlehem. "Go find him and report back – I'll need to know where I should go and join in the party celebrations."

9-10

The new boys in town make for Bethlehem. The attention-seeking star they've been tracking from the east stops; they work out the coordinates – right over where the lad is.

11

In danger of embarrassing themselves with excitement, they arrive at the house and see the baby in his mum's arms. They kneel, awestruck by him.

Once they recover from the impact, they open their presents for him: gold, incense oil and myrrh.

12

That night one of them gets a memo in a God-dream: "Avoid Herod like he's contagious!" The Astrologers make a detour on their return trip.

Not keen on competition! Matthew 2:13-18

13-15

Joe also downloads another God-dream (the sequel) where an angel's getting the Davidsons ahead of the game: "Go to Egypt with the family. Stay there till you get the okay. Herod's put a price out on the baby's head."

[Matthew 2:9] How did they find the new Davidson baby? A better question is how could they not, since the Sheep Security guys had blabbed off about it since the first night.

[Matthew 2:11] Which "house"? Were the new family in proper rooms by now? Had they sorted the family rift or set up on their own?

And how big is this? That the Astrologers react? Getting into the Jewish mind would show how big: check out the song lyrics from the original Davidson family in Psalm 72:10 – 15 for the full version. The catchy bit goes, "Dignitaries from lands you can't pronounce will announce their presence, and give their presents to this boy."

There's other stuff about the boy "being on the side of the sidelined, recharging the pride of the much maligned". And much more! Look it up. Won't take long.

The Jews News Interviews

Star quality!

Did you spot it? Did you look up? You couldn't have missed that humungous star hanging over Bethlehem in recent weeks. Dr F.N. Cents is one of the world authorities on star spotting and he's in town, so we tracked *him* down and asked him, "What it's all about?"

JN—So, Dr Frank, having traced this record-breaking star all the way from the land of the rising sun, were you relieved when the star finally lost its travel bug?

FNC—Well, more excited than relieved. We'd been building up for months to this. Since we first located the star. But probably not as excited as (you Jews would be) you have been building up to this since, what, seven hundred years minimum?

JN—Yes, but we've also had more false alarms than you. Probably more than you've had rice dinners.

FNC—Ah, right. I had not realised.

JN—And it wasn't anticlimactic, then, after your long road trip, that it was hovering over Bethlehem and not the more glamorous Jerusalem?

FNC—We did wonder if we had, as first, got our calculations wrong. But when we saw the boy. . .

JN—Could you tell? I mean, say you'd just walked in off the street, would you have realised this was a special baby?

FNC—Well there was no aura, no sparkling halo, so I do not know – but we had worked it out, so we *did* know. So it was goosebumps-on-your-goosebumps time. All the potential of the Jewish Liberating King packed into one little bundle of skin and bone. Hands that would, presumably, hold a sword splattered with Roman blood, just curled round his mother's little finger. Lips that would kiss the future Queen of Israel, just dribbling, gurgling. Awe inspiring!

JN — So you could say, with respect of course, that the Geek Squad have turned God Squad?

FNC — Sorry, "Geek"?

JN — Never mind. It gets lost in translation.

They decide they'll skip breakfast and exit Bethlehem while it's still dark. They follow the road signs for "Egypt, Northern Africa" and stick around down in pyramid land till Herod's number is up. This asylum-seeker existence fits with old courier Hosea's line where God's saying, "Ready to round up my son, I pointed the loudspeaker down Egypt way."

16

Back in Jerusalem, Herod's fuming at being outsmarted by his foreign visitors. Playing back their conversation in his head, the boy could be anything up to two years old by now. So his troops get the order to carry out Action Plan B: Infanticide. Herod the (not-so) Great spells it out: "Kill every boy aged two and under in and around Bethlehem."

17-18

Look it up: Jeremiah Hilkiahson saw it all coming. His ancient poem proves it:

"Listen up. Hear that wailing coming out of Ramah Town?
Shrieking, screaming, a scraping of the soul.

[Matthew 2:13] Question. Did the Davidsons sell the gold in the markets of Egypt for the down payment on a pad? Did they keep the incense for the Religious HQ once they returned? Did they keep the myrrh burial oil for any deaths in the family?

[Matthew 2:15] How long do the Davidson's hang around in Egypt? History books tell us that Herod probably dies about five or six years later, so does Jesus start speaking with an Egyptian accent?

[Matthew 2:16] How many boys is this? It could be at least a dozen from a small town like Bethlehem. Depends how wide Herod circles his red line on his wall chart. If it was big enough to include Jerusalem up the road, then Herod was giving orders for more like a couple of hundred toddler boys to die.

[Matthew 2:17] Just how does a human being become so desensitised to be able to kill so easily? Herod's secret graves include his own wife, a whole generation of Bethlehem baby boys, and the movers and shakers of Jericho (a deathbed order from Herod to ensure there's tears at his own funeral!). Just how does this "competitor cleansing" happen?

[Matthew 2:17 – 18] Jeremiah 31:15 in a proper Bible.

Old Mother Rachel grieving for her missing children.
Uncontrollable?
No, more. Inconsolable? No, more. Grieving for her
children who are no more."

How many Herods? Matthew 2:19-23

19-20

Big state funeral. Herod the Great is dead! One of God's angels
does another walk-on part in Joe's dream life. The angel makes
his speech. "On your feet Joe. You're taking mother and child
back up to Israel. Those set on spilling his blood are out of the
picture."

21-23

Joe makes the trip. "One-way ticket to Israel for two adults
and one child, please." But he gets word that Herod's boy,
aka Herod Archelaus, is running Judea in the south and (not
surprisingly), Joe's a bit wobbly about stoking the fire of old
family vendettas. Another dream gives him the plotline; he
tiptoes off up north to the back waters of County Galilee. They
find a pad in their old home – the sleepy nowheresville town of
Nazareth – and start putting out the "home sweet home" signs.
More old-time courier predictions getting ticked off:

"The tag on his holdall handle will read, 'From: Nazareth'."

Zitty? Luke 2:40-52

40

And the boy grows up to be a strapping lad. He's packed full
of wise lines and God's good stuff just oozes off him.

41-45

Fast forward about a decade. (Bar Mitzvah time for the Davidson lad?) It's the traditional family annual jaunt to Jerusalem

Don't Like This? [Matthew 2:17-18] How come we never sing this carol by candlelight? You know the tune. … "Bad King Herod last looked out. When he'd ceased believing. / Blood and guts lay all about. / Deep and crisp and even." © Joe Davidson. Spoils things a bit, no? Especially with children around. And Christmas is for the children, isn't it?

Really **Don't Like This?** [Matthew 2:17-18] "La, la, la, la, la." Grab those earphones. Play something sweet and Christmassy: "O, little town of Bethlehem, how still we see thee lie. Above thy deep and dreamless sleep, the silent stars go by…" Keep the carol karaoke compilation pumping out the syrup and you should be okay.

[Matthew 2:19] Why does history only record rich people's dates? We know Herod the Great died in 4 BC; it's just that we don't know how far before year zero it was when Jesus arrived. How bizarre is it that Jesus was probably born BC?

Some calendar calamity in the Middle Ages did it. Hurrumph!

6 **Flyby Festival = Passover.** A major Jewish Religious festival, like our Easter/Christmas. It celebrates God liberating their ancestors from the sweatshops of Egypt. The name derives from when the angel of death passed over/flew by Jewish homes.

7 **Religious HQ = Temple.** Jerusalem's focal point of the Jewish Religion. Literally a house for God. Question is, how much does God get let out?

for the Flyby Festival[6] national holiday. After the party a whole posse are making their way back to Nazareth. Mary and Joe are gabbing away, assuming Jesus is with friends and family up front. After checking, no one's seen him since Jerusalem, so Mary and Joe leg it back to the Big City.

46

After three days (of panic-searching) and three nights (of sleepless fretting), they track him down to Religious HQ[7] and they're in one of the foyers – where everyone hangs out – and he's sitting there, cool as you like, with the official teaching staff. He's soaking everything up and quizzing the Big Beard Academic with his profound questions.

47-48

The whole crowd are stunned by his grip on spiritual things and the answers he's coming out with. His parents spot him and break up the seminar. "How could you do this to us?" his mum asks. "Your dad and I have been looking all over, worried sick!"

49-50

"Was I that hard to find?" the trainee teenager asks. "Didn't you work out I'd be getting stuck into my Dad's business affairs?" They have no idea what he's going on about.

51

He goes back up to Nazareth with his family and grows up. All we get is that he's not a typical teenager – he does what he's told!

His mum bundles up all these precious moments in her deepest places.

52

The boy Jesus grows through puberty into manhood, through experience into wisdom, through relationships into popularity with God and the community. Quality lad!

[Luke 2:49] Who's right about who Jesus' father is? Mary reckons Jesus' "dad" has been helping her organise the search party. Jesus reckons he's been working on his "Dad's" business. Who's right?

Chapter Three

Do the Prep

Eighteen years later... Mark 1:1

1

This is where stuff really kicks off – the breaking headline news: a good news story featuring Jesus The Liberator, God's Son.

Famous names Luke 3:1-2

1-2

Famous name check: It's 15 years into Tiberius Caesar's stint on the Rome Throne; it's Pontius Pilate's shift as Governor of Judea; it's the

---

[Mark 1:1] Has it *really* been 18 years since we've heard anything?! How has this child prodigy now hit 30 with no press cuttings to his name? Did the wisdom just instantly appear or was he doing the "Liberator" prep alongside his carpentry apprenticeship? And just how good a handyman was he?

Check out the dictionary: "Jesus", aka Joshua in Hebrew: "Je" = Jehovah/God/Lord. And "Sus" = saves/sorts/straightens out. So cut-and-paste them together and you'll see Jesus is short-speak for "God'll sort it". Not far off anyway.

---

[1] **Top God Rep = High Priest.** The main man, the head honcho responsible for all the people's spiritual health. His job description states he's the middleman between God and the people; a "go between" for all negotiations . . . in both directions. No pressure then?!

[2] **Heaven on Earth/God's New World Order = The Kingdom of God.** Like with monarchies, but with God in charge, so not like with monarchies. There's also a sense of "sort of already/but not yet" paradox. We get to download glimpses now, but the full package would cramp our hard drive's style.

[3] **God's Courier = Prophet.** Personal message delivery service direct from God. Think any package delivery corporation, but think "quick". Although, thinking about it, with their record, the depot for uncollected packages would've been pretty chocka by the end of the Old Testament.

time of the brotherly double act of Herod and Philip as rulers of Galilee and Iturea/Traconitis (respectively) – same time when Lysanias was ruler of Abilene; it's the time when Annas and Caiaphas were Top God Reps[1].

And God gets his message through to John Zechariah-son who's hanging out in the desert.

Do a one-eighty Matthew 3:1-2

1-2

It's the time when John "Baptizer" Zechariahson starts stirring things up in the Judean Desert. He's going, "Turn round! Do a U-ey! Turn your lives round a full 180 degrees – over here – yes, Godward! 'Cos God's New World Order[2] is just round the corner and you're staring the wrong way."

Mark 1:2-3

2-3

Check it out ... it's the same guy the courier[3] Isaiah Amoson predicted:

> "And I quote: 'Look sharp! I'm sending my publicist out on the "Preparation Gigs".' "

A lone voice, his insights echoing off wasteland stones and landfill zones:

[Luke 3:1 – 2] So how come God didn't get his memo through to all these big cheeses of the day? Men with big titles on their office doors like: "Caesar", "Governor", "Jewish Ruler", "Religious Leader". Were they all tuned into different spiritual frequencies? Had God tried to leave messages for them and given up?

[Mark 1:2] Actually, the first bit isn't Isaiah's copyright at all – it's nicked from Malachi 3:1 (see a proper Bible). So does Malachi miss out on royalties since Isaiah gets credited?

[Mark 1:3] Do the crowds sing along? This is one of Isaiah's greatest hits – it'd be in most people's compilation CDs. Especially if they were looking to get all misty-eyed about a Liberator making his arrival. And with the Roman Occupying Forces rubbing their Jewish noses in it, "Liberation" sounds pretty sweet.

"Give us a motorway, a freeway, a quadruple highway.
Make the streets straight.
Fix the lights on green
For God's cavalcade to be seen."

Luke 3:5-6

5-6

"Level the land,
Flatten out the geography.
Lay the tarmac, roll it extra smooth,
'Cos God's Liberation is on the move.
Level the land,
Flatten out the geography.
For all humanity to see:
God's sorting out the Big Rescue.
Whoa, look, just coming into view."

Water proof Mark 1:4-6

4-5

So John Baptizer's blasting away about people turning their lives back round 180 degrees to God and getting their mess straightened out and sorted. He's pumping away at proving it by going public with baptism.

John's like a magnet pulling in capacity crowds, drawing people out from all over Judea as far down as Big City Jerusalem. All shapes and budget sizes are hitting the wasteland and throwing out all the messed up stuff they've been into and signing up for baptism in the Jordan River to show they're serious about facing God's way again.

[Mark 1:4 – 5] How exciting is this? Finally! After 400 years of God's self-imposed silent retreat. After the Jews take all that guff from the Egyptians, the Assyrians, the Babylonians, the Syrians and now the Romans. Again a courier from God talking "Liberation" takes centre stage: one who'd kick the Romans where it hurt and trump all their pagan claims of Zeus and his cronies running the show.

6

John looks the biz on the wild catwalk: he's wearing an outrageously retro courier clothing line of camel hair leggings and a top, held together by a simple but effective leather belt. He's looking lean and fit on his alternative cuisine diet of Sun-Baked Locust and Wild Honey Crunch.

Winning key friends? Matthew 3:7-10

7-10

Then John B sees the Religious Leaders[4] and Traditionalists[5] mingling with the Baptism queues. Not known for his seminars on tact, John launches into, "Snakes! Look! Snakes!" John keeps going for the Religious jugular, "Who got your pulses up? Who rattled your cage? Got you panicking about God's anger brewing up for a storm? Well if you're so worried, if you really are going to turn your lives round to God, then prove it. Let's see the evidence in your lifestyle. We want to see fruit, not just leaves. And don't start spouting off, saying, 'But Abraham's our Father Figure!' You're not so special. God could morph these boulders into new children for Abraham. Get a move on; God's chain saw is nicely revved up and ready for action. It's got its job spec – 'take down any tree marked with a big black "W" – for "Waste of Space"'. No fruit? No escaping the saw mill bonfire."

Interactive sermons Luke 3:10-18

10-11

The crowd press the red button and go interactive with John. "And? What are we to do then?" they ask.

[4] **Religious Leaders = Pharisees.** A faction calling themselves literally "the separated ones" – "the exclusives" perhaps. Big into Rules, running a well-oiled propaganda machine which seemed to be fuelled by people's guilt.

[5] **Religious Traditionalists = Sadducees.** These guys were only into Moses' first five books of the Instruction Manuals; anything later was to them liberal hoo-ha to be sniffed at. One of their big things was that all this rising from the dead malarkey was indulgent hogwash, brought in by liberal lightweights like Daniel, among others. Not natural partners for the Religious Leaders.

Don't Like This? [Matthew 3:7-10] Just play the "Redirect the Sermon" game. It's dead easy. Even if the preacher's directly eyeballing you, just deflect the rant towards the people groups you've decided need to hear it more than you. Works a treat. Shame John B's target audience hadn't heard of it!

[Mark 1:6] So what's with John's image? Was his self-designed fashion an anti-materialistic statement or a back reference to Elijah's God courier uniform? Or did he just have minging taste? Was his special diet a protest against dietary indulgence, or did he actually *like* insect salad?

[Matthew 3:7] The Religious jugular is just above the overactive control gland, I believe.

John gets practical, going, "Simple: You got two jackets? Give one to the homeless guy who hasn't. You got a fridge full of food? Ditto!"

12-14

One of the Outland Revenue Officers[6] (aka Roman lackeys) also wants a pointer. "Coach," he shouts from his corner, "what about us lot?"

John's on the money with, "Don't round the figures up for your own funds."

Then some of the soldiers (aka Rome's hand puppets) want some answers. "What about us?"

John's blunt enough to say, "Cut the backhanders, quit framing innocent people just to improve the conviction stats … oh, and 'game over' on using poor pay as an excuse for confiscating what's not yours!"

15-16

The audience is leaning in, on the edge of their rubble-and-sand seats, asking, "Is this John guy The Liberator, or what?"

John's not holding back, he's coming back with, "My job's confirming changed lives with good ol' H_2O baptism. But you ain't seen nothing yet! Side stage, waiting in the wings is a guy with much more class than me. I'm not even good enough to be his roadie. This guy doesn't use H_2O; he uses God's Holy Spirit; he uses fire no less."

17-18

"And he's in action-mode: he's going to sort the good stuff from the gunk; the stuff he can use from the stuff he'll chuck. The pile marked

[6] **Outland Revenue = Roman Tax Department.** Where the Empire collected its taxes from the minions. Hence Outland Revenue Officers weren't exactly popular.

[Luke 3:10 – 14] How did John answer — were these wild guesses? Were they direct inject wisdom from above? Or was he more up with current affairs than you'd imagine for a guy stuck out in the desert?

So why didn't John come back with Revolution slogans? Why did he implicitly endorse the status quo and insist on Justice within the system? Which would be more radical?

[Luke 3:15] Is it the proximity of Herod's soldiers that keeps the crowds from shouting out this "who is he?" question? Isn't Herod Antipas technically the King of the Jews who's supposed to be doing the Liberating? So why's he spending all his time choosing wallpaper for the Better-Than-Ever Jerusalem HQ project?

The Jews News Interviews

John Baptizer's old mum comes clean

John Baptizer's totting up the tabloid column inches – everyone's got an opinion about this Desert Wild Man. But how do we know who the real J.B. is when he refuses to give a press conference? We sent Reuben Jobson to catch up with John's ageing mum Elizabeth in her nursing home and capture her thoughts on her boy's career, his amazing voice and whether he's eating his greens. Question is whether the rather senior lady has got the picture straight. What do you think? Contact us on www.jewsnews/yourviews.co.il.gos.

I'd not expected much; a frail old lady – she had him late in life – but on walking into the day room she just stood out. John's ageing mum was happy to chat away about her boy and his cousin Jesus. They could talk, this family!

"Well they'd known each other since they were youngsters, of course," she was straight into top gear. "What with our family get-togethers, and we'd always catch up at Flyby Fest time. Zech, John's father, and I made sure he knew his cousin well since John was always destined to be Jesus' PR man. Zech would've been so proud. Quite a thing for a God Rep to see his only son go into the ministry, except he actually didn't quite *see* it, God rest him. But he *knew*! Of course it's not the usual route into a Religious career, but our John always did things differently. He was a leader, never a follower. Apart from when the Davidsons were over. Oh, they used to play stories and John could talk, ah, could he talk! But when Jesus was over he always played emcee or just drew in the crowd with that voice of his and let Mary's lad loose with a story or nine."

I noticed she had The Good Book open on her lap, and I squeezed in a question about what she was reading at the moment. She looked down at the open Scriptures as if she'd forgotten they were there and almost told me off. "Oh, I'm not reading ... no need when you've known it by heart for the last thirty years." I must've looked a bit blank. She had pity on me and said, "See, if Jesus is the One and our John's the one before the One, then it all makes sense – the energy, the love of the outdoors, the voice – everything was leading to this great career. For decades to come: the two J's, the Cousins' Cooperative. Just think: our John – The Liberator's right hand man in Jerusalem's Palace!"

I was still working out, *the one before the One!* But when she recited the bit from Isaiah 40:9–10, it all flooded back: memory verses from Saturday School way back. "You! You want to spread the good news? Shift yourself! Get up that mountain. You! You want Jerusalem to know? Project, from the diaphragm; give it all you've got and holler. Don't choke on it; free your mouth up and yell, 'Ladies and gentlemen, it gives me great pleasure to introduce to you – your God! Arriving centre stage, totally in control, power pouring from every pore – your God! With his diamond-studded trailer behind, holding rewards for you, prizes for you.'"

And she was word perfect! I checked! Not bad for an old lady. Now I'd caught up and she seemed to come over all thoughtful. "Can you get a message to him for me?" What was I to say? *No, I've been out Wasteland Way twice, and if work isn't paying the travelling expenses then you'll have to get your Zimmer frame oiled and get out there yourself, darling!* I nodded. Of course I would! She scribbled me a note for her boy, crumpled it firmly – really quite firmly – into my hand. And that was it. Interview over. Yes, being a journalist, of course I checked the private note later. It read: "I'm worried that you're not eating well. Lots to do still, keep your strength up. Don't get into trouble. Love, mum."

I'm glad I did. I took it the day "cousin Jesus" turned up. Next day off I had, I went back in ... told her all about it. This John's going to go far – good family stock!

Don't Like This? [Luke 3:17 – 18] Whoa! Where's "gentle Jesus, meek and mild" gone? Where's all this Jesus "The Incinerator" Davidson stuff come from? Well, assume it's just the desert sun playing games with John B's excitable nature.

'burn' will get lowered into the incinerator that's stuck on 'full power'."

This is just a brief sound bite from one of John's mega-speeches, egging them on and coaching them about the breaking good news.

Jesus takes a dive Matthew 3:13 – 17

13 – 14

Then Jesus turns up. He's trekked down from Galilee to the Jordan to get baptized by John. But John's not keen, spluttering, "No way! I'm so out of my depth! Is this some weird role reversal thing? *I* should get baptized by *you*. How come *you're* asking *me*?"

15

Jesus comes back, "It has to happen. It's the right thing – let's do it just so."

John goes with the flow.

16 – 17

Straight after the baptism, Jesus is hardly out of the water when it seems like the clouds split and God's Holy Spirit is flying down from heaven and landing on him in dove disguise. He hears a voice rumbling like thunder through heaven's sound system, saying, "You're my son. I love you. I'm wild about you. I'm well into everything you are."

Guess that's a "no" then Matthew 4:1 – 11

1 – 3

Next up, Jesus gets the nudge from God's Holy Spirit and follows him further out into the wasteland for more prep in the Testing Resolve department. He's there 40 days: no food, no home comforts; his belly's screaming, "Feeeed meeee!"

[Matthew 3:13 – 15] Hold on! Isn't baptism about turning your back on your mess and living right? So how come Jesus wants to be done? Did he have mess to sort? Or is Jesus just associating himself with John B's great social movement of people connecting with God?

[Matthew 3:16] Question is, who *is* Jesus? We've no records of his adult life so far. Would previous descriptions help? Check out Isaiah's character assessment of God's chosen One in Isaiah 42:1 – 7 in a proper Bible.

Just when he's at his weakest, in strolls the Tempter Meister, the Devil himself, who's needling away at his resolve, hissing, "If you're God's Son, let's see some proof. Do a trick! Turn these boulders into big, beautiful fresh-baked bread loaves. Smell that dough!"

4

Jesus has an answer already prepared. "Moses in The Good Book[7] says, 'You won't survive if you just eat bread. It's God's words you need to get down you.'"

5 – 6

So, rethink: The Devil drags Jesus off on an animated sightseeing tour of Jerusalem. They're perched at the top of the Religious HQ[8] high tower. Now the Devil starts (mis)quoting one of the Instruction Manual's song lyrics:

> "If you're God's Son, jump!
> 'Cos The Good Book states categorically,
> 'The angels have their orders, orders straight down from the top.
> They'll catch you. Carry you. Set you down gentle.
> You won't even get to land on all fours,
> 'cos these out here are uneven floors.
> You won't even turn an ankle.
> So jump! Get yourself some proof!'"

Don't Like This? [Matthew 4:1-11] No problem; just think of "the Devil" as a literary device to portray dementia that comes from food deprivation.

[7] The Good Book = Old Testament. The bit of the Bible they had in first century Judah. Aka God's Instruction Manual.

[8] Religious HQ = Temple. Jerusalem's focal point of the Jewish Religion. Literally a house for God. Question is, how much does God get let out?

[Matthew 4:3] Was the Devil listening in on God's voice-over, just 40 days back, "You're my Son ... I'm into everything you are"?

[Matthew 4:4] How much of the Scriptures could Jesus just reel off? Just how mentally sharp are you after 40 days with no food and no water? Had Jesus already considered the bread-making option before the Devil's "helpful" suggestion?

[Matthew 4:6] See Psalm 91:11,12 located midway through a proper Bible.

7

But Jesus has another answer that was made much earlier. "Moses in The Good Book also says, 'God's not sitting down at your desk to take your tests.'"

8 - 9

Rethink. Next location: the Devil whisks him off to the top of a mountain the size of an office block. He's pointing out the offices of all the major players, the power brokers of the world, saying, "All these networks, all these mobilizers and empire builders – they're on my payroll, and I'll lease them out to you at very reasonable rates. They're at your disposal. They'll jump to your text messages. They'll make it all happen for you. All I ask is ... you work on my terms."

10

"Back off, Satan!" Jesus pulls another answer from the same Book. "Moses in The Good Book says, 'Give God what he's worth, which is everything. Work only for him; don't moonlight for any dodgy extras.' That's my final answer."

11

Next thing Jesus knows, the Devil's gone. Jesus is surrounded by angels who are giving him the spa treatment, getting him back up to full strength.

Say "no" to being a yes-man Luke 3:19-20

19-20

Back in "civilisation", John Baptizer lays into none other than King Herod Antipas on the whole marrying-your-brother's-wife thing, with his brother Philip's ex now being Mrs Queen. Well, it's not just this illegal Queen issue, there's a whole list, which John (helpfully) runs through for him. So Herod adds one more item to his list of broken rules – he imprisons a political dissident. John's doing time.

[Matthew 4:7] **See Deuteronomy 6:16, an early chunk of a proper Bible.**

[Matthew 4:10] **Just before the last quote, Deuteronomy 6:13.**

[1] **Heaven on Earth/God's New World Order = The kingdom of God.** Like with monarchies, but with God in charge, so not like with monarchies. There's also a sense of "sort of already/but not yet" paradox. We get to download glimpses now, but the full package would cramp our hard drive's style.

[2] **Taking God at his word = Faith/Belief.** Faith is more than just a Religious Club you belong to. Belief is more than just a vague whim. This big word is an active, gutsy, practical concept. Aka "trust".

Chapter Four

Liberator Launch

Whose line is it anyway? Mark 1:14-15

14-15

D'you want the good news or the bad? Headline: bad news of John Baptizer being imprisoned; meanwhile Jesus kicks off his "God's good news story" tour of Galilee. He says, "Synchronise watches! Get in line with my time zone: ETA for God's New World Order[1] is in final countdown stage! It's just round the corner and you're looking the wrong way! Do a full 180 degrees: clean up your lives; turn and take God at his word[2] about the great news hitting your screens."

[Mark 1:15] God's New World Order was the big event Jews were up on their toes for. For most, the big priority was political revolution and the overthrow of enemy forces. For most, top of the wish list was the Romans upping and offing out of Jewish ancestral territory and taking their weird Western culture with them.

[3] **Local Religious HQ = Synagogue.** Local meeting place for Religious Jews to worship their God. Central point of any Jewish community.

The Liberator's job spec Luke 4:14-30

14-15

Jesus' One Man Revival Tour has moved north and all Galilee's talking about it. The Galilean broadcast channels can't get enough coverage of him. Each Saturday he's there in some local religious HQ[3] and the people's vote is a unanimous "10 out of 10"!

16-17

He hits his home patch, Nazareth, and does his usual thing by taking a pew in the local religious HQ. He gets to go up front and do the honours for today's passage, so he scrolls down Isaiah's book to chapter 61, verses 1 and 2 and reads:

18-19

"The Spirit of God is coursing through every part of me. He's commissioned me to announce the breaking news – fantastic news for the poor! He's sent me to liberate those slammed up in dark prisons. He's sent me to liberate the blind from their darkness. He's sent me to liberate those just existing under the weight of oppressive forces. He's sent me to announce the news that this is the era of God doing people good."

20-21

Jesus hands The Complete Works of Isaiah back to the altar boy and sits down to coach the congregation. All eyes are locked onto him like wisdom-seeking viewfinders. His sermon is just, "Today! All these words have come to life. Right here. Right now. In 3-D."

[Luke 4:14 – 19] Does he look out on the audience, sorry, *congregation,* and remember jobs he did for different people? A table and bench for the Jacobsons over there; a barn extension for farmer David and his family. Does he still know who's poor, who's going blind, who's more oppressed than most? Is he delivering these lines personally?

[Luke 4:18 – 22] Is this the shortest sermon ever? And is this *why* they love it?!

[4] **God's Courier = Prophet.** Personal message delivery service direct from God. Think any package delivery corporation, but think "quick". Although, thinking about it, with their record, the depot for uncollected packages would've been pretty chocka by the end of the Old Testament.

22 – 23

They love it. Positive vibes bounce off the walls of the local religious HQ. Jesus' generous words pour out of his mouth and stun the people. They need to check, "Isn't this Joe Davidson's boy? Isn't he one of our own?"

Jesus pushes it further and says, "Let me guess, which one-liner are you going to quote back to me? 'Doctor – solve your own stuff! Press action replay on the supernatural specials you pulled off in Capernaum – do something spectacular here too!' Is that what you'll spout?

24 – 26

"I'll tell you straight," he says. "There's no such thing as 'local boy made good' in the world of God's couriers[4]. Take it from me, when Elijah did his stuff, there were plenty of widows in his own country. Remember the bit where the rain clouds shut up for three and a half years and the shelves were begging for some food to carry? And where did old Elijah get sent? To one of these poor true Jew widows? Nope! To a foreigner – a widow way up past the Israeli border in Zarephath, Sidon, Phoenecia.

27 – 30

"And take it from me, when Elisha was really on fire, there were plenty of people with chronic skin diseases in his homeland of Israel. Remember the bit when Army Officer Naaman got baby-soft skin? And was Naaman Jewish? Nope! He was a foreigner. A Syrian no less!"

The people in the local religious HQ were initially proud of their local hero, but now Joe's boy is really pushing it. They're incensed. They're

[Luke 4:23] Why did Jesus move into supernatural mode in Capernaum, which is packed full of non-Jews? How weird is this for these Jews to get their heads around? Is God into people without Abraham DNA in their circuits? How about only people with Adam/Eve DNA? Did old man Simeon get it right, back 30 years or so when he predicted that Jesus will be "the eye-opener for outsiders, the pride and joy for the Jews"?

[Luke 4:28] Talk about pressing all the wrong buttons! Why were they so incensed at Jesus' "unpatriotic" stance? Did they see Jesus' words as undermining the people's national identity?

Did they realize that Jesus actually skipped the last line of Isaiah 61:1 – 2 ("the day of God's pay back for his enemies")? Isn't this the best bit if you're an oppressed people with a 1,000-year-long history of begging God to kick out the occupying forces?

on their feet and driving him out of town. The lynch mob back him
up to the top of the hill where they don't intend to stop till he's over
the cliff and hitting the rocks at the bottom at terminal velocity.
That's the plan anyway. But what *actually* happens is that he walks
right through the fuming gang without a scratch!

New tour base Matthew 4:13-16

13-14

So Jesus shifts operations up to the main business artery of Galilee
Lake itself. His new business cards now read "Capernaum Town".
From this top left (northwest) edge of Galilee Lake he tours the whole
area of Zebulun and Naphtali ... just like old Isaiah said he would,
way back when. You ready for this?

15-16

"Zebulun and Naphtali and the whole area around
Where the Jordan and the Galilee can be found.
Where the non-Jews choose to settle down:
Capernaum Town. Capernaum Town.
All eyes down, adjusted to the dark, like they've always done,
And then they're dazzled by a light full up, full on.
They're groping around, Death standing tall, blocking out the sun.
And his shadow landing on everyone.
Then they're dazzled by the light as it dawns on them...
The morning sun has finally come."

Recruitment drive Luke 5:1-11

1-3

Jesus is standing there on the beach of Galilee Lake, coaching a whole
crowd who are huddling in, well up for hearing God's take on things.

[Luke 4:28 – 30] Not the best of starts then. Cousin John B in Herod's dungeon and Jesus' old ties in Nazareth
snapped. Wouldn't it have been easier for John and Jesus to have played to the crowd a bit – some "we're going
to kick us some Roman butt" bravado – and not made quite so many enemies this early on in the project?

[Matthew 4:15 – 16] See Isaiah 9:1,2 in a proper Bible.

He spots two fishing boats doing nothing in particular, so he walks over and gets into the one marked "Si and Drew – we fish for you". Si comes over from net-washing duty – just tying up a few loose ends (literally) – and Jesus asks him to give the boat a bit of muscular shoulder, so Si shoves the boat out into the lake. Jesus makes himself at home and coaches the beach full of fans from his improvised seat of learning.

4 – 5

Jesus winds up the seminar and calls over to Si, "Okay, let's go deeper. Right out to the middle. We'll let your nets catch us some fish, eh?"

Si comes back, "Boss, we've worked our buttons off all night and we've not caught zilch ... but ... if you say so ... here goes." Si and his brother Drew push out and humour the landlocked life coach by going through the motions with the nets.

6 – 7

Wham! Bam! The nets are so chocker with next month's salary of fish they're going to snap any second. The adrenalin kicks in and Si and Drew are screaming over to their partners (Jim and Jonno of "Zebedee and Sons – Fishery Supplies"), "Get your boat here, sharpish – it's a boomer!" Even with both boats and four hardened fishermen, the catch is so massive it's threatening to sink the mini-fleet.

[Luke 5:1 – 3] The zigzagging coastline of cliffs jutting out into the lake doesn't just create picturesque crescent beaches, it also makes for great acoustics. Once you're out in the lake and your voice is bouncing back off the cliff face, it's a natural amphitheatre, like a surround-sound cinema.

[Luke 5:3] Were Si and Drew excited about the extra work they were going to generate from this sponsorship promotion of their boat? Thousands of people seeing their logo has to be good for future business, no?

[Luke 5:4] So what was Jesus talking about in his seminar? The only hint regarding content is his standard line, "Heaven on Earth's just round the corner and you're looking the wrong way! Do a full 180 degrees: clean up your lives, turn and face God, and get some personal conviction going about the great news hitting your screens."

[Luke 5:4 – 5] Has Si's language been cleaned up for the sake of decorum??

5 **Rest Day = Sabbath.** Rule No. 5 in Moses' Big Ten: "You'll keep my rest day special." By now this "special" had been defined down to the nth degree. There were plenty of things you shouldn't do.

6 **Religious Law Enforcers = Teachers of the Law/Scribes.** Experts in Moses' law. Academics, who sadly, often became "academic" in the sense of "irrelevant".

8-10

Si, aka Pete, connects with what's just happened and kneels down (fish up to his waist). "Boss, back off – I'm a total mess. You don't want to hang around with the likes of me." Jim and Jonno in the other boat are nodding like he's their spokesman; they're so blown away by the record catch.

Jesus says to Si, "Don't panic. From here on in, you'll be fishing for people."

11

They drag their boats up onto the beach and leave the bumper bonus for the locals to haggle over. They're out of there. They're sticking with Jesus.

What does the enemy know? Mark 1:21-28

21-22

Still Capernaum Town, fast forward to Rest Day[5]: Jesus gets an invite to talk in the local religious HQ. The locals are stunned by his coaching, 'cos he's not just a quote machine like the other Religious Law Enforcers[6], peddling their secondhand thought-for-the-day. No, he's got his own ideas ... and clout to go with them!

23-24

Then, mid-talk, some guy who's (dis)possessed by a demon hears the words come out of his own mouth: "Why you hassling us, Nazareth's Jesus? What you going to do? Snuff us out? I know who you really are – God's Divine One."

[Mark 1:21 – 23] Replay the scene but change the backdrop to your local community centre. A capacity crowd is listening into the speaker; suddenly this guy from the middle row starts manifesting a demon – but instead of the bile you'd expect, the voice from hell starts endorsing the guy with the microphone as God's Man of the Moment.

25-26

"Shut it!" shouts Jesus, full-on fierce.

He follows through with, "You're evicted, NOW!" The evil spirit doesn't go without one last convulsion; one last shriek, but then the guy's clear.

27-28

Forget the congregation's "stunned-ness" before. Now they're *really* STUNNED – if not cranking up a level to GOBSMACKED, in fact! "What *is* this?" "New ideas and with what clout!" "He clicks his fingers and the demons scramble; one word from him and they wing it!"

The grapevine is on gridlock with so much gossip flying round Galilee County.

Mobile miracle clinic Mark 1:29-34

29-31

Straight off, after exiting the local religious HQ, they're hitting Si (or Pete) and Drew's place for a big Saturday roast. Jonno and Jim are round the table too.

Simon's mum-in-law's ill. She's horizontal, shivering hot and cold, fever seeping out into the bed sheets. They mention it to Jesus. He goes in, just takes her hand and helps her up. She hits vertical and the fever's out the window. She gets back to work: her job description – "Fulltime Homemaker and Caterer". She dishes up personally.

Don't Like This? [Mark 1:21-28] This exorcism stuff give you the heeby-jeebies? What did they know about this stuff back then? Write it off as epilepsy or something. Forget the fact that epileptics aren't usually so coherent mid-seizure. Also block out the fact that Jesus could cure the condition by just words.

[Mark 1:25] Is this a pattern? When Jesus is healing people, he talks to people; when he's clearing out demons, he bypasses the person and talks direct to the demon.

[Mark 1:29] Tradition was (a) do the Religious thing, then (b) have a big meal. Is this where the phrase "hunger after righteousness" comes from?

[Mark 1:29 – 31] Note to self: Resist all mother-in-law gags.

The Jews News Interviews

Zebedee loses boys

Local fishing stalwart, Zebedee Galton, talks of mixed emotions on seeing his boys – and his retirement fund – walk off with the new life coach sensation Jesus Davidson.

JN—It must be tough, seeing your boys go off like this.

ZG—I was warned that it'd be hard, you know, if my boys ever walked off, left the family business. It's rare, but it does happen. And I'd always dreaded it.

JN—Quite! What if they go off the rails? Now you can't steer the family boat, as it were?

ZG—I know! What if this is some weird sect? We don't know if he's kosher or not, this Davidson boy. Seems good, but if he was dodgy…

JN—Exactly. Could you see yourself doing what all good Jewish dads should do?

ZG—The whole "Jim who?/Jonno who?" thing? I don't know. Could I wash my hands of my two boys? Not sure I could go through the motions that they were dead to me, like I should. Dunno. Jury's still out on this latest Liberator wannabe, so until then … dunno!

JN—So you'll close down the family business?

ZG—I might keep some of the hired hands on, but we might be looking at dry docking the family boat.

JN—And the bumper catch? What's happening with all the fish?

ZG—I've salted most of the bonus catch so at least I'm fine for the winter.

JN—And Mrs Z? She's not been seen around. Where's she?

ZG—She's off with them! The missus is talking about making sure they don't get looked over when it comes to promotion and perks. "First in, first up," she keeps saying.

JN—So she thinks this is going to be really big?

ZG—Yup. So they're launching their new careers; slamming the champagne bottle onto the side of their new adventure. Like the partner boat logo says, "Si and Drew – we fish for you." Still works, she reckons. She thinks it's a really good career move...

JN—And what'll you do now?

ZG—Me? Well, oh, I think I could do with some lie-ins, mornings.

JN—Sounds like a plan!

32-34

Soon as it's dark, the locals are lugging some right sorry cases – the diseased, the demon (dis)possessed – into the house to see Jesus. The whole town's at Si's in-laws' door as if Jesus' mobile clinic has the "Open for Business" sign flashing above the roof. Jesus is notching up loads of successes for the sick – one word from him and they're leaping round the place. He's making whole networks of demons homeless, and he's still blocking demonic endorsements: sticking a silencing order on them as they make their exit – 'cos they know his true ID.

Flashback Matthew 8:17

17

All this clicks into place nicely with what God downloaded through Isaiah's classic poem,

> "But whoa!
> Step back a sec!
> Weren't those our weaknesses he took on?
> Wasn't that our damage he carried?"

Mark 1:35-38

35-37

Way before there's even a hint of dawn, Jesus is up and out of the house, escaping for a bit of space to connect with God. Si and the others send out a search party, and when they track him down they moan, "Everyone's looking for you!"

[Mark 1:32] Why wait till dark? Are they ashamed? Nope, it's all about the Rest Day "No Carrying" Rules. But once dusk lands, they can legally lift heavy weights again without getting any turbo tutting from the Religious Suits.

[Matthew 8:17] One of Isaiah's Greatest Hits (Isaiah 53:4). Is Matthew being restrained not to include the whole thing, or is he banking on his readers knowing it by heart? Look it up in an official Bible or wait till Chapter 20 of this offering (see page 362).

38

Jesus comes out with, "Let's move on to other villages. It's not just about getting people back on their feet, focused, feeling fine here. My mission statement's about presenting ideas in other places too."

The "God's New World Order"[7] tour Matthew 4:23-25

23

So Jesus tours round Galilee County, hitting the local religious HQ venues, taking the coaching slot any Rest Day he can and wowing them with his all new presentations. Between Saturdays, he does his outdoor gigs, talking up God's New World Order. And for the capacity crowds in both locations, there's his supernatural doctor role where he sorts out symptoms and root causes of every ache and pain in the book.

24-25

We're talking major celebrity. We're talking household name, even if your postcode is right up in Syria – you've heard of him. Queues of people at his open air impromptu clinics – the diseased, the disturbed, the (dis)possessed, the epileptics, the paralysed – all getting eased, settled, freed, liberated. All fully functioning again and crediting Jesus with the miracle cure. He's hitting capacity crowds from all over. Different accents saying the same thing in their own ways: Galilean gabble, Decapolisian Grecian ghetto talk, Judean burrs, Jerusalem vowels, Jordanian jowls all working up the reputation of Jesus the Miracle Doc.

(Dis)enfranchised Mark 1:40-45

40

In one of the towns, this guy with an infectious skin disease kneels directly in front of Jesus and says, "If you're into the idea, you can give me baby-soft skin."

[Mark 1:40] It's not just his smooth skin he wants back; it's his social life, his family, his life! Why? Leviticus 13:45,46 sums up his problem: "The person with such an infectious disease must wear trashed clothes; wear his hair matted; wear a face mask and must shout the warning, 'Contaminated! Contaminated!' He must live alone, outside society."

Infectious skin diseases – basically, if you've got one, you're a no one.

---

[7] **Heaven on Earth/God's New World Order = The kingdom of God.** Like with monarchies, but with God in charge, so not like with monarchies. There's also a sense of "sort of already/but not yet" paradox. We get to download glimpses now, but the full package would cramp our hard drive's style.

41-42

Jesus isn't just "into the idea"; his heart melts for this "reject" (their term). So – shock, horror – he touches the untouchable; he makes contact with the contaminated outsider! He says, "Oh, I'm well into the idea all right! Your medical records will show a clean bill of health." Instantaneously, the guy's clear. The sores are sorted.

43-45

Jesus' parting words to him are stern. "All this is on the quiet, understand? No mouthing off about what I've just done. I'm serious! Go do the legal necessaries with the Religious authorities, get your medical papers cleared – like Moses laid down – but don't go blabbing off on a 'I was Mr Elephant Man' freak show tour. Understand?"

So what's the guy do? He goes on all the chat shows and, for a while, becomes a minor celebrity. He blows his benefactor's cover so wide open that Jesus can't even step foot inside a town without being mobbed by crazed fans. So Jesus parks himself in solitary backwaters. Which *still* doesn't sort it – the crowds just get mobile and turn the countryside into a Spot the Celeb. Contest.

Upping the stakes Mark 2:1-12

1-5

A few days on, Jesus pulls in at Base Camp Capernaum. Word soon spreads that Jesus is back home and the house/garden/street is packed – all ears bent toward Jesus' coaching session. Four guys turn up (late), with a paralytic mate on a makeshift stretcher. No way are they going to get their buddy to Jesus through the door, so they grit their teeth and haul the paralytic up the outside stairway to the roof, dig up the thatch and earth, tear off the tiles, and lower the guy through the beams to Jesus, who's in mid-flow. Jesus looks up, clocks their conviction, sees how they're taking God at his word, and tells the paralytic, "Chin up son, your mess is wiped off your slate – all you've

[Mark 2:1] Maybe Jesus backing off from Capernaum earlier in the week seems to have done the trick. Now he's back – possibly in his own pad – and they're actually listening to him talk, not just gagging for spectacular show-stopping stunts. Although … speaking of show-stopping stunts…

ever done to mess people up and wind God up is straightened out and
sorted. You're in the clear!"

6 – 7

Switch to the reaction of the Religious Law Enforcers sitting bolt
upright. You can almost read the twisted thought bubbles above their
heads: *What d'he say? That's God's job! Who's he think he is? He's way out
of line here!*

8 – 9

Jesus reads them like a book – a children's book with large print and
pictures. He goes, "Why so cynical? Which is the tougher call, eh?
To tell the disabled guy, 'Okay, your slate's clean with God' or to tell
him, 'On your feet, pack your stuff; you're walking out of here'. Which
of the two is simpler?

10 – 12

"But in case you're in any doubt whether The Man himself has the
kudos down here on earth to wipe slates clean for God". He turns to
the paralytic and says, "Listen up: on your feet, pack your stretcher,
stick it under your arm and make for home under your own steam." In
full view of everyone there, the guy's getting up, packing his stuff and
striding off into the sunset (once he gets past the crowd, that is).

It's like all the audience has been hit with a turbo-charged stun gun.
Once they recover, God gets all the credit for supplying the supernatural juice to make this happen. The standard line is, "Never seen
anything like it … never!"

[Mark 2:7] Most Jews thought nobody could wipe slates clean for people. Only the Son of God/Divinity/Deity
had the clout to call the shots on total slate cleaning. Only God.

[Mark 2:10] "The Man": Bit of a weird way to talk about yourself, no? Well, no, not if you know your classic
Daniel publications (7:13,14). "In my vision I looked and, smack, bang in my face is one like The Man surfing in
on the clouds. He skids to a halt in front of the Ancient of Days and is escorted into his throne room. Inside, this
Man gets given all the clout, kudos and credit for running the whole show and every nationality knows he's
worth every bit of respect he gets, and some! His position in top spot is permanent; his New World Order will
never get wasted." Nice name badge!

---

[8] **Outland Revenue = Roman Tax Department.** Where the Empire collected its taxes from the minions. Hence Outland Revenue Officers weren't exactly popular.

[9] **Religious Leaders = Pharisees.** A faction calling themselves literally "the separated ones" – "the exclusives" perhaps. Big into Rules, running a well-oiled propaganda machine which seemed to be fuelled by people's guilt.

Eating with the wrong people? Matthew 9:9-13

9

Jesus moves on and spots a guy, Matt Alphaeusson, sitting at an Outland Revenue[8] kiosk. Jesus tells him, "You're retiring early: you're joining my Team." Matt doesn't even file the papers away. Just walks off from his desk and joins the growing Team.

10-11

Later, Jesus is eating on Matt's patio with a whole gang of Matt's old work colleagues – shady characters and dodgy dealers, all probably messed up in some sort of money laundering scam for the Roman Occupying Forces (allegedly).

Course the Religious Leaders[9] soon catch on to the fact that Jesus is all buddy-buddy-feet-under-the-table with such a rabble. They corner Jesus' Team and quiz them, "Give us one good reason why your boss is eating with these undesirables, these low-life scum?"

12-13

Jesus tunes into their (possibly overly loud) enquiry and tells them direct, "Who needs a doctor more, fit people or ill people? If you're sure you've got a clean bill of health, then what d'you need a doctor for? But if you're struggling to get through the day with all your aches and pains, you know the doctor's number off by heart. Clear off and mull over this one-liner from God's courier Hosea: 'I'm into giving people slack, not giving things up.' I'm here to get the

[Matthew 9:9] Has Matt's tax kiosk got Jewish hate graffiti scrawled across it? Something like, "Roman lackey" or "Pilate's puppet" or worse?

[Matthew 9:10] How much is Matt walking away from? Not just the job, but paid holidays, health insurance and pension contributions.

So, why throw a dinner party? Was it a leaving do? Or a chance for his ex-workmates to meet the new boss? Were all these Roman Customs Officials corrupt fraudsters? Were they all making a fast buck for themselves while creaming off Jewish money to fund the Roman Occupation? Maybe not *all*, but try mentioning you're a tax collector at a first-century Jewish party and you'd soon pick up how the locals felt about their hard earned money being siphoned off to Rome!

jaywalkers back on the road to God. Not to have picnics in the middle of the road with those who think they're doing fine."

New and old Luke 5:33-39

33

Jesus is on the receiving end of the third degree. "John B's crew go without, The Suits' fan club go without, but your lot fill their faces, partying with the worst of them – explain, do!"

34

Jesus grabs for an image. "Picture your typical wedding reception, yeah? Are the guests tucking in or abstaining? Are they partying or mourning? Answer: They're having a great time 'cos the bridegroom's there with them and it's all new and exciting.

35

"Okay, fade up the sinister backing track. Say the groom gets dragged off – now who's eating? Now who's drinking?

36-39

"Or focus on the wedding clothes. Rewind to a week before the wedding and one guest finds a rip in the knee. What sort of clothes repair service would stitch in a matching bit of cloth without checking if it's pre-shrunk? A soon-to-be bankrupt one! With the first wash the patch shrinks and your best wedding suit's only good for doing the garden."

[Luke 5:34] So what's the problem with fasting? Isn't it part of the whole Religion deal? It's typically about grieving past tragedies and/or focusing the mind to lobby God to bring in his New World Order. So what about here when the mess is actually being sorted in front of their eyes and Heaven on Earth is physically being beamed down and taking shape before them?

[Luke 5:35] Is this "dragging off the groom" a clue as to Jesus' own exit? A second read has this line jumping at you for attention, unless someone nudged you on it or pointed you toward Hosea 2:19 – 20 where God's making his wedding vows to his people. "I'll marry you: In the here and now and in the future; in good living and in justice; in love and in passion; in loyalty and in acceptance. I'll marry you, my wife."

Don't Like This? [Luke 5:33-39] Fasting is hard work, but less so if you just see it as an add-on Religious motivation to lose a bit off your waistline – a sort of "divine diet". If it helps, use the strap line: "low fat cheeses for Jesus". Just don't check out Isaiah 58:1 – 9 if you can't stomach the idea of what real fasting should be about.

[10] **Big Ten Rules = Ten Commandments.** Dictated by God to Moses on the top of the Sinai Mountain and the basis of Christo-Judaic law since then. Check out Exodus 20 for the breakdown.

[11] **Religious HQ = Temple.** Jerusalem's focal point of the Jewish Religion. Literally a house for God. Question is, how much does God get let out?

Jesus throws out another visual. "Pull focus from the wedding suit to the wine on the table: check the year on the label, rewind to just before the fermenting process. What sort of wine merchant would put new wine in old containers with no room to expand? A soon-to-be unemployed one! New wine needs space to express itself in new wine containers! And which philistine downs the old wine and then craves the new stuff? No, he's convinced, 'The old wine's way better!'"

Rest Day Rules? Matthew 12:1-8

1-2

Spot the dilemma: Jesus and the Team are taking a shortcut through some wheat fields. The Team are peckish and start picking off the organic groceries. But the diary page clearly states "Rest Day". The Religious Leaders have their spies out and confront Jesus. "How dare they? By working like this, your excuse-for-a-team are deliberately contravening Big Ten Rule[10] No. 4, Sub-Clause 738, paragraph 25."

3-5

Jesus' reaction? "Did someone nick your Instruction Manual and rip out the page where David and his posse were starving? Or have you just not read it? Save you looking it up, what happened was this: David goes into God's Religious HQ[11] and helps himself to the sacred bread. Worse! He dishes it out for his fellow outlaws to tuck

---

[Matthew 12:1 – 2] So what's the problem? Is it the shortcut? Nope. "Public Footpath" signs everywhere. Is it the theft of local produce? Nope. "Pick Your Own" signs for travellers dotted around the place. Is it the eating on a Rest Day? Nope. No law against that. Is it that they're, technically, harvesting crops – ie "working" – on a Rest Day? Yup! Now that could be a problem.

[Matthew 12:2] How come *Jesus* wasn't reported as tucking into the local produce? If their spies had circumstantial evidence of the main man breaking the law, wouldn't they have pounced on it? But if he's so convinced about his argument, then why not pick away?

into – totally illegal according to Moses' Instruction Manual ... unless you're a God Rep[12], which David wasn't. Or go back even further into Moses' Rule Book itself. Technically, every God Rep who lifts a finger to take a service in the Religious HQ on a Rest Day is breaking Rule No. 1 of the Rest Day protocol. But who pulls them up for it? Nobody.

6

"I'm telling you, there's someone round here who's bigger than your oh-so-crucial Religious HQ building; way bigger than your oh-so-very-important Rest Day Rules; soooo much bigger than your oh-so-ever-so-very-fundamentally-essential Religion.

7 – 8

"Like I say, 'I'm into giving people slack, not making them give things up.'" Worked out what Hosea's line is getting at yet? Obviously not, or you wouldn't be wasting your energies acting like lifestyle police and spot-checking the wrong people. 'Cos The Man is Boss of the Rest Day Rules, not vice versa."

Plot thickening Mark 3:1 – 6

1 – 3

Different time, same territory: Jesus is back in the local religious HQ on a Rest Day and there's this guy with some sort of hand paralysis. Some of the Religious Establishment are bent on catching Jesus off guard and finally getting some mud to stick. Will he/won't he work his supernatural skills on a Rest

[12] **God Reps = Priests.** The "go between" for God and his people – not to be mistaken for the "get-in-between." Years back, this guy named Aaron was the very first God Rep, and since then only his family line was eligible for the post.

[Matthew 12:3] Wasn't David totally out of line? Yes, but click on "search" for any hint of David having his knuckles wrapped for it and you'll come up "no results found, retry?" So does God waive the rules? Or are there more important things? And why were the Big Ten Rules made in the first place?

[Matthew 12:7] See Hosea 6:6 in a proper Bible.

[Mark 3:1] What's going on behind the closed doors of the Religious Establishment? Are there internal memos flying back and forth? "Is he winding us up deliberately? Is all this Rest Day civil disobedience his way of locking horns? We'll set the bait, next Rest Day – if he bites, then we know what we're up against" ... Or not?

[Mark 3:1 – 3] Probably a plant: front row – bit obvious.

Day? They watch his every move until Jesus takes the bait, several moves ahead of them. He says to the guy with the bad hand, "On your feet then, so everyone can get a good view." The disabled guy's centre stage.

4

Jesus gets provocative. "What's legal on a Rest Day? Press 'A': to do people good; or 'B': to do evil. So that's 'A' to help someone get a life or 'B' to snuff out a life?" The Suits didn't come prepared. No chance to confer. They pass.

5 - 6

Jesus looks them in the eye, absolutely furious with their stubborn, waste-of-time wrangling. So pedantic! He turns back to the guy and says, "Stick your hand out." He thrusts out the limb in question and doesn't recognize the back of his own hand! It's fully functional, strong, skilled, normal.

The Religious Leaders storm out all dramatic. They call an emergency meeting with strange bedfellows – Herod's cronies. Only one point on the agenda: "How to eliminate Jesus."

Broader fan base Mark 3:7-12

7 - 8

Jesus exits the area. He and his Team get back to Galilee Lake and the locals tag along, as ever. But not just locals, it's building – and, surprisingly, in non-Jewish areas as well as Jewish strongholds. Loads boost the Galilean tourist trade by coming from the south – Judea,

---

[Mark 3:4] What's the disabled guy thinking through all this? He's still standing there, wondering if he gets to do handstands again, if he's going to get his craftsman job back, or if Religion's going to get in the way. Torn? Confused? Miffed?

[Mark 3:5 – 6] Isn't calling a meeting and engaging in heated discussion about ways to get a man on death row also, technically, "work"? Especially if they have to go out of their way, or make the coffee, or sharpen the pencils!

Jerusalem, Idumea; from the east – across the Jordan including Perea and the Ten Towns of Decapolis; and the northwest – Tyre and Sidon.

9 – 12

The sheer numbers force Jesus' hand, and he tells the Team to sort a small boat as a makeshift stage for him. This reduces the chances of Jesus getting trampled in the stampede – so many had been seen just touching him and getting instant cures. Result? Plenty more pushing through for some of that kind of medicine! And every time there's demonic forces being ousted from their trespassing on human lives. Every time the dark spiritual forces spot him they hit the deck and scream, "You're God's Son!"

Every time, he gives the demons strict orders to, quote, "shut it!" unquote.

Not your typical celeb. Matthew 12:15 – 21

15 – 16

Jesus is aware of the Religious Leaders' game, and he's out of there, but he doesn't shake off the crowds. They leave with him and people's health carries on getting sorted at a 100 percent success rate. He tells them straight, "Don't let on who I am."

17

Why's he so not into the Golden Prize of word-of-mouth buzz publicity? So that the whole thing fits with the picture old Isaiah painted:

[Matthew 12:16] Is this some sort of reverse psychology or does Jesus really *not* want people spreading the news that he's God's Son? Is it about the Religious Leaders' scheming to get him eliminated?

Does he not want to get in trouble with the Romans for establishing himself as the Jewish Liberator? Or is it more about John B's nemesis, Herod Antipas, not being too keen on Jesus setting up shop as an alternative King of the Jews? Or does he just not want publicity from unreliable sources, likely to spin things their way? Or is it just like Isaiah prepainted the portrait in 42:1 – 4?

18-21

> "Take a good long look at the servant I'm backing.
>
> I'm so proud of the one I've picked out.
>
> I rated him, saturated him with my Spirit.
>
> So he'll teach the nations the meaning of the word "justice".
>
> He's not the loudmouth, self-publicist type.
>
> He's not the media machine, with celebrity hype.
>
> He won't step on a slug or leave a helpless turtle on its back to die.
>
> He's totally focused on making his Justice For All campaign
> really fly.
>
> Countries you've never heard of will rely on his ideas for their laws,
>
> And for the prospect of upholding their cause."

The unusual suspects Mark 3:13-19

13-19

Jesus calls his Team together. He goes up a mountain and they go with him. There are 12 of them. The plan: to hang out together, with Jesus as mentor/teacher/coach. Then to send them off to communicate, both to people (good news stories) and to evil spiritual forces (bad news stories). And ... the 12 finalists, the Team Twelve are: Si – who Jesus rebranded as Pete, Jim Zebson, his brother Jonno Zebson – Jesus gave the brothers the nickname "Boanerges" or "Sons of Thunder", then there's Drew, Phil, Bart, Matt, Tom, Jamey Alphaeuson, Thad (short for Thaddaeus), Si Keeno and Judas Iscariot, who ratted him out later.

[Mark 3:13 – 19] Twelve? Random number or symbolic of the twelve tribes of Jews? Have they cottoned on, asking, "Is this some sort of new nation?"

Chapter Five

Team Training Session

Coaching on the level Luke 6:17-20a

17-20a

Jesus goes down from the mountain peaks with the freshly picked Team Twelve and finds a plateau packed full of his devotees and loads of others from all over Judea, from as far south as Jerusalem and from the northwest coast of Tyre and Sidon. This lot had heard the rumours and legged it this far up the mountain to tap into the coaching and the curing. Those hassled by evil spirits lost the demonic voices and everyone scrambled to get a finger on this supernatural power-pack of a teacher as he was pouring out health and wholeness on them all.

He's eyeballing his crew and coaching them...

[Luke 6:17 – 20a] Is this just the condensed notes of Jesus' famous Team Training Session? If so, how long was the original seminar?

Who's laughing?*

3

"I'll tell you who'll laugh last: the people who don't think too much of themselves; who *know* their spirituality scores are poor – their ticket to heaven's already in the post (special delivery).

4

"I'll tell you who'll still be laughing: the people who know about grief, who don't shove the mess behind the sofa, but face it. God himself is going to put his arm around them.

5

"I'll tell you who'll laugh the longest: the modest, gentle types who don't go round grabbing – they'll be given the world.

6

"Who'll be laughing? The people who only want to do the right thing, like it's their food and drink – their 'good news in-tray' will be piled high.

7

"Who'll be laughing? The people who don't hold grudges, who forgive and forget – they'll get treated likewise.

8

"Who's laughing deep down, already? The pure people who aren't polluted with stuff that mugs the heart – they'll get to see God.

* See Appendix at back of book for definition.

Don't Like This? Tune into the Sermon on the Mounted TV: [v. 3] "We'll tell you who the sad cases are: Those who've got no pride in themselves, who know they're a mess and don't lift a finger to change it – they're sad. No chance of escaping the poverty trap. Losers! Sad!"

[v. 4] "Sad cases? Those who mope about, crying over spilt milk. They'll get no sympathy till they get on with their lives. Hey, get over it! Losers! Sad!"

[v. 5] "Sad cases? The timid types – they are sadness itself. They get nothing, not in this world. These days you've got to sell yourself, push yourself forward, 'cos if you don't, no one *else* is going to. 'God helps those who help themselves' and all that. Who needs 'timid'? Losers. Sad!"

[v. 6] "More sad cases? Those who try to be good – they're just so full of themselves. People hate all that 'holier than thou' stuff which usually just makes trouble for everybody else. So quit the higher ground and stop rocking the boat, you bunch of goody-two-shoes losers. Do-gooders? Sad cases!"

[v. 7] "Sad cases? We'll tell you: The easygoing people who let others get away with murder; who don't keep tabs on those who've let them down before. They'll just get ripped off again and again. You've got to be cruel to be kind, and violence is the only thing some people understand. 'Easygoing'? 'Soft touches' more like. Sad cases!"

[v. 8] "Sad cases? The 'pure', always claiming the 'moral high ground'. They need to come off their cloud and get hands dirty in the real world. The 'pure'? Sad!"

[Matthew 5:3] So when does all this world-turning-upside-down happen? Soon? Much later? Bit by bit?

9

"Who's laughing, deep down? The people who stop fights and start friendships, who turn fists into high fives – they'll be known as God's children.

10

"Who's laughing? The people who get slapped down for doing the right thing – they're given the security codes to heaven's gates.

11-12

"And *you're* laughing if people despise you and pick on you. If they libel you 'cos you're on my side – throw a party! Paint the town – your bonus in heaven's hitting the humungous mark. 'Cos that's exactly what they did to all God's couriers[1] who predicted my arrival."

Who's crying? Luke 6:24-26

24

"But bad news for you lot who are rolling in it – your designer sofa is all the comfort you're going to get.

25

"Bad news for you lot who super-size every meal – your stomachs are going to forget what food feels like.

25b

"Bad news for you smug lot with your belly laughs bouncing round the bar – you're about to face the mourning after the night before.

[v. 9] "Sad cases? Those 'peacemaker' types – they just get beaten up. Don't get involved; it's not you're problem. Don't get sucked in. Save it for your own battles. Sad!" [v. 10] "Sad? Those who are victimised for doing the right thing. Don't they realise it just makes the rest of us look bad? Rules are there to be broken, so live a little. 'Do-gooders'. Sad!" [vv. 11-12] "And you're sad when people rip into you because you're a Jesus freak. If they're victimising you for your Religion, then you're obviously taking it too far. Work on your people skills, or grease some palms and start doing some serious networking. Keep your options open, keep them guessing where you're coming from. 'Jesus freaks'. Sad cases!"

[1] **God's Courier = Prophet.** Personal message delivery service direct from God. Think any package delivery corporation, but think "quick". Although, thinking about it, with their record, the depot for uncollected packages would've been pretty chocka by the end of the Old Testament.

Don't Like This? More Sermons on the Mounted TV: [v. 24] "Good news in the happy stakes for the rich. They've got opportunities; they can take the high risk/reward option and it won't matter if it all goes pear-shaped. Even if they're not that happy, they can at least be miserable in comfort. The rich: winners. Well happy." [v. 25] "Good news in the happiness department for the well-fed. Fullness in the face shows a rich lifestyle – it's a sign of success. And if the rounded look isn't in, then a gym membership is just a drop in the Jacuzzi, and even liposuction isn't beyond budget. The well-fed: winners. Well happy." [v. 25b] "Good news on the happy-o-metre for those who laugh a lot. It's great exercise. It reduces stress and everyone loves someone who can see the funny side of life. Those with well-toned laughing tackle: winners. Well happy."

[v. 26] "Good news up the happier end of the mood spectrum for Mr and Mrs Popular. They've obviously got that likeability factor, that winning smile. People will do anything for them, including their crucial word-of-mouth marketing for their next project. The popular: winners. Well happy."

[2] **Big Ten Rules = Ten Commandments.** Dictated by God to Moses on the top of the Sinai Mountain and the basis of Christo-Judaic law since then. Check out Exodus 20 for the breakdown.

26

"Bad news for you flavour-of-the-month people, you popular ones – it's just history repeating itself, regurgitating itself more like. Their forefathers slapped the backs and bought the drinks for the corrupt couriers back then too!"

Salt of the earth? Matthew 5:13-16

13

"You lot, my Team – you're the world's natural preservatives. You stop the world from going old and moldy. Like salt, you bring out the flavor. But if you go bland on me, what use is that? You might as well be chucked out and go join the wasters at the landfill site.

14-16

"You lot, my Team – you make the world visible. You bring light. You can't camouflage a fireworks display. You don't put floodlights behind a brick wall, so don't pull curtains across the good things that brighten up people's lives. Let people see your right lifestyle, and let God get some great reviews for what he's done in your dark corners."

Dusted and done Matthew 5:17-20

17-18

"It's time to rumble the rumours: I'm not here to bulldoze through Moses' Big Ten Rules[2]. I'm not here to do a character assassination job on God's couriers. I'm not here to finish off the Instruction Manual. No, I'm here to complete it.

[Matthew 5:13] If salt was used as a preservative, as a flavour enhancer and even as a fertiliser, then why is "today's team" accused of just rubbing their salt in the wounds of the world?

[Matthew 5:14] If light is supposed to give direction, safety and even warmth, then why is "today's team" accused of using their light to interrogate the world for its crimes?

"Straight up, on the level, nothing's getting deleted from Moses' Contract – not the smallest dot from your paper print-out; not the tiniest pixel; not the faintest watermark – zip. Not till every ending, from main theme to smallest subplot, gets wrapped up and filed under 'C' for 'Complete'.

19-20

"Anyone who scribbles out the smallest clause of the Contract; or who gives the nod and the wink to others that it's okay to bend the Rules; anyone messing with the Contract will find God hacking in and changing their new Heaven on Earth[3] e-mail address to 'lowestofthelow' (yes, that's lowercaseallone-word). But anyone applying the lifestyle requirements in the Contract will get big visual links to their personal website marked 'Star Site' – top spec. We're talking major kudos in God's New World Order.

"I tell you straight, your right lifestyle has to overtake; no, has to leave behind; no, has to lap the service of the Religious Leaders[4] and Law Enforcers[5]. If it doesn't, there's no way you'll get to see Heaven on Earth."

Anger management Matthew 5:21-26

21

"You know your stuff: Locate the Big Ten Rules in your memory banks. Scroll down to number six. What's it say? 'You won't snuff out a life, stop someone's clock, blow anyone away, bump anyone off, dole out the big chill, erase, drop, hit, top, waste anyone.' And you know that anyone who flies in the face of this should be brought to trial.

22

"But *I'm* telling you, anyone who loses their cool with some-one for no reason should *also* stand in the dock. *I'm* telling you, anyone who disses someone – slagging them off with

[3] **Heaven on Earth/God's New World Order = The kingdom of God.** Like with monarchies, but with God in charge, so not like with monarchies. There's also a sense of "sort of already/but not yet" paradox. We get to download glimpses now, but the full package would cramp our hard drive's style.

[4] **Religious Leaders = Pharisees.** A faction calling themselves literally "the separated ones" – "the exclusives" perhaps. Big into Rules, running a well-oiled propaganda machine which seemed to be fuelled by people's guilt.

[5] **Religious Law Enforcers = Teachers of the Law/Scribes.** Experts in Moses' law. Academics, who sadly, often became "academic" in the sense of "irrelevant".

[Matthew 5:21] Is Jesus working from a script or just making it up as things come to him? Or is he getting it direct on the hotline from God?

stuff like 'you've got space-for-brains' – *they* should be up before the Jewish Supreme Court*. Anyone who's fluent in the dialect of slander-ese is on a one-way trip to hell's lake of burning sulphur. And not as a visiting tourist!

23 – 24

"So, picture the scene: You're in a Religious service, about to bring some sort of contribution to the front and what image lands in your head? That ex-mate who's really miffed with you. What d'you do? Carry on? No! You press pause on the Religious stuff, get in a taxi and go sort it with your mate. THEN you get back to the Religion and lift the pause button to make your contribution up front.

25 – 26

"Or, you've got an on-going dispute; the wheels have fallen off some business deal and it's got to the 'legal letters stage'. What d'you do? Come on confrontational with lines like, 'I'll see you in court, pal!'? No! You sort it, sharpish. Even if it's as late as standing on the steps of the courthouse, you settle the bills, you settle the argument, you settle your stomach. You become mates. THEN you won't see the inside of the courtroom or hear the judge's hammer or even get a close-up view of the police officer's truncheon. There'll be no fine to pay; no sentence to serve."

[Matthew 5:21 – 26] Whoa! They're hard enough as it is! So what's this talk about "Do not kill = do not lose your temper"? What's Jesus' problem with it just being a simple "to-do" list? What if we simply revert back to seeing the Big Ten as a list of "do's" and "don'ts" to be scored on? At least we know where we are then. Simply end the day by totting up your scores: "Did you murder anyone today? Nope. One point. Did you steal anything? Nope. Two points!" Anywhere around six points in a day has got to be pretty good, no?

[Matthew 5:22] Could this one be triggered by the memory of a row between two of the Team members? How *did* they get on – Pete the big-mouthed fisherman and Matt the ex-Roman lackey? Throw Simon the anti-Roman Zealot into the mix and who's to say it's never come to fists after some mealtime debate got out of hand?

Wandering eye syndrome Matthew 5:27-30

27-28

"You know your stuff: Press recall on the Big Ten Rules again. Scroll down to number seven. What's it say? 'You won't sleep with someone else's husband or wife. You won't put it about, cheapen yourselves.' But *I'm* telling you, anyone who spots a 'real looker' and locks on and fantisizes, letting their lust cells work overtime, undressing the object of desire in the cinema of their imagination – if they drool like this then they've already slept with them in their heart.

29-30

"If your right eye messes you up, gouge it out and kiss it goodbye. Isn't it better to chuck out one bit of you than to end up with all your bits, but frying in hell? And if your right hand's messing you up, hack it off and kiss it goodbye. Isn't it better to chuck out one bit of you than end up with all your bits but frying in hell?"

Decree absolute Matthew 5:31-32

31-32

"You're also well up on the clause in the Manual where Moses says, 'If you're divorcing your wife, give her the proper legal papers.' But *I'm* telling you that anyone who divorces his wife 'cos he's gone off her or there's a younger model on special offer, forces his wife into breaking Rule No. 7 when she finds someone else. The only legit reason for divorce is if she's been putting it about with other lovers. By the same logic, the guy remarrying your ex for little or no reason is also messing up on Rule No. 7 by sleeping with her, 'cos technically she's still married."

[Matthew 5:27 – 28] Was this bit sparked off by Jesus spotting one of his Team Twelve eyeing up one of the local women in the tag-on crowd? Surely not! Not one of the holy twelve apostles! They'd not have an issue with lust!

[Matthew 5:29] So is a wandering eye really the fault of the spherical organ located in your eye socket, or is it deeper than that?

The Big Ten Rules

Moses holds the copyright on the first five books of the Bible, known in Hebrew as the Torah, which contain the history and the legally binding constitution of the new Nation of the Jews. It's built around Moses' Big Ten Rules. Here's Exodus 20:1–17 according to *the word on the street*:

1–3
God dictates to Moses:
No. 1: I'm your God, your God who liberated you from slave labour in the sweatshops of Egypt. I get total priority. You won't have any other gods taking your attention away from me. I'm it, the only God! No other god's worth squat.

4–6
No. 2: You won't idolize anything else of any shape. Nothing that *is* something, or *represents* something – you'll waste no time polishing them or showing them off to your mates or looking to them for the big answers of life. 'Cos I get jealous! And when I'm jealous, I'm ruthless. I punish families even three or four generations after those who hated me have rotted in their graves. But those who live by my rules, I show *them* incredible love for thousands of generations of their family line.

7
No. 3: You won't use my name lightly, as some sort of magic word, which is supposed to blackmail me into action. You won't use it as a swear word. If you do, you won't go unpunished. Handle my handle with care!

8–11
No. 4: You'll keep my Rest Day different, distinct, special. You'll do what the word means – stop. You'll work six days, do all you've got to do, then the seventh day is my day. You won't work, your family won't work, your staff won't work, your equipment won't work, your guests won't work. 'Cos I made everything you see in six days. Then I took a break on the seventh. So will you.

No. 5: You'll treat your parents with respect. Then you'll live long and prosper in this new land I'm moving you into.

No. 6: You won't snuff out a life, stop someone's clock, blow anyone away, bump anyone off, dole out the big chill, erase, drop, hit, top, waste anyone. You won't.

No. 7: You won't sleep with someone else's wife or husband, put it about, cheapen yourselves. You won't.

No. 8: You won't thieve: nick, lift, blag, fleece, half-inch, swipe or get sticky-fingered. You won't.

No. 9: You won't deceive: lie, fib, fudge about someone, in or out of the witness box. You won't.

No. 10: You won't drool over your mate's house, their wife/husband, their garden, staff, equipment, gadgets or anything they have and you don't. You won't.

The Ten Amendments

Not happy with being tied into the Big Ten Rules? Neither were the Children of Israel. So having considered what they saw as God's "Ten Suggestions", they sent someone back up the mountain to negotiate a "more realistic" Contract. It's believed to have gone something like this (look it up in a proper Bible to do the old "compare and contrast" thing):

1st amendment: Yes, you are our God who brought us out of the land of savoury into a dessert made of all manna of things including milk and honey and lovely sweet things in general, especially chocolate. We're happy enough with this one.

2nd amendment: Okay, we shall not make for ourselves an idol in the form of anything in heaven above or on the earth beneath or in the waters below. We shall, instead, delegate those under us to make our idols, which we shall buy with our ample disposable income. Clever, more practical idols, in new metallic shapes, shiny and not like anything in God's creation — above, beneath or below. So that's all right then, surely?

3rd amendment: Okay, we shall not misuse the name of our God. But we shall franchise it and set it all up properly, so that God's name will serve to endorse all our ideas and projects and be the magic word at the end of all our prayers to ensure we get what we ask for in God's name. Yes, very happy with this one too.

4th amendment: Fine, we shall remember the Sabbath day by keeping it wholly for ourselves. Four and a half days we shall labour and do as much work as gets done, then we shall enter into a recreational establishment and drink there until the clubs open. The sixth day is a day to be kept solely to be irritable with the offspring of our loins and, of course, more consumption of the amber nectar. The seventh day is a day wholly for hangovers to be recovered from while watching sport and lounging on the couch. We find a six-day working week completely unacceptable – we're only human after all!

5th amendment: Yeeesss, we will honour our father and mother and give them the respect they deserve, which obviously isn't much given their outdated ideas and embarrassing attempts to dress like us. We're willing to nod and smile and eat their Sunday roasts and turn to them eagerly whenever we require an injection of monetary funds. So as long as that qualifies as honouring them, then we're fine with this one too.

6th amendment: We shall not murder, if we can possibly help it. But if someone threatens us, we'll be well within our rights to inflict grievous bodily harm in self- defence and possibly even commit manslaughter if we're so angry that it qualifies as diminished responsibility, especially if we can prove we've been under a lot of stress lately.

7th amendment: Of course we shall try our very hardest not to commit adultery, unless of course we were a little bit drunk, and/or it was subdued lighting, and/or we were seduced. But we shall probably end up sleeping with our boy/girlfriend (depending) since neither of us is married. So how can it be called adultery, technically, mmm?

8th amendment: We shall not steal, but if we don't feel our boss is paying us what we're worth, then we shall see the taking of manifold office freebies as only right and proper compensation, which we shall duly call a form of unofficial bonus package – tax free, obviously. We would also make the point that stealing from people who've got more than enough and wouldn't miss it if it went walkies isn't really the same as stealing in the proper sense when you think about it, surely?

9th amendment: We shall not give false testimony against our neighbour unless they had it coming to them or it's really juicy gossip or it's really funny (or all three) and we couldn't resist telling the gang … or it's for prayer, obviously.

10th amendment: We shall not covet our neighbour's house, because it's exactly the same design as our house, being on the same estate. It's just different wallpaper which we don't like anyway since they have no taste. But when it comes to that house overlooking the park, then surely you've got to have something to aim at, haven't you? We shall not covet our neighbour's husband/wife, because he/she's looking quite rough for mid-50s, but there's no harm in ogling our neighbour's son/daughter when he/she's back from college for the summer and is sunbathing in the back garden. There's no harm since we're not going to do anything about it and they should be getting a holiday job. Anyway, they don't even know we've got tinted binoculars in the back bedroom, so what's the harm?!

And verily, they took these Ten Amendments back up the mountain, but God was no longer present on the mountain top, and since the negotiator was not struck down by lightning from the heavens, the people took it as a "yes", which suited them fine.

On **my mother's life!** Matthew 5:33-37

33-37

"You know all this! What's in the drop-down menu under Rule No. 3? 'You won't use my name lightly.' The sub-clause says, 'You make God a promise … you keep it!' Some of you bring God into everything you say, going, 'In God's name, I'm straight up here.' But *I'm* telling you, don't swear by anything. Don't swear by stellar positionings; the stars are God's recliner. Don't swear by planet Earth; it's God's footrest. Don't swear by Jerusalem; it's the Great King's top location. Don't blurt out, 'On my mother's life.' Don't blather, 'On my life, honest!' 'Cos you're getting on, you're going grey. You can henna all you like, but the roots show their true colours soon enough. Let people talk behind your back and say, 'He said "yes", so he means "yes".' Or 'he said "no", so he means "no".' Any top ups and add-ons to this – any ifs, any unlesses – anything extra at all, and they're coming straight from the Evil One."

Ha**ve** ano**ther** go Matthew 5:38-42

38-39

"You don't need me to tell you. On the same page as the Big Ten, what's it say? 'Eye for an eye. Tooth for a tooth.' But *I'm* telling you: Don't do anything in self-defence, even if someone comes at you with fists flying. They whack you on the right cheekbone – drop your defences and let them have a crack (maybe literally) at the left one.

40-42

"Someone sues the shirt off your back – throw your jacket in with the settlement. Someone threatens you with violence if you don't carry their stuff a mile down the road – take it two miles, take it all the way

---

[Matthew 5:36] What's this grey hair thing? Always thought of the disciples as similar in age to Jesus? Around late 20s, early 30s? Who's to say some of them weren't older?

[Matthew 5:41] Was Jesus getting at the typical Roman soldier's game of rubbing Jewish noses in it by enforcing their right to freebie taxi services from civilians? They'd make them carry their equipment a mile both to give them a break and to remind them who's boss. Is Jesus pandering to the status quo or being revolutionary in a different way?

home and carry it to the doorstep! Don't suddenly go all deaf when someone's looking to borrow some cash. If they ask, you give."

Love, father style Matthew 5:43-48

43-44

"And this one. Again, familiar territory. The famous bill sticker slogan, 'Pour out love on the guy next door so there's only pure hate left for the guys across the road.' But *I'm* telling you: 'Keep some love back for the ones you can't stomach, and ask God to do them good when they victimise you.'

45

"This way, you'll be the spitting image of your Dad in heaven, showing a real family likeness. God knows how to do equal opportunities. He gives the sun its wake-up call and lets it loose on everyone in range, whether they deserve it or not. Same with the rain: it doesn't get instructions to go up or down a gear depending on who's down below and what their lifestyle's like.

46-47

"If you only love those who love you back, don't come to God expecting a gold star for good behaviour. Even the tax fraudsters at the Roman Tax Office do that. If you only shake hands with your buddies in the holy-huddle-in-crowd, how are you any different from any other club? Even the godless look after their own.

48

"You've got to be the best. Like God, your Dad in heaven, is the best."

Fund your enemy's project Luke 6:34-36

34-36

"And, okay, so you loan out the cash. But only because you know you're going to get it back! So where's the kudos in that? Even messed up people set up loan schemes for their fellow messed up, 'cos they know they're going to get it back. But, big 'BUT', love your rivals; do good to your archenemy. Fund their projects — on a donation basis, not as a loan and not with strings attached. Now we're talking major gold stars! Now you're starting to look like a chip off the block of the Most High God. 'Cos that's *his* style, that's typical of *him*: doling out good things for those who've forgotten the word 'thanks'; dishing up the quality goods for those who've locked onto 'evil' as a lifestyle.

"Imitate God your Dad. He gives people slack, so should you!"

Who's your audience? Matthew 6:1–4

1

"Watch yourself! Don't just do the right thing to boost your image as a 'nice guy'. Don't time your good-deed-for-the-day to synchronise with the bumper crowds. If you do, Father God will cancel the bonus he had lined up with your name on it in heaven.

2

"Some guys, when they're filling out their charity donation form at the bank, they get their mates to phone their mobile so they can tell the whole lobby area what they're doing. Don't you! Some guys milk the fact that they're helping old Mrs Brown to the shops, even giving cheesy grins to the CCTV cameras in case anyone's watching the footage. How sad is that? I'm telling you straight, these performers get their good reviews with their public, but that's it. Don't ape them.

3–4

"No, when you're filling out the charity form, don't even let your left hand know what your right hand's putting in

---

[Matthew 6:1 – 4] So where d'you draw the line between the warning here and the bit before: "Let people see your right lifestyle, and let God get some great reviews for what he's done in your dark corners"?

If this principle was actually applied, how would it change the world of corporate sponsorship? Is it ever better for some things to happen and the sponsors to waive their "heaven bonus" than for events and projects to die a death from lack of funding? Discuss.

[6] **Local Religious HQ = Synagogue.** Local meeting place for Religious Jews to worship their God. Central point of any Jewish community.

the amount box. Keep it marked top secret in your filing cabinet. Then your Dad in heaven, who has X-ray vision, will see what you do and sort out your bonus."

Template for talking to God Matthew 6:5-15

5

"And these same performers, they're chattering away to God with their mumbo-jumbo-sized prayers on main stage in the local religious HQ[6] or at bus stops or anywhere a crowd might form. They're giving it, 'Oooooh God!' full on from the diaphragm, using all the vocal tricks to get maximum effect with the audience.

"Straight up, I'm telling you, they're having *zero* effect on God. They've had their bonus, and it's not *God's* cashier who's signing the 'I promise to pay the bearer...' notes. All they're getting is a short-term fee in the plummeting currency of human brownie points. Dumb deal!

6-8

"No, when you're on the hotline to God, don't do it on public transport at rush hour – do it behind closed doors. And don't hang a notice on the handle, 'Do not disturb: saint in prayer.' Keep it invisible, like your Dad in heaven is invisible. It won't go unnoticed, 'cos doors mean nothing to God's planet-piercing vision. And he's all that counts since he's the one issuing the reward cards that matter.

"And don't go on and on and on, with boatloads of empty jargon designed to baffle and bluff. This is the script churned out by people with no relationship with God. They reckon they'll wow him by just pummelling his answering machine with their rant. No. God's got a list of what you need before you press the 'send button'. Don't doubt it.

9-13

"I'll give you a template for when you're talking to God...
'God in heaven, you're our Dad.

[Matthew 6:6] "Behind closed doors" might take on new meaning when you think that, back then, the only room in most people's houses that would have had a door was the bathroom/WC. Imagine the combination of laughter/disgust (depending) from his audience. Is Jesus using toilet humour to make a point?

Don't Like This? [Matthew 6:9-13] Always resented being forced to mumble your way through the "Lord's Prayer" in formal public gatherings? Here's an alternative version:

"Our father, who art in heaven where everything's just fine. / Shallowed be your name. / Your kingdom come, your will be done anywhere on earth that doesn't adversely affect me. / Give us this day our three square meals plus snacks and cappuccinos and parking spaces in town and most other things we neeeeeeed as and when we see the advertisements for them. / Forgive us our trespasses, but turn a blind eye to all our other mistakes, and we might tolerate those who trespass upon our own personal space. / And help us to steer as close to temptation as possible but deliver us from anything evil otherwise we'll shake our fist and scream, where were you God? / For ours is the personal kingdom that we've built down here, / Ours is the power to keep you well out of it, / And ours is the glory for all we've achieved without much help from you. / For ever and ever / Ah well."

We respect everything you stand for. We want others to stand up for you too.
Please bring Heaven on Earth: people living life your way, like the angels do.
Please bring us what we need to keep us going each day.
Please acquit us, as we cancel our grievances and throw them all away.
Please pull us back from the edge of evil, stop it from sucking us in.
'Cos you're all that matters; you're able to do it and you're to take the credit.
You're on your own.
It's your throne.
Absolutely!'

14-15

"'Cos this is the deal: you wipe the slate clean of grudges against people who've done the dirty on you, and God'll wipe *your* slate clean. And the opposite's true too: if you seethe over how you've been messed around by others, God will leave your slate of mistakes untouched by his heavenly scouring pad."

More than a diet? Matthew 6:16-18

16-18

"When you give up food (or whatever) for Religious reasons, don't do your impression of those in the 'Milking It School of Acting' who ham up their hunger, grimacing away to get it noted that they're

[Matthew 6:16 – 18] Question is, how many status games go on in today's Religious get-togethers? Who's caught standing when they should be sitting, or vice versa? Who's feeling out of it 'cos they can't close their eyes and still sing the song lyrics? Who's got their hands up or their knees down and when?

Once you graduate to a level of influence, do you forget how alien you felt in the company of these terribly Religious people?

oh-so-ever-so-very-especially Religious. They even let their hair go all frizzy/greasy/lanky/yucky/mad – all this just to up the visual effect. I'm telling you straight, they've had all the bonuses they're going to get. When you go without for God, hide it. Bluff that you're fine. Camouflage any telltale side effects so that no one would have the first clue that you've not eaten for hours/days/weeks (delete as applicable). Do this, and your Dad in heaven will see what you do on the quiet and sort out your bonus."

Long-term investment strategy Matthew 6:19-24

19-21

"Don't spend (pun intended) your life stockpiling goods with a sell-by date. Don't put your money into stuff that can just get nicked. Build up your balance in heaven's bank vaults, where nothing rots, where nothing dates, where nothing gets walked off with. Want to know where a guy's heart is? Track down where he invests his stash and his heart won't be more than an arm's length away.

22-23

"Your eyes are your body's windows. If your eyes are kept clean and healthy, loads of light will get into your soul. But if your eyes are all clogged up with gunk from the streets, there'll be no light bouncing onto your soul. And if even your soul is shrivelled up from light-deprivation, then how dark is that?

24

"No one can have two full-time bosses and do two full-time jobs. They'll either be well into the first one and resent having to turn up for the second, or they'll hate the thought of the first and look forward to clocking on for the second. You can't work for both God and gold."

Don't Like This? [Matthew 6:19 – 24] Best start underlining lots of other bits away from here. See page 100 for the advantages of this tactical use of highlighter pens. If this doesn't work, for a small investment in paper glue you can stick pages together and then avoid certain passages altogether – another useful catchall approach to these trickier sections.

[Matthew 6:19 – 24] So what about the "spiritual descendants" of the Team Twelve? How well has the church applied this principle with its property investment programme? How many quintillions are locked up in bricks and mortar? Or is this stuff more about working all the hours to get the latest gadget/vehicle/apartment (delete as applicable)?

7 **Taking God at his word = Faith/Belief.** Faith is more than just a Religious Club you belong to. Belief is more than just a vague whim. This big word is an active, gutsy, practical concept. Aka "trust".

Anti-stress programme Matthew 6:25-34

25-27

"So, I'm telling you, don't get all stressed by the pressures of life, moaning, 'There's nothing in the cupboard!' Or 'I haven't got a thing to wear!' Life's not just about what you're going to fill your face with next. Life's more than just knowing which pair of shoes to wear with what outfit. Lift your chin and look up. See those birds? They don't 'speculate to accumulate' or develop a five-year plan, but your Dad in heaven feeds them fine. And how much more worth are you than birds? Hitting the panic button is not going to get you an extension on your life.

28-30

"Anyway, why get so paranoid about labels and clothes? Lower your chin and look down at the lilies. D'you see them bent over a sewing machine? No! But I'm telling you, not even old moneybags Solomon Davidson could afford such an extravagant clothing line as they're modeling. And if that's how the lavish God kits out ordinary park plants, which will only get the sharp end of a lawnmower soon enough and join the rest of the organic waste on the compost heap, then how much more will he make sure you're walking down life's catwalk with? Why don't you ever take God at his word[7]?

31-33

"So don't stress! Stop all this, 'what'll we eat?', 'what'll we drink?', 'what'll we wear?' tripe. Those are standard lines reserved for people who don't know God, and they reel them off at random. Your Dad in heaven knows what's on your needs list. So make your life focus

---

[Matthew 6:25 – 34] So are we not to bother getting out of bed then? Nope! Ever seen how hard a bird works? Why has the phrase "the early bird catches the worm" become a cliché? Because it's true! Isn't the point more that they don't *stress* over it, they just do it? And isn't stress more likely to shorten, not lengthen, your life expectancy?

So if Jesus is talking to people who have next to nothing and don't know where their next meal is coming from, then how does this stuff apply for those of us who have most of what we need except that gadget upgrade?

Don't Like This? [Luke 6:39 – 42] Uncomfortable with the idea of Jesus being funny? This should help: Develop a mental image of the most unfunny person you know and imagine *him* delivering these lines. Some people can kill the wit in even the most sparkling of speeches. Keep this surrogate least-funny-person-you-know handy for other bits of Jesus' coaching sessions.

all about God's New World Order; all about getting in sync with a right lifestyle, and then God will lob in all these trimmings on top.

34

"So don't stress about things that might never make tomorrow's plotline. Tomorrow can take all that on the chin. Today's got enough to get to grips with without wasting worry beads on what might or might not kick off next week."

Don't play judge Luke 6:37–42

37

"Don't sit in judgement over people. 'Cos soon enough, the tables will swivel and you'll be the one getting the verdict handed down. Don't set yourself up as a life and death critic 'cos soon enough someone will be writing the review from hades on your precious lifework. Wipe the slate clean for others and you'll get the same treatment for *your* mess.

38

"Give and you'll get given – loads, compacted and piled into your lap, and then more on top so it's spilling onto the floor. 'Cos it's very much in-the-style-of-you: how you've been with people – you'll get the same treatment coming back round full circle."

39–40

Jesus also sets up a visual scenario: "Do blind people get through the interview stage for the job of guiding other blind people? Don't think so! Download this video trailer: 'Two blind people, one leading the other across the road. Just before they get to the other side we see the drain cover's off and lying in the gutter, and ... ffffsshhhwwwp ... the blind guys are six feet down in the sewer wondering what the smell is!'

"You don't train someone to be great by hiring a so-so teacher. Best case scenario is that they'll know as much as their teacher knows!

[Luke 6:38] Shakespeare's play *Measure for Measure* was based on this one verse! Mmm. Bit of culture for ya!

41-42

"Why d'you focus on the speck of house dust in your mate's eye when you've learned to live with the dirty, great big steel girder sticking out of yours? How can you keep a straight face when you're telling him, 'it's alright ... I can see it ... nearly got it ... keep still'? You plonker!

"Listen up, here's the plan: Phase One – get on the waiting list for the girder-ectomy operation on your own eye, then, Phase Two – have a good go at helping get the dust out of your mate's eye."

Keep on keeping on at God Matthew 7:6-12

6

"Don't waste sacred stuff on the stray mongrels who rip into your bin bags; don't posh up the farmyard pig with a twin set and pearls. They'll just growl or grunt and tear into you for disturbing their alfresco feast.

7-8

"Keep on keeping on at God. Keep asking – you'll get it. Keep searching – you'll find it. Keep pushing the doors – you'll get through.

9-11

"Your son asks you for a bread roll, d'you give him a rock? He asks you for fish and chips, d'you give him a venomous snake with a cyanide side salad? So, despite being messed up, you can still give good things to your kids. So multiply that by infinity squared when God's doling out good things to those who ask.

12

"Shall I sum it all up – the Rules of the Instruction Manual; the complete God Courier Files? It's this: 'Look out for other people as you'd like them to look out for you.'"

[Matthew 7:7 – 8] It's logical really. If you don't ask, how will you recognize the answer? If you don't search, how will you remember what you're looking for? If you don't push the door, how are you going to know if it's been unlocked?

[Matthew 7:9 – 12] Why keep on at God? Doesn't God know what we want? Or is that just the way he wants "the family" to work: with the kids asking/getting/not getting/having to wait/learning what's good for them/ knowing their dad and what he wants for them? Isn't this the same process every toddler has to go through?

Don't **follow the** crowd Matthew 7:13-14

13

"You're standing there with two gates in front of you.
Which one d'you go through? You check out the big one.
Peer through the chunky wrought iron frame and there's
a huge, state-of-the-art airport conveyor belt of people. It's
wide as you like, with trendy cafes at regular intervals into
the distance. Looks good! Apart from the fact that, if you
stop your fashion gazing for a sec. and look, there's a huge
sign straddling it, saying, 'Route 666 straight on; use all 13
lanes, no delays ahead'.

14

"Mmm. Second thoughts. You go to the poor relation of
a gate next to it. You peek through the rusty railings and
see a rough-looking mountain path going up, really steep,
hardly anyone on it. Looks tough going! But what's that on
that tree trunk? It's a handwritten sign that says, 'Life –
this way.'"

Charge **up your** Integrity **Detector**
Matthew 7:15-20

15-20

"Charge up your Integrity Detector and set it to alert
mode. You'll need it whenever you're within voice range of
a self-styled courier wannabe. They're like a pack of wolves
getting past the bouncers at a fancy dress party for sheep
by the simple scam of kitting themselves out in cute little
lamb costumes.

"And how does this Integrity Detector device work? Its
action sensors pick up on any evidence of right lifestyle.
If there's no signal, there's no proof of good things done,
so don't listen to a word they spin. If you do, it'd be like
wading through stingy nettles fumbling for blackberries.
You want fresh fruit salad? Do your homework and pick the
right bush. A good tree can't produce dodgy fruit, and you
don't get good fruit from a rotten tree. And we know what

Don't Like This? [Matthew 7:13 – 14] Assume that the modern concept of democracy has made this illustration redundant. Our developed, civilised world is committed to the democratic process – and that, surely, includes voting on whether God's way is the best way. People vote with their feet – or their four wheel drives, in our case – so obviously the most populated road would also be, by definition, the right road, no?

So feel free to skip this snub to the power of the immoral majority, not just because you don't like it, but in the name of democracy … let the market decide!

Don't Like This? [Matthew 7:15 – 20] Relax, there is no integrity detector. As you well know, you can fool most of the people most of the time and, let's face it, that's enough for most of us.

happens to a rotten tree: it gets chainsawed and chucked into the incinerator. So check the produce. You'll know."

Saying v doing Matthew 7:21-23

21-23

"Not everyone who calls me, 'Boss, Boss' gets to be part of Heaven on Earth. Only those who live in line with what Dad in heaven lays down. Fast forward to Judgement Day: there'll be crowds of people going, 'Boss, Boss, didn't we broadcast under your name? Wasn't it up there in neon lights? Didn't we end our begging letters with "In God's name"? Didn't we clear out the demons using your name? Didn't we tap into the supernatural using your name? Didn't we?'

"I'll tell them straight, 'I've got no idea who you are. Get lost! You're just into evil.'"

Rock solid crew Matthew 7:24 – 8:1

24-25

"So, anyone who takes all this in and applies it, then turns it into a lifestyle – they're like the guys from 'In The Know Construction Co.' who have checked their geology and only build on solid rock. The rain sheets down, it's declared a Flood Disaster Area. Gale force winds and worse rattle through the girders. But the building stays standing 'cos it's built on solid rock.

26-27

"But anyone who hears all this and does nothing to change their lifestyle – they're like the slackers from 'Dumb and Sons Builders' who buy up cheap land that's not even sandstone, just sand, and do the construction work with fingers crossed. Same rain sheets

---

[Matthew 7:24 – 27] How does this parallel apply in our Western world of stringent building regulations? Isn't such shoddy workmanship less likely to be allowed to happen here and now than in the unregulated building industry of Jesus' time?

So what's another parallel for "hearing but not doing", for "taking in but not applying"?

down, same flood alert, same gale force winds. End result? Mangled girders and shattered bricks."

28–29

Jesus stops speaking and everything's silent. The crowd is gobsmacked! "He's so different from the bog-standard Religious instructors – he's got ... what? Clout!"

8:1

And have they heard enough? Or do they want more? He comes down from the mountainside, and there's a whole posse jostling for part two of the Team Training Programme.

[Matthew 7:28] So just how brilliant/engaging/captivating/intriguing a public speaker was Jesus? The crowd probably turned up to see more of the spectacular miracle cures or even to get some of the supernatural quick fixes for themselves, but did Jesus oblige? No evidence of anything but word-of-mouth coaching. So having come with typical "bless me" motives, they leave wanting more of the hard stuff!

Why wasn't the video camera invented earlier?!

Chapter Six

Who's "The Man"?

Remote control healing Luke 7:1-9

1-5

Jesus winds up his Team Training Session, listened in to by the huge fringe contingent. They all follow him down past the "Please drive your camel carefully through our town" sign coming back into Capernaum. The Army Officer based there has a major crisis: one of his best coworkers is confined to his quarters, stiff as a shield, going loopy with pain. It's looking like the guy won't make it through. The Officer's up to speed on Jesus' medical track record and sends a delegation of Jewish Community Leaders with a request for an impromptu healing session. The senior Jews deliver the message, full-on keen to get a

---

[Luke 7:1-9] Yes, the fringe followers are impressed. Yes, they're intrigued enough to hear him out. But have they really worked out who he is? How many are still assuming he's going to lead the Revolution against Rome, or has some of that Sermon on the Mount stuff shifted their expectations? Especially since loads of his audience come down the mountain with him and are eyewitnesses to this encounter where he actually helps the "enemy"! What's going on? How are they putting the clues together?

[1] **Local Religious HQ = Synagogue.** Local meeting place for Religious Jews to worship their God. Central point of any Jewish community.

[2] **Taking God at his word = Faith/Belief.** Faith is more than just a Religious Club you belong to. Belief is more than just a vague whim. This big word is an active, gutsy, practical concept. Aka "trust".

[3] **Heaven on Earth/God's New World Order = The kingdom of God.** Like with monarchies, but with God in charge, so not like with monarchies. There's also a sense of "sort of already/but not yet" paradox. We get to download glimpses now, but the full package would cramp our hard drive's style.

green light from Jesus. "Our Officer friend has really earned this – he's well into all-things-Jewish; he built our local religious HQ[1] for us!"

6 – 9

Jesus goes with them. He's almost at the drive of the house when the Officer sends other mates out with the message, "Boss, I don't want to be any trouble. I'm so out of my depth, I can't have you actually step in under my ceiling. That's why I didn't consider myself qualified to just walk up to you in public. No, just give the order from there – remote control – and he'll be up on the next work shift, raring to go. I know about orders – I'm an army man! I take orders, I give orders. I say 'dismissed' and the soldiers are off; I say 'attention' and they're on alert; I say 'march' and they're shifting."

Jesus hears this and is stunned. He turns to the posse around him and tells them, "Straight up, I've never met anyone who takes God at his word[2] at this level. Not even in the whole of Israel."

Matthew 8:11–13

11–13

Jesus pushes the point further: "I'm telling you, when Abraham, Isaac and Jacob are honored guests at the opening party for Heaven on Earth[3], there'll be plenty of strangers sitting at the top table too. But the very people you'd think should have VIP passes will be chucked out into the dark-

---

[Luke 7:6] Was the officer also thinking Jesus would get bad press for entering a non-Jew's house?

[Matthew 8:12] And who are the people gnawing through their unused VIP passes? Are there Jews among them? Those with a heritage of being in on God's plans for rebuilding Heaven on Earth?

So Jesus isn't changing his tactic in the light of his Nazareth experience. Back home he was nearly lynched for this pro-foreigner, apparently un-Jewish talk, and he's still at it! So is he anti-Jew? Or just not exclusively pro-Jew? He's pro-Jew, pro-non-Jew, pro-half-Jew … pro-person, basically.

ness where the shrieks go right through you and the sound of teeth grinding against the pain makes you batty."

Jesus turns back to the Army Officer and says, "Go! It'll happen exactly as you said it would." Turns out the worker got a clean bill of health, right that minute.

Funeral? What funeral? Luke 7:11-17

11-13

Pretty sharpish after this, Jesus treks down to the town of Nain, County Galilee, with the Team and a whole train of hangers-on. He's within view of the town gate when he sees a funeral procession trudging his way. The open coffin has the only son of a woman who's already lost her husband. It's a big funeral. The whole town is "with her" in taking the boy to be buried next to his dad. Jesus sees her and fills up, telling her "don't cry".

14-15

He goes to the open coffin and . . . touches it. The pallbearers stop in shock. Jesus says, "Lad, I'm telling you – get up!" The dead man sits up and starts chatting away. Jesus gives the widow woman the best present ever – her dead son back.

16-17

The crowds are blown away. They're celebrating God. From the hub-bub you can hear snatches of, "A top-notch courier[4] of God has hit town" and "God's shown up to help his people". This is front-page

[4] **God's Courier = Prophet.** Personal message delivery service direct from God. Think any package delivery corporation, but think "quick". Although, thinking about it, with their record, the depot for uncollected packages would've been pretty chocka by the end of the Old Testament.

[Luke 7:11 – 17] Yes, this is a different widow from the one Jesus talked about early in Chapter 4 (see Luke 4:25, page 69). Did people think Jesus was insensitive by telling her "don't cry"? Why did he risk being labeled ceremonially unclean by actually touching the coffin (go to Numbers 19:11 in a proper Bible if you're wondering)? If he knew he was only going to give the word, couldn't he have avoided the sniff of controversy by just giving the word and not getting his hands "dirty"?

Does this ring bells with the local crowd? Wasn't it not far from here, about 800 years before, that the courier Elijah pulled off that legendary funeral stopper by raising another widow's son (see 1 Kings 17 in a proper Bible)? Were there people in the crowd who were direct descendants of the son of the Shunammite widow who got another chance courtesy of Elijah/God?

---

news on every paper; the story on everyone's lips in Judea and
beyond its borders.

Is **he "the One"**? Matthew 11:2-19

2-3

Scene changes to Herod's palace and John Baptizer's prison cell.
John's just got word on what The Liberator Jesus is up to. He tells
his crew: "Ask him, 'Are you really the One. *the* One as in THE
ONE, you know, *THAT ONE?* Or should we keep searching the
radar screens for ANOTHER ONE?'"

4-6

Jesus gets John's communiqué and sends the message back, "Tell
cousin John what you see, what you hear. The blind play 'I Spy';
the lame go jogging; the scab sufferers get baby-soft skin; the deaf
start up their music collections; the dead check their pulse and the
disadvantaged, disenfranchised, disenchanted and the just plain
dissed get fantastic news. Who's God going to make happy? The
ones who don't trip up over what I'm making happen here."

7-9

John Baptizer's crew have their answer and they're off. Jesus starts
talking up John to the crowd: "Why did you queue up for your
return tickets to the wasteland? To see a weedy guy struggling

---

[Matthew 11:2 – 3] So why were people having doubts about whether Jesus was The Liberator? He'd been hitting the headlines for around a year already and still no sign of the Roman Occupying Forces considering their exit strategy. Even John B, Jesus' own cousin, wanted confirmation about Jesus' Liberator qualifications.

[Matthew 11:4 – 9] All these results would've rung bells with John B on the predictions of the Liberator in Isaiah (check out the juicy poetry in Isaiah 29, 35 and 61). Jesus was paraphrasing some of Isaiah's most famous passages which John would've eaten up as Liberator "pre-biographies".

But was John B still wondering where the judge part of The Liberator's character was hiding? "Judgement" had been a big part of John's wasteland talks and most of the evidence is of Jesus building people up, not knocking them down. How come? Was Jesus not The Liberator? Or was he just a different sort of Liberator than the one they were expecting?

against the dust storms? No? Were you expecting some slick dude in a designer suit? No, you should exit at the palace stop if you want to go fashion spotting. So what got you off your backsides and out into the dusty wasteland? A real live courier from God and some! And some more!

10-11

"This is the one Malachi spotted on the horizon 400 years back:

'I'll send my message delivery man ahead of you.
      He'll do the prep for you.
So there's nothing stopping you from coming on through.'

"I'm telling you straight, no mum has given birth to anyone with more kudos than John Baptizer. And yet even the lowest of the low in God's New World Order has more clout than him.

12-15

"Since John Baptizer started up, God's New World Order has been progressing under enemy fire, with forceful characters trying to hijack it. But before John's time, way back in the 'olden days', God's Contract with his people and his couriers were building up the suspense. Scene after scene just building the anticipation, developing the plotlines. And, reading between the lines, you might well set John up as the second Elijah whose big entrance was predicted way back. If you're hungry, like I say, chew it over.

[Matthew 11:10] See Malachi 3:1 in a proper Bible. Prophets/God couriers were thought to be extinct. They'd become an endangered species around Malachi's time and hadn't been spotted in the 400 years since. John turning up in the wasteland is almost the equivalent of a zoologist spotting a dinosaur in the desert and then organizing trips for people to see the "Johnosaurus Rex".

[Matthew 11:11] Did Elizabeth, John B's mum, ever get to hear this? Did she need to? Didn't she already know her boy was special?

[Matthew 11:12] John knew about forceful characters trying to roadblock the entrance of The Liberator – why else was he down in Herod's dungeon? But did he assume that this sort of opposition would melt away when The Liberator showed? How come it was shifting up a gear?

---

[5] **The Man = Son of Man.** Jesus' term for himself – lifted from Daniel 7, where it's a pretty blatant clue that this is no mere mortal: "the Son of Man … surfing in on the clouds … where the Ancient of Days … gives him … all the credit for running the show … and permanent position in the top spot." Nice name badge.

16 – 17

"What is it that you guys want?
'We pressed play, pumped out our dance tunes,
But did you get down to the vibe?
No, you stayed propping up the wall.
We changed the tune, played the depressing stuff
and you didn't even frown,
Let alone get down.'

18 – 19

"Work this out: John didn't do the party thing, and the reviews are full of libel about him having demonic connections. But The Man[5] whoops it up at all the best parties, and you're all claiming he's got a drinking problem and a weakness for rich food! They even dig up the dirt on the other guests on the invite list, pre-judging my mates as messed up money launderers.

"Still, a quotable quote for you to chew on:

'Wisdom will have a knowing smile across her face when she's proved right by walking the walk'."

180 degrees – radius or temperature?

Matthew 11:20 – 24

20 – 22

Then Jesus starts laying into the towns listed on the back of the tour t-shirts. All the places that have recent CCTV footage of his supernatural showings get the sharp end of his tongue, 'cos they won't

---

[Matthew 11:16 – 17] So Jesus' big gripe seems to be about people keeping their distance,

being too cool to get involved,

too cynical to give anyone the benefit of the doubt,

too depressed to risk caring in case they're let down again,

too scared to actually commit to something,

too educated to want to be confused with inconvenient facts,

too determined to keep an open mind while sitting on the fence with both ears to the ground.

Mmm! This would've resonated with John too – he was totally an all-or-nothing guy.

---

turn their lives back round 180 degrees to God, despite the spectacular proof.

"Bad news in your inbox for you, Korazin City! Bad news on your answer machine for you, Bethsaida Town. If the supernatural stuff that made the headlines in your local tabloids had happened way back when in the Phoenecian Riviera of Tyre and Sidon, they would've turned their lives back round 180 degrees to God long ago, big time. I'll tell you straight, the fire of Judgement Day won't be turned up as hot for old Tyre and Sidon as it'll be for you.

23-24

"And Capernaum! What's the future looking like? Will it be 'sky's the limit' for you? Or will it be quite a dive? And the answer is ... it'll be a full-on nose dive, no parachute, no safety net. If the supernaturals you've seen had been on the front page of the Sodom Express way back when, the place would still be on the map. But, on the level, the fire of Judgement Day won't be as daunting for the Sodomites as it'll be for you."

Don't Like This? [Matthew 11:20 – 24] Prefer the gentle Jesus, meek and mild? You're not alone – there are courses you can attend in Apparent Discipleship and Bluffing Your Way Through Christianity where you learn a lot of nodding and smiling techniques which seem to work well enough. Many people swear (gently) by them since they allow you to pick and mix the bits you like and leave the outlandish behaviour for the fanatics or the lonely (often the same people, it seems).

[Matthew 11:20 – 24] What's Jesus doing?! Does he really want to press self-destruct on setting up the Peoples' Liberation Army? Evidently. Not only is he losing his footing in the popularity charts, he's also losing the potential sponsorship of some very influential people. Has he got a different strategy to fulfil his Liberator mission?

[Matthew 11:23 – 24] These were local towns. Capernaum was his home base for the last year. So why's he suddenly coming out with such harsh things? And what exactly happened in Sodom in 2000 BC-ish? The fire and brimstone bit is famous enough – where God uses his incendiary bomb to blast the city for its dedicated services to hedonism. But less well-known is Abraham's shuttle diplomacy with God on the part of these debauched foreigners. He got God to change his mind and agree not to "nuke the place" if there were 50 decent people in the city, then he nudged God down to 45, then down to 40, then 30 and finally drove a hard bargain with the God of the cosmos that if there were just ten decent people in the place then God would agree to call off the rockets.

Negotiating with God? How's that work then?

Access denied - retry or cancel? Matthew 11:25-30

25-26

Just then, Jesus redirects his conversation upwards. "I celebrate you, Dad! You, Boss of the cosmos and planet Earth – you get the credit for blocking the high-speed connections of the educated elite who are trying to tap into all this. And who gets to open the files marked 'Godstuff' instead? The kids – that's who! Nice one, Dad. I know you're just loving it!

27

"Dad's given me full scope to call all the shots on the whole caboodle; everything comes under my jurisdiction. No one knows me like Dad does. No one knows Dad like I do ... and those I let in on all this.

28-30

"Anyone here burnt out? Anyone running on empty? Pull in at my service station and I'll give you a break. Agree to carry my cases. Copy me on how to carry them best. Listen to my quietly spoken advice that I'll never shove down your throat, and your soul will think it's on a luxury holiday. 'Cos what I ask you to carry for me is light and streamlined to cause least resistance. It'll be so part of you, you'll hardly notice its weight!"

[Matthew 11:25 – 26] So are the crowds who've just heard his scary Judgement Day rant still listening in or is this a private conversation with God?

[Matthew 11:27] If they're listening, the Religious ones (most of them) might just be twitching at all this overfamiliar "Dad" stuff. If a Religious Jew is reading out loud and spots God's name, "Jahweh", they'll then swap it for "Adonai" (meaning "Lord") so as to be sure not to somehow break Rule No. 3 and take God's name in vain.

So, "Dad"! Is he being presumptuous, deluded or what?

[Matthew 11:28] Seems like it's an open conversation with God that all people are allowed to tune in to. Doesn't it seem like he's not so much as making an appeal, but more like praying an appeal? Or doesn't Jesus distinguish so rigidly between talking to people and talking with God?

How grateful? Luke 7:36-50

36-38

Jesus gets an invite to a dinner party with one of the Religious Leaders[6]. Just after the hors d'oeuvres, a woman with a baaaad reputation enters, stage left, and gives Jesus a deluxe foot-washing service, involving perfume, her tears, her long hair and, like, 1,000 kisses.

39-40

Jesus' host – the Religious Leader – sees this and thinks, "Some prophet! He can't even tell that this masseuse is as 'pure' as the filth on his sandals."

Jesus reads the thought bubble above his head and says, "Simon, a story for you..."

"Sure, Coach," he replies.

41-42

'Two guys, right? Both up to their hairlines in debt. Trouble is, one guy's almost bald – he owes about two years' wages. The other

[6] **Religious Leaders = Pharisees.** A faction calling themselves literally "the separated ones" – "the exclusives" perhaps. Big into Rules, running a well-oiled propaganda machine which seemed to be fuelled by people's guilt.

[Luke 7:36 – 50] What was the motive of the Religious Leader in inviting Jesus? Was he genuinely interested? And why was Jesus RSVPing "yes, I'll be there"? Did Jesus still hold out some hope of winning the Religious Establishment over? Or was he just hungry?

So what's the problem with using her hair to apply the foot cream? Just that, back then, only a prostitute would untie her hair in public. Gives a whole new meaning to the phrase, "let your hair down"! Was she oblivious to the inappropriateness of her gate-crashing at so pure a party as this? Or if she was a prostitute, was this her way of announcing to all the men in the room that she was different now?

Might this have been a clue for Jesus as to the agenda behind the invite? Not to get offered foot-washing water – well, it's not exactly welcoming! If Jesus had come hoping to win over the guy and the other guests, just how far did his heart sink when he was snubbed at the door like this?

So who was this woman? Was she part of the crowd at one of Jesus' open healing clinics? Has she been healed of something, maybe even something she'd picked up from her (allegedly) iffy lifestyle? Whatever happened, it was obviously big to get this reaction! Makes sense – if you'd been given the reins to your life back, you'd be pretty grateful, no?

has a full head of hair and only owes about two months' wages.
Both have no cash to even get close to paying it off, so the creditor
cancels both accounts. They now both have a clear credit rating.
Which of the two will be more grateful?"

43-47

Simon says, "Well, I suppose the bald one, who had the bigger
debt written off."

"Spot on!" says Jesus. He turns to the woman and says to Simon,
"See this woman? I come in with the usual animal filth caked on
my sandals and toes. D'you get me a bowl of water and a towel?
No, but she uses her *tears and her hair*! D'you even give me a slap
on the back? No, but she's not stopped kissing my *feet*! I'd been
out in the sun all day and d'you pass me the face cream or hand
cream? No, but she wastes good perfume on my feet! How much
debt d'you think she's been released from? Exactly. Must be loads!
From her response she's obviously been let off a ton of dark stuff.
But for someone who's done little wrong, we're right down the
other end of the spectrum – not that grateful really!"

48-50

Jesus says to her, "Your mess is cleaned up. You're straightened out
and sorted in God's books."

The rest of the table are now mouthing to each other, "Who's he
think he is? He can't wipe slates clean for God!"

Jesus lets the woman go. "You take God at his word and that's
what's got you through this. Walk away content."

On the road again Luke 8:1-3

1-3

After this episode Jesus goes back on tour. Notching up the
towns and villages and broadcasting the great news about Heaven
on Earth. It was Jesus, the Team Twelve plus a posse of women
who'd been wiped free of demonic (dis)possession and a whole
medical dictionary worth of diseases. The cast list kicks off with:
Mary from Magdala town, who'd lost seven demons since meeting Jesus; Joanna, who was Cuza's wife – managing director of

Herod's domestic arrangements; Susanna; plus loads more. Together these women managed to fund the tour from their own independent financial means.

Crazy or evil? Mark 3:20-22

20-21

Jesus goes into a house and the celeb. factor is taking the numbers way past capacity – there's not even enough elbow room for him and the Team to eat. Switch scenes to Nazareth where news of Jesus' workload filters through to his family. They set out to sort things, going, "he's lost his mind!" and "he's crazy!" and "totally nuts!"

22

The Religious Law Enforcers[7] from Jerusalem had a stronger theory: libelling Jesus as demonic. "He's possessed! He's only throwing his weight around with all these exorcisms 'cos he's in cahoots with the Big Boss Demon – Beelzebub, none other! Indeed – possessed!"

Enemy forces Matthew 12:22-37

22-24

The people bring a demon (dis)possessed guy to Jesus. His bully of a demon has blinded his eyes and shut up his mouth. Jesus does the eviction business and the guy not only sees things again but does the

[7] Religious Law Enforcers = Teachers of the Law/Scribes. Experts in Moses' law. Academics, who sadly, often became "academic" in the sense of "irrelevant".

[Luke 8:2 – 3] How radical is this? Okay, so Jewish society was far more open to girls/women getting themselves an education than the Romans and the Greeks around them. Jewish women had been known to fund other Religious Teachers, but this was still pretty radical of Jesus to have women on the road with him. And just how sorted was Jesus not to have to be the breadwinner? These women were obviously assertive and capable business women to have built up their cottage industries to such a point as to have surplus funds to reinvest in something they really believed in.

[Mark 3:20 – 22] So who is this Beelzebub? The name goes back more than eight centuries before Jesus, when Beelzebub was the name of the Philistines' "god-in-residence". The Religious Leaders "borrowed" the term and reworked it into another name for the Devil. Check out 2 Kings 1:3 in a proper Bible for the full story.

running commentary as well! The crowd is stunned. The question ricocheting off the walls is, "What are the odds on this being the Davidson Liberator?"

The Religious Leaders hear the gossip and make the counter claim, "We say it's only by Prince Beelzebub of the Demon Division that this showman shows demons the door."

25 – 28

Jesus knows their thought processes and brings the debate out into open territory. Jesus goes, "Picture a map of a country – civil war ripping it apart with the loyalists to the west and the rebels to the east. You may as well crumple up the map. In a civil war the whole place gets trashed. If Satan sabotages Satan's own work, he's got a civil war that neither side will win.

"How's he going to survive that? Listen, there's only two ways I can give demons their eviction orders: (a) via Beelzebub or (b) via God's Spirit. If it's answer (a), via Beelzebub, then on whose say do *your* people kick them out? How will your Exorcism Experts react to that?! And if it's answer (b), via God's Spirit, then God's New World Order is here already.

29

"Or put it this way: You can't go 'breaking and entering' the mafia boss' palace and fill up your van with his stolen art collection, unless you've tied up the top man first. Only then can you make off with the family silver.

30 – 32

"Let's not blur the edges. If you're not with me, you're against me. If you're not pulling people in, you're pushing them away. So I'm giving it to you straight. Every mess-up, every badmouthing of God that

---

[Matthew 12:24] Why is it that when something's too good to be true, people always ask "where's the catch?"? Why are the conspiracy theorists here incapable of just taking things at face value?

[Matthew 12:29] When was it that Jesus "tied up the top man"; when did he win this turf battle with Satan? Was it back in the wasteland of Chapter 3 (see Matthew 4:1 – 11, pages 64 – 66), when he swatted off Satan's tempting offers of power and fame?

goes on – it's not indelible, your slate can still be wiped clean. But if you slander the Spirit by crediting his work to Satan – calling good evil – then, whoa! This is the unshiftable stain written on your slate in permanent ink. This'll never be wiped, erased, deleted. No, this mess goes on going on.

"It's one thing to slag off The Man; we can handle that. But if you go round libelling God's Holy Spirit then it'll stay on your record right through to the end of time and into the next world.

33

"Best way of playing 'Name That Tree'? Wait till the fruit pickers are in line for casual labour, check what it says on the truck, follow it to the shop and read the label. Check with the supermarket fruit buyers – they'll tell you. You only get good fruit from healthy trees. Sick trees produce rotten fruit.

34 – 37

"You bunch of snakes! You only get rotten words from evil people. Question: Where do words grow? Answer: In the back garden of the heart. If you've got a good heart, you'll grow good words. If your heart's evil, you'll come out with evil words. I'm getting you ahead of the game: on Judgement Day everyone will stand in the dock giving evidence and trying to explain why they let all those words slip out. Words are big – they'll dictate whether the hearing ends with the word 'innocent' or 'guilty' and what sentence follows."

Bigger than Jonah and Solomon Matthew 12:38 – 45

38

Next up, some of the Religious Leaders and Law Enforcers approach Jesus. "Coach, we're looking for spectacular proof – something symbolic."

Don't like This? [Matthew 12:30 – 32] Best to avoid this idea of some stains not being shiftable by focusing on pictures of Jesus being lovely to everyone. Just pick and mix the bits you like and create your own personal Jesus – Jesus-lite, if you like. A more radical solution would be to take a thick marker pen to every reference to God being a God of judgement. Oh, and don't go anywhere near Daniel, the Minor Prophets or Revelation . . . not if you don't want to run out of ink.

[Matthew 12:30 – 32] Why can't the unshiftable stain on a soul be wiped? Is it 'cos sticking your heels in with an "I'm right" attitude means you really don't *want* your slate wiped clean, since you don't reckon it's dirty? And when you're right, you can afford to be dogmatic, no?

[Matthew 12:38] Given that "Coach" (or Rabbi/Teacher in a proper Bible) comes from the Hebrew for "great" and was a hugely respected prefix, does this mean that these Religious Suits were well into what Jesus was about or just that they know how to be smarmy?

39-41

He answered, "Ah! What a bunch! Only an evil and two-timing society would ask for watertight proof of something supernatural. Well, tough! You're not getting any pyrotechnics from me. You want something symbolic? Jonah Amittaison in the stomach of a huge fish for the best (or worst?) part of three days. Want something else symbolic? The Man in a grave for the best (or worst?) part of three days. The reluctant courier Jonah got the message to the Ninevites and they turned back round to face God. Come Judgement Day, they'll stand in the dock and give damning evidence against you lot. Why? 'Cos they did a one-eighty when they heard Jonah and you lot get a prophet of far higher rank than Jonah, but you dig your heels in with your back to God.

42

"Next witness for the prosecution on Judgement Day will be the Queen of Sheba herself. Her Yemeni dialect will be translated into only one word: 'guilty'. She went out of her way – like, over one thousand miles out of her way – to get Solomon Davidson's wisdom firsthand. But now you lot get a King of far higher standing than Solomon right on your own street.

43-45

"When a Satanic squatter gets kicked out of its human home, it flicks and flaps its way round the wastelands looking for some other poor sucker to be lumbered with the role of landlord to a destructive tenant. When it can't find any openings, it says, 'Hang on, I'll check out if my old pad's still vacant.' When it finds the previous victim still empty, its laugh echoes round the cleaned out den, as it sends the message through to seven other, more menacing demons: 'Old pad's free. Come

[Matthew 12:39 – 41] Eventually! Ever had a package delivered ages after it was sent? The Ninevites back in Jonah's era could relate! Check out the plotline in the Old Testament book with this beached prophet's name on it.

[Matthew 12:43 – 45] What's the opposite of demon possessed? Is it self-possessed or God-possessed? Certainly seems like the vacuum option isn't a goer.

on over!' With a whole posse trashing the place, the poor guy's in a worse state than before. That's this evil society. That's you lot."

Family ties Mark 3:31-35

31-32

Just then, Jesus' mum and (half)brothers turn up. They park themselves outside the house and send an errand boy in to "go get him". Jesus is centre of attention and the message gets through: "Your mum and brothers are outside — they want words!"

33-35

Jesus shocks everyone by asking, "Mum? Brothers? Do I have a mum? Are there brothers?"

Jesus deliberately scans the crowd around him, eyeballing them and saying, "My mum's in here; my brothers are in here with me. Don't get it? My real family is anyone who lives God's lifestyle. They qualify as true blue Davidson — my bro, my sis, my mum."

Don't Like This? [Mark 3:31–35] More into the romanticised view of Mary, Mother of Jesus? Well we don't actually get any quotes from her, so maybe she'd voted against the family conference decision and was only here to see her boy.

[Mark 3:31–32] Back earlier in this chapter (see Mark 3:20–22, page 121), Jesus' family had been having a powwow about their famous family member's workload. Decision made, the Davidson clan send their delegation on the 30-mile trip up from Nazareth to sort things out for their big bro/oldest son who, they're convinced, has lost the plot.

[Mark 3:33–35] So is Jesus trashing the Big Ten Rules here? Rule No. 5 reads: "You'll treat your parents with respect. Then you'll live long and prosper in this new land I'm moving you into." Or does the Sermon on the Mount show he's still into this concept and just redefining "family"? Controversial or what?! No, worse – scandalous! You don't hire Demolitions R Us to do a job on one of the ancient pillars of Jewish society like the family. You do not undermine the family unit, not in Israel in Jesus' day. Does Jesus need a PR consultant? Or does he know exactly what he's doing?

[1] **Deep-as-you-like stories, riddles and images = Parables.** From the Greek word to "put things side by side" (ie, parallel). An ancient craft where you say things different ways; where an earthly story can take on a heavenly meaning ... if you dig.

Chapter Seven

Just Stories

Good acoustics Mark 4:1-2

1-2

Again, Jesus kicks off a lakeside coaching session. Again, numbers are pushing the patience of the Health and Safety Officer in the crowd. Again, Jesus opts for the good ol' fishing boat approach. He's sitting there on his floating stage, moored just off a beach full of people who are all ears. Again, he's clueing them in on things with his deep-as-you-like stories, riddles and images[1].

Riddled with it Matthew 13:4-23

4

Jesus goes, "A farmer's out sowing seeds. He's chucking seeds out all over the place. Some hit the footpath. The seeds don't even get to the starting line; they're out of the race – only good for the birds to grab for their lunch 'to go'.

[2] **Heaven on Earth/God's New World Order = The kingdom of God.** Like with monarchies, but with God in charge, so not like with monarchies. There's also a sense of "sort of already/but not yet" paradox. We get to download glimpses now, but the full package would cramp our hard drive's style.

5-6

"Some seeds hit the rockery. They grow okay in what little soil there is, but they're more sprinters than long distance runners so their scorched leaves soon droop and drop off in the blazing sun.

7

"Other seeds rebound off the brambles. They set out at a good pace, but as they grow they get throttled by the thorns and end up as 'did not finish'; just marked down as 'also rans'.

8-9

"But other seeds hit good soil. They benefit from the good conditions there and hit the finishing tape, getting a great result."

The crowd look at him as if to say, "And...?"

Jesus just says, "If you're hungry – chew it over!"

10

The Team quiz him by asking, "D'you forget the moral, or what? And why's it always stories with this lot anyway?"

11-12

Jesus spells it out: "You guys have the inside story on what Heaven on Earth's[2] going to look like. But not all that lot are there yet. If you've made a start, you'll get shifted, bit by bit, further along the journey. You'll get a bit of momentum going and make loads of progress! But

---

[Matthew 13:4 – 23] So what if, when trying to engage with those still dubious/unsure/interested/intrigued, Jesus pulled the plug on the preaching and just told stories from everyday life, instead, leaving it up to them to delve into the spiritual dimension if they wanted?

[Matthew 13:10] Before you read Jesus' explanation, you might want to have a stab at the meaning for yourself! Why were the Team so shocked that Jesus used deep-as-you-like stories, riddles and images to make his point? Wasn't this standard practice for many Religious life coaches of the time? Was Jesus being more cryptic than most teachers? Maybe their run-of-the-mill stories had obvious "big arrow pointing" morals and didn't need thinking about. And why does Jesus seem to be making it deliberately difficult for people to tie him down?

if you've not even bothered to get moving, you won't just stay where you are; you'll drift backwards.

13 – 15

"That's exactly why I use stories, riddles, images in public:

'So they'll watch, but not see.
So they'll listen and not hear what I say.
So they'll just not get it; glaze over and drift away.'

"It's totally what Isaiah said would happen:
'You'll hear every syllable, but the words won't go in.
You'll see every action, but the lights won't go on.
'Cos these people have got a dodgy heart condition;
They've got a hardening of the spiritual arteries.
They're spiritually dead. And the symptoms spread:
Ears all gunged up with wax.
Eyes all blocked up with cataracts.
Otherwise, they'd listen and hear.
Otherwise, they'd watch and see.
Otherwise, they'd find the meaning appear,
And they'd turn around to the new things they'd found.
And I'd heal their fear.'

16 – 17

"But you lot are laughing, 'cos you've got sharp vision; you've got crisp hearing. I'm telling you, whole lists of ol' time couriers of God[3] lost sleep straining to catch a flicker of what you see – but it was miles off, all blurred and out of focus in the distance. Good people were up nights, craving for what you hear – but it was still a distant whisper.

[Matthew 13:13] See Isaiah 6:9 – 10 in a proper Bible.

Is it that Jesus doesn't *want* them to get it? Or is he being ironic with his "otherwise they'd get it" lines? Or is it that he doesn't want to just "wow" people into the kingdom with his considerable powers of persuasion; that people need space to work it out themselves? Question is, would Jesus get kicked out of Church Evangelism Training taking this approach today?

---

[3] **God's Courier = Prophet.** Personal message delivery service direct from God. Think any package delivery corporation, but think "quick". Although, thinking about it, with their record, the depot for uncollected packages would've been pretty chocka by the end of the Old Testament.

The Jews News Interviews

Just stories

Yesterday Jesus Davidson regaled hundreds more people on the Galilee beach with his stories. But does anyone really know what he's getting at? We interviewed several eyewitnesses to Jesus' recent presentation and asked them what they made of the show, and one story in particular – the inefficient arable farmer. Here's what people said:

Maria Danson: "He's soooo captivating on that floating stage of his! He just grabs your attention and doesn't let go. But I hadn't really thought what the stories were actually about, not till you asked me. I suppose they're about Religion and such, but more than that, I'm not sure. I'll have to think about it!"

Rabbi Zacharias Engels: "Well, of course, it was a thinly veiled reference to the judgement passages of the prophet Joel, specifically Joel 3:13: 'Swing that sickle – 'cos the harvest is ready for the blade. Stomp on those grapes – for the vat's jam-packed.' Not that most of the audience members would've spotted that without it being spelt out, which he failed to do. So for me – or rather for them – I fear he missed the boat … so to speak!"

Hannah Capston: "It was amazing! I was there, miles away, back in Eden Garden, imagining God walking through Paradise Gardens with Adam and Eve. God strewing out seeds all over the fields; Satan dropping his snake costume and adopting a new bird disguise and stealing some of the seeds; Eve telling Adam, 'How many times have I told you to cut back those brambles!' Only then I thought there wouldn't have been brambles in paradise would there, and I got distracted and missed the end of the story. But it got me thinking and it was just great being there!"

Joe Epherton: "I reckon it's a teaser. I was mulling it over all night. I reckon it's something to do with him casting himself as the good seed and recreating himself thirty times, sixty times, even one hundred times. He's started with the twelve guys and his female crew, but if he's going to liberate us from the Romans, he's going to have to aim a lot higher than just one hundred strong forces! So I don't really get it, still working on my theory I guess."

Sam Aaron: "Well, I'm a farmer, so I was totally with him all the way. The way he told it got me thinking, *I do that! And what a waste!* I spent most of the rest of the afternoon scribbling down ideas for a machine; a new tool that throws out the seeds more tidily to cut back on the wastage that Jesus was so strongly against! I can't go into details here 'cos I've not patented the idea yet, but it'll revolutionize my farm, and maybe I can set up a sales department and shift loads of them to other farmers. Don't know why I'd not thought of it before. Anyway, no more clues."

Ben Perez: "Well, I reckon the seeds were people, probably, and it got me really thinking about that classic bit from Isaiah (40:8): 'People are like blades of grass. Their best years, like the short flowering season, don't last – they're gone. Grass gets mown down; flowers droop and drop off, but the Boss' message stands strong and long.' It's always been a big favourite bit of mine, but it came back full force – that I didn't want to just produce flowers that'd die, but crops and fruit, something that'll do some good while I'm down here. Really got me thinking about how I react to what he's saying. Which seed am I?"

Josh Calebson: "Well, they're just stories. Fair dues to the guy, he tells them well, but he's not going to change anything by just entertaining the crowds with stories. I don't see what the fuss is about. Some people get off on reading all sorts of other worldly stuff into it; shoe-horning morals into what are basically just fun stories. They spend hours dissecting every word and reading some crazy Religious ideas into it. Me? I'm not against what he's doing, but some people just take it too far!"

Add your views to those above by going to www.newromantimes.co.it.gos/jesusdavidson/yourseedideas.

Don't Like This? [Matthew 13:4 – 23] Not happy with all this "wrestling with the story" approach? Prefer someone else to explain it for you? Well, maybe the Bible's not the book for you then. Best avoid most of the Old Testament and loads of the Jesus bits. Your best option is to go straight to the "epistles from the apostles" where it's generally far more direct. So maybe ditch the Bible altogether – given that it's about 51 percent story, 29 percent poetry and only 20 percent explanation. Best get hold of a seriously thick book of Systematic Theology which'll tell you what you should think.

18-19

"Okay. Ears in gear?" Jesus explains. "Here's the inside story on the seeds and soil story. Ever wondered why some people hear the great news about God's New World Order and it leaves them blank? It's basically a hit-and-run heist by the Evil One: swooping down into their heart and making off with the seed – like it's bounced off concrete.

20-21

"Ever wondered why some people hear the great news, get all pumped up about it, but a couple of weeks later, all the joy's burnt off? It's about depth – or lack of! When there's more rock than soil the seed's got nothing to get its roots into, so when hassles or victimisation crop up, it's got no grip to keep things together. It's over.

22-23

"Ever wondered why some people hearing the same news just get sidetracked by stress levels and money troubles? The seed of an idea just gets throttled by the sly suggestions and anxiety

---

[Matthew 13:18 – 23] Jesus used images from everyday life, so how about TV as an image: Think of a TV producer and his new programme, "God's New World Order". Some would-be viewers never tune in; those evil rival channels steal them with their own programmes. These non-viewers miss out completely 'cos they're tuned in elsewhere.

Second viewer category: these guys watch "God's New World Order – part I", and they're into it at first but don't have the concentration to stick around through the commercial break and go channel flicking. They never tune back in for "part II".

Third viewer category: this lot watch, get well into it, but then after the break things go pear-shaped (toast burns/pipes leak/stock markets crash, whatever) and they leave the room to sort it and miss out.

Final viewer category: these people watch the whole thing, record it, play it back till the tape goes fuzzy, then buy the series on DVD, check out the website and subscribe to the fanzine. They're out there getting 30, 60, 100 of their mates into it.

"Results!" thinks the TV Producer. "I've connected."

attacks of modern life. With that noise pollution clogging up your brain, there's no way you can think about an end product.

"But there are seeds thrown out which land on good ground. These people take it in, mull it over, make connections and then start spreading the news. Ever wondered why these people get the same seed but multiply the effect by one hundred, by sixty, by thirty times? Why? We're talking 'quality soil'."

Levels Mark 4:21-25

21-23

Jesus gives the crowd another mental image to play with. "Question: Do you buy a lamp to (a) just shove it in the cupboard or under the bed? Or to (b) attach it to the stand that's still in the box? Look, what's blurred now will come into focus. What's just a series of dots will suddenly show a great image – if you look long enough. Replay the riddle and work it out yourself. If you've got ears, use them.

24-25

"And don't let any old noise pollution bounce around your eardrums! The more you live out my words, the more you'll get out of them, and some! Those who've got will get given more on top; those who've got zilch, even the 'zilch' itself will be cut and pasted, leaving them with less than zero.'

Sleep on it Mark 4:26-29

26-29

Another Jesus sound bite: "Want to know what God's New World Order's like? This guy chucks out seeds onto the ground. And then ... does nothing ... not one thing ... diddly-squat. What difference does it make if he sets the alarm and gets up early, or if he dosses around

---

[Mark 4:24] Is it like a computer game? Might he have used that image today? Staying at level one is dead tame. But work at it, get up to the higher levels, and it's way better. Level two isn't just twice as good as level one; level three isn't just three times as good – no, we're talking exponential: ten times as good; 100 times as good! Focus on collecting the points and you'll get *more* points; stop bothering and you don't stand still – you go backwards, losing points by the minute, till your score hits "worst ever".

Don't Like This? Finding all these different stabs at describing Heaven on Earth a tad frustrating? For your convenience, the majority of Jesus' parables have been compiled into one neat story. Read on....

A certain man sold all he had to buy a field. He set his hand to the plough with his two equally yoked oxen, but he had ears to hear the plough as it hit something underneath the good soil. He knelt down to dig, and he found a treasure chest of great worth covered in pearls of great price that had clearly never been thrown before swine. He knocked and knocked and, verily, the lock was duly loosed on earth. The lid sprung open to reveal an old wineskin, which he shook and 100 tiny mustard seeds fell out: some fell on the thin soil, some fell among the weeds, some fell on the good soil, but the 100th seed fell on the footpath and was immediately taken away by a bird which flew off towards the northern range of hills.

The bird dropped the 100th seed on a farm in a far off land run by a rich farmer who was tearing down his barns and building bigger ones. The demolition made a loud noise and he begged forgiveness from his Samaritan neighbour who forgave him. But then when the Samaritan threw a party to celebrate him finding his lost coin, the rich farmer didn't love his neighbour but instead had him thrown in jail for anti-social behaviour. Soon the farmer went off on a long business trip, but he still had ears to hear about the great storm that had just washed away his new barns, which he'd built upon the sand. When he realised how foolish he had been, he died that very night of shock.

in bed all day? The seed still works its magic. And he hasn't the foggiest idea how! He's not out there on all fours coaching, cajoling, coaxing them, saying, 'Come on, you can do it, focus on the tree you'll be – push through the pain barrier, come on!' Nope, the seed just does its seed-thing; pushing itself up as a stalk, stretching out as a head and then morphing into full-grown grain. Then it's time for the guy to actually do something – just slicing the grain off and transporting it to the warehouse."

Enemy sabotage Matthew 13:24-30 / 24-26

Jesus is on a roll. He tells the crowds another story. "Want to know what Heaven on Earth looks like? It's like a farmer getting hold of top quality wheat seed and planting it in his field. Job done, his staff workers are off duty, sending up some hard earned zzzzzzzs. But the CEO from the rival production firm is wide awake, decking himself up in night gear and infrared goggles and emptying a truckload of darnel weed onto his competitor's field and then legging it. When the plants spring up, one of the farm staff spot the weeds growing next to the wheat.

[Mark 4:26 – 29] Is Jesus hinting at Noah's famous Seasons Song from Genesis 8:22? "As long as there's a planet called Earth, / Day and night will play tag, cold and heat will take turns; / The seasons will run and hand over the baton to each other, / And nothing's going to stop them again."

In what way is Heaven on Earth going to grow without our help? Are we off the hook and don't have to lift a finger – apart from on the TV remote? Or is Jesus trying to point out what his audience would possibly take for granted?

27-28

"The worker makes an urgent appointment with the boss and gives his report. 'Sir, it was top quality seed you planted back last spring, yes? 'Cos the place is, like, totally covered in darnel weeds.'"

" 'This is sabotage!' the boss shouts. 'Enemy sabotage!' " The coworker takes initiative, 'So, I'll get the De-Weeding boys in then, yes?'

29-30

" 'Whoa!' says the boss. 'No way, you'll just mess up the good crop. We'll have no wheat left! No, here's the plan – let both grow free till the distribution trucks turn up, then I'll send a memo round to all the staff telling them to work in three phases:

    Phase 1 = wait,
    Phase 2 = bundle up the dodgy darnel and
        stick it on the trucks heading for the
        incinerator,
    Phase 3 = warehouse the wheat and stack it
        up high.' "

Meanwhile, the mustard seed deposited by the bird in the damaged farm grew larger than any of the other trees in the region. But there was a drought and it became overgrown with weeds. Its leaves were scorched in the sun and the mustard tree was left bare and completely alone in a far off land separated from his family by a huge range of mountains. Then the tree came to his senses, saying, "my farmer's other ninety-nine mustard seeds have each other as neighbours, and I am completely alone. I will call up all the faith I have and command the mountain range to throw itself into the sea." The faith was enough and once the mountains were sinking into the sea, he could see his homeland in the distance where the farmer was still searching for the one lost mustard seed.

The farmer saw how the lost mustard seed had grown when he was still a long way off. He ran toward him and threw his arms around his trunk and began to prune the tree. He brought the branches back and began to graft the branches into each of the ninety-nine trees that grew safely in his field.

But the ninety-nine older mustard trees said, "Why should we waste even ten percent of our sap on these prodigal branches?" The farmer called all his friends together for a garden party to celebrate, but his friends made excuses saying they had just got married, bought fields or cattle and so couldn't come. So he called the tramps and strangers and they enjoyed a banquet where every guest was given a party bag to go home with made out of new wineskins and containing a pearl of great price and food so lavish that even the dogs under the table couldn't finish off the crumbs that fell. That is what Heaven on Earth is like. Much clearer now?

[Matthew 13:24 30] **Blank on this one? Jesus is about to give the Team a decoded version backstage, so hold your horses ... If you were on the beach with the crowd you'd have had to work it out yourself or just not bothered and taken someone else's word for it.**

[Matthew 13:25] **Darnel weed? It does what it says on the bag, "Caution: Darnel appears exactly like wheat in early stages of growth, but is easily distinguished from its rival when ripe."**

It's the little things that count Mark 4:30-32

30-32

Another story: "God's New World Order? What image really captures it? How about the mustard seed? Go to the shops and ask for a pack. It's probably the smallest seed they've got in stock. But once it's in there, wow! It'll put your other garden plants in the shade! There's no stopping it. Ask any mustard seed what it wants to be when it grows up and it'll say, 'A tree! I want to be a tree!' Wind the clock on a generation and the same seed will be sending out signals to all the local birds, 'Nesting or Just Resting – facilities to let'. It just keeps growing till its branches are big enough to throw gazebo parties for the local birds."

Influential Matthew 13:33

33

Jesus gives them another angle: "What's Heaven on Earth look like? Got a bread maker? How small is that packet of yeast!? And what's it say on the directions? 'Mix thoroughly into twenty-two litres of flour.' Must be a misprint! 'Twenty-two litres'!? But it works wonders when you 'mix thoroughly' into the dough."

[Mark 4:30 – 32] Which Old Testament courier's bouncing round heaven going, "that's one of mine" this time? Ol' Ezekiel gets one of his hinted at by the master storyteller in his list of influences (see Ezekiel 17:24). "Ask any of the trees of the field, and they'll all tell you, 'God snaps the trunks of the look-at-me tall trees and makes the we're-not-worthy saplings stand tall and strong; same God dries up the show-off green trees and makes the cracked dry trees flourish.'"

Apparently from millimetres small to three-metres-plus tall – good yardstick (only it's metric) for the growth of the Jesus Liberation Movement. Twelve timid cap twiddlers to tens of thousands of radical committed crew – quite a turnaround in a season of just weeks. But that's about two years off yet, back to now…

[Matthew 13:33] So is Heaven on Earth about quantity or quality? By setting up both the mustard seed and the yeast images, is Jesus hinting that it's about size *and* influence; about growth *and* infiltration; about numbers *and* calibre?

Just stories Mark 4:33 - 34

33 - 34

So, with loads of riddles, deep-as-you-like stories and coded visual images, Jesus teaches his public about God's ways. He feeds the people as much as they can take in without giving them indigestion. He says nothing to them without using some sort of riddle, image, picture, symbol of some sort. But when he's "backstage" with his Team he explains everything.

Always telling stories Matthew 13:35

35

All this "storyfying" links back to what God's old couriers wrote about him:

> "If my lips are moving, I'm telling stories, riddles, images —
> deep-as-you-like.
> If my voice box is open for business, I'm unlocking the padlocks
> on the time box of all that's profound,
> Buried in the ground when the world was made.
> Finally found when I come around."

[Mark 4:33 – 34] So is this storytelling approach a new tactic brought on by the increasing opposition, or is this the way Jesus always taught the general public? Up until now, the main coaching session on record was the marathon on the mountain plateau in Chapter 5 (see pages 87 – 109), which was a hybrid of parables and some pretty direct stuff. But that seems to have been mostly aimed toward the Team Twelve (plus *x* number of women crew and other devotees). Sure, the crowds were allowed to listen in, but it seems more as a trailer for what they'd be letting themselves in for if they signed up as crew.

[Matthew 13:35] Check out Asaph Berekiahson's song lyrics, Psalm 78:2 in the Old Testament. Matthew uses his poetic license, tweaking the words a bit, but, interestingly, the early verses in this old hymn are all about not hiding the old truths from the children, and yet it's still talking about using stories/parables! Wouldn't that confuse the kids or is this 'cos children click onto stories straight off and it's the adults who are metaphorically challenged?

Backstage debriefing Matthew 13:36-43

36

Jesus takes a break and goes backstage into Pete and Drew's house. The Team clobber him for explanations, saying, "Uh ... you know your story about the weeds? Well ... we don't get it."

37-39

Jesus switches into left-brain mode and explains, "Okay, cast in order of appearance:

- The boss farmer who sows the wheat seed = The Man
- The field = Planet Earth
- Top quality seed = Members of God's New World Order
- The darnel weeds = Children of the Evil One
- The saboteur = The Devil
- Harvest time = The climax of world history
- Farm staff workers = Angels.

40-43

"The violent ending, where the weeds are pulled up and burnt? 'Wrap It Up' time (just before Judgement Day). The Man will give the angels their work order: Two words, 'Get weeding'. They'll pull up by the roots everything that messes things up, everyone that's into evil. They'll bundle them up and drive them personally into the incinerator. Over the noise of the roaring flames will come the stabbing shrieks of grief and the muffled sound of teeth grinding against the pain. Cross

---

[Matthew 13:37] You know the usual cop-out clause, "Scenes and characters in this story are entirely fictional and bear no resemblance to real events or people"? Well, Jesus is saying scrub that for this story. Could this story be true – it just hasn't happened yet?

[Matthew 13:40] How well did the Team know their Old Testament quotes? Could they spot that Jesus was casting himself in the roles normally associated with God himself – the sower, the farmer and even more classic God-roles coming up? Did they pick up Jesus' use of the handle "The Man" from Daniel 7 where it's clearly an image of God finally sorting the mess out? (See Daniel 7:13 in a proper Bible.) Is this getting near to an answer for all those times we've all said, "Why doesn't God step in and sort out the evil stuff"? Is he waiting till Judgement Day itself? If so, why?

fade to those with right lifestyle, shimmering in the reflected sun of
Dad's New World Order. If you're hungry – chew it over."

What's it worth? Matthew 13:44-46

44

Jesus also says, "Heaven on Earth? It's like one of those guys in a
field with his metal detector. The thing's going 'wee wah' crazy, so
he digs down and finds ... well ... d'you want the good news or the
bad news? The good news? It's a metal safe packed full of diamonds.
The bad news? The field's not his so he can't touch it. What's he do?
He cashes in the metal detector, everything he owns, sells his flat and
everything in it – he's got to get hold of that secret stash of diamonds.
He sits tight and waits till the field comes up for sale. That's what
Heaven on Earth is worth!

45-46

"Or put it this way. Heaven on Earth? It's like a jewellery dealer coming across the-ultimate-mother-of-all-pearls. Once she's picked her jaw
up from the shattered glass counter, she goes off and sells everything
she owns – all her pervious pearl stock, her wheels, her pad – everything! Then she comes back, steadies her hand to write the cheque and
walks out as the proud owner of that football-size pearl. That's what
Heaven on Earth is worth!"

Trawling techniques Matthew 13:47-52

47-50

"Another one? Heaven on Earth is like the net from an industrial
trawler. The crew lower the net into the water and when it registers
as full, the fishing crew winch it back into the boat. The fish fill the
hold and the sorting team start their work, picking out the good fish
and sorting them into baskets. The dud fish left over are chucked out.
Strong image for how things are going to get wrapped up when the

[Matthew 13:44 – 46] What's the spiritual equivalent of a metal detector? What does the bleeper sound like
in your head when you realise there's something of Heaven on Earth in the room? Is that what goose bumps
often are – just your Heaven-on-Earth-alert detectors trying to get your attention? Or are goose bumps an
entirely physical phenomenon completely detached from your spirituality?

history books close for business. Look again at the fishermen: they've got wings, they're angels! Look at the fish: they've morphed into real people! Two types — the double-tongued evil-eyed predators and the right-backed wave breakers. The angels are hurling the evil-eyed into the fire; the crackling of burning flesh doesn't quite drown out the shrieks of grief and the grinding teeth against the pain.

51-52

"Vivid enough for you?" Jesus checks. "D'you get it now?"

"Loud and clear," say the Team.

Jesus adds, "So every graduate from the University of God's New World Order, having specialised in 'Heaven on Earth' studies, is like a host throwing a party and surprising his guests with all sorts of goodies: new and old; innovative and traditional; cutting edge and established."

Don't Like This? [Matthew 13:47 – 52] All this weeping and wailing and grinding of teeth stuff could be scary if it's applied too close to home. So, feel free to deflect it towards those "really evil people" – those people in categories that we demonise and label as "beyond redemption." Make sure you act as if you're the centre of the universe and then your standards of behaviour become the norm. This makes "evil people" easy to spot as people who are worse than you. Whatever you do, don't imagine anyone you know being tortured in this way – it'll be a bit more digestible with just world tyrants and the like.

Chapter Eight

Last Galilee Gigs

Who is this guy? Luke 8:22-25

22-23

One day Jesus says to the Team, "Let's get some waves behind us; let's go across to Galilee east side." They push off from the beach and Jesus takes a power nap. The weather forecast said "calm", but gale force winds whip up the lake with the waves acting like they're auditioning for an ocean disaster movie.

24

The Team shake Jesus awake, wide eyed and worried and yell, "Boss, Boss, we've had it. We're going under!"

He takes his head off the cushion and stands up to the gale force winds. "Whoa! Calm down. Enough!" The wind drops everything; holds its breath and the waves sulk like told-off toddlers. The lake is ironed out – flat as an indoor swimming pool.

[Luke 8:22 – 25] Is Jesus weary from tour fatigue or from being with people 24/7?

25

Jesus quizzes the Team, "Did you bail out on taking God at his word¹? How come your trust dive-bombed overboard?"

Now they're more scared of Jesus than they were of the wind; more wowed by him than they were at the strength of the storm. When they regain the power of speech, they're going, "Who is this guy?! He's even got the elements eating out of his hand!"

Destructive tendencies Luke 8:26-39

26-29

Jesus and the Team sail east and moor up in Kersa, County Gerasene. The second Jesus gets his feet on terra firma, he's "welcomed" by this nutter who's leaping out from the tomb caves and is obviously (dis)possessed by evil forces. The guy had forgotten what clothes and houses look like, because tombs have been his natural habitat for so long.

The guy's groveling flat out in front of Jesus shouting full throttle, "What's your business with me, Jesus, Son of Big God? I'm begging, no torture, pleeeeease, no torture!"

Why the pitiful pleading? Jesus had given the eviction order for the demon to leave the man alone. He'd suffered so many demonic

---

[Luke 8:22-25] Play a word association game with most Jews of the day and what would their Religion-soaked subconscious throw out at the word "water"? They'd probably come back instinctively with words like "danger" or "judgement" or "catastrophe". Their land-dominated history is packed full of water-causing worries. Right back on Day Three of history: "God says, 'Too much water! We need something to walk on, a huge lump of it – call it Land.'" (Genesis 1:9)

Would their minds have played song lyrics like: "God our Liberator . . . who smoothed out the crashing oceans; / who shut up the roaring seas; / and with such ease, calmed the chaos of countries, / disarmed the fear of nations far and near?" (Psalm 65:7)

Or this one: "You rule – the mountain waves. / You rule – the surging seas. / When you have your say – the surgings cease?" (Psalm 89:9)

And the classic: "God came down hard on the Red Sea, / split it down the middle; / he led them through the ocean floor, / their footing on the dry land sure." (Psalm 106:9)

seizures. He'd been victim to so much sabotage on his life: the locals would chain the guy up by his hands and feet, but his demonic-charged adrenaline snapped the chains like their best blacksmith only had soggy newspaper to work with. His demons had driven the guy into virtual solitary confinement out in the wasteland spaces.

30 – 31

Jesus orders, "Name?"

"Legion," he spits out – 'cos there were loads of them in there! He is (or they are) begging Jesus, over and over, not to banish them to hell's black hole. "Not The Abyss, please, not that black hole! Not The Abyss."

32 – 33

There's a herd of pigs in the next field. The demons in their panic are still thinking quick enough to beg Jesus, "If you're going to kick us out of our accommodation, send us into those pigs."

"Okay," says Jesus, "pigs it is. Go!"

And the demons exit the man; a whole herd of pigs get dodgy lodgers and go crazy – stampeding down the steep bank and hurtling themselves into the lake where they sink and die.

[Luke 8:30] Just how many demons were in there? A "legion" of soldiers in the Roman Army was 6,000 men. Had the man forgotten his real name? Or wasn't he allowed to speak for himself?

[Luke 8:32] Pigs might be a strange sight in a Jesus bio pic, but this east side of Galilee Lake is non-Jew territory, so it makes sense.

[Luke 8:32 – 39] Does Jesus like the symbolism of sending the demons into nonkosher, unclean animals? Should Jesus expect hate mail from animal rights activists? Did the demons drive the pigs off the bank, or did the pigs commit mass suicide to escape the demons? Did Jesus know what would happen? What does it say about the destructive power of the enemy? Why are the locals not into the idea of Liberation from destructive evil forces? Why are they more concerned about the profit margins of their local enterprises than the Liberation of one guy?

How else might the crowd have reacted? Options from the following:

    1. "Oh, yes, really pleased for the poor guy."

    2. "Wow, God's amazing!" (continued on next page)

---

34 – 36

The pig security team run off to the town telling everyone, "What could we do? It wasn't our fault! The pigs just suddenly went mad." Sensation in small town Kersa! Big, angry crowds, striding out to see who's been messing with the livestock? They track Jesus down to the beach and think there's been a body switch. "Is this Legion's long lost brother or what?" and "Whoa! This is freaky – it is Legion! Only he's so … well … so, self-possessed." The eyewitnesses give the locals a full running commentary on how the demon (dis)possessed guy had been brought back to his beautiful self.

37

The crowd are so scared rigid that they go, "Get out of here you freak show magician!"

Jesus ups and offs, back into the boat, back onto the lake.

38 – 39

But the Legion guy, well, he's up to his waist in the water, begging Jesus to let him come with him.

"Nope!" says Jesus, giving the signal to the boys to leave shore. "Go back to your family, get them up to speed on what God's done for you, on how he's given you so much slack."

So the guy doesn't just talk up Jesus with his family; he goes round the whole town getting all passionate about the difference Jesus has made to him.

(continued)

     3. "Look forward to getting to know the real bloke."

     4. We'll have a bit of whatever this healer's got."

But no, it's option number five: "Get out of here you freak show magician." The guy formerly known as "Legion" needs a new name – the old one just doesn't sit right anymore.

Is this a change of policy; Jesus giving permission for the guy to spill the beans on who did the healing? Or is it different tactics 'cos they're not in Jewish territory anymore? Is it that people here won't get the wrong end of the javelin when they hear the word "Liberator"? They don't have the same baggage as those Jews who saw it as the catalyst for some violent political revolution to kick out the Romans, so maybe Jesus thinks it's okay for the guy to talk God up.

Blood and death Mark 5:21-43

21-22

Jesus sails back over to the west side of the lake and the crowds on the Galilee beach are having to take it in turns to breathe again. Soooo many people! Then one of the big guns from the local religious HQ[2] – Lay Deacon Jairus, no less – turns up.

23

Jairus spots Jesus and swallows his pride by hitting the sand, getting horizontal and face down at Jesus' feet. He's giving it everything, saying, "My little girl's dying, dying! Please, won't you come and do your healing hands thing – then she'll be fine again?"

24-28

Jesus goes with him, as do the hoard of hangers-on. Then ... shift focus onto an obscure-looking woman who's obviously got bad self-esteem and is stuck on the wrong side of people's jibes. Flashback: semi-blurred images of bleeding/haemorrhaging/ year-long periods; calendar pages flicking through twelve long years; library footage of her in surgery after surgery; her writing hand filling out checks to clinics for extortionate amounts; distressing images of her getting worse and worse until her eyes light up when she hears about Jesus. She's elbowing her way

[2] **Local Religious HQ = Synagogue.** Local meeting place for Religious Jews to worship their God. Central point of any Jewish community.

Don't Like This? [Mark 5:21 – 43] Guys, find all this talk of women's periods a bit off? Most of this episode is a bit women's issues ('scuse the pun), so if this doesn't apply, just flick on through. Look at it this way, if it was a film, you'd probably offer to make a cuppa at this moment. "No, don't worry about pausing it, I'll pick up the thread, thanks."

[Mark 5:21 – 43] Was Jesus going for the Inaugural Male Feminist Award? This sandwich structure story has both the bread and the filling with Jesus focusing on women's stuff. This is radical back then – especially when one is not only female, but "just a kid" (their term) too!

[Mark 5:21 – 22] Jesus has sorted "infectious skin diseases" and "tombs", now he moves onto "blood" and "death" – all stuff that marks people out in Jewish society as "contaminated goods", "rejects", "dross". Think AIDS/HIV back before we understood how you did/didn't catch it and you're getting the idea.

[Mark 5:23] Quite a sight, no? A senior figure in the town, swimming against the white water rapids of the Religious Establishment's growing animosity towards Jesus. So why the shift? Well, when your 12-year-old girl's dying, you don't give a stuff about what your colleagues think or what you thought only days before. You'll do anything. Blessed are the desperate!

through the mass of people, determination on her face, she's thinking, "If only I ... if I can ... just ... touch his ... just touch his coat – I'll be whole." She's stretching out her hand; she gets a finger on his coat.

29 – 31

Yessss! No more blood. She knows it – physically, psychologically – her trauma's timed out. Same moment, Jesus realizes a surge of supernatural power has left him. He turns round accusingly and asks, "Okay, who touched my coat?"

The Team are non-plussed and answer, "Uh, probably about twenty of us! What d'you mean 'who touched my coat?'?"

32 – 33

Jesus ignores them and just keeps looking round. The woman knows what's happened; she comes clean by hitting the deck and telling the whole story in front of the whole crowd.

34

Jesus goes, "Daughter, d'you know what's healed you? Taking God at his word and doing something about it – that's what! You're whole now: physically and spiritually whole. Walk off a different woman, content that your misery's a thing of the past. Go enjoy life!"

35 – 36

Jesus is still sending the lady off to her new life when Jairus' staff run in, bringing bad new from the house. "She's dead. Jairus sir,

---

[Mark 5:25] What's so terrible for the lady isn't just the pain or the crippling debt but the label "reject" that everyone projects onto her. They were keen on their Leviticus (15:25): "When a woman has her period and it drags out longer than normal, she'll be 'contaminated' and so labelled a reject. You'll be keeping the law by sidelining her, putting her in her place."

[Mark 5:29 – 33] What's Jairus thinking? "Come on ... come on Jesus! Hellllooo! Everyone touched your coat! Hello! Come on, don't get sidetracked. This woman isn't dying, my little girl IS."

How countercultural is Jesus here? Jairus is an official; the woman is an outcast. Jairus has a life-threatening crisis; the woman has a chronic condition. But both are desperate, so both get his time.

your daughter's dead! No point in taking up any more of the coach's time, eh?"

Jesus ignores the messenger boys and tells the Lay Deacon, "Don't freeze with fear. Take God at his word."

37–39

Jesus whittles the observers down to just Pete, Jim and Jonno, Jim's brother. They get to Jairus' house and Jesus sees the organized chaos supplied by the "Don't Bottle It Up School Of Grieving". They're all earning their pay as Grief Stimulators and it's just too in-yer-face for Jesus. "Why all the noise pollution? The child's sleeping. She's not dead."

40–43

Quick switch of extremes: they shift from tears of tragedy to rolling around belly laughing at Jesus.

He gets rid of them and takes his inner three Team and the girl's parents into the room where the child's body is laid out. He holds her limp hand, lifts it up and says, "Talitha koum!" If your Aramaic's a tad rusty, this means "little girl, I'm telling you – get up!" Within the nanosecond, the girl's up and walking around like any other twelve-year-old. "Stunned" is not the word. There is no word for it!

Jesus insists that no one gets to hear about this. He's also the first to spot that she's probably peckish and suggests a snack.

"See no evil, speak no evil" Matthew 9:27–34

27

Jesus gets moving again, away from Jairus' place. Two blind men follow him. The clatter of them crashing into dustbins doesn't drown out their yelling, "Give us some slack, Mr Davidson; liberate us, eh?"

[Matthew 9:27] Did these two guys sense that Jesus was The Liberator? 'Cos if he was, then eyesight would be one of his specialties, as they'd heard it read from Isaiah (35:5 – 7) ... check it yourself!

The Jews News Interviews

Yesterday two of our female community members got their lives back – one literally, one symbolically. We speak to the father of Ruthie Jairchild and also to the lady who nearly spoilt his day...

Jairus – the longest hour

"It was the longest hour of my life. I'd been morose, playing out how life was going to be without our Ruthie. Then someone says Jesus was in town with his "mobile miracle clinic". Finally, there was something I could DO! I'm racing down to the beach, wondering if I'd track Jesus down in time, elbowing my way through the crowds. There was that heart-stopping moment when I didn't know what Jesus would say about my little Ruthie; then the exhilaration, the flood of relief when he agreed to come to the house. Then – oh – unbelievable! Then this stupid woman – sorry, but that's what I thought then – was virtually killing my daughter by faffing about with her 'women's problems'. Not exactly life threatening, come on! Of course, I was pleased for her when Jesus sorted it, but the clock was ticking, my heart was ticking like a time bomb about to blow my world apart. Then my people rush in. Before they said it, I knew it was over. Kaboom! I was back to all the thoughts from before about life without Ruthie, only now they were even darker, having dared to hope. But the healer was asking me to trust him! I guess seeing the woman sorted was like a turbo injection of faith and I sort of did, until he came to the house and it hit me – *maybe he's just paying his respects.* Was he deliberately messing with my head? I need a top up of trust! Don't know how, but he brought her back! We've got a signed plaque above our fireplace, just the words, 'Talitha koum'. I can't walk past it without filling up."

ers.

Sudden popularity

"People always treated me differently, but now it's a different type of different — if you see what I mean. Before Jesus — BJ — it was snubs and jibes and snide comments, all sort of justified by the Instruction Manuals. It's not that I blamed them; they were just doing things by the book. Even seconds before getting to Jesus I was getting shoved away, treated like I've got the lurgy — especially in the desperate face of Jairus. We've laughed about it since, over a meal we had at his place, but at the time he was burning the word 'DISAP-PEAR' into me with his laser glare.

"But after Jesus — AJ — the way people treat me is so different. Now I'm the one they all want to meet. People listen to what I've got to say just 'cos Jesus did his wholesome thing on me. And the laugh of it is that, frankly, I've got no more to say than I did before. It's just that people wrote me off back then, assumed I had nothing worth hearing and sidelined me.

"If anything, it's really made me think about what I say. 'Cos when people pay you this sort of attention; when they shut up when you're just clearing your throat, you want to make sure it's worth saying. So now, maybe I've actually got *less* to say, but it's more worth saying. It's totally different now after Jesus. It's not just my health he's given me back — it's my voice too."

Was Jesus right to push Jairus' patience by delaying? Does the happy ending justify the trauma our local official was put through? Should Jesus have walked on past?

Your thoughts to www.newjewsdaily.co.il.gos/stayorgo.

28

Jesus goes inside. The blind guys feel their way through the door. He checks, "You going to trust me on this?"

"Totally, Boss," they chorus.

29-31

He touches their eyes with his hands and says, "Since you're so convinced, it'll happen." Instantly, they're enjoying 20/20 vision. Again, Jesus cuts through the celebrations, goes all stern and warns them, "Don't broadcast this round. Keep this on the quiet!" So they do the exact opposite, hiring a vehicle and doing the chat show circuit, sending their story across the region.

32-33

They're hardly out through the door when a demon-(dis)possessed guy piles in. His demon-in-charge has zipped his mouth shut and the guy can't even whisper his symptoms. Jesus gives the eviction orders to the demon and the guy says his first words for yonks. The public are scrabbling around for words themselves, words big enough to fit this spectacular stuff. All they can manage is, "never before" and "not in all Israel."

[Matthew 9:28] Why did Jesus go inside? Was it a (not-so) vain attempt to dampen the hype after the last spectacular healings? You bring a child back from the dead and you have plenty of people shaking your hand. Or was he testing their resolve; seeing just how determined they were? Why did Jesus touch their eyes? Before, the Army Officer got his coworker healed by "long distance remote control". Does Jesus treat every situation differently? Why do we sooo want there to be a formula?

[Matthew 9:31] Normally Jesus is anti-fame, so why does he press the healing button at all? With the number of times Jesus has dismissed a healed patient with the "don't tell" instructions, it can only be concern for the guys needing the health injections.

Was Jesus always torn, always wrestling over the question, "If I heal this person, the publicity ratings will rocket, but if I don't, their lives will stay wrecked. What do I do, Dad?" How different is this from "spiritual healers" today?

34

The Religious Leaders[3] are quick to find a different word for it: "demonic." That's what they think — "He tells demons where to go 'cos he's demonic."

Local reception Mark 6:1-6

1-2

Jesus finishes being the Miracle Doc for a while and goes back home with the Team. Not Capernaum home, but home "home", as in Nazareth. First Rest Day[4] he takes the gig in the local religious HQ. He's doing his coaching thing and they're all blown away by his originality. "Where'd he get this stuff?" they ask. They're nudging and whispering mid-talk, "Talk about wisdom! Plus the supernaturals to back it all up!"

3

They blab away, "Isn't this the local handyman — the guy who used to stop our tables wobbling?!" "Great with hammers and nails!" "Yeah, it's Mary Davidson's runaway-to-be-famous oldest." "But aren't those his brothers: Jimmy, Joe Jnr, Simon and Jude!?" "Look, all his little sisters are still around too!" They sniped away at him behind their hymn books from the safety of their pews. "He's forgotten his roots he has." "Yeah, got a bit too big for his sandals."

[3] **Religious Leaders = Pharisees.** A faction calling themselves literally "the separated ones" — "the exclusives" perhaps. Big into Rules, running a well-oiled propaganda machine which seemed to be fuelled by people's guilt.

[4] **Rest Day = Sabbath.** Rule No. 5 in Moses' Big Ten: "You'll keep my rest day special." By now this "special" had been defined down to the nth degree. There were plenty of things you shouldn't do.

[Matthew 9:34] Why will there always be some cynics who'll find a way of putting the kybosh on people's good news?

[Mark 6:1] Do they stay with his mum and half siblings? Do the family still think he's a few ingredients short of a fruitcake? Do they take it in turns to talk him round to being "a little more sensible"?

[Mark 6:3] Thirty years later on a "Where are they now?" programme, they couldn't track down Joe Jnr or Simon. But they had no trouble tracing Jimmy and Jude through the Bible publishers; they both got a book into the bestselling Life Manual. Jude's e-mail is only brief, but James (Jimmy) Davidson gets the most on-screen minutes as he's a major name in the Jerusalem branch of the Jesus Liberation Movement by now. He's holding the fort while Paul Benson and Pete Jonahson go off on their Euro-Tours. So when did they change their opinion about Jesus?

---

[5] **God's Courier = Prophet.** Personal message delivery service direct from God. Think any package delivery corporation, but think "quick". Although, thinking about it, with their record, the depot for uncollected packages would've been pretty chocka by the end of the Old Testament.

[6] **Heaven on Earth/God's New World Order = The kingdom of God.** Like with monarchies, but with God in charge, so not like with monarchies. There's also a sense of "sort of already/but not yet" paradox. We get to download glimpses now, but the full package would cramp our hard drive's style.

4 – 6

Jesus sees the irony. "There's no place like home! It's history stuck on repeat! Most other places a courier from God[5] gets the red carpet treatment, but in his own hometown it's only zero respect!"

He couldn't bring himself to spark the supernatural – hardly got into gear at all, just touching and healing a few people. Now it's Jesus' turn to be stunned – they just can't seem to take God at his word.

Job vacancies Matthew 9:35 – 38

35 – 36

So Jesus hits the road again taking the tour around all the towns and villages, coaching the people at the local religious HQs, communicating the fantastic news about God's New World Order[6] and sending all the ill people back home skipping like big kids. Every time he sees the crowds, jostling for poll position, his heart leaps for them. He sees the stress on their foreheads from a mile off; he sees the weight on their shoulders dragging their sights down to the gutters; he knows they're like lost kids, with no tour guide, no guard, no minder, no mentor – so vulnerable to ruthless abusers.

37 – 38

Jesus darts a quick aside to the Team. "Look, they're so up for this! So ready. Ripe as a juicy olive! But you just can't get the staff. Ask the Big Boss; lobby him to take on more workers; to blow the advertising budget and get the troops in place to handle all these lost people queuing up for life."

[Matthew 9:38] Were there really so few signing up? Were the terms and conditions so hard that there weren't enough staff? Or is it just that even with an army of staff the job's still overwhelming? What does Jesus do to up the numbers? Does he lower the entrance requirements? Read on...

Working conditions Matthew 10:1-42

1

Jesus calls a powwow with the Team Twelve. He commissions them as Jesus Reps with the clout to kick out demons and clear out diseases.

2-4

And the 12 names again? The Team Twelve are firstly Si, who Jesus renamed Pete; Si's bruv Drew; Jim Zebson; Jim's bruv Jonno; Phil; Bart; Tom; Matt (ex-Outland Revenue[7] Officer); Jamey Alphaeuson; Thad (short for Thaddaeus); Si Keeno and Judas Iscariot, who ratted out on him later.

5-7

Jesus sends them off with a big coaching session: "Don't go to the non-Jews. Don't even go to the Samaritans. Keep it 'in-house' for now. Focus on the lost kids of Israel. Your catchphrase: 'God's New World Order — just round the corner.'

8

"If they're ill — heal them. If they're dead — bring them back. If they're outcasts on account of their skin — sort it for them. If they're demon (dis)possessed — drive out the Satanic squatters. You've had so, so much; don't get all tight fisted on doling things out like there's no tomorrow, without keeping tabs.

9-10

"You're travelling light. Don't take any petty cash with you in your wallet. Don't take an overnight bag. Don't take a spare jacket, shoes or walking stick. No, if you're working, then you're worth your bed and full board.

[7] **Outland Revenue = Roman Tax Department.** Where the Empire collected its taxes from the minions. Hence Outland Revenue Officers weren't exactly popular.

[Matthew 10:2 – 4] Why 12? Was Jesus deliberately going for the symbolism of the twelve tribes of Israel? Did the women who were on tour with him (mentioned in Chapter 6, Luke 8:2,3, pages 120 – 121) stay put?

[Matthew 10:5] So Jesus wasn't into holding their hands, wrapping them up in cotton wool then? Talk about throwing them in the deep end! Did he think they were up for it? Did he think they'd cope? At least they couldn't say he didn't warn them.

11-13

"On passing the 'Welcome to Our Town' sign, track down someone worth their weight in heaven gold and kip down in their spare room till you're off, even if you get offered an upgrade somewhere else once the locals get into what you're doing. Say 'hello' as you cross the welcome mat. If the place deserves you, let your serenity rub off on them. If it doesn't, make yourself scarce and your peace will slide off them and come back to you.

14

"If they won't take the door off the chain for you or even listen to you through the intercom, then take a stick to your shoes and clean off the street gunk as you clear off out of there.

15-16

"I'm telling you straight, it'll be better to be in the Sodom and Gomorrah cell when Judgement Day comes round, than for the people in that place. I'm sending you off like lost children among ruthless predators. So be as streetwise as a city fox while staying as innocent as a pet dove.

17-18

"Don't be naïve. Go into this with your eyes wide open: They'll stitch you up, hand you over to the Big Wigs on the city council and dole out the punishment beatings in their local religious HQs. You'll stand trial in front of local judiciary and even royals – all 'cos of me. But your evidence will hit the papers and get the story out there.

19-20

"And when you're handcuffed, don't freak about how to defend your case; what to say, how to phrase it, which tie would win the judge over best. No. You'll get your script from the Prompter just before you deliver each line. It won't seem like it's you talking. It won't be! It'll be the Spirit of your Dad. He'll be speaking. You'll just be his PA system.

21

"Brother will turn informer on his own brother and hear the judge pass down the death sentence. Dad will turn in his own daughter, knowing she's up for a capital offence. Kids will stitch up their parents and watch them face the lethal injection.

22 – 23

"You'll be national hate figures, 'cos of me. But those who take it on the chin will be straightened out and sorted by the end. If victimisation hits you in one town, move house, but straight up, you won't have covered all the towns on the map before The Man[8] shows up again.

24 – 25

"A pupil can't exactly pull rank on his teacher. A staff member doesn't get more privileges than her employer. The pupil gets no better deal than the teacher. The worker gets no more perks than the boss. And if they slag the chief off, laying into him with slander like 'Beelzebub' or 'Demonic Prince', then what sort of dark defamation of character are they going to hit the rest of his Team with?!

26 – 27

"Don't lose sleep over these bullies. It's scheduled in: A time when the top secret files will be open to the public; when the cover-ups will be blown apart. I'm telling you in private, but you're to get it out there in the public domain. I'm whispering this stuff into your ear, but you're to broadcast it via satellite.

[8] **The Man = Son of Man.** Jesus' term for himself – lifted from Daniel 7, where it's a pretty blatant clue that this is no mere mortal: "the Son of Man ... surfing in on the clouds ... where the Ancient of Days ... gives him ... all the credit for running the show ... and permanent position in the top spot." Nice name badge.

[Matthew 10:22] So when's the world going to get so "Christophobic"? Was it like that for the Jesus crew's first solo tour, or was Jesus looking further into the future?

[Matthew 10:26 – 28] Mmm! Could this pep talk possibly be why "the workers are few", why "you just can't get the staff" (Matthew 9:38, page 152)?

Is it wise to advertise a job which expects – not "has the possibility of", but "expects" – terrible working conditions, family division, corporal punishment and regular imprisonment? What sort of crew is Jesus looking for?

28

"Don't waste adrenalin over the guys who can shoot you in the head, but have no way of getting a bullet anywhere near your soul. I'll tell you who should get your undivided attention – the one who can wipe out both your body and soul . . . in hell.

29 – 31

"How much do they get for two sparrows? About one pence. But not one sparrow dive-bombs without God seeing it hit the deck on his control room monitor screens. You lose a hair on you pillow over-night – God knows what number hair it is. So don't get a sweat on about these thugs making threatening noises; you're down on God's balance sheet as a major asset, worth way more than the figure next to the stock of sparrows, even when they've rounded it up.

32 – 33

"Whoever makes it clear in their conversations that they belong to me – I'll also own them out loud when I'm talking with my Dad in heaven. But whoever goes quiet, avoids eye contact, looks at their shoes when my name crops up – I'll have to tell my Dad, 'Nope, can't speak for them.'

34

"You're making assumptions here. If you jump to the conclusion that my mission statement is for everything to be serene, you're way off the mark. I'm not here to make everything lovely and squidgy, with families skipping through a field of daisies together, holding hands and laughing.

35 – 37

"No, I'm here to stir up trouble. I'm into swords, not sofas; tough choices, not the easy life. There'll be:

[Matthew 10:29 – 31] That might be number 2,338 out of 9,382; fewer for some!

[Matthew 10:35] Check out this Old Testament bit in a proper Bible, Micah 7:6.

'Dads turned against sons.
Mums with cold shoulders to their daughters.
Feuds between daughter-in-law and mother-in-law.
Arch enemies behind the same front door.'

"If you put your nearest and dearest up there before me on your priority list, you're not worth calling one of my crew.

38

"If you don't take the strain under the weight of your own execution equipment and if you don't pull your weight and carry on with me through thick and thin, then you're not worth calling one of my crew.

39

"If you fight to do things your way, going, 'it's MY life', then it'll slip out of your hand and hit the deck. If you open up your palms and give it all up for me, it'll fly! You'll get to grab hold of real life.

40-41

"If someone waves you in, all smiles and open arms, they're opening the door to me and, by definition, they're welcoming the one who sent me here. You give one of God's couriers your spare room 'cos of what he does, you'll get a courier-size bonus. You let someone who does the right thing stay with you 'cos of his lifestyle, your bonus will match the one they're in for.

42

"And if you give a bottle of still water to even the smallest member of my Team because he's one of my crew, I'm telling you, you won't lose out on your bonus."

Don't Like This? (Matthew 10:1 – 42) Is this pep talk not in sync with what you signed up for? "They told us our burdens would fall from our backs, so what's all this about having to pick up our cross? They told us we'd get a life, so what's all this about losing it?"

Do assure yourself that this discrepancy between Jesus' idea of being "on the Team" and the church's idea is mostly due to a misunderstanding about "different levels of buy in." Surely what Jesus is talking about here is only for those opting into the highest level of commitment – for the real fanatics, or just for the Team Twelve back then perhaps, or just for the full-time Christian workers right now, or for those in far off lands with dictators for rulers. Surely, it's not us. We signed up for something altogether more realistic . . . didn't we? Something more in line with Jesus' line "my yoke is easy". Yes, we like that one.

Ambassadors Mark 6:12-13

12-13

And they're off! The Team Twelve leave and talk up the need for people to turn back 180 degrees to God; evicting whole estates of demonic squatters; healing loads of people, smearing sacred oil on them.

Price of confrontation Mark 6:14-29

14-15

Shift scene: King Herod is all ears; his spies are on permanent over-time. Herod has to have the latest briefing on all goings-on. Jesus and his trainees' antics are top of the report pile. Herod ploughs through the paper work:

> theory A = Jesus is John Baptizer come back from the dead;
> theory B = Jesus is actually Elijah;
> theory C = Jesus is a new courier in the old mould.

16

Herod's own (guilt-riddled) "eureka moment" lands on, "He's John Baptizer. I decapitated him, but he's back from the dead!"

17-20

Wave after wave of flashback scenes plunging deeper into the roots of Herod's paranoia:

> Back before this, we see Herod giving the orders for John to be slung into the back of an unmarked vehicle and put in his place — namely, chained to some prison wall.

[Mark 6:12–13] How did the Team react to this trial by fire? Did it all go smoothly, or were there teething problems? And what's with the oil?

[Mark 6:14–15] In case anyone thought Jesus might've been over egging all that victimisation stuff from above, here's what happened to John B when he applied God's New World Order to the nitty gritty.

So what's with Theory B? Why Elijah? Could be 'cos there's no record of Elijah actually dying. The Good Book has him going directly to heaven in a chariot of fire without dying (check out 2 Kings 2:11 in a proper Bible). He probably should've got a percentage on the Performing Rights Society money for the old spiritual, "Swing low, sweet chariot". It swung low enough to scoop him up into heaven. Hence the theories that it'd be Elijah who'd turn up again around the inauguration of God's New World Order. See also Malachi 4:5 in a proper Bible.

Before this, we see Herodias, Herod's brother's wife – the lady
he'd just stolen and married – and she's nagging her new hubby to
silence John Baptizer.

Before this, we see John shoving placards under Herod's nose.
"Wife stealer!" and "Rule No. 7 – look it up!" Add to the mix
John's in-yer-face soapbox speeches going, "Your marriage is illegal!
You wife's still married to your brother! Sort it!"

No surprise then that Herodias hates John's guts and, when she's
feeling low, imagines him rotting six feet under to bring a bit of zing
back to her life. But she's stumped 'cos Herod's got this thing about
John – half fear, half intrigue, half respect.

The fear's stoked by Herod's reports of John being a good man, an
outstanding man. The intrigue is just that, despite trying not to,
Herod really likes listening to the guy speak, and the respect is fuelled
by John's radical lifestyle.

21-23

Cut to the (un)chaste: Herod's birthday. Big banquet. All the Suits are
there. All the Uniforms are there. And Herodias' fit daughter is dancing. Broad smiles on the faces of all his dinner guests as she's "shaking
her beauty"! Herod's besotted with the girl, totally intoxicated with
her moves. He opens his big mouth and shouts over the dance track,
"It's yours! Anything you like. Just ask and it's yours!"

He's swearing by this, that and the next thing, saying, "Whatever! I
just draw the line at over half my realm!"

[Mark 16:17 – 20] Quick bio of Herod Antipas' new "wife", Herodias: She's family – having called Herod the
Great "granddad"; she had just walked out on Antipas' brother, (and her uncle) Philip. But since Philip's still
alive, the whole dynasty soap opera is defying Moses' Big Ten Rules. Plus Leviticus 18:16 – check it out in a
proper Bible.

[Mark 6:21 – 23] We're not talking dancing as in "ballroom", probably more like dancing as in "pole". This was
somewhere on the spectrum between sensual and soft porn.

24

She goes off to the little girls' room with her mum to discuss the offer. "What? What? What do I really want?"

Herodias just says, "John Baptizer's head."

25

Straight off, before anything changes, the girl sweeps back into the King, picks up an empty meat tray and purrs, "This tray's missing something – yes – John Baptizer's head, please."

26–28

Shift in atmosphere or what?! The king's sweating. Everyone's stock still frozen. All the Uniforms. All the Suits. He's thinking, *I can't rat out on my word, I'm a Herod.* All eyes are locked on him, seeing if he'll wheedle out or deliver. He caves in and gives the order, "Head of John Baptizer, here, now, on that tray."

So the on-duty Death Squad Officer does the deed and makes a big presentation of the plate with the unplanned delicacy "courier head in cold blood sauce". The girl, in turn, hands it to her mum.

29

John's previous team hear the news and collect the rest of his body and give it a decent burial.

Chapter Nine

Super Natural

Spiritual retreat Mark 6:30-31

30-31

Just checking in from their "in the deep end" training exercise, the Team Twelve report back to Jesus and exchange stories on what happened on their sortie: all the action, all the coaching. They've created more of a buzz than before and don't even have time to eat on the go. Jesus calls "time", saying, "Right, what's needed here is a spiritual retreat. Just us, on our own. You guys could do with a bit of R&R."

Jesus reads the headlines Matthew 14:13-14

13-14

Round the same time, Jesus gets the news about John's execution, and it hits him hard. He takes off in a boat for some badly needed quiet time. Fat chance! Local rumour merchants pick up the latest sightings and chase round the lake blabbing away, telling everyone where he is.

[Matthew 14:13] What was going on in Jesus' head when he heard the John B news? Was he angry? Scared? Sad? Was he wrestling with his Dad about "why"?

Jesus moors up and sees the huge welcome committee. His need for time on his own is blown away by concern for the crowds. He starts healing the sick people they've carried to him as if he were some kind of "mobile miracle clinic".

Thousands plus for a picnic Mark 6:34b-44

34b

Jesus saw the crowds as, like, a bunch of teenagers without a hero; like a tourist party without a guide; like a party without a DJ; like a team without a coach. So he's coaching them with loads of things.

35-36

It's later in the day. The Team interrupt Jesus in between stories with, "This place is a marathon run from anywhere and it's already getting dark. Best wind up the coaching session, eh? Send them off to the nearest shops; get some food inside them before the day clocks off."

37

Jesus comes back with the line, "You feed them!"

One of the Team blurts out, "To feed this lot, the budget would be, oh, what? About two-thirds of a year's paycheque! You're not proposing we blow that much on the catering, surely?"

[Matthew 14:14] No comment on the reaction of the tour-weary Team: probably unprintable!

[Mark 6:37] Is Jesus winding them up? Earlier he told them not to take food or money with them, now he's telling them to feed a massive crowd! With what?

Wouldn't you love to know which disciple had calculated the catering budget? Pete was often first off the mark, but then "Matt the Tax" was good with figures, and Judas Iscariot was proud owner of the Team Treasurer name badge – so, any guesses?

Didn't we learn earlier that the team of x number of women did the catering from their own resources (see Chapter 6, Luke 8:3, pages 120 – 121)? So how come he asks the Team to sort the problem? Or is this part of their mentoring scheme? Does Jesus hope one of them will think of tapping into supernatural supplies? Why didn't they?

38

Jesus pushes it further, asks, "Okay, you got any pita bread between you? Check it out."

They come back saying, "Uh, we've rustled up five – five pita breads. Oh, and, uh, two sardines."

39-41

Jesus gets the people to sit down in groups of 50s and 100s on the lush green grass. Jesus takes hold of the five pita breads and two fish, looks up, thanks God, and rips into the bread, giving out chunks to the Team as he breaks them off. He's splitting the fish up too and doling out handfuls.

42-44

They all tuck in – everyone gets plenty. They're all getting that full-after-your-mum's-best-meal feeling. The Team keep to the country code and collect up all the leftovers: there's 12 huge doggy baskets left over! Five thousand hungry guys – not to mention women and kids – had eaten alfresco.

Extreme sports – water walking Matthew 14:22-33

22-24

Straight after this Jesus sends the Team back by boat to the other side of the lake. He adds a personal touch and sticks around to send the people home. Eventually they've all left, and he climbs up the mountainside to talk things through with God long into the night. Meantime, the Team is well out on the lake and the waves are looking nasty.

[Mark 6:41] Does he debone the fish?

[Mark 6:44] Is the catering figure 5,000 or Is It actually more? Well, the original source material says 5,000 *men*. Yes, they only counted the men! Not that iffy back then, but it'd certainly have been more if the men brought their wives and kids. So, if half the men brought a wife and one kid, we're talking 10,000 total. If more men made it into a "family fun day" then the total could get up to what? 14,000? 20,000? More? Your guess is as good as mine!

New Roman Times

Mum shares family lunch with 15,000+

Last week Jesus Davidson pulled off another amazing stunt — feeding a crowd of up to an estimated 15,000 fans from one woman's lunch pack. We tracked down the mum — Rebecca Jenson — to get the inside story. She told us:

"Well, it wasn't like my lot at all. Normally they'd be nagging me for snacks and nibbles by mid-morning, and they don't leave any food unless they're ill. But we were just so captivated, we forgot about our stomachs. So when Jesus' Team went round calling out for any food, I thought it was for the Coach. Well, it must burn up some energy, all that storytelling, and my lot hadn't mentioned food since we arrived that morning, so I thought, *it's the least I can do.* Then he just keeps on doling it out, doling it out. We watch it go through the crowds, everyone getting some of my homemade bread! Was I proud?!

"Funny thing was, when we told the kids we were going to an outdoor rally, you could see them think, *oh, booorrring!!* The oldest did the old 'I've got a bellyache' thing – which he's overused lately so he didn't get away with it. I told them, 'You'll love it; he's not your normal coach'. And they were locked onto every word. Course they didn't admit I was right – that *would* be a miracle."

25 – 26

Sometime, three maybe four in the morning, Jesus walks out to them across the waves. Freaked out, they all scream, "Ghost!"

27 – 28

Before they'd time to scream again, Jesus shouts, "Whoa! Don't panic! It's me!"

Pete yells back, "If it's you, Boss, let me have a shot at the water walking thing too, yeah?"

29 – 30

"Come on then," offers Jesus, "go for it!" So Pete swings his leg over the boat and his foot doesn't go under! The other leg joins it. The water takes his weight. Seconds later he's walking across the lake towards Jesus – on the water! He's stepping over the waves, making his way out to Jesus when a face full of wind slaps him back to normality. He panics, loses focus, and starts going under, screaming, "Boss, grab me!"

31

Straight off, Jesus grabs him and holds him there, saying, "Couldn't you take God at his word[1]? You were trusting me so well – what happened?"

32 – 33

Soon as they get back in the boat, the wind stops playing with the waves and goes calm. The Team are far from calm. They can't take their eyes off Jesus; they improvise a worship session, coming out with their own variations on, "You're the real thing – God's Son!" "You're him! You are!" And other stuff like, "Wow!"

[Matthew 14:28 – 30] What are the other 11 (plus women?) thinking of Pete's impulsive reaction? Are they impressed by his blind belief or secretly relieved when they see him go under?

[Matthew 14:33] Isn't worship supposed to be reserved only for God? Isn't that Rule No. 2 of the Big Ten: "You won't idolise anything of any shape, etc"? (See Exodus 20 in a proper Bible.) So how come Jesus, who's big into Moses' Big Ten, doesn't make them quit? Who *is* he?

Magnet for the messed Mark 6:53-56

53-56

The rest of the trip's plain sailing. They moor up at Gennesaret,

they get onto the beach and Jesus is spotted straight off. It's the same wherever he goes – a montage of people: ill people on stretchers, whole people leaping off stretchers. Wherever the paparazzi spot him – beaches, shopping centres, middle of nowhere – it's always full of people. Some people desperately reach to get even just a fingernail on the edge of his coat; other people dance away from the crowd, delirious at the new dance moves their healed bodies are pulling off.

Religion! Mark 7:1-23

1-2

The Religious Leaders[2] and Law Enforcers[3] in Jerusalem had Jesus as the main point on the agenda for most of their meetings. The Suits from Jerusalem travel north to stalk Jesus and soon they're getting picky with his Team's lifestyle – they're not dotting the "i's" or crossing the "t's" of orthodox Religious practice.

[2] **Religious Leaders = Pharisees.** A faction calling themselves literally "the separated ones" – "the exclusives" perhaps. Big into Rules, running a well-oiled propaganda machine which seemed to be fuelled by people's guilt.

[3] **Religious Law Enforcers = Teachers of the Law/Scribes.** Experts in Moses' law. Academics, who sadly, often became "academic" in the sense of "irrelevant".

[Mark 6:53] Was this where they'd been heading before being blown off course? Possibly not.

Rough Guide to Gennesaret: Great nature spot for Capernaumites. They often head west down the Galilee Lake coastal road on the weekends; big tourist pull in the summer, passing the road signs: "Gennesaret – Garden of Galilee".

[Mark 7:1] Time for a quick swot up on Religious Leaders. One iffy thing about them is that they're not what's advertised – they're more about using Religion to score points politically rather than practicing the real thing (allegedly).

So "Religion and politics" isn't a new issue then?

[Mark 7:2 – 7] Ever wondered where the term "obsessive-compulsive disorder" originated? Sure, rules are rules but might this be just a tad over the top? Might there be their other agenda creeping in here?

---

3 - 4

Bit of background for non-Jews: The Religious Leaders in particular and Jews in general don't eat a crumb until they've done the Washing Ritual (up to the elbow!) as per the Daily Life Rulings from Senior Religious Giants. They come in from doing the shopping and don't even nibble a crust until they've gone through the big Washing Ritual. And it's not just their hands! It's cups, jugs, kettles – if it's in the kitchen, it needs the good ol' Washing Ritual.

5

Up for a tiff, the Religious Leaders and Law Enforcers challenge Jesus. "Why don't your Team take on the lifestyle of the Daily Life Rulings? Specifically, why do they grab their grub with filthy fingernails?"

6 - 7

Jesus comes back saying, "Isaiah was definitely talking about people like you lot when he was ranting on about hypocrisy, and I quote:

'This bunch are all mouth, their vocal chords spout
all the right things.
But their hearts are miles off.
It's lip service worth diddly-squat – they're paying "respect" to me.
They spout urban myths they've picked up, and they claim it's
coaching wisdom from above.'

8

"You've lost your grip on God's Rules; they sink to the bottom of the ever growing list. You replace them by downloading new ones from

---

[Mark 7:5] History briefing: Ever since the Babylonian army dragged the Jews out of Judah 600 years back, the Religious Leaders have been outdoing previous generations with more and more detailed Daily Life Rulings. Every Jew for half a millennium would almost instinctively know all the "do's" and "don'ts" of what later became the bestselling, "A Million Tricky Steps To Being A Proper Jew" (aka the Talmud). It's all based on Moses' Rules but taken to the nth degree and beyond. Break them, and you were spiritually and socially "contaminated" – a reject. Notice how Jesus will argue in their language – that of the Old Instruction Manuals.

[Mark 7:6 – 7] See Isaiah 29:13 in a proper Bible.

DIY wise-guy sites like, 'systemsofcontrol.nets' or 'keepingcrowdsin-tow.orgs' or 'thingsyoushouldknowaboutrunningtheshow.con'.

9-11

Jesus is on a roll. "You're so slick at sidelining God's Rules to concentrate on sticking obsessively to your DIY Religious traditions. Like this one: Moses' Big Rule No. 5, no less: 'You'll treat your parents with respect. Then you'll live long and prosper in this new land I'm moving you into.' And Moses adds later in the Manual, 'If you curse your parents, it's the Death Penalty for you.' Clear enough? Obviously not, 'cos your Daily Life Rulings have this oh-so-handy little get-out clause which gives you the green light to look your poor, ageing parents in their good eye and say, 'You know the savings I've had in my Parents' Pension Account, well, I've just stamped it "Gift With God's Name On" so we'll just have to downgrade your nursing home.' ('Gift With God's Name On', aka 'Corban' = 'a gift earmarked for God' in Hebrew.)

12-13

"You actually create Rulings which give people a loophole to cop out on the responsibility to look after their own parents! You wipe out God's fifth Big Rule just because some historical boffin figure got 'creative' with the legal files. And that's just one of loads of ways in which you twist God's Rules to suit you."

[Mark 7:9 – 11] How sneaky is this? Not only did they not have to fund their parents' dotage, but also by channeling the funds through the Gift With God's Name On route (aka "Corban"), they didn't even have to actually cough up any money to the Religious HQ! Having adjusted the portfolio, they were free to siphon off cash for their own holiday fund whenever they liked. Is this just a clever financial advisor's trick to legally exclude the parents from eating in their old age, or did God see it as fraud?

The Religious Leaders were big fans of Numbers 30:2: "God's orders are: When someone swears by God or takes an oath/pledge/promise (delete as applicable) – no way must they rat out on their word; they must stand by everything they said they'd do."

Handy one, especially if the pledge in question gets you out of your responsibility to look after your parents in the days before government or private pension schemes.

---

14 – 16

Jesus broadens it out from a Religious debate with the Powers That Be to a coaching opportunity for the general public. He draws the public in, saying, "Listen up, you know the line 'you are what you eat'? Twaddle! There's nothing in the world you can swallow that'll make you 'contaminated' spiritually. Nothing! It's not what goes in that counts, it's what comes up out of you that 'contaminates', so change the cliché. How about, 'You are what you throw up'?"

17 – 19

Jesus leaves the crowd to mull on that and goes indoors. Backstage with the Team, they're after him, asking, "You going to unpack the riddle?" "Yeah, spell it out Jesus!"

Jesus is miffed and says, "You really that thick? Isn't it obvious that nothing going in can get you 'contaminated' spiritually 'cos it just bypasses your heart, goes into your stomach and then eventually expells through, uh … natural channels. Basic biology guys!" (Just to spell it out: "A-l-l f-o-o-d i-s o-k-a-y", quote, Jesus.)

20 – 23

Back to Jesus' in-house explanation for the Team. "It's what comes up out of someone that makes them spiritually 'contaminated'. 'Stomach'? No! Wrong organ. It's the heart that makes you have dark ideas; the heart that screws you up sexually; the heart that drives you to nick stuff; the heart that fuels the 'killer' in you; the heart that betrays a partner by sleeping around. It's the heart that feeds your desperation for having more stuff; the heart that fires your cruel streak; the heart that cheats people; the heart that celebrates filth; the heart that ogles other people's kit; the heart that tears people down; the heart that puffs you up; the heart that makes you act like an idiot. All this mess comes riding out of the conveyor belt of the heart – that's what makes people spiritually 'contaminated'."

[Mark 7:20 – 23] Was Jesus reworking Jeremiah 17:9? "Don't let your heart pull a fast one on you: / the heart's specialism is deception. / There's no operation that'll stop it cheating on you; / no way to understand that old heart of yours."

Not just the Jews Matthew 15:21-28

21-22

Jesus makes tracks away from Israel and goes 30 miles (just short of 50 km) northwest to the non-Jew country of the costa del Phoenicia near the big cities of Tyre and Sidon. A local Phoenician woman rushes at him, crying, "Boss, Mr Davidson, sir, give me a break! My little girl's going through hell with a demon pulling her around like a puppet."

23-24

Jesus says zip. She gets on the Team's nerves and they come to Jesus pulling their hair out and moaning, "Make her get lost! She's giving us brainache!"

So he tells the foreign woman, "My mission statement only mentions the lost Jewish kids."

25-26

Not taking no for an answer, she kneels down and begs, "Boss, help. Please help!"

Jesus explains, "How wrong would it be to steal bread from the toddlers and throw it to the dogs?"

[Matthew 15:21 – 28] Was Jesus needing a break from his fellow Jews? He certainly still needed some space, but why cross the border? Was the plan to finally enjoy their postponed Spiritual Retreat?

Rough Guide to Phoenicia (today's Lebanon): A bustling land hugging the Mediterranean coastline with magnificent cities dripping with commercial success and cultural sophistication. There's a breadth of Religious influence here: Greek Hellenistic architecture combined with Caananite Pagan burial sites. Not exactly home territory for Jews then!

[Matthew 15:24 – 28] Racial tension, certainly, but given what we already know, was Jesus inciting racial hatred or just adopting the terms everyone else used? Does it change anything that he was probably speaking to the lady in his second language, Greek? Seems he was just quoting the standard terms used by both Jews and non-Jews about each other. Scary thing is there's a stronger word for dogs he *could've* used, but chose to avoid. To an outsider, "dogs" seems strong enough, but at least it's the word for "a cute family pet", not "a scavenging mongrel".

The Audience

A Monthly Magazine For Up Front People

Talking their language

What is it that makes Jesus Davidson's public speaking so effective? How can he switch from dueling with the highbrow intellectuals one minute to connecting with the working classes the next?

Prof. Rachel Cohen is head of Religious Communications at the University of Jerusalem. She's been analysing Jesus Davidson's approach to his audiences since he hit the scene 18 months ago. Here she draws out principles for other would-be persuaders:

"In my research a key conclusion I've drawn is that Jesus Davidson doesn't have one speaking style — he has several. I have been fascinated by his use of multiple communication techniques, which he tailors to his different audiences.

"A recent episode provides a fascinating example in which the self-styled life coach faced three different audiences within the space of an hour. He addresses the same issue using three different styles of communication:

Audience One: Jesus talks technical with the academics
"Here Davidson is primarily activating the left hemisphere rational part

of his brain by entering into technical debate. He listens and reacts; he uses logic; he quotes authoritative material; he speaks the vocabulary of his combatants. But he's not shutting down the creative right hemisphere of the brain, for he's still using visual images; he's still creating metaphors; he's still using humour. Clearly he's speaking their language without losing his voice. What distinguishes him from many other communicators is his ability to bridge the divide by honouring the standard approach but introducing elements of surprise. A powerful and effective combination.

Audience Two: Jesus talks poetic with the people

"Once Davidson has won the argument with the Religious Leaders, he focuses his attention on the general public who have been drawn in by his natural authority. By using picture stories it seems he is being deliberately cryptic; he turns a well-known expression on its head while refusing to explain it. He certainly leaves the crowds with plenty to mull over – if they're hungry, he gives them something to nibble on.

"Davidson tends to use images that even the least educated would spot if they are intrigued enough to work out the abbreviations and symbols. Here intellect isn't the important currency, but rather tenacity. Interestingly, if they choose not to think through his message then they're not driven away by feeling preached at. This wisely leaves the door open for a possible future encounter.

Audience Three: Jesus talks direct with the Team

"Finally, Davidson spells it out with the signed-up. Now he goes into detail because they are clearly hungry to learn more. Here he returns to the more left-brained approach of direct explanation, but he's still using visual imagery to explain difficult material. It's clear from this episode that he takes on a different style in a Team seminar than in a Religious lecture and a public presentation.

"So to take on Religious language, Davidson uses:

- apologetics for the Religious intellectuals;
- mystery for the general public; and
- exposition for the converted.

"A fine balance which recognises and honours each audience group without just giving them what they want.

"The question Davidson's approach raises for the Religious Establishment is this: Will other Religious Communicators adapt to this broad range of approaches, or will they continue to explain the minutia of Religious doctrine to people who aren't interested? Will they risk lower response numbers by not manipulating those vulnerable enough to be swept along by the power of the live performance? Or will they build a community of people who subscribe to The Movement from the firmer base of true ownership of belief?

"As a result of both the supply and demand ends of Religious communication being so entrenched in the need for 'boxed in answers', anyone taking on board the lessons drawn from Davidson's multiple communication styles will have to be strong to make progress against tradition. The crux of the matter is likely to be whether people consider Davidson to be the genuine article. Those who accept what Davidson is saying are far more likely to incorporate his breadth of approach, which will lead to rich, creative and imaginative portrayals of life's big issues; while those who disagree with Davidson's position are likely to reject his approach as well as his message. This will lead to a compounding of the rational/academic approaches as the primary method of representing their belief system. We will watch carefully how things develop."

To enter further into this debate, go to:
www.jerusalem.gos.il/religion/arewegettingthrough.

27

"Wrong enough," she says, but she's not giving in. She comes back with the quick-witted answer, "But hey, children are messy eaters! Even the household puppy gets to tidy up the breadcrumbs that the toddlers chuck out of their high chairs."

28

Jesus loves her answer. "Now, lady, that's what I call trusting. Nice one! It's win-win: You've got what you came for!" he tells her.

And her girl was demon-free – whole – from that time on.

Talk, don't talk Mark 7:31 - 37

31 - 32

Jesus' personal navigation system reads: "North 25 miles (40 km) to Sidon City, return south 50 miles (80 km) to Galilee Lake and then southeast 40 miles (64 km) to the western edge of the region of The Big Ten Towns." When they arrive, some people bring a profoundly deaf guy to Jesus. He's got a related severe speech impediment, and his mates are going, "Please, Jesus, do the whole healing touch thing with him, won't you?"

33 - 34

Jesus gives him the personal approach and loses the crowd for a one-to-one with the deaf guy. Once on their own, Jesus puts his fingers into the guy's ears. Then he spits onto his hands and puts the saliva

---

[Matthew 15:28] By agreeing with the woman, is Jesus giving his watching Team practical proof of what he'd been hinting at in his coaching back down in Galilee? The clean/unclean or reject/accept barriers are going out of fashion ... fast.

By healing her little girl, surely he blows any "anti-foreigner" label out the water? Doesn't it all fit with his Nazareth post-sermon seminar when he talked up the way both Elijah and Elisha helped foreigners (see Chapter 4, Luke 4:24 – 27, page 69)?

[Mark 7:31 – 37] Is Jesus keen to stay in non-Jew territory? He seems to go a roundabout route to get to the same area where "Legion" had lost his demons for good a while back.

onto the guy's tongue. He looks up to heaven and with a heavy sigh he breathes out a one-word prayer, "Ephphatha!"

Quick translation: "Ephphatha" = Aramaic for "open"/"release".

35 – 37 ·

That nanosecond the guy's ears are opened and his tongue's back in work with its spokesperson role. He's whole again.

Jesus' debrief is the standard ultimatum not to go spreading the story. But the guy who was dumb can't keep mum and the more Jesus pushes this "keep it quiet" policy, the more his fan club of ex-ill people gossip it round the houses. People are so stunned they can't function properly! "Every little thing he does is awesome. He's even giving music back to the deaf; giving a voice back to the mute."

Supernatural supper – action replay

Mark 8:1 – 10

1 – 3

Round the same time, more crowds, similar in scale (pretty humungous). They'd eaten nothing and Jesus' passionate side kicks in. He calls a powwow with his Team and tells them, "Look at these poor people! We're into day three of our outdoor teach-in and there's no catering trolley in sight! Do I send them home? No way! They'll flake

---

[Mark 7:33 – 34] How does the deaf guy know that Jesus is putting in a healing request to God? He's stone deaf! And why the Aramaic word? Jesus spoke Greek before to the Syrian woman, so why's he back to using his first language?

[Mark 7:35] So just how big is this? Is it "just" one guy getting a life-changing supernatural operation and regaining control over two of his five senses? Or is it more than that? Is this a coded signal that things are happening? Is it symbolic evidence of Jesus being The Liberator? How many people connected back to Isaiah 35:5 – 6a? If The Liberator's here... "Then, oh then, Blind eyes – wide eyes. / Then, oh then, Deaf ears – clear ears. / Then, oh then, Dead legs – leaping legs. / Then, oh then, Limp tongues – free tongues."

[Mark 8:1] How humungous is "humungous"? Pretty huge if you realize that the population stats for towns like Capernaum and Bethsaida had 3,000 max each. The question isn't so much who was there as who *wasn't* there. Wouldn't this level of profile activate the jealousy gland of the Religious guys who dream of these sorts of numbers eating out of their hands ('scuse the pun)?

out and faint before they get halfway. Some of them have clocked up some serious miles to get here."

4

His Team come back with the negatives, telling him, "But we're miles from anywhere. There's no way we could rustle up any catering for them. And where we going to get any bread from round here?"

5 – 6

Jesus asks the Team, "What's the pita count looking like?"

"Seven!" they tell him.

Jesus announces that his audience should find a piece of grass and park themselves on it. He collects the seven pita breads, thanks his Father, doles them out to the Team whose job it is to lay out the picnic for the people. They follow Jesus' orders.

7 – 8

The Team also had the beginnings of a fish course, so Jesus thanks his Dad and gives the nod for his Team of makeshift waiters to serve the people. Everyone stuffs themselves. After the meal, the Team go round collecting the leftovers – seven jumbo-sized baskets full to the top.

9 – 10

We're talking a crowd of 4,000 – and that's just the men! Once Jesus has sent the delegates home, he gets into a boat with the Team and gets in some lake behind him heading west for the Dalmanutha area...

[Mark 8:2 – 3] Is this a different motivation from Jesus than his catering for 15,000+ earlier in the chapter? Jesus sparked the supernatural then 'cos they were like a bunch of lost sheep. This time it looks like it's just practical – three days is a long time without a meal, especially in the heat – and it sounds like there's no local snack trailer close. Interesting that the 15,000+ gig was in-house for Jews, but this crowd is mostly non-Jews!

[Mark 8:8] Search for the same Greek word for "jumbo-sized basket" and the results come up with Acts 9:25 – where the Jews were after Saul's blood and he escapes from an upstairs window in a, quote, *jumbo-sized basket*. Pretty big basket if you can hide a full-grown Religious Leader in it. And yes, it *is* a different word from the, quote, "huge doggy baskets" in the Picnic for 15,000 + mentioned before.

"We want supernatural proof!"

Matthew 16:1-4

1

The Religious Leaders and Religious Traditionalists[4] are pooling resources in setting up hurdles for Jesus to jump over. "We want proof! Supernatural proof! Something with heaven's registered trademark on it."

2-4

Jesus isn't jumping: "Evening comes; you check the weather forecast for the next morning. First thing, you look out the window, you're thinking, 'Looks like rain, take my waterproof coat.' You know how to check the sky; you've got your weather stations in place; you've got your regular bulletins; you check the atmosphere in a room. But d'you bother reading the atmosphere of the times? Nope. You've not got the first hint of a clue of what's coming down here. So you ask for supernatural proof. Isn't it just totally typical of a wicked, two-timing society to crave supernatural proof?! I'm just saying one word: 'Jonah.'" And he walks off.

[4] **Religious Traditionalists=Sadducees.** These guys were only into Moses' first five books of the Instruction Manuals; anything later was to them liberal hoo-ha to be sniffed at. One of their big things was that all this rising from the dead malarkey was indulgent hogwash, brought in by liberal lightweights like Daniel, among others. Not natural partners for the Religious Leaders.

Don't Like This? [Matthew 16:1-4] Far prefer conclusive evidence that all this stuff is worth investing your life into? Be more specific: Don't just ask for writing on the wall, ask for a cryptic message that only *you* would recognise. Then sit back and wait. If there's no divine typing, then it's not your fault, is it? There either is no God, or he can't access that font you requested.

[Mark 8:9] Like before, with the picnic for 5,000+ (see Mark 6:35 – 44, pages 162 – 163), the catering figures of 4,000 don't include women and children – not so unPC in those days. But if half the men brought a wife and one kid, we're talking 8,000 total. If more men made it into a "family fun day", then the total could get up to 10,000, 12,000, 16,000? Who knows?

[Mark 8:10] Dalmanutha just so happens to be where Mary Magdalene grew up. So she's accompanying Jesus back to her hometown! What sort of reception is she expecting? How will her folks respond to her now that she's clean of her seven demons courtesy of Jesus?

[Matthew 16:1] Proof. And then what? Is the Religious Establishment genuinely up for getting into Jesus' version of Religion if he can come up with the supernatural proof? Do they really want him to leap over the hurdles and prove himself to them? Or are the hurdles put in place for him to clatter into them and polish the running track with his chin?

[Matthew 16:3] Or should that be "atmosfear"?

Use your loaf Mark 8:13-21

13-15

They go back across to the northeast side of Galilee Lake, get there and the Team's all, "Who's got the bread?" "D'you bring the bread?" "No, I thought you had it!" They've just got one stale sandwich between them – and that's been in the boat for a while.

Jesus picks up the theme and says, "Red alert, guys! We should definitely boycott the evil yeast cosponsored by the Religious Leaders and King Herod."

16-18

The Team think he's on about actual bread. They're saying, "It's 'cos someone had a blank on bringing the sandwiches on board." Jesus knows how their minds are jumping to the obvious and asks, "What are you on about actual bread for?! D'you still not see it? D'you still

---

[Matthew 16:4] "Jonah"! What's Jonah got to do with anything? This bunch know their history – 800 years back Jonah goes AWOL and tries to cop out of his God courier duties by taking a boat trip west instead of trudging east to Ninevah. God blocks Jonah's attempted escape by making the boat do its seesaw impression, which gets Jonah thrown overboard and swallowed by a remote controlled whopper of a fish. Jonah's stuck in the fish's stomach to weigh up his career options – fish food v God courier? Three days later the fish has a severe case of projectile vomiting and Jonah lands on a beach with a second chance to "go preach to the foreigners". But check out the bit they rarely cover in Sunday school – the less famous ending where Jonah gets really narked with God for going easy on the World Super Power scum when they do a U-ey and turn back round to his ways causing God to call off the lightning bolts.

Do the Religious cream spot the symbolism of Jesus' answer or have they made up their minds already so they refuse to be confused with the facts?

[Mark 8:13] Why this zigzagging across Galilee Lake? Is Jesus on some "lake miles" bonus scheme? Or is it the only head space he gets?

[Mark 8:15] What's a Jew think of yeast? Probably brings the word "Liberation" to the tip of the tongue. Yeast goes right back to when their ancestors escaped from being slave labour in the sweatshops of Egypt (flick to Exodus 12:17 in a proper Bible for the story). Bread without yeast lasts longer than bread with yeast; you can travel places with yeast-free loaves ... even through a desert.

not get it? Are your deep places still so stone stupid? D'you have eyes, but you don't see it? D'you have ears, but you don't hear?

19 - 21

"And if I was talking about actual bread, just how short are your memories? When I dished out the five pita breads for the five thousand guys – how many doggy baskets did you guys fill up with leftovers?"

"Twelve," they mutter.

"And when I dished out the seven pita breads for the four thousand guys – how many jumbo-sized baskets did you stuff full?"

"Seven," they mumble.

Jesus just rounds off with, "And you still don't get it?!"

Eye opening Mark 8:22 - 26

22 - 24

They hit Bethsaida Town and some people bring another registered disabled person to Jesus. This guy's blind. The crowds are begging Jesus to touch him. Jesus grabs the guy's hand and walks him beyond the outskirts of the village. Jesus spits in the blind eyes and touches the guy. He wants feedback. "D'you see anything?" Jesus asks.

Don't Like This? [Mark 8:22 – 26] What's all this about then? Don't like the idea of Jesus apparently running out of his "Popeye-branded Spiritual Spinach"? Best blame it on the person being "helped". There's a whole list of accusations you can use when faced with stubborn ailments: Patient not taking God at his word. Hidden sin. Or, even better, just write off any possibility of supernatural healing in the present day and this tricky bit doesn't even need solving.

[Mark 8:18] Ouch! This must've really stung! This "d'you have eyes, but you don't see it" is the same line Jesus used back in Chapter 7 (see Matthew 13:13 – 15, page 129) when he was slagging off those who aren't "in the know". Now he's using it for his troubled Team!

[Mark 8:22 – 26] Geography briefing: Bethsaida Town is on the northeast (top right) coast of Galilee Lake.

[Mark 8:23] Is it really necessary to gob in someone's eyes to heal them? Why did it take two goes?

Did Jesus not realise what a tricky case this would be? Was it that the guy was delivered by friends and wasn't so into the idea himself? Or is it not about the person?

Does Jesus sometimes heal gradually? Was the two-phase approach to wholeness deliberate and symbolic of people opening their spiritual eyes gradually?

Was there a spiritual battle going on, blocking Jesus' first try? Or was Jesus fully in control and just proving he wasn't restricted to any formula?

The guy looks around, says, "Yesss! But are people really so ... well ... blurred? Do they just look like tree trunks? I thought trees couldn't walk about like that?"

25 - 26

Then Jesus puts his hands on the guy's partially sighted vision. This time the guy gets perfect eyesight – he sees everything, clear and precise. Still minimizing the hype, Jesus tells him, "Go straight home, yes? Not back into the village."

1 **The Man = Son of Man.** Jesus' term for himself = lifted from Daniel 7, where it's a pretty blatant clue that this is no mere mortal: "the Son of Man . . . surfing in on the clouds . . . where the Ancient of Days . . . gives him . . . all the credit for running the show . . . and permanent position in the top 'spot." Nice name badge.

2 **God's Courier = Prophet.** Personal message delivery service direct from God. Think any package delivery corporation, but think "quick". Although, thinking about it, with their record, the depot for uncollected packages would've been pretty chocka by the end of the Old Testament.

Chapter Ten

Team Catches On

More eyes opening Matthew 16:13-20

13-14

Jesus hits the Caesarea Philippi area. He asks his Team, "What's the gossip? What are people saying about who Yours Truly, The Man[1] is?"

The Team come back with, "Depends who you ask: some say John Baptizer." "Others go back to Jeremiah or further to Elijah." "Some won't commit, saying just 'one of the God couriers[2]'."

15-16

"And you guys?" asks Jesus. "What *d'you* reckon?"

Pete jumps right in and answers, "You're The Liberator. God's Son."

[Matthew 16:13] Geography briefing: Caesarea Philippi was straight up from Galilee Lake about a 20-mile trip past the Jewish border and well into "here be foreigners" territory. Twin-towned with Costa del Caesarea on the Med. Coast.

³ **Councillors = Elders.** The non-Religious element of the ruling of the people. Sort of civil servants.

⁴ **Big God Reps = Chief priests.** If "God Reps" (priests) were the "go between" for God and his people, then *chief* priests were the ones with real clout. This eminent group are the ones who've done their year's stint as Top God Rep (High Priest).

⁵ **Religious Law Enforcers = Teachers of the Law/Scribes.** Experts in Moses' law. Academics, who sadly, often became "academic" in the sense of "irrelevant".

17-19

Jesus answers, "Simon Jonahson, you'll be glad you said that! You've not picked that up secondhand from office gossip or pub chat; you've downloaded that direct from God in heaven. Your name means 'rock'. And this is the rock-solid foundation I'm going to build my new community on. And the powers of death won't win through against them, no way! I'll tell you the security codes of heaven: If you block something happening down here, heaven will make sure it stays blocked; if you give something the green light down here, heaven will make sure it goes through."

20

Then he changes moods, gets stern and tells them not to spill the beans on him being The Liberator.

Appointment with Death Mark 8:31 – 9:1

31

From here on in Jesus lets them in on what the prospects are looking like for The Man:

- He's going to hurt, big time;
- He's going to get major rejection by the big noise Councillors³, Head God Reps⁴, Religious Law Enforcers⁵;
- He's going to be executed;
- He's going come back to life two days later.

[Matthew 16:20] **Why?**

[Mark 8:31 — 9:1] **Does Pete's "aha" moment of "you're The Liberator" shift the team into a new paradigm? Has Jesus waited till now – when they really get it – to fill them in on the plotline for the rest of the story? Is this the trigger point for Jesus kicking off a new course of instruction for the Team with the title, "How To Lose It All"?**

[Mark 8:31] **Is this the greatest comeback of all time? Okay, so he's pulled off the big one bringing back the widow's son from Nain, but bringing yourself back?! Or will someone else do the honours for him?**

---

32 – 33

He lays this out and Pete takes Jesus to one side and starts telling him off; trying to get him thinking more positively. Jesus looks back over at the Team, makes eye contact, and turns the tables on Pete, telling him off. "Back off, Satan! You're locked onto human agenda, not fixed on God's plans."

34

Jesus then unloads more heavy-duty news. He calls a crowd and the Team round him and says, "Anyone want to come my way? Do the prep by ditching your life goals, chucking in your personal ambitions and thinking of yourself as already dead. Picture yourself carrying your own execution equipment.

35 – 37

"And I'll tell you why: The people who get precious about their life, only looking after No. 1, will lose it. The people who are up for the ultimate sacrifice, losing their life – for me, for the good news story – they'll keep it. What's the point in taking over the whole world if your soul goes out the window in the process? What's the recommended retail price on a soul? Have you got enough to buy it back?

38

"If you're going to disown me and my coaching in the face of this two-timing, messed up society, then The Man is going to disown you when he comes back with his Dad's dazzling entrance and his multiple angel escort."

Don't Like This? [Mark 8:35] Mmm, this is tricky. Back in Chapter 8 (see Matthew 10:38 – 39, page 157), we established an all-purpose escape route by saying all this carrying your own execution equipment was probably only for the real fanatics – the Team Twelve, etc. Problem is, now Jesus is saying the same death wish material publicly! So now maybe it's only relevant for those in far off lands with dictators for rulers. There's got to be a way he doesn't actually mean us, no?

[Mark 8:33] What d'you think: might Jesus be already regretting telling Pete "whatever you block down here will be blocked in heaven" from before? (see Matthew 16:19, page 184) Should Jesus have put a clause to include "And no blocking of me!"? Or did he know we'd blow it?

[6] **Heaven on Earth / God's New World Order = The kingdom of God.** Like with monarchies, but with God in charge, so not like with monarchies. There's also a sense of "sort of already / but not yet" paradox. We get to download glimpses now, but the full package would cramp our hard drive's style.

Mark 9:1

1

Jesus wraps up with, "I tell you straight, some of you lot standing here right now won't get your appointment with Death till you're eyewitnesses of God's New World Order[6] cranking up the power.

All "heavened-up" Luke 9:28 - 36a

28

Jesus leaves for about a week to let his big speech to sink in, then he takes just the inner three, Pete and the Zebson twins, Jim and Jonno, up a skyscraper of a mountain to engage with God.

29

As Jesus is in chat-mode with God, he morphs into something from a sci-fi blockbuster – he gets all heavened-up: His face radiates with supernatural brilliance, like he's wearing some light-generating face make-up. His clothes are dazzling white, again shining like they're plugged into a star-charging generator.

[Mark 8:35] What happens if you replace the word "life" with other words like, "reputation" or "image"? Is this a fair barometer of conviction levels?

Is this the appointment with Death that Isaiah was on about in Isaiah 53:1,3 – 5?

"Who'd have foreseen this plotline in God's Liberation story? He was dissed by most, given the cold shoulder by many. There was a sadness about him. You could see in his face he was on personal terms with grief. He was messed up for our mess. He was knocked down for our slipups. The slapping we should've got – he got. And we got serenity instead. His punishment beating left him half-human and us whole and fully human."

[Mark 9:1] Is this a specific event? What exactly are some of these people still going to be alive to see? Options seem to be from… (a) The Transfiguration, where Jesus gets all "heavened-up", (b) Jesus' execution and coming back from death, (c) The impact of the Holy Spirit's arrival at the Jewish Thanksgiving Holiday, (d) The spread of the Jesus Liberation Movement through the Roman Empire, (e) Maybe even, in some weird way, the destruction of Jerusalem by the Roman military forces in AD 70.

[Luke 9:28] Was this Mount Hermon – more than 9,000 feet high – looking down its ridge at Caesarea Philippi? Or could it have been Mount Tabor, County Galilee – less than 2,000 feet?

---

7 **Big Ten Rules.** = **Ten Commandments.** Dictated by God to Moses on the top of the Sinai Mountain and the basis of Christo-Judaic law since then. Check out Exodus 20 for the breakdown.

30 – 31

Then a cameo appearance from Moses (of the Big Ten Rules[7] fame) and Elijah (top guy from God's couriers), also modelling dazzlingly bright outfits and working through plans with Jesus about his exit strategy which was pending in Jerusalem.

32 – 33

Pete and the twins are knackered and sending up the zzzzs. They wake up and wonder who turned the sun up a notch or five! Clocking onto the fact that the floodlights were coming out of Jesus, Moses and Elijah.

The two old-timers are making to go when Pete finds his voice and says, "Boss, this is awesome, totally awesome! How about we get busy making some monuments, one each for you, for Moses and for Elijah?" He didn't have a clue what he was going on about; they were all pretty freaked.

34 – 36a

Mid-gabble, God interrupts, camouflaged by a sun-saturated cloud. Pete, Jim and Jonno are frozen with fear when God's voice comes out of the cloud and says, "This is my son, I'm wild about him; when he speaks, you listen."

After the heavenly PA system clicks off, they look around and it's just Jesus with them; Moses and Elijah have been beamed out of there.

[Luke 9:30 – 31] Is it significant that both these Old Testament heroes have no recorded burial? Both legends say that they somehow cheated proper death: Moses dies alone and God buries him according to Deuteronomy 34:5 – 8. From this the rural myth spread that Moses didn't actually die, he just got on the heavenly moving walkway. And Elijah gets taken up to heaven in a chariot of fire with a whirlwind providing the uplift according to 2 Kings 11.

So is this a pep talk from the old boys? Or just a reminder for Jesus of what's on the other side of his mission?

Processing new info Mark 9:9-13

9-11

They're on their way down the mountain and Jesus gives them direct orders not to blab their mouths off about any of this: "No one gets to hear about this, right? Not till I've come back from the dead."

This kicks off this massive Team debate about what "come back from death" means.

They ask Jesus, "Uh, so why do the Religious Law Enforcers drone on about Elijah coming before The Liberator on their time line chart?"

12-13

Jesus agrees, "Elijah makes his entrance, sorts things out, gets things ready. But then how come The Good Book[8] talks about The Man being victimised and kicked out? I'll let you in on this, Elijah's already been and gone and they've done what they wanted with him, just like it's written in The Good Book."

So John B = Elijah! Matthew 17:13

Just then, the lights come on. The Team clock onto what he's on about ... the part of Elijah in this Tragedy Production was played by John Baptizer.

[Mark 9:11] The Religious Establishment were into quoting the Old Testament courier of Malachi (4:5,6a): "Before Judgement Day comes, I'll send Elijah the courier to you. He'll renew the bonding between fathers and sons. Fathers will burst with love for their sons, and children will love their fathers."

But the question is this: Why didn't our trio ask him what they were *really* arguing over – this "come back from death" thing? Does he mean when they *all* "come back" before Judgement Day, or is this just "*him* coming back from death"? Were they such bluff merchants that they couldn't admit they didn't get it? Or are they just in flat denial about all this "death" talk, full stop?

Empire News

Who Is He? The Davidson Survey

A week ago we asked you, our readers, to give us your take on whom this Jesus Davidson really is. We had a sack full of answers, and we've listed them below in order of when people first encountered Jesus Davidson (as far as can be established). Please note the views expressed below are not necessarily the views of Empire News and should not be taken as such. If you don't agree or would like to add your views on the phenomenon that is Jesus Davidson, go to www.empirenews.gos/davidsonsurvey.

What have people made of him? Read on:

	Elizabeth Abijahson, John Baptizer's mother
Jesus is a nephew	Mary Davidson
Jesus is a miracle baby	Ditto
Jesus is the great status leveler	Joe Davidson, Jesus' stepdad
Jesus is a challenge	Bethlehem Sheep Security Team
Jesus is The Liberator spokesman	Simeon (surname withheld)
Jesus is a sniper's bullet through his mother's soul	God courier Anna (surname withheld)
Jesus is Jerusalem's ransom payment	Eastern Astrologers' Travel Book report
Jesus is a future Jewish King	Mayor of Bethlehem
Jesus is a tourism boost	Herod the Great's Press Officer
Jesus is hardly proper competition	An Egyptian neighbour
Jesus is an asylum seeker	A Nazarene neighbour
Jesus is a carpenter's boy	Religious Leaders from Jerusalem Religious HQ
Jesus is a child prodigy	Galilean Tourist Board
Jesus is a local celebrity	The Nazareth Against Jesus Movement
Jesus is an escapologist	Capernaum Guild
Jesus is a guaranteed crowd puller	Local Fishermen's Cooperative
Jesus is a productivity guru	Mrs Zebedee
Jesus is a good partner for my boys	The hooligan formerly known as Legion
Jesus is an exorcist	

	The Jesus Healed Me Club
Jesus is a spiritual healer	The Jesus Healed Me Club
Jesus is a reluctant star	Pete's mother-in-law
Jesus is a new lease of life	Skin Hospital Outpatients Dept. spokesperson
Jesus is an expert dermatologist	Rabbi Ram Sandalson
Jesus is a dangerous subversive	Rabbi Saul Gideon
Jesus is a worthy debater	Religious Leaders Press Office
Jesus is demonic	Wine Suppliers Group
Jesus is a party animal	Prof Rachel Cohen, University of Jerusalem
Jesus is a master communicator	Team Twelve spokesman extraordinaire
Jesus is a life coach	Centurion Campese
Jesus is a military general	Jews Only Society
Jesus is a pro-foreign, anti-Jew heretic	Anonymous widow's ex-dead son
Jesus is new life	Anonymous widow
Jesus is new life	John Baptizer RIP Fan Club
Jesus is the One	Name(s) withheld
Jesus is a drunkard	Joanna, wife of Cuza – manager of Herod's Household and multiple Anonymous entries
Jesus is a feminist visionary	Family spokesman – Jimmy Davidson
Jesus is a nutter	Multiple entries
Jesus is a master storyteller	Multiple entries
Jesus is a Heaven on Earth tour guide	Pig Farmers Cooperative of Gerasene
Jesus is a farm saboteur	Ruthie Jairuson
Jesus is new life	Jairus
Jesus is a wonder	Ex-Blind People For Jesus
Jesus is sight	Multiple entries
Jesus is a one man catering crew	Religious Leadership Today editor
Jesus is disrespectful and unhygienic	Ex-Deaf People For Jesus
Jesus is music	Multiple entries
Jesus is a reincarnated John Baptizer	Multiple entries
Jesus is Elijah revisiting planet Earth	Multiple entries
Jesus is Jeremiah back from heaven	Multiple entries
Jesus is a God courier in the old mould	Pete Jonahson
Jesus is The Liberator, God's Son	

Part 2

Dead Man Walking

1 **Religious Law Enforcers** = **Teachers of the Law/Scribes.** Experts in Moses' law. Academics, who sadly, often became "academic" in the sense of "irrelevant".

Chapter Eleven

Choosing Sides

Can't get the staff! Mark 9:14-27

14-16

Jesus and the inner three trek down the mountain and rejoin the other nine who are mid-argument, mid-crowd, mid-crisis: the Religious Law Enforcers[1] are slamming into the Team. The second the crowd spot Jesus, they get all starstruck and rush him.

Jesus asks them, "So, what's the big row?"

17-18

This guy in the crowd speaks up and answers, "Coach, I tracked you down for my son. He's (dis)possessed by a demon and he's mute – the demon's nicked his voice! Whenever the demon grips him, my boy's

---

[Mark 9:14 – 16] Why's the crowd so overcome? Was it the precision timing? Or just the nature of celebrity? Or was there still some excess shimmering going on, as with Moses back in Exodus 34:29? "Moses treks back down Mount Sinai, with the two patio-sized stone slabs of God's dictation in his hands. He's totally unaware that his face is like a torch on overdrive 'cos he'd just been chatting with God."

[2] **Taking God at his word = Faith/Belief.** Faith is more than just a Religious Club you belong to. Belief is more than just a vague whim. This big word is an active, gutsy, practical concept. Aka "trust".

crashing into the stone floor, demented, foaming at the mouth, grinding his teeth and going stiff as a board. I asked the rest of your Team to kick the demon out, but no result! The demonic squatter's still putting his feet up, making himself at home."

19-20

Jesus groans, "This society just doesn't take God at his word[2]! How long is my job contract to coach you? How long do I have to keep at it with you? Bring the boy here."

They bring the boy to Jesus. The evil spirit sees Jesus and freaks, triggering the boy off on another wild convulsion, rolling across the floor, dirt and dust mixing with foaming saliva.

21-22

Jesus quizzes the dad and asks, "How long's he been in this state?"

"Since he was a kid," the dad comes back. "I've lost count the number of times it's tried to kill him, targeting the fire or a local pool to try to fry him or drown him. But if you can do anything, give us a break and help us."

23-24

Jesus bounces the question back to him, asking, " '*If* I can'? What d'you mean '*if*'? Sky's the limit, if you're going to trust."

Straight off, the boy's dad says, "I do trust; I just need you to fill in the cracks — there's gaps where my trust goes AWOL."

25

Jesus sees more fans turning up so he gets on with it before they arrive. He does some straight talking to the demon making all the

---

[Mark 9:25] Again, why isn't Jesus making the most of the publicity? Is he so anti-fame that he rushes the job to try not to be spotted? The face-off with Satan in the wasteland of Chapter 3 was about Jesus not locking onto fame. He won that biggie and looks like he's determined to keep on winning it. But then if he's going to Jerusalem to die — like he just announced — then maybe he has no reason to maximise the celebrity moments?

trouble and barks its marching orders. "You deaf and mute spirit, I'm ordering you out of this boy. Get out and stay out!"

26 – 27

A repulsive scream from the demon, more fits and then exit. The boy's lying there on the floor – looking like a corpse – oblivious to the crowds muttering, "He's dead." Jesus grabs the boy by the hand and the boy gets up.

Mountain v mustard seed Matthew 17:19-20

19

The Team tap Jesus for more clues on their de-demonising nightmare. Jesus continues his private debriefing and they get some answers to their big question: "How come the demon wouldn't shift when *we* gave it the eviction order?"

20

Jesus lays it out, telling them, "'Cos you just don't take God at his word. Straight up, imagine you could bottle 'trust'. If you just have one tiny bit stuck in the corner of the bottle, about mustard-seed size, that'll do nicely. You could take it with you to the local mountain range and give it. 'Mountain! Shift location – here to there, sharpish!' With just a crumb of trust you'd see the thing pick up its foothills and leg it to the exact spot on the map you're pointing at. Take God at his word and nothing would be in the 'impossible' category for you."

Mark 9:29

29

Jesus sums up with, "Different league that demon. Some hard-core types only come out with a real hotline connection to God."

[Matthew 17:20] Is Jesus deliberately referring back to the previous lesson in Chapter 7 (Mark 4:30 – 32, page 136)? Wasn't a mustard seed an image he used to describe what Heaven on Earth looks like?

The Jews News Interviews

Check you get the main man

Aaron Bromberg, the father of the mute boy recently healed by Jesus Davidson, speaks his mind about the encounter with Jesus and his entourage:

JN—So it was a pretty traumatic time for you, Aaron?

AB—How d'you think I felt? I've got a chronically ill boy, we're on a knife's edge as to when his demon's going to push him over the edge from self-harm to suicide, and I finally track down the miracle doctor who might just sort it. I'm on the edge of getting my boy back and what do I find? The main man's off on some mountain retreat with his "chosen few" and I'm left with his second tier skeleton staff "umming" and "ahing", going, "Well, it normally works" and "No, the Boss has let us do these jobs before, should be fine." Pah!

JN—And that wasn't your only problem, was it?

AB—No, those callous Religious Law Enforcers were using my poor boy as an excuse to pounce on Jesus' Team's failure and launch into a theological attack. That's pastoral of them – not! How are the boys supposed to remember how it all works with the boffins bending their ears?

JN—But things changed when Jesus rolled up?

AB—Significantly! He timed his entrance a bit tight, but yes, when he did eventually show, he dealt with it. Jesus was amazing to us. I couldn't fault him even when I wasn't totally convinced. But those hangers-on! Personally I wouldn't have the time of day for that lot.

ers.

JN—So Davidson's still pretty crucial to the project?

AB—Indispensable, I'd say. I tell you, if anything happened to the Big J, it'd all fall apart at the seams. If he's got any hopes for retiring and watching The Movement grow, he should either readvertise or write a book – it'd be a bestseller. But that bunch of lads are never going to make the grade.

Spiritual retreat Mark 9:30-32

30-31

The Team leave their memories of failure and go with Jesus through Galilee. He's adamant that they get their much-needed private coaching retreat. He tells them, "Yours Truly, The Man[3] is going to be handed over to the authorities; they'll execute me, then, two days later, I'll come back from death."

32

But they don't get it; not a clue what he's on about, and they're too nervous about his reaction to push it with him.

Do royals pay tax? Matthew 17:24-27

24

Jesus and the Team arrive home in Capernaum and who's at the door of their digs? The tax man! Worse: *two* tax men ... from the Religious HQ[4] Revenue Department looking for this year's payment of two days' wages for the Religious HQ Refurbishment Fund. Pete's staring at the bottom line while they're probing, "Your Coach, would he be currently in a nil balance position with our Department or is he in danger of leaks to the press about tax fraud?"

25-27

Pete's adamant in saying, "Jesus is paid, in full, up to date, nil balance owing; I'm sure of it."

[Mark 9:31 – 32] Was this what the Team wanted to hear? Not your normal talk from a mentor who takes his Team away to refocus. Was this his way of saying, "You've got to learn, 'cos I'm off soon"?

Yes, this is mention number two of the death-and-return plotline, so why can't the Team quite get it? They were only just getting the hang of taking Jesus' words and peeling off the literal for the deeper meaning, but at this stage Jesus is just talking straight. He's alone with the Team so he's in direct mode. No metaphors. When he says "death", he means "death" as in "not alive".

[Matthew 17:25] How come Matt – the retired tax man – doesn't deal with this? And why does Jesus call Pete "Si"? Could it be a gentle nudge to remind him of their previous lives, and therefore might it be a hint that people like Matt Moneybags also had a previous life in tax?

Pete comes back into the house and Jesus breaks the silence first and asks Pete, "Question for you Si: Kings and Queens, right? Who do they send a tax bill to? (A) Just their immediate family, letting every other resident off scot-free, or (B) every address in the country *except* their immediate royal family?

Pete's straight in with, "Well (B), obviously!"

Jesus pushes it further and asks, "So the royal Princes have some sort of special Tax Exemption Code then, yes? But look, I'm not into stirring up unnecessary aggravation, so nip out the back, pick up your fishing tackle and angle for some fish. First bite, open up its mouth 'cos you'll find it's been chewing on a coin. A coin that'll get both our tax statements stamped, 'PAID IN FULL'. Go to the Religious HQ Revenue Office and hand the money over the counter for both of us, eh?"

Soft spot for kids Mark 9:33 - 37

33 - 34

They get back to their digs in Capernaum and Jesus probes, "What was the big debate on the way here?"

Embarrassed silence. They'd been jockeying for position, arguing about who gets to be vice captain of the Team – second behind Jesus – basically earmarking the high profile roles for themselves.

35

Jesus sits down for a Team Twelve coaching session. "You want the top job? Go to the very bottom of the ladder and give the others a leg up. You want a front row seat? Go right to the back, let others go first."

Don't Like This? [Mark 9:33 - 37] Of course, Jesus' famous "first shall be last" sound bite doesn't account for the fact that most of those who are not out-front-leader types don't even want to be first. They're happy following. So no worries then about all this talk of the followers rising up and overtaking the know-it-all leaders, since it's not about to happen!

[Matthew 17:26] How does Pete feel about going back fishing? Does he reminisce, or doesn't he have time as the Lesser Spotted Coin Eating Carp is munching on the hook within minutes? Or did the fish get instructions to delay: give Pete time to chew things over?

[Mark 9:34] Is it any wonder they started staring at their sandals? How exactly do you tell your mentor, "Well, *you* were talking about being executed and *we* were talking about what's in it for us; *you* were saying something about your impending death sentence, and *we* were arguing about how we're best going to cash in on the media opportunities"? Tricky.

[5] **Heaven on Earth/God's New World Order = The kingdom of God.** Like with monarchies, but with God in charge, so not like with monarchies. There's also a sense of "sort of already/but not yet" paradox. We get to download glimpses now, but the full package would cramp our hard drive's style.

Don't Like This? [Matthew 18:3 – 5] Argue that little children are actually often really selfish, spiteful and cruel, so it's obviously best not to populate the world with childish grownups. Okay, so it's missing the point, but it should do the job.

36 – 37

He picks up their hosts' toddler, stands the little lad next to him, hugs and cuddles him and, with this visual aid in front of him, says, "You make time for one of these because of your connection with me and d'you know what? You make time for me! And if you make time for *me,* d'you know what? You're making time for my Dad who sent me."

The trust of a toddler Matthew 18:3-5

3 – 4

"Straight up, unless you have a radical turn around and morph back into being like a trusting, simple, open-hearted kid again, you won't ever get your passport into Heaven on Earth[5]. But to answer your question, whoever shifts into vulnerable, innocent, pure mode – whoever shifts and makes like this kid – then you're talking about truly great in God's New World Order.

5

"Like I say, make time, spend energy on a, quote, 'mere child' like this 'cos of me and it's like you're making time for me; it's like you're spending energy on me."

Competition? Mark 9:38-41

38 – 39

"Coach?" Jonno interrupts. "You know we've got competition, don't you? Some other exorcist has set up business, nicking your name and logo and setting up as 'Davidson Exorcism' – and he's getting results! Course, we told him to pack it in, not being registered as one of us."

[Mark 9:36] Children were cute, their parents adored them, but back then they had no rights, status or standing. They didn't legally "become someone" till what today is known as bar mitzvah age (13). So is this the level of zero prestige Jesus is recommending for The Liberator's lads?

[Matthew 18:3 – 5] Why is Jesus giving more coaching on climbing the ladder in God's system? Is it so obvious they just can't handle the role reversal?

Don't Like This? (Mark 9:38 – 41) Not sure about Jesus' line on who's in the club? Follow these simple rules: Ask people to sign your Statement of Faith. Only work with people who've signed your Statement of Faith. In fact, only work with people who are endorsed by people who've signed your Statement of Faith.

"You told him what?!" Jesus asked. "Don't tell him to shut up shop. He's tapping into my authority, so he's not about to slag me off in his next breath, is he?

40 – 41

"Quit all this 'Club Exclusive' thing, will you?! If someone's not attacking us, they're attacking *with* us. I tell you straight, if anyone even just gives you one glass of tap water because of your connection with The Liberator, they're not going to miss out on the bonuses due."

Don't mess with the kids Matthew 18:6 – 8

6 – 7

"But anyone who messes with one of these kids, making them crash out of their childhood, whoa! They'd be better off up to their neck in a skip full of concrete and getting chucked overboard a mafia yacht in the Mediterranean. Bad news fills every current affairs programme, hourly, daily, worldwide. Dark things happen. But it's bad news for the people who fill the streets with enough of this gunk to trip anyone up.

8

"If you've got wandering hands, chop them off and chuck them out; if you're feet are a magnet for trouble spots, chop them off and chuck them out. How much better will it be to go through life in a wheelchair than to have all your extremities frying in hell?"

[Mark 9:38] So are they still smarting from drawing a blank with the foaming mute boy fiasco earlier? Are they still so paranoid about other peoples' spiritual careers overtaking theirs on the inside lane?

[Matthew 18:8] Does this ring bells from the Team Twelve's initial training talk back in Chapter 5 (see Matthew 5 :29 – 30, page 93)? How sad is it that Jesus has to go back to square one with them?

Don't Like This? [Mark 9:47 – 50] Find it disconcerting that Jesus is talking about hell so much? Highlight the bit about Jesus being lovely with the children, or inclusive with the women, or just a great storyteller. Then maybe when you flick through you won't land on the harsher aspect of Jesus' team teaching.

No added salt Mark 9:47-50

47-48

"Ditto," says Jesus, "say you've got a wandering eye. It's going to be better to be an active part of Heaven on Earth with an eye patch, than to get a fully focused wide-screen view of hell. How does old Isaiah put it when he winds up his book with the words? And I quote, 'Where the maggot doesn't die, where the fire never dies down.'

49-50

"No exceptions: Everyone will get salt-style purification by getting a roasting. Salt's great!" Jesus says. "But if you go bland on me, what use is that? How d'you get its zing back? Keep yourself strongly salted and stop your infighting. Let's have some serenity around here."

Looking out for the wanderer Matthew 18:10-14

10

"Make dead sure you're not looking down on these kids; make dead sure you're not writing them off till they've 'arrived' (your term). I'm telling you their Personal Angels back in heaven are in regular eye contact with my Dad in heaven."

12

"What d'you reckon? If a teacher's got a hundred little kids on a geography field trip and one of the 'poor lambs' goes AWOL, what's he going to do? Right! He's going to leave the ninety-nine safe on the hillside and bust a gut looking for the one in danger of exposure/cliffs/rivers/wolves/worse. We *all* would!

[Mark 9:47] Jesus doesn't actually use the word "hell", he taps into local knowledge by using the word "Gehenna" – an actual place southwest of Jerusalem with a dark history of fiery child sacrifice to the so-called-god, Molech. Check out 2 Kings 23:10 on what King Josiah did. This Gehenna valley became Jerusalem's smoldering rubbish dump – maggots outbreeding those that die in the smoldering fires set to burn up the piles of rubbish. Pretty vivid image of future prospects for hell's inhabitants!

[Mark 9:48] See Isaiah 66:24 in a proper Bible.

[Matthew 18:10] So was Jesus delivering all this hell fire team coaching in front of the little boy? What does this say about Jesus' opinion of what kids can cope with?

Don't Like This? [Matthew 18:15 – 20] Not into this confrontational stuff? Find it all a bit scary? Mull over the line "time is a great healer", then ignore the person who's naffed you off until the wound has been healed by the salve(ation) of time. There's always the outside chance that the wound will go septic, but most likely there'll just be a nasty scar which clothes or cosmetics can cover up quite easily. The great thing is that churches are often big enough these days to not have to speak to someone for years on end.

13 – 14

"And if he finds him, I'm telling you, he's more buzzing about the one that went wandering off than the 'flock' of ninety-nine that've been hugging their compasses in the safety of the campfire and singing 'Bind us together'. Want to get a sense for how your Father in heaven feels about anyone wandering off from him like a lost sheep? Mull on that image – should get you close."

Plural power Matthew 18:15 – 20

15 – 17

"If your brother/sister messes you around, don't just bottle it up. Plan A: Show them the wound ... in private. If they realize what they've done and back down, then great! You're like brothers/sisters again. But if they're sticking their heels in, shrugging their shoulders, denying all knowledge, then not so great!

"Plan B: Get official. Take one or two others round with you to take minutes of the meeting; to vouch for you that it was all above board. If your brother/sister's still not shifting, then double not so great!

"If there's still no progress then, Plan C: Send a general memo round the whole of my Jesus Liberation Movement community. But if they won't even listen to a group of my people, then treat them like they have no links with God, like they're traitors.

18 – 20

"Straight up, if you block something happening down here, heaven will make sure it stays blocked; if you give something the green light down here, heaven will make sure it goes through. And, I'm telling you, if just two of you down here on earth have a meeting of minds on something you're lobbying God for, then it'll happen, my

[Matthew 18:15] So is this housekeeping confined to your blood-related siblings or is this "siblings in the Lord"? The later stuff is loud and clear that this "family" is bigger than just your domestic unit; it's about the whole church.

[Matthew 18:16] As per Moses' Rule Book (see Deuteronomy 19:15 in a proper Bible).

[Matthew 18:17] Is this a rare glimpse of Jesus being aware of setting up the church movement/community?

Dad will guarantee it. For if there are two or three of you and you're together 'cos of me, then I'm there with you upping the numbers by one."

Bad debts Matthew 18:21-35

21-22

Pete strides up to Jesus and says, "Say someone close does the dirty on me. I know I've got to wipe their slate clean. But what if they keep doing it? Where's the line? Seven times?"

Jesus answers, "No, not seven. More in the range of seventy-seven times or seventy times seven.'

23-25

Jesus moves into storytelling mode again. "Want to know what Heaven on Earth's like? Picture the scene: A CEO of a multinational wants to settle the accounts of his creditors. He's asking his finance director who owes him what and for how long. First on the black-list is a middle manager owing billions. The guy brings in his bank statements and it's obvious he can't pay up. So the CEO pulls out the form, which outlines 'payment of debt by sale of all assets and the use of family members in the sweatshop labour unit'. The CEO signs the dreaded form and hands it to the manager.

26-27

"The guy's down on the floor, giving it the whole works. 'Just give me some time and I'll get all the money to you, I'm begging you!'

"The CEO stuns the guy by saying, 'Okay, then.' He rips up the debt statement and lets the guy off free. Free!

[Matthew 18:20] Is it just "upping the numbers by one"? Or is having Jesus on board more like having a majority?

[Matthew 18:21] Pete probably thought he was being over the top with his "seven times", as most life coaches of the day recommended biting your lip just three times. Anyway, why was Pete asking this? Which of the Team were really getting up his nose?

[Matthew 18:22] Some Bibles quote Jesus saying "seventy-seven", some quote him saying "seventy times seven". Either way, it's a paradigm shift away from "seven"!

---

28 – 29

"The manager guy's skipping away and spots a coworker in the corridor who owes him about a hundred … a measly hundred! He grabs him by the throat and demands, 'Cough up the cash you owe me, now!'

"The guy owing him is begging, on his knees, 'Just give me some time and I'll get the money to you, I'm begging you!'.

30 – 33

"But this isn't good enough. Oh no! He goes straight to the Police Debt Collecting Service and has his coworker arrested and locked up till the debts are settled.

"Course, he's spotted, his colleagues make sure the CEO sees the CCTV footage and the main man blows a gasket – livid! The manager guy gets a swift recall to the top office. 'You evil little tyke! How ungrateful can you get? I rip up the papers. You walk away a free man. Why? 'Cos you begged me! And you can't even give out a little slack after I write off all that for you!'

34 – 35

"The CEO is struggling to remain professional and hands the guy over to the jailers specializing in torture techniques with the strict instructions, 'No breaks till he's paid off the billions.'

"And it'll be ditto with you," says Jesus, unpacking things for the Team. "Same treatment from my Dad in heaven unless you resist the urge to slam down on those who owe you; unless you wipe your coworkers' slates clean and mean it."

[Matthew 18:35] This is in-house, just the Team of 12 plus x number of women there. So Jesus tags on the moral, just in case they missed it.

Wonder at what point did Pete work out the arithmetic? Hardly worth counting if he's got to forgive 490 times … or is that the point?

New Roman Times Letters Page

Exorcism franchise

"I agree with your editorial last week where you commented on the apparent sharp rise in reported cases of demonic activity. In my work as CEO of Davidson Exorcism, I've seen the problem spiralling out of control over the last few years. Whether this is due to the high profile of Jesus Davidson himself is not for me to say, but my fledgling company is now inundated with requests for assistance. And these clients are not just your 'overly superstitious' types or those some may judge as 'mentally vulnerable', this is an epidemic of vast proportions which is affecting a wide cross section of our society. This is an issue that needs to be acknowledged and dealt with by the appropriate authorities.

"Having worked in the field, I'm convinced something is shifting in the unseen world of spiritual forces. There's something building, some sort of heightened activity in the lower echelons of the spirit world. Jesus Davidson himself implicitly acknowledged this when he went public with his Open Arms policy. His track record in this area is phenomenal, but it's a measure of The Man that he hasn't been interested in creating a monopoly situation, despite the advice he was getting from his coworkers. He's obviously aware the demand is more than he can treat.

"So we were thrilled to receive his endorsement — obviously it's been good for business — but ultimately we're just trying to do the right thing and release people from this demonic (dis)possession. We've not been able to hook up with the rest of his Team for idea swapping or networking — they're still keeping us at arm's length — but we carry on working under his fine name in our small corner of Galilee. Getting the thumbs up from the main man and working under the Davidson logo is enough for us."

If you are concerned about friends or family exhibiting symptoms of possible demonic activity and you've not been able to attend a Davidson clinic, then why not set up an appointment with www.davidsonexorcism.org.gos.il?

Chapter Twelve

Southbound Highway

Jerusalem calling Luke 9:51-56

51-53

The date and time of Jesus' return trip to heaven is ticking closer, and Jesus locks his personal navigation system onto a southward direction, tapping in the word "Jerusalem" as the final destination. Part of the prep is to send out "scouts" ahead of him into the midland villages of Samaria, but the locals turn the cold shoulder when they pick up he's not hanging around but "going down to Jerusalem".

[Luke 9:53] Was the "cold shoulder" the same one they had the chip on? Samaritan animosity towards the true blue Jewish capital of Jerusalem goes back seven centuries and continues to this day.

Samaritans had a blanket "No B&B for Pilgrims" policy. Loads of northerners took the hint and went down to Jerusalem the long way round by avoiding what is today's West Bank and going down the east side of the Jordan River. Anything to minimise the hassle of racist slurs or attacks.

So, if there was an alternative route, why did Jesus go through the heart of anti-Jew territory?

Don't Like This? [Luke 9:57 – 62] Not too tricky this one: before really getting serious about your faith, just make sure your really "must do" things are not the same as listed here. So, "Just need to get married" is probably fine; "Just need to get the family settled" is no problem; "Just need to get my career established" is not specifically mentioned as an outlawed excuse. Easy when you know how.

[1] **Heaven on Earth/God's New World Order = The kingdom of God.** Like with monarchies, but with God in charge, so not like with monarchies. There's also a sense of "sort of already/but not yet" paradox. We get to download glimpses now, but the full package would cramp our hard drive's style.

54 – 56

Team members Jim and Jonno are up for doing their best Elijah impersonation. "Boss, d'you want us to order some of heaven's incendiary bombs to 'shock and awe' these pseudo-Jews back to their senses?"

Jesus turns and lays into them, "No!" Then they hit the road again to another village in Samaria County.

Only the 100 percenters need apply

Luke 9:57 – 62

57 – 58

Jesus and Team are "trucking on south" when this guy says to Jesus, "Coach, I'm with you. Permanent. Wherever you go, I'm there!"

Not convinced, Jesus just says, "Foxes run to their holes. Birds fly to their nests. Me? I have to write 'No Fixed Abode' on my registration documents. Nowhere called 'home'."

59 – 60

Jesus says to another guy, "Come on! You joining up?!"

But the guy goes, "Boss, count me in; just let me sort my old man's funeral first, yeah?"

But Jesus says, "You in or what? It's make-up-your-mind time. Let the dead bury their dead. You need to go and announce Heaven on Earth's[1] arrival times."

[Luke 9:54] What's with this flame throwing from heaven's barricades? Check out 2 Kings 1 in a proper Bible for what was at stake when Elijah triggered the pyrotechnics – a lot more than just whether the Team get nice overnight accommodation followed by a full Samaritan breakfast.

[Luke 9:60] Is it that Jesus is insensitive to someone mourning their old man, or is it that the guy's dad's still alive and so he's actually saying "I've got to wait for my dad to die first"!?

Most Jews would've seen the job of burying their dad as *the* most holy duty of a son, so is Jesus saying that broadcasting Heaven on Earth's arrival tops this?

61-62

Another guy comes on all keen and says, "I'm in, Boss. But I've just got to tell my family I'm off, okay?"

Jesus goes, "No one who puts his fingerprints on the tractor steering wheel and then looks back is suitable material for bringing in God's New World Order."

Seventy-two times Jesus Luke 10:1-16

1

After this, Jesus commissions 72 crew members. He pairs them off and throws them out into the deep end of the Samaritan towns on his pending tour schedule.

2-3

He briefs them with, "Look, the olives are juicy and ripe, but you just can't get the staff. Ask the Big Boss; lobby him to take on more workers, to blow the budget and get the people in place to handle all these lost ones lining up for life. Go! I know it's stacked against you, like packs of wolves verses little lambs; like lost children against ruthless predators. But go!"

4-6

Jesus tacks on, "You're travelling light: Don't take any petty cash in your wallet. Don't take an overnight bag. Don't take a spare jacket, shoes or walking stick. Don't stop and natter on the road.

"As you cross the doormat, say, 'Serenity to soak through these four walls!' If people of peace are living there, your serenity will top them up. If aggression is more the accepted currency, then your serenity will slide off them and come right back to you.

7-9

"Kip down in their spare room, eat whatever is plonked down in front of you – that's fair! You're worth your wages. Don't switch and swap if you get a better offer; no, stay there till you're out of that town.

"On passing the 'Welcome to Our Town' sign and on getting a decent reception, eat what's on the menu. Set up your own "mobile miracle clinic" and broadcast the news that God's New World Order is just round the corner.

10-11

"If you enter a town and get a chilly reception, go out on the street and announce, 'I'm taking a stick to the gunk from your town that's clogging up my treads. I'm removing the last memory of me ever having been here. But get this, just this: God's New World Order is just round the corner.'

12-14

"I'm telling you straight, people from Sin City – yup, Sodom itself – will look out and be freaked by the levels of grief that'll hit that town! Bad news for you Korazin City! Bad news for you Bethsaida Town. If the supernatural stuff that made the headlines in your local tabloids had happened way back when in the Phoenecian Riviera of Tyre and Sidon, they would've turned their lives back round 180 degrees to God long ago. I'll tell you straight, the fire of Judgement Day won't be turned up as hot for old Tyre and Sidon as it will be for you.

15-16

"And Capernaum! What's the future looking like? Will it be 'sky's the limit'? No, it'll be a scary nosedive – no parachute, no safety net, nonstop into the depths of Hades itself. If someone listens to you, nodding and taking it all in, they're agreeing with me. And vice versa: blank-

[Luke 10:7 – 8] Is this dietary advice about picky eaters, or is it more theologically profound information about eating ingredients that true Jews might've found sticking in their throats? Is it a case of "when in Rome..."? Only this is Samaria – almost the same difference, to a Jew!

[Luke 10:11] What's it mean that the announcement, "God's New World Order is just round the corner" is used both as good and bad news?

[Luke 10:12] How's this bad news bit fit with the more chummy stuff above? Is Jesus feeding the Crew Seventy-Two with this hellfire and brimstone material so they can vent their spleen at their cousins, the Samaritan half-Jews? Or is Jesus just providing them with the motivation to make sure they really get the "serenity soaking through these four walls" message loud and clear so that none of this ugly stuff needs come into play? Which fits best with your grasp of Jesus' character so far?

ing you out means they're blanking me out. But also, by definition, they're blanking out the one who sent me here."

Kids outpoint the boffins Luke 10:17-24

17-18

Transition of time. The Crew Seventy-Two come back buzzing at the stuff they've seen happen, saying, "Boss! Even unbudgeable demons shift when we drop your name!"

Jesus gets reminiscent, saying, "I can see it now – Satan plummeting down from heaven's balcony; bombing like a comet on a collision course with planet Earth."

19-20

He switches back to the Crew Seventy-Two and says, "I've given you the spiritual clout to stomp on snakes, to stand on scorpions, to win against the power of the enemy – with not even a scratch to brag about! But I'm telling you, don't get high on the fact that evil spirits jump when you say 'jump'. No, get high on the fact that your names, photos and fingerprints are all kept on file in heaven."

21

Jesus is on a high too. Courtesy of the Holy Spirit, he's going, "Credit to you Dad, all the credit flying up to you, Boss of Heaven, Boss of Earth, 'cos this is stuff that you've kept under lock and key; stuff that the boffins and academics have debated for centuries, and who gets a look in? It's the kids, the uneducated kids. And you love it, Dad. I know you just love doing this!

[Luke 10:19] Why snakes? Is Jesus conjuring up images that have symbolised Satan from way back when God sentences Adam and Eve in the garden?

In Genesis 3:15 God predicts a descendant of Eve will, "stomp on the snake Satan's head and give it some juicy bruises." If Jesus is doling out the authority to do some serious snake stomping, does this mean that God was referring to The Man right back when the planet got messed up in the first place; right back as far as when Death first strolled in?

22 – 24

"God, my Dad, has given me full access; there are no limits on my jurisdiction here. No one's got the full picture on me apart from my Dad. And no one's got the full picture of my Dad apart from me, and those I choose to let in on things."

He turns to the Team and, just for their ears only, says, "You're laughing, full-on belly laughs at seeing this stuff. I'm telling you straight, whole lists of God's couriers² lost sleep straining to catch a flicker of what you're seeing, but it was still miles off, all blurred and out of focus in the distance. Kings were up nights, craving to get hold of what you're hearing, but it was still a distant whisper."

Samaritan **helpline for the Jews** Luke 10:25 – 37

25 – 26

One time, this Religious Law Prof stands up and tries to catch Jesus out. "What have I got to do to get this limitless life?"

Jesus responds with a question back, "You're a lawyer. What's the law say?"

27 – 29

He rolls off the pat answer: "Love God, your Boss, with everything you've got; with all your emotions, all your decisions, all your physicality, all your imagination; plus, love your neighbour as you love yourself."

"Good answer," says Jesus. "Do it and you'll get a life!"

[Luke 10:25 – 37] Who are these Samaritans? The Jewish definition might go "second class, low-life, mongrel scum, pseudo-Jews" or something even less polite. Brief history: After the Assyrians trashed Samaria (capital city of northern kingdom of Israel) in 722 BC, loads of true blue Jews were deported as slave labour. Some of those left behind intermarried with local Gentiles. These half-Jewish offspring are the Samaritans. Jews despised them for many reasons, two of the biggies being they only read the first five books of the Instruction Manuals ("pah!") and they didn't recognise Jerusalem as the place to do Religion ("double-pah!").

Where in today's world is a similar heritage of deep-seated prejudice? What are the realistic chances of peace in these virtual war zones?

---

[3] **God Reps = Priests.** The "go between" for God and his people – not to be mistaken for the "get-in-between". Years back, this guy named Aaron was the very first God Rep, and since then only his family line was eligible for the post.

[4] **Religious HQ = Temple.** Jerusalem's focal point of the Jewish Religion. Literally a house for God. Question is, how much does God get let out?

But the Prof couldn't resist posing: "But who qualifies as, quote, my 'neighbour'?"

30–31

Jesus answers him with a story. "There's a guy leaving Jerusalem on the Jericho Road, okay? He gets mugged, left in the gutter half-naked and two-thirds dead. One of the God Reps[3] is passing. He sees the poor bloke and crosses the road ... to avoid him.

32–35

"Then a Religious HQ[4] worker goes past, sees him and does the same – crosses the road to avoid him. Next up, Sam Aritan goes past. Sees him and, well, what d'you reckon? Believe it or not, his heart melts for the guy. He cleans the guy's injuries, lifts him onto his donkey, walks him to the next country B&B, pays for bed and full board, promising to cover the excess if the bill tots up to more."

36–37

Jesus throws it back to the Law Prof. "So which of the three is down in the characters list as, quote, 'neighbour'?"

The slick lawyer mumbles, "The Sama- ... uh, the guy who looked after him."

"So, go do the same," Jesus says.

Workaholics anonymous Luke 10:38–42

38–40

Jesus and the Team are still getting more of the north behind them, still moving down through Samaria, when they take up the offer of B&B from a woman called Martha. Her sis – Mary – is getting stuck in the impromptu coaching session while Martha's getting all flustered with having to pull a big meal together. She finally drops her multitasking and stomps into the seminar and says, "Boss, don't you give a fried fig that that my sister's sitting on her backside while I work my butt off? Tell her to help, won't you?"

41–42

"Martha, breathe!" Jesus says. "Go on, breathe, Martha! Your stress points are off the chart; you're driving away at stuff that doesn't really matter. Only one thing counts for anything. And Mary's gone for that option! So, no, I'll not take that away."

Two-way conversation with God Luke 11:1-13

1

Another time, Jesus is locked in conversation with God and one of the Team is waiting for him so he can quiz him. "Done? Uh, boss, give us some tips on this God conversation thing. John B coached *his* team; will you coach us?"

2–4

Jesus nods and replies, "When you're talking with God, say,

'God in heaven, you're our Dad!
We respect everything you stand for.
We want others to stand up for you too.
Please bring Heaven on Earth – people living life your way, like the angels do.
Please give us what we need to keep us going each day.
Please acquit us, as we cancel our grievances and throw them all away.
Please, pull us back from the edge of evil, stop it from sucking us in.'"

5–7

Jesus then says, "Say one of you has a buddy and you turn up at about midnight at their place going, 'Mate, I've got surprise guests. They've

---

[Luke 10:40 – 41] What if Martha had just bottled up her resentment against her sister till Jesus left? Would Mary have had the confidence to say similar lines as, "Only one thing counts for anything and I went for that"?

[Luke 11:2] Again, is this Jesus going over Lesson No. 1? He'd given them this prayer in Chapter 5 (Matthew 6:9 – 13, pages 101 – 102). But had they lost the script? Why's he feel the need to repeat himself?

just turned up, and I've not been shopping for yonks. Lend us three loaves of bread, will you?'

"The muffled voice from behind the curtains goes, 'Don't hassle me now! I was just nodding off, and I've only just got the kids settled. No way am I getting up now!'

8–10

"I tell you, the only reason the not-been-shopping-for-yonks guy gets his midnight toasted sandwich supplies is not because he's a mate. No, what gets the result is that the guy with the catering crisis just goes on and on and doesn't quit till he's got what he came for.

"So? Keep on keeping on at God. Keep asking – you'll get it. Keep searching – you'll find it. Keep pushing the doors – you'll get through. 'Cos everyone who asks has an answer come through; everyone who searches gets results popping up; everyone who pushes doors gets to hear that great creaking sound when it opens wide.

11–13

"Say your son asks you for fish and chips, d'you give him a venomous snake with a cyanide side salad? Or he wants scrambled eggs, d'you dish up live scorpion surprise? So, despite your evil part, you can still give good things to your kids. So multiply that by infinity squared

---

[Luke 11:9 – 10] Are they still asking/searching/knocking like they were way back in year one of the Heaven on Earth tour? Seems that way. So is Jesus' answer even more encouraging than before? If you don't ask, you won't realise what you've got is the answer. If you don't search, you won't recognise it when you find it. If you don't push the door, how are you going to know if it's been unlocked?

So is God a sleeping friend? Or does it just seem like that sometimes when your "shopping list" of prayers are rebounding back at you from the ceiling?

Every riddle can be pushed too far; the main point is, if you give up after the first ask, then you're probably not that sure about wanting a response.

No good dad gives bad things; no good dad gives everything the child asks for; no good dad spoils the child with their every little momentary whim. So is this Religion thing just supposed to be a natural relationship with the best Dad ever? And how easy is it to see God as dad, if you've not had the best experience of fatherhood?

Don't Like This? [Luke 11:37 – 54] Of course you could argue that all these Religious rituals were nutty as a peanut butter jar with the warning label "may contain nuts". And if you're in the category of "Religious Leader", simply assure yourself that the Pharisees back then were wrong and you are right. Then reassure yourself because you're unlikely to sit down for lunch with Jesus and so he's not about to point out where you've gone wrong … not for a while yet anyway.

[5] **Religious Leaders = Pharisees.** A faction calling themselves literally "the separated ones" – "the exclusives" perhaps. Big into Rules, running a well-oiled propaganda machine which seemed to be fuelled by people's guilt.

when your Dad in heaven is doling out the Holy Spirit to those who ask."

Religious Leaders for lunch Luke 11:37-54

37-38

Jesus calls time on his coaching and straight off gets an invite for lunch from a local Religious Leader[5]. Jesus gets his feet under the table, but without first going through the ceremonial hand-washing rigmarole. The Religious Leader doesn't know which to do first – roll his eyes or tut!

39

Jesus says to him, "You Religious Leaders scrub the bowls and cups so they're sparkling on the outside, but then the inside you leave for the bacteria of greed and evil to fester and grow.

40-41

"Just how stupid are you? Did God make the outside and delegate the inside to someone else? No! Sort out your sick, putrid hearts. Give the cash strapped some of what you're keeping from them, and you'll be a whole lot cleaner.

42

"You Religious Leaders have got bad news round the corner: You give God his ten percent commission on the garden herbs but you blank out justice and love of God. Fine, do the calculations of all the ten percents, but don't let it cut into the time where you practise the justice and love stuff.

[Luke 11:38] So was Jesus deliberately winding them up by not going through the ceremonial hand-washing thing?

Earlier accusations from similar quarters just picked on Jesus' Team, not Jesus himself. Does this imply Jesus usually *did* keep to the rule book? Was he looking for trouble? Didn't he realise these powerful people could ruin him? Or was that the idea?

[Luke 11:39] So it's not about looking the business?

[Luke 11:42] So it's not about doing the business?

[6] **Local Religious HQ** = Synagogue. Local meeting place for Religious Jews to worship their God. Central point of any Jewish community.
[7] **Religious Law Enforcers** = **Teachers of the Law/Scribes.** Experts in Moses' law. Academics, who sadly, often became "academic" in the sense of "irrelevant".

43 – 44

"You've got bad news round the corner, 'cos you love posing around the local religious HQs[6] with your permanent reserved signs screwed into the best pews. You love hanging out at the shopping malls where the people do all their nodding and scraping, looking up to you like you're VIPs.

"You've got bad news round the corner, 'cos you're like concealed mass graves that people walk over without knowing."

45 – 46

One of the Religious Law Enforcers[7] interrupts and asks, "Coach, when you rant away like this, you know you're insulting *my* fine profession as well?"

Jesus says, "Yup! 'Cos you Religious Law Enforcers have got bad news coming round the *other* corner. You load people down with guilt and then just tut when they stumble under it, not wanting to catch them in case you break a precious nail.

47 – 48

"You've got bad news coming 'cos you cut the ribbon to celebrate opening new Tombs of Honour for God's old couriers, but it was your ancestors who killed them! So it's like you're accessories to the crime; your memorial tombs just endorse the deaths of God's couriers when your predecessors got away with blue murder!

[Luke 11:43] **So it's not about people saying you're the business?**

[Luke 11:44] **So it's not about hiding the dirty business?**

[Luke 11:46] **So it's not about telling others to get their business in order?**

49 - 51

"This is exactly why the all-wise-God said, 'I'll send them couriers and messengers and, yes, some of these they'll execute, some they'll victimize.'

"Which is why it'll be your generation who'll have to answer for the leaking blood of the whole *Who's Who List of God Couriers* from day one to right now; from the blood type of Abel right through to the blood type of Zechariah who was martyred at the altar of the holy place. Yup, this generation – you lot – you'll have to face the music for this A to Z of cold-blooded killing.

52

"You Religious Law Enforcers, you've got bad news coming 'cos you've got the keys to the doors to knowledge, but you've locked the keys away. Okay, so you don't want to walk into the Knowledge Room, but you've blockaded the doors and nailed up 'not open to the public' signs so no one else can get in either!"

53 - 54

Jesus leaves the Religious Leaders and Law Enforcers seething. They up the ante on their opposition campaign and inundate him with trick questions, desperate to catch him out, trip him up and then kick him when he's down.

More tips for the Team Luke 12:1-12

1

Meantime, Jesus has a crowd of thousands stepping on each other to hear what he's saying. But he's coaching his Team and letting the others eavesdrop. "Red alert! Build up your immune systems against the two-faced hypocrisy of your Religious Leaders.

[Luke 11:52] And, finally, it's not about minding your own business. Maybe it's not about "business" at all? By turning the whole structure of love and justice that Jesus highlights in verse 42 into a business, isn't there the danger of giving a whole new meaning to the old expression "making a profession of faith"?

2 - 3

"There's no top secret files that won't be front page news; there's no conspiracy that won't be blown wide open. What's been sent to a secret e-mail address and then encrypted will be blown up on an illuminated billboard; what's been whispered in the corridors of power will be released as a chart topping single.

4 - 5

"Don't wobble over those who can shoot you in the head but can't get a bullet anywhere near your soul. I'll tell you who should get your undivided attention – the one who can wipe out both your body *and* your soul ... in hell. Yeah, now he's worth raising your pulse about.

6 - 7

"How much do five sparrows cost? About two pence? But not one sparrow hits the deck without God seeing it on his CCTV screens. You lose a hair on your brush and God knows what number hair it is. So don't get in a tizzy, for you're down in God's books as a major asset, worth way more than forests full of sparrows.

Don't Like This? [Luke 12:1 – 12] Not so into this fanatical devotion? More interested in a friendly club of people who have similar interests as your good self? Fortunately, 2,000 years of devotion have created many variations on a more relaxed take on the faith. There were plenty of the thousand-strong audience back then who also found acceptable ways of not getting sucked into an overly radical Religious expression. So you'll be in good company.

[Luke 12:2 – 3] Is Jesus talking about the Religious Leaders' files or his own Team's plans being overheard by Herod's or Roman spies? Either way, the tension's building and it's all going to blow wide open pretty soon.

[Luke 12:4] Haven't we heard some of this before (see Chapter 8, Matthew 10:28, page 156)? Yup! And has it sunk in yet? Nope! So is Jesus going over some past papers in the hope that when he's gone the Team will remember it?

Religious Times

Davidson must be gagged!

Jesus Davidson's recent outbursts against the Religious Establishment have caused much controversy in Religious circles up and down the Nation. Rabbi T. R. Levison, a senior figure in the Religious HQ in Jerusalem, calls for a gagging order to be issued against Davidson:

"I would be the first to admit that Jesus Davidson has remarkable charisma. I would also concede that there is no doubting the man's dedication to social action and the medical assistance of some of the poorest, most disadvantaged people in our troubled society. But he has no right or reason to launch into a tirade of character assassination against some of the most successful and influential public servants of our land — honourable people who have also dedicated their lives to help the people.

"I was one of the Religious Leaders present at the now legendary debut of the twelve year-old Davidson when he thrilled us all in the Religious HQ, Jerusalem, with his answers on a wide range of Religious topics. Back then, we all thought he was going to grow up to become a great asset for our Religious system. Some of my then-colleagues even tipped him to become one of the youngest Top God Reps ever — one who would negotiate the difficult path through an occupied land and back out into some semblance of freedom.

"What we now see transpiring in Davidson's public career is all the more tragic because of this early promise. This hope disappointed is part of the reason why the Religious Establishment must now, after allowing him free reign for almost two years, show great fortitude in bringing him into a more disciplined position or, if he refuses to conform, gag this once exciting talent altogether.

"I submit just three points from a growing list of reasons why this loose cannon cannot be allowed to rumble around the decks of a ship already buffeted by stormy waters:

1. **Anti-Jew:** "His endorsement of historical figures such as the foreign Queen of Sheba simply serves to distract the public from a focused determination to rebuff the

eroding influences of Greek and Roman values on our unique and God-given Jewish culture.

2. Aggressive Jibes: "His vitriolic verbal attacks on our respected Religious Leaders and Law Enforcers will inevitably erode the public's trust in these devout public servants. I call upon those Religious Leaders to weaken his standing by taking him to court for defamation of character.

3. Anarchistic Jesus: "By attacking not only the personnel but also the structure of our God-given Religious System, Davidson is threatening to steal from those people he claims to want 'liberate', the very mechanism for their political, financial and personal freedoms. He must not be allowed to even question, let alone begin to dismantle, the structures designed to connect the people with their God.

"I would agree that, regrettably, not everything within the workings of our Religion is necessarily as it should be. But given the adverse conditions of an alien army occupation, we can hardly afford to be so cavalier about our faith. If we implemented even just some of Davidson's proposals for radical change, surely the Roman Procurator, Pilate himself, would command legions of Roman soldiers to blockade the entrances to our Religious HQs both here in Jerusalem and up and down the country. This is just one of the areas where his approach has obviously not been subjected to the rigour and challenge of the collective wisdom of the seasoned Religious Leaders of our day.

"So I call upon the people of our proud Nation to stand with their local Religious Leaders in a display of solidarity by boycotting any further Davidson rallies held for anti-establishment propaganda and incitement to anti-Religious activities. If we allow him to continue the demoralisation of the vulnerable and the manipulation of the gullible, then this could be more than just a trend of disillusionment; it could spread into an irreversible dismantling of our ancient traditions which are instituted to bring us closer to our God. This must not be allowed to happen. So help us God."

Rabbi T.R. Levison, Jerusalem

To sign an online petition calling for a gagging order on Jesus Davidson, visit: www.religiousfreedom.bis.il.gos/davidson/gag.

8-10

"I tell you, whoever makes it clear in their conversations that they belong to me — I'll also own them out loud and proud when I'm talking with Dad's angels in heaven's HQ. But whoever goes quiet in company and swallows their pride in me — they'll be disowned before God's angels too. And if you diss The Man[8] your slate can still be wiped clean. But if you slander the Holy Spirit, that stain on that spoilt slate of yours will never be wiped, erased, deleted.

11-12

"And when you're handcuffed and standing in the dock of the local Religious HQ, with the Religious Leaders frowning down at you, don't go all tense about how to argue your position. No. You'll get your script from the Holy Spirit who'll be prompting you just before you deliver each line."

The rich idiot Luke 12:13-21

13-15

This guy in the crowd shouts out, "Coach! Tell my brother he's got to split the family inheritance with me!"

Jesus shifts the focus. "Hey, who set me up as judge and jury for your family feuds?"

Then he broadens it out to the crowd and says, "Red alert! Watch you don't get hoodwinked by a whole load of different disguises of greed! Your life is not defined by your bank balance; your value isn't about what you drive, drink or dust."

[Luke 12:10] So why won't you be able to press "delete" on this stain? 'Cos the very action of slagging off the Spirit means you're not about to come asking for your slate to be cleaned up. So, by definition, it won't get the cleaning treatment.

[Luke 12:12] No winning one-liners assured? No guarantees that the Holy Spirit will give you the magic line that'll wipe the floor with the prosecution's argument? Just that you'll get God's lines for the situation.

[Luke 12:13] Is this heckler's question a clue as to the real reason why many of the crowd were there? Were they just waiting for the space where they could squeeze in *their* agenda?

16 – 17

Jesus launches into one of his deep-as-you-like stories[9]. "So there's a guy whose factory has great productivity figures. He's scratching his head, thinking, 'Problem — where do I keep all this surplus produce?'

18 – 19

"Then the coin drops. 'Eureka! I'll set up an expansion programme! I'll bulldoze my poxy little storage facility and build a spanking new whopper of a warehouse! And then I'll sign my own early retirement package and chill a bit, eat out more, get a bit tipsy, take a couple of sun soaked cruises and live life to the max!'

20 – 21

"Want to know what God thinks of this entrepreneur's expansion programme? God's line goes, 'You idiot! Tonight's your appointment with Death himself. So who's going to eat out, drink over the limit and get suntanned on the company profits now?'"

Jesus wraps up with, "Which is about the size of it for anyone who just ploughs his profits back into his Me, Me, Me Account and has a piffling little bank balance in heaven dollars with God."

[9] **Deep-as-you-like stories, riddles and images = Parables.** From the Greek word to "put things side by side" (ie, parallel). An ancient craft where you say things different ways; where an earthly story can take on a heavenly meaning . . . if you dig.

[Luke 12:16 – 21] How does this hit you? To the privileged among us it might sound a bit harsh; to those of us in the poverty trap it might sound right on. But what if this assessment of relative wealth suddenly moved to a global scale? What if we had to shift our place along the spectrum from "relatively poor" to "pretty darn wealthy" compared to around four billion paupers?

How's it sound now? Not quite so comfortable?

[Luke 12:20] Does this mean that everyone's got a pre-ordained date with Death? Or is this story just a tool to make a different point?

Does this mean that Jesus isn't into people retiring and enjoying sun, sea and Shangri-la? Or is this just a character in a story that is making a different point? How many other ways can we get sidetracked and miss the main point?

[Luke 12:21] Not sure you can wait till heaven to go on a spending spree with your heaven dollars? Who said anything about waiting till you die to get your hands on the God cash? Isn't the point of bringing in Heaven on Earth that heavenly currency is acceptable down here too? Hey, "spiritual retail therapy"! How good is that?

Don't Like This? [Luke 12:22 – 34] Find all this "hippy chill" stuff a little unrealistic? Argue strongly that what Jesus didn't realise was that being stressed would become a major weapon in the one-upmanship games of twenty-first century life. Sing the driving theme song of the National Association of Workaholics: "You ain't no one if you're not frazzled! / You ain't no one if you're not stressed. / Not got an illness? Not a stranger to stillness? We're not impressed! / No anxiety attacks? No hidden Prozacs? No hidden Prozacs? / Just not impressed? / Not got a migraine? Not going insane? / We'll say it again, We're not impressed!

"Taking God at his word = Faith/Belief. Faith is more than just a Religious Club you belong to. Belief is more than just a vague whim. This big word is an active, gutsy, practical concept. Aka "trust".

Stressing the point Luke 12:22-34

22-23

Then Jesus switches his focus back to his Team and says, "So, this is why I've always said, don't get all stressed by life, by food, by image worries. Life's so much more than recipes; your body's so much more than what you cover it with.

24-25

"Lift your sights. See those ravens? They don't 'strategise to realise'; they've not sweated over their career plan; but your Dad in heaven sorts them. And how much more worth are you than a bunch of birds?

26-27

"Notching up the stress points is not going to get you a new lease of life. And since you can't do this, why worry about the rest? Focus down on these lilies. Are they working their petals off to look that good? No! I'm telling you, not even rich old Solomon Davidson could look this good.

28

"And if that's how much TLC God gives to the flower garden, which'll soon enough be topping up the bonfire, then how much more will he sort your dressing dilemmas? Why won't you take God at his word[10]?

29-31

"Don't panic about the meals and drinks! That's what people who don't know God have to do. Your Dad in heaven knows what you need. Make your mission statement all about bringing in some Heaven on Earth. Then God will throw in loads on top.

[Luke 12:22 – 34] Back to the Team Teaching Session and a replay of the very first chunk of material he plonked in the Team's mental in-tray back in Chapter 5 (see Matthew 6:25–34, pages 104 – 105).

So is this Jesus driving home his Back to Basics curriculum?

[Luke 12:26] Isn't stress more likely to shorten, not lengthen, your life expectancy? Was Jesus deliberately illustrating his principles with the visual aids available on the side of a lush mountain?

32 - 34

"Hey, my tiny Team! Don't let life get the frighteners on you. Why? 'Cos your Dad in heaven has been thrilled to hand you down Heaven on Earth, no charge. Sell up! Donate the proceeds to those caught in the poverty trap. Build up your balance in heaven's bank vaults, where nothing rots, nothing dates, nothing gets walked off with. Want to know where someone's heart is? Track down where they invest their stash and their heart won't be more than an arm's length away."

Batteries charged? Luke 12:35-48

35

Jesus is saying, "Roll up your sleeves! Be dressed, ready for action! Keep your batteries well charged!

36 - 37

"Imagine a bunch of ushers waiting for their boss to come back after a wedding reception meal. Their main man knocks the door and they're opening the door within seconds. What a result for the ushers! He'll come in, don his serving clothes and dish up a banquet for them to enjoy! Total role reversal.

38 - 39

"A cracking result, especially if it's not till the early hours that he turns up. But get this: If a thief makes an appointment ahead of his heist, leaving his card that reads: 'I called but no one was in, so I'll

---

[Luke 12:29] What would Heaven on Earth look like in the area of stress-related diseases? How can we add more calmness and yet still get on with our daily dealings?

Was Jesus delivering these lines from a pressure-free position, or did he have some pretty heavy deadlines on the horizon? So how come he could still talk about scything down the stress?

[Luke 12:36] How close were they to the annual Flyby Festival? Why do I ask? 'Cos the traditional re-enacted meal of their ancestors' Great Escape from Egypt was eaten with their travelling boots laced up and their windproof jacket zipped. The idea of being ready for action was hardwired into their culture — they did it every year about this time.

[Luke 12:37] What's all this big return and wedding imagery about? Is Jesus so definite about using his return ticket to heaven that he's briefing the Team on tactics for when he's off the scene?

return tomorrow at 5:30 pm.' What's the householder do? He has the police staked out waiting and surely he won't be making an insurance claim.

40-41

"Now apply this closer to home: The Man will come back sometime, so look lively."

Pete's needing it spelt out. "Boss, is this story for us or for everyone?"

42-44

Jesus answers with a counter question: "What's loyalty to the boss look like? What's wisdom in the workplace? A manager's put in charge of the workforce, special duties in looking after staff meals. It'd be a good career move if the workers are mid-mouthful when the boss turns up unexpectedly? The guy will be looking at promotion, bonuses, bigger office and more interesting work.

45-46

"Or switch to the alternative ending where the same middle management guy gets to thinking, 'the boss has been off jet-setting for ages now', and he starts harassing the workforce and uses the office space for drunken binges with his mates. Sure enough, the boss opens the door mid-party. The manager gets cut to shreds and his career path turns a corner into 'No Commitment Cul-de-sac'. He's fired!"

47-48

Then Jesus says, "The worker who knows what his boss wants and doesn't deliver will get a good beating. But the worker who's not fully briefed on what his boss wants and messes up will only get a bit of a slapping. You've been well briefed? Your targets are set right up there. You've been well invested in by the boss? Your results are expected to be more."

[Luke 12:47] So is the answer to Pete's question about *who's this meant for*? not "either/or" but "both/and"? Was Pete still looking blank and Jesus needed to drive the point home? Looks that way.

Don't Like This? [Luke 12:49 – 53] What's wrong with pretty things and peaceful lives? Face your favourite cute kitten poster with the soft focus edges and comforting Bible text and ask that all this negativity would soon disappear.

Controversy Luke 12:49–53

49–50

"Why am I here? To light the fires! Oh, if only they were already blazing! But I've got a date with my baptism and it's huge pressure … looming closer every day till I've gone through with it.

51–53

"What!? You think I've come to bring pretty things and peaceful lives? No, me being here is going to cause controversy; my arrival marks a dividing line. From now on families will fall out with each other: take a family unit of five – three pro-Jesus, two anti-Jesus. Dads at loggerheads with sons, sons mouthing back at dads; mums dissing daughters, daughters blasting back at mums; in-laws becoming out-laws, families morphing into war zones."

Spiritual climate change? Luke 12:54–59

54–55

Jesus ups his voice to reach the crowd listening in. "You know how to tune into the weather forecasts. 'Clouds sweeping in from the west will bring rain to most parts' – and what happens? Rain! Or 'strong winds will be pushing the warm weather up from the south' – and what happens? A heat wave!

56–59

"You bunch of double standard specialists! You're virtual meteorology profs when it comes to the weather, so how come you miss all the signs

---

[Luke 12:49] Is this going to be the work of some of those who'd given up on Jesus since he wasn't the sort of all-action Liberator they were looking for? Are the insurgents finally going to get into gear and burn some Roman Army barracks? Or is this a different type of arson?

[Luke 12:50] Hasn't he had his baptism already? Didn't the late and great John Baptizer do the biz at the public launch back about two years ago? Or is this some other sort of baptism of fire?

[Luke 12:51] So was Simeon right, back in Chapter 2 (see Luke 2:34,35, page 48) when he predicted to new mum Mary, "This is going to impact everyone, one way or the other – pulling them up or knocking them down. I'm talking controversial. He'll expose people's thought bubbles; he'll uncover hidden attitudes. It'll be a sniper's bullet through the soul for you, mum."

of the spiritual climate change happening right here? Use your brains! What's going on here? Somebody make a judgement call! If you're on the road to Courthouse Crescent, do everything you can to sort it before you and your opponent arrive. That is unless you want the judge to convict you and get you taken down to the cells by the Court Heavies. I'm telling you straight, you won't be seeing open skies till you've worked off the whole debt!"

Fertilizer! Luke 13:1-9

1

Some of the crowd want Jesus' comments on the recent incident with Pontius Pilate's massacre of Galileans, where he had the blood of the pilgrims mixed and muddied with the blood of the animal sacrifices.

2-3

Jesus' angle on the horrific murders was, "What? D'you think the Galileans were getting their comeuppance for their messed up lives 'cos they got a gruesome ending (dis)courtesy of a Roman sword? No! I tell you, if you lot don't do a U-ey and turn round 180 degrees to God, then you'll face the same ending.

4-5

"And what about those eighteen people in the news a while back? Those Jerusalem guys crushed by the Siloam Tower collapsing? D'you think they were somehow worse than those in the next street? No! I tell you, if you lot don't do a one-eighty back to face God, then you're looking at the same gruesome ending."

[Luke 13:1–9] So Jesus' sermons weren't all one-way traffic then? How come we mostly hear his side of it? How many other questions, comments, disagreements was Jesus reacting to from the floor? And how did Jesus deal with those wanting his sound bite on current affairs?

Did he launch into pointing the finger at the victims of the recent atrocity as some sort of Divine judgement? How did these would-be current affairs pundits feel when he suggested they used the tragic events to take stock of their own lives?

6-7

Then Jesus serves up this image to chew over. "A wine producer plants a fig tree next to the vines, but when he starts rustling the leaves for juicy figs he just keeps on rustling – no figs to feel! The vineyard owner goes to the Chief Vine Inspector and says, 'It's three years now. Three years! Every year I check for figs and every year, hey, no figs! Sharpen your electric saw; that tree's a waste of good soil.'

8-9

" 'Sir,' " says the Chief Vine Inspector, 'give it another year, eh? I'll dig around it, pile on the fertilizer. Should do the trick. If not, we can always use some extra fire wood.' "

Stand up for Jesus Luke 13:10-17

10-11

Change of scene: A local religious HQ on a Rest Day[11]. Different place, different time, but Jesus is still coaching the crowds. It's the Saturday service time and this lady's there with curvature of the spine – trademark sign of a dark spirit. She'd been bent double for 18 long years.

12-13

Jesus sees her and waves her forward and says, "Lady, you're straight-ened out and sorted – literally!" He plants his palms on her and her spine stands to attention. She's eyeballing the congregation and giving God the credit.

14

The boss of the local religious HQ gets all huffy, ad-libbing a notice to the pew fillers: "It should be made quite clear there is plenty of available time on non-Rest Days for such work related activities. So do please come and avail yourself of this clinic on days other than Rest Days. Thank you for your cooperation."

15-16

Jesus bursts out, "You two-faced ham actors! Which of you hasn't, this very day, parked his chosen mode of transport or topped up its fuel supplies? So how come you break sweat moaning about this lady – this fine true-blooded Jewish lady – who's been crumpled up by Satan for eighteen years? How come you're not into her getting straightened up ... whatever day of the week it is?"

17

Jesus buttons it, and the HQ Secretary and his cronies are totally put down. Most others are high as kites on a windy day with the amazing stuff Jesus is pulling off.

Chapter Thirteen

Change Community

Small door Luke 13:22-30

22-23

Jesus' personal navigation system is still locked onto a southward direction; still targeted for "Jerusalem" as final destination. He's on the move through the local towns; coaching on the go. Someone poses the question, "Boss, who's going to be straightened out and sorted? Is it only limited entry numbers to Sortedville, or what?"

24-25

He says, "Sortedville has a very small door, so you'd better bust a gut to get in. I tell you straight, loads of people will give it a go and jack

---

[Luke 13:23 – 25] What sparks this question? Has Jesus filled beaches, crammed local religious HQs and squeezed mountain slopes full of fans, but only a fraction of the numbers are actually "signed up" as crew?

If Jesus was "doing evangelism" today, would he be reprimanded for his poor result ratio?

If the door's that tiny, what are the luggage restrictions at the entrance point?

[1] **God's Courier = Prophet.** Personal message delivery service direct from God. Think any package delivery corporation, but think "quick". Although, thinking about it, with their record, the depot for uncollected packages would've been pretty chocka by the end of the Old Testament.

[2] **Heaven on Earth/God's New World Order = The Kingdom of God.** Like with monarchies, but with God in charge, so not like with monarchies. There's also a sense of "sort of already/but not yet" paradox. We get to download glimpses now, but the full package would cramp our hard drive's style.

[3] **Religious Leaders = Pharisees.** A faction calling themselves literally "the separated ones" – "the exclusives" perhaps. Big into Rules, running a well-oiled propaganda machine which seemed to be fuelled by people's guilt.

it in as too tough. Once the owner shuts the door you'll be out in the cold, begging, 'Sir, open up! It's us!'

"He'll call back out through the letter box, 'I've got no idea who you are or where I don't know you from.'

26 – 28

"You'll shout back, 'You remember us, we had meals, we were your drinking partners, you coached us in the streets. Us!'

"And his answer? 'I've got no idea who you are or where I don't know you from.' With the add-on flourish, 'Clear off you dealers of dark stuff!'

"You'll sneak a look in through the key hole, spot the Founding Fathers: Abraham, Isaac and Jacob. You'll see all God's couriers[1] who were part of setting up God's New World Order[2] – but you'll be outside trying to bargain with the bouncers. There'll be big tears and the sound of teeth grinding in frustration.

29 – 30

"You'll also see plenty of non-Jews from all the continents finding their name cards on tables reserved for those with invites to the big banquet – the party to celebrate Heaven on Earth going live. Like I say, there are some at the bottom of the ladder who'll end up with great views from the top; and there's those who've grown acclimated to life at the top only to free fall back down to the bottom rung."

Sad old Jerusalem Luke 13:31 – 35

31

Just then a scowl of Religious Leaders[3] are trying to help Jesus. "It has come to our attention that King Herod has a

---

[Luke 13:31] Were these Religious Leaders tipping off Jesus out of genuine concern? Yeah, and pigs might fly into a Jewish burger! Was this just a fabricated piece of news to get him off their patch? Is there some plan they know of from Head Office Jerusalem? Or is it just a line to clear him out of their territory?

4 **Rest Day** = **Sabbath.** Rule No. 5 in Moses' Big Ten: "You'll keep my rest day special." By now this "special" had been defined down to the nth degree. There were plenty of things you shouldn't do.

contract out on your life. We strongly recommend that you cross over our county line and continue your journey."

32-33

Jesus is straight back with, "Tell that sly, overgrown rodent, aka King Rat, that I've got two more days exorcising demons, making people whole then, on day three, I'll hit my destination. More to the point, no self-respecting courier could possibly die anywhere else but Jerusalem!"

34

He cries out, "Oh, Jerusalem City! Jer-u-sa-lem City! You specialist in killing the couriers! You expert in the sport of stoning those messengers sent your way! How many times have I pictured myself cuddling your kids, like a mother hen snuggling the tiny chicks under her wings. But no! You wriggle away; you fight my every attempt to get close.

35

"And now, look through the settling dust: your Jerusalem Town House is a derelict disaster area; a shell of its former self. You'll not set eyes on me again till you deliver the famous line, 'Welcome! He's laughing all the way to the throne – the one who marches in here for God.'"

Table tactics Luke 14:1-14

1-4

Rest Day[4] rolls around again and Jesus is eating out on the Religious Leaders – this time at a top notch Big Wig's place.

[Luke 13:34] How strong are the protective instincts of a hen? Have you heard the story of a farm burning down and the clean up team finding a dead mother hen with live chicks chirping under her barbecued wings? So is Jesus deliberately setting up this parallel of the sacrificial act waiting for him to complete in Jerusalem?

[Luke 13:35] What famous line? From Psalm 118:26 – the line Jews keep reserved for when they finally spot their Liberator, who will kick out the alien forces in Jerusalem and finally set up the New Era.

[Luke 14:1] So it's not warm hospitality then? It's probably more a competition – who can twist something he says to catch him out?

[5] **Religious Law Enforcers = Teachers of the Law/Scribes.** Experts in Moses' law. Academics, who sadly, often became "academic" in the sense of "irrelevant".

Jesus' every move is under fierce scrutiny. Just in front of Jesus is a guy with swollen limbs – "dropsy" for the medics – so Jesus quizzes the Religious Leaders and Law Enforcers[5], asking, "What's the law say on this? Is making people healthy on a Rest Day kosher or not?"

No one says a syllable. Nothing. Awkward silence. So Jesus grabs the guy with limb trouble, sorts his condition and sends him off whole.

5-6

Then Jesus breaks the silence and asks, "So! Who here owns a set of wheels? Who's got a son? Well, say this lad's driving your multi-purpose vehicle and he loses it on a tricky corner and veers off into someone's front water garden feature. Oh, and – crucial plot detail – it's Rest Day! What d'you do? You'd be down there in a pulse, dragging your boy, your wheels, out of trouble, no?"

Still they're silent – zip to say.

7-9

So Jesus changes the subject: He'd not missed the earlier game of picking-the-best-seat-without-being-obvious. So he tells a story: "You turn up at the hotel stated on the gold-lettered wedding reception invite. Here's a tip: Don't just bag the top table. What if someone even more distinguished is also on the guest list? What if the host has to relegate you to a table down with the plebs, and with everyone watching? 'Sorry we're going to have to move you! Notice the name card for this seat is extra long – to allow for all the letters behind their name!' How embarrassing!

10-11

"No, here's the tactic: turn up with your invite and go straight for the worst possible chair. Then the host will spot you and say, 'No, no,

---

[Luke 14:5] What's Jesus daring them to say? "No, I won't pull my boy out of the crumpled vehicle. He'll have to stay there till Monday morning – I'm religious!"

[Luke 14:8 – 10] As ever, with Jesus' deep-as-you-like stories there are levels: On the first level he's actually just giving them a tip, being practical. On the higher, or deeper, level it's also a metaphor for the Heaven on Earth Inauguration Banquet at the end of time.

no! Someone of your standing can't possibly sit down here. No, come and join us at the top table!' And, again, everyone's watching! Result! Why? 'Cos those who set themselves up on a pedestal will be knocked off; and those who know their place will be escorted to higher things."

12-14

Jesus turns to the host and says, "When you have people round to lunch or a dinner party don't run through your address book of friends and family; don't see it as a networking opportunity with that rich guy up the street. You go down that route, and you'll get the polite return invite, so you'll just be evens. No, when you throw a dinner party with your best recipe, best dishes, best linens – invite the poverty stricken, the homeless, the ones on disability allowance, that tramp on the crutches, the blind beggar from the corner – then you'll be laughing! Can they return the favour? No way! They can't invite you back, so you'll get your payoff when those with the right lifestyle get brought back from death."

Sad excuses Luke 14:15-24

15-17

From across the dining table someone chips in, "Well happy are the guys who get their feet under that table; who tuck into the banquet of God's New World Order!"

Jesus sparks off this, saying, "Talking of banquets ... this guy, right, he's planning a big party – sit down food, waiter service, posh drinks, live music, the works. All the prep is done and his personal assistant gets the nod to go and invite the guest list personally. The assistant reads the invitation card into the gate intercom of the well connected: 'Preparations for the party are complete. My boss is delighted to inform you that your company is requested forthwith.'

18-20

"But they all start ratting out on him saying, 'I've just expanded my farming business and I have to inspect my recent purchase. Do send my apologies.' Another guy's RSVP goes, 'I've just invested in some new equipment for the factory and I've got to do the test runs. Send my apologies. Still another says, 'I've just got myself a wife and we're spending some quality time together. Apologies.'

21

"The personal assistant finds a way of telling his boss that the party's looking like a total non-starter. The boss throws a wobbly and blasts his assistant back out onto the streets with the new brief to 'get out there, hit the back alleys, the subways, go under the bridges and hand out the invites to the homeless, the ones on disability allowance, the blind beggar from the corner, that tramp on the crutches.'

22-24

" 'Consider it done, sir! But by my calculations we still have available places set at the table, sir.' "

The boss comes back, "Then get another batch of invites from the printer and confetti them around the streets. I want this place heaving. Oh, and don't shred the original guest list; make sure the bouncers have a copy — I don't want any of that lot getting their taste buds tickled by even the party nibbles in the lobby!"

Fair-weather fan club? Luke 14:25-34

25-26

Jesus' trip south is virtually turning into gridlock with big crowds hanging on the tail gait [sic] of the passing celebrity on his Jerusalem journey. One time he tells them direct, "You want to sign up as crew? You do know about the 'forget your nearest and dearest' clause, yes?

[Luke 14:18 – 20] Can't these people come up with better cop-outs than this? What kind of successful businessperson buys extra capacity without inspecting it first? What kind of professional invests in new equipment without checking it out beforehand?

Okay, the third guy may have a point, but it's not like he's on honeymoon, so can't they leave their marital bed for a little fresh air and a massive party?

[Luke 14:22] What state would the tablecloth be in with these riffraffs leaning their grubby elbows on the table and digging into the munchies? Does the host of the party care? And where on earth did we get the idea that heaven would only be full of nice people?

Well, shove them down the pecking order! Oh, and you know about the 'forget your own life' clause? Yes, strike the 'me, me, me' stuff off the list! Basically, it reads: 'No one qualifies as Jesus' crew unless they've put me top of their priority list.'

27 – 30

"Like I say, you can't be one of my crew unless you've ditched your life goals, jacked in your personal ambitions and pictured yourself as dead already – carrying your own execution equipment. Look, say one of you guys wants to build a skyscraper. What's first, digging out the foundations or sitting down and working out the budget? You'd look a right duffer if you've done the foundations and then have to pull the plug on the building work 'cos your bank balance is looking about as red as your face. All the locals would rip into you with, 'not much of a building!' and worse, 'this guy started, but he can't finish!'

31 – 32

"Or say a world leader is on the verge of declaring war on another world leader. What's first, pressing the 'war' button on his control panel or sitting down with his military advisors and working out if his ten thousand troops can kick the butts of the enemy's twenty thousand? If he gets frowns and head shakes from his generals, he's going to send in the diplomats, not the troops, and see if they can't negotiate a peace deal.

33 – 34

"This is what I'm getting at with expecting people to cross off everything but me on their priority list, if they're serious about

Don't Like This? [Luke 14:25 – 35] Not so eager to give up family and your own life to sign up as a Jesus devotee? Don't worry, there are plenty of things Jesus failed to mention; plenty of things you don't have to let Jesus have priority over – as long as you can justify them not being for you or your family. Handy examples include: 1. Career – if it's benefiting society in some elastic, stretching it, sort of way. 2. Gadgets – if it's saving valuable time and/or employing poor people in the manufacturing process. 3. Hobbies – if it's a provable method of winning friends and influencing people. 4. Cosmetics – if it's only applied out of concern for what others have to look at. 5. Shoes – if they really do make a difference in how you feel and therefore enhance your performance in the service of others. (Feel free to add your own items to the list.)

[Luke 14:26] So is Jesus suddenly going cold on Big Rule No. 5, "respect your parents"? How would that fit with his earlier pro-family stance with the guys who were finding small print excuses not to finance their parents' nursing homes? (See Chapter 9, Mark 7:9 – 13, page 169.)

So, if he's not into people "forgetting their families", then is it more about priorities? Is it more about him being number one on a list of, well, one?

signing up as crew. Salt's great! But if it goes bland, then what use is that? How d'you re-inject its zing? It's not even any use in the garden or on the compost heap. Non-salty salt is just for chucking."

He winds up with his cryptic catchphrase, "If you're hungry, chew it over."

Losing stories Luke 15:1-7

1-2

Jesus is surrounded by a whole range of "undesirables" – alleged Outland Revenue[6] money launderers and a gang of the generally messed up. 'Course, the Religious Leaders and Law Enforcers spot this and start their "tutting and frowning" routine again, going, "This chap doesn't only talk to these lowlifes; he actually shares his lunch with them!"

3-4

So Jesus hits the Tutting Club with a deep-as-you-like story[7]: "Say one of you guys starts dealing in wool supplies. Say you've got your stock of sheep up to the round one hundred. What if one of them goes off jaywalking? D'you write off the wanderer as a bad debt or d'you leave the ninety-nine in the safety of the field and go find the poor thing that's gone walkies? 'Course you do – you go tracking.

5-7

"Fast forward to the moment you find the poor lamb: excitement or what! The sheer adrenalin hauls the sheep onto your shoulders and fuels the long trek back home, with still loads in the tank to

[6] **Outland Revenue = Roman Tax Department.** Where the Empire collected its taxes from the minions. Hence Outland Revenue Officers weren't exactly popular.

[7] **Deep-as-you-like stories, riddles and images = Parables.** From the Greek word to "put things side by side" (ie, parallel). An ancient craft where you say things different ways; where an earthly story can take on a heavenly meaning . . . if you dig.

[Luke 15:3] So what experience would clergy have with sheep rearing? Not a lot, but their sacred books are packed full of poetry about Religious Leaders being shepherds for the directionally-challenged Jews.

Then there's Ezekiel 34:2,3: "Mortal boy, get this message out to the leaders of my people; tell them: This is what the God who runs the show says: 'You're in big trouble! You're supposed to look after my people, be like a shepherd to the lost sheep. But you're too busy looking after number one. You're happy wearing the woolly jumpers, filling your faces with lamb stew. But what d'you do to protect the flock? A big fat zero!'"

get your mates and extended family round for a celebration. 'Come on, party with me – I got my endangered sheep back!' I'm telling you, you'd see the happy ending party scene and you'd almost think it was the angels up in heaven, celebrating one of the messed up doing a U-turn and coming back to God. They'll be a load more buzzed than they get over the ninety-nine who never needed turning back to the safety zone."

Losing stories – the sequel Luke 15:8-10

8

Jesus is on a roll and the Frowning Fraternity get the follow-up story. "Or change the picture: Say this woman has ten days' pay saved up; each day's pay in a separate envelope. She's checking it's all there and – freak – one's missing. What's she do? Get all philosophical; shrug her shoulders and say, 'Ah well, win some, lose some.' Or does she turn all the lights on maximum and turn the house upside-down looking for the elusive envelope? 'Course she does, she gets busy.

9-10

"And when she finally locks eyes on the savings, she rings round all her friends to come celebrate. 'Come over, it's party time – I've got my paycheque back!' Again, it's a carbon copy of the party atmosphere in heaven when one of the messed up does a U-turn and comes back to God."

What does "prodigal" mean? Luke 15:11-32

11-12

Jesus tells the third in the trilogy of deep-as-you-like stories: "This factory owner guy has two sons, right? The kid brother gets it into his skull that he's had enough. He goes to his dad, and as much as wishes the old man dead: 'Dad, I want my chunk of the inheritance, sharp-

---

[Luke 15:9] Not convinced? Shift the time dial forward 2,000 years. What if you're toiling over a computer and suddenly you realise you've lost a whole day's work? Apart from cursing the fact that you hadn't pressed "Ctrl-S" all day, wouldn't you search out the darkest corners of your hard drive trying to retrieve the document?

Still don't think you'd throw a party at finding a lost sheep/coin/computer file? If so, do you think this points to how throwaway our society has become?

ish!' The dad sits down, does the sums, sells some shares and hands over the boy's part.

13-15

"The son doesn't even hang around to hear his dad's top ten tips for survival. Within weeks he's in foreign climates, spending the nights filling the glasses of the designer set with his liquid assets. He has such a great time he can't remember any of it the next day. 'Course, the money goes down the toilet. So do the 'friends' when they realise he's skint. Double jeopardy – there's a major recession. He's beginning to wonder where the next meal's coming from. So he surfs around and finds a site called www.worstjobsposs.cos. He scrolls through the search results and ends up cleaning out the pigsties!

16-19

"He's craving the gunk the pigs are scoffing; he's considering the options of muscling in on the trough and munching away on the carob seed slurry. Well, no one else was offering! He's there with his shovel, scratching away and suddenly a light bulb goes on just above his head: *What am I doing? The worst job in the old man's empire is, like, jet-setter status compared to this. If I had any food in my stomach, I'd be throwing up. I'll hitchhike home!* Work on a speech, something like: *Dad I've messed*

[Luke 15:12] Are the Religious Leaders and Law Enforcers anticipating where this story's going? Are they expecting the dad to reject the request and reestablish his patriarchal control over the family and its finances?

How shocked are they (and the crowds listening in) when the dad coughs up the cash and waves the lad off? Is this some sort of endorsement of our desire to explore? What had happened before this? Why did the kid brother want to get away? Could it have something to do with the repressed stay-at-home party pooper of an older brother?

[Luke 15:16] How does Jesus' Religious audience react to a Jewish boy's career taking such a dive that he ends up feeding the pigs? Is Jesus deliberately upping the shock factor to make an impact?

[Luke 15:19] Are some of the Religious Law Enforcers thinking they've heard this one before? Isn't this the one where the good Jewish father puts his foot down with a firm hand and declares the errant son as "dead to him"?

---

up — messed up with you and with God. You don't have to think of me as family, but please, give us a job?

20-24

"So after the long hot trip home, he turns the corner onto his old street. His dad spots him and runs out into the street in his slippers, throws his arms round him, lifts him up, spins him round and kisses him.

"The son starts his speech, saying, 'Dad I've messed up — messed up with you and with God. You don't have to think of me as family, but. . .'

"But the dad cuts in, telling his secretary, 'Arrange the biggest street party ever. Get the boy's tuxedo, some smart shoes, all the gold accessories. Blow the expenses budget, get the best caterers booked — let's party! 'Cos my son was as good as dead, and he's come back. We had the "Lost Boy" signs pasted up around town and now he's turned up.' So they kick off the party.

25-27

"Don't you just love a happy ending? Sorry, not this time! See there's still the big brother issue. He's coming home from work; he turns the same corner and thinks he's in a scene from an old musical: dancing, music, tables right up the middle of the street and everyone having far too much fun. He calls over one of the waiters and says, 'We just win the lottery, or what?' The employee answers, 'Better than that, sir, your brother's back — "safe and sound" I believe is the phrase — so your father's blown the whole entertainment budget on the party!'

28-30

"That's the trigger. The big brother loses it. Furious, he stomps off, boycotting the extravagance and thinking about organizing a petition

---

[Luke 15:24] "More parties!" think the Suits. "Okay, parts one and two of the trilogy were passable party cases, but just how can you justify this? The sheep didn't know better and the coin is an inanimate object, but people can't be allowed to get away with prodigal wastage of family assets, surely?"

[Luke 15:28] Is the Religious thought bubble reading, "How dare Jesus portray the loyal, devoted and supremely sensible son as 'the baddie'?"

to have it closed down. He's kicking lampposts, ranting and swearing. His dad catches up with him, but he has to fend off words he'd never heard before from his eldest 'Look! I've slogged my guts out. Slaving over your accounts. Doing exactly what you told me to do – I've not even gone on the sick when I fancied a day down at the beach – and did you ever, ever throw a paltry party for me and my mates? No! But when this waster son of yours comes crawling back, having been guilty of the prodigal wastage of a huge chunk of the family asset on, I don't know ... well ... prostitutes probably! Oh yes, he gets the red carpet and the full treatment. Well, thanks for nothing!'

31–32

"'Son,' his dad says, grabbing him by the shoulders and eyeballing him, 'you're around all the time, and I love it. What's mine is yours. But how could I not throw a party – as far as I knew, your brother was dead! Now he's alive. He could've been anywhere! And now he's here, with us.'"

More on "wasteful" Luke 16:1–9

1–2

Jesus shifts back to mentor mode for his Team. He tells them, "There's this Big Noise Mr Moneybags who has a middle manager employee who's up for a disciplinary hearing for allegedly wasting company funds. The nervous manager guy is sitting in the boss' big office and

---

[Luke 15:32] Why doesn't Jesus unpack this one? He's normally happy to be direct with this bunch. What's his thinking in just leaving the Religious Suits simmering with the cliff-hanger ending? Does he want them to ask the question "does big brother join the party or not?"? Did he want them to secretly wish that the sequel would have the two brothers slapping backs and toasting each other? And what does the word "prodigal" mean? "Wasteful" or "lavish" ... or both?

[Luke 16:1] Was this story straight off the back of the Prodigal Dad Greatest Hits? Even if it wasn't, are the Team still mulling on the "wasteful/lavish" kid brother in that memorable tale? Is Jesus drawing on that story as a deliberate backdrop to this one? If so, why does he wait to just tell it for the Team's ears only?

[Luke 16:2] Was it that he was inefficient or actually a crook? Either way, the boss was losing money and didn't like it.

the boss asks him straight out, 'What's up? Are the "wasteful" allega-
tions true? I want a full report before I sack you.'

3 - 4

"The manager guy's scurrying down the corridor thinking, 'What
should I do? He's fired me! I'm too much of a wimp to do manual
work; I'm too much of a poser to go on the social.' Then an idea hits
him: 'The clients don't know I'm no longer authorised to deal, so
what's to stop me from pulling some scams so at least I'll be the flavour of the month when I'm out on the street?'

5 - 6

"So he sets up appointments with his boss' whole database of debtors.
First up, he asks the worried debtor, 'How much you owing my boss?'

" 'Eight hundred gallons of olive oil,' he admits. The canny (soon to be
ex-) manager tells him, 'No you don't! 'Cos it's just ticking round to
our special Half Price Hour. Here, take your bill and round it down to
four hundred, no worries.'

7 - 8

"Second appointment, similar deal, he asks the debtor, 'How much
you owing?'

" 'A round one thousand wheat bushels,' he owns up. The sharp (soon
to be ex-) manager says, 'Today's your lucky day – it's 20 Percent Off
Tuesday. Here, change the document. Write in just eight hundred.'
No worries.'

"And the boss man marked it down to the sharp manager's credit that
he'd obviously been taking his 'shrewd tablets'. So what's the point?
That normal people out there on the street are usually far more astute

[Luke 16:5 – 7] Wasn't it illegal for Jews to charge interest on money? Yup, so this set up could've been an
accounting scam with the bills written up in commodities, not cash, so as to camouflage the hidden interest.

The manager would've been in on this, and it could be that his partial amnesty is just him slicing the interest
off the top. Plus the boss can't argue since his company shouldn't have been piling the interest on anyway!
Not to mention the goodwill won for the company for those clients who had debts. So it's a win-win-win situation! No wonder the boss had to give credit where it was due to the sharp manager.

in the way they handle their own kind of people than you lot who are supposed to be enlightened!

9

"I tell you, use the 'dirty dollar' to win friends and influence people for good, then, when it's spent, you'll get an open door reception when you turn up at Heaven Mews."

Response ability Luke 16:10-13

10

Jesus is still coaching the Team, telling them, "It's about responsibility! If you can keep your integrity with the small fry stuff, then you can be trusted with the bigger jobs too. But if you're straight as a bent banana in the little things, then you're not going to suddenly turn into integrity itself when you get promoted to a more responsible position.

11-13

"So, if you've never quite played by the rules with mere money stuff, then who's going to trust you with things that are really worth something? And if you've not looked after someone else's stuff well, then who's going to give you your own things to look out for? Like I say, no one can do two full-time jobs, have two full-time bosses. They'll either be well into the first and resent having to turn up for the second, or they'll hate the thought of the first and look forward to clocking on for the second. You can't be on the payroll for both God and materialism."

[Luke 16:9] So what is it that Jesus is impressed with? Obviously not the "creative accounting". Big Rule No. 8 is pretty clear on God's anti-thieving policy. Isn't it more the fact that the guy was looking down the barrel of a gun called "ruin" and he got proactive, he took the initiative, he did something about it. Is this Jesus' point then?

[Luke 16:13] When did Jesus say this before? Way back on the first Team Training Session up a mountain with crowds listening in. (See Chapter 5, Matthew 6:24, page 103.) How confident is Jesus that they've taken in the early lessons now that the clock's ticking and soon he's history?

Heaven and hell Luke 16:14-18

14-15

The Religious Leaders – who just lurved their money – were eaves-dropping on all this Team Coaching Material and sniggering at Jesus behind their bling-busy hands.

Jesus confronts them with, "You're the experts at creating the right image! But God sees through your fake perma-tan, past your perfect teeth, and down your lying throats into your hole-some [he spells it out, H-O-L-E-some] hearts. What gets into the magazines as the ultimate rank puller with people is just stomach churning gunk with God.

16-17

"Your sacred books: God's Instruction Manuals and the Courier Files, these were being broadcast 24/7 till John B turned up. Since John, the great news about Heaven on Earth is getting loads of column inches, and people are clambering their way forward to get into it. Not that we're ditching the Instruction Manuals or the Courier Files – no way! It's more likely that earth gets vamooshed off the cosmic charts; it's more probable that heaven itself will go missing without trace than The Good Book[8] goes out of circulation!

18

"So, yes, if you're wondering, this one's still in: 'Anyone who divorces his wife 'cos he's gone off her, or there's a younger model open to reasonable offers; anyone who's giving it all that "my-wife-doesn't-understand-me guff"' – I'm telling you, he's still breaking Big Rule No. 7.

[8] The Good Book = Old Testament. The bit of the Bible they had in first century Judah. Aka God's Instruction Manual.

[Luke 16:14] Most of the (designer) Suits subscribed to the formula "EW = SH," ie, Earthly Wealth equals Spiritual Health. Their motto was, "If you've got it, God's given it." Their theological position was that God was handing out big dollops to his particular favourites, making Jesus wrong. According to this, you could serve both bosses.

How they squared this with wealthy tyrants like Caesar or Herod is not clear. And how they got through reading Psalms like 73 and 37 would've involved some creative scholarship.

[Luke 16:18] Why did Jesus pick out this one from the Big Ten to make the point that the Contract still applies? Was he aware of a bit of self-justified wife-swapping going on among the Religious Suits?

And the guy who does the 'I do's' with someone else's ex-wife, is also beating up on Rule No. 7."

The sound of tables turning Luke 16:19-31

19-21

Jesus goes for another deep-as-you-like story. "Two guys, yeah? Introducing – Bill Ian Heir, wearing his purple designer suit and curled up in luxury's warm lap. And introducing, Laz R Us, wearing whatever he could rustle up from the trash to wrap up his open sores and stop the stray dogs from panting and drooling over his pustules. Now patch the two worlds together: see, technically, they're neighbours 'cos the street beggar's regular pitch is the sheltered bit just outside the rich guy's palace gates.

22-23

"Both peg it: The beggar gets an angelic cavalcade direct into Abraham's big hug of a welcome. The rich guy ends up in a torture chamber in hell. From the window of his cell he looks up and sees Laz enjoying Abraham's hospitality suite.

24-26

"He yells up, 'Abraham, give us a break, eh? Send what's-his-name ... Laz ... send Laz down with some water for me? Just a damp fingerfull of moisture might give my tongue a break. Come on! These flames are licking the life out of me!'

"Abraham comes back, 'Sorry old boy! But no can do! It's all changed. You had all the breaks in your previous life, and Laz here got the rough end of the deal. Now it's vice versa. He's living it up and you're dying to die. Anyway, even if he wanted to come down, he couldn't – it's blocked off. There's no through traffic ... either way.'

[Luke 16:23] We're back to Psalm 73 from before. Look it up, make sure you get to the "aha" moment in verse 17.

Jesus is using images and language that the Religious Boys had probably all trotted out in their sermons: all this Abraham's side stuff, the cool water in paradise, the flames in hell. It's just that, for the Suits, the casting is all confused – they're playing the wrong parts!

---

27 – 30

" 'Okay, but I'm begging you,' says the rich Bill guy, 'please send Laz back to my five brothers then, yes? They've got to know hell's worse than the worst horror story they've heard.'

"Abraham calls back down, 'So Moses and the whole list of couriers weren't good enough, huh?'

"The rich guy's really struggling now: 'But surely, with respect Abraham, if someone actually comes back from the dead; you know, turns up from the grave – surely, this'll get their attention; they'll be all ears and turn back round 180 degrees to God.'

31

"Abraham doubts it. 'They were all mouth with Moses, and it was worse with the other God couriers. Nope, they're not shifting even if someone comes back from the dead!' "

Just doing our job Luke 17:1–10

1

Jesus switches back to the Team and says, "There's bound to be a whole range of products which will make for a messed up world; these things that trip people up are bound to keep hitting the shelves. But bad news round the corner for the guys who manufacture, market and move the evil merchandise out into the street.

[Luke 16:27] Oh, so now he's concerned for someone else not to get fried! How thoughtful of him. Is he learning some new skills here?

[Luke 16:31] Is Jesus just piling it on now? He's already told the Team more than once that he's going to be executed and then come back for the sequel. Are they finally getting the point? Doesn't seem so.

[Luke 17:1] So is Jesus not into boycotting, banning and blasting the factories where people make these products? Is he happy to leave the manufacturing process running since he knows the board of directors are going to get their Bad News Dividends soon enough? But what about all the "vulnerable ones" (aka "suckers") who buy these things? Is there ever a case for pulling the plug on the conveyor belt? Is there even a case for sabotaging the belt itself? Discuss!

2

"Like I say, they'd be better off up to their neck in a skip full of concrete and getting thrown overboard, than for them to mess up the vulnerable ones.

3 - 4

"So set your own alarm bells and check the batteries are live. If a crew member does the dirty on you, confront them. If they hold their hands up to the foul, then wipe their slate clean. Even if their foul score is up to seven a day and they've held their hands up, come clean and apologised, saying 'it won't happen again' seven times, still keep on wiping that slate clean as the day you bought it."

5 - 6

The Team Twelve come back with, "Boss, we're going to need trust-boosting injections for this!"

Jesus counters, "If your trust supplies are just the size of a seed of mustard..." he spots a mulberry tree "...then you can order this mulberry tree about, 'Oy, tree, pick up your roots and relocate in the Ocean.' And you'll see the mulberry march off to the coast!

7 - 9

"Say one of you has a farm and the guy on Ploughing Duty or Sheep Security comes in from the fields. Would you, as his boss, fuss about him, saying, 'Here's your chair and I've made your steak supper — rare to medium, just the way you like it.' 'Course not! The boss would expect the farmhand to do his catering duties first: 'Slice the vegetables, do the prep and dish up my dinner, then when I'm well fed with

---

[Luke 17:2] When did he say this before (see Chapter 11, Matthew 18:6-7, page 203). And it was the same watery grave for those who mess with the kids as those who produce evil merchandise.

[Luke 17:3] And why does Jesus change the subject and switch the talk to forgiveness? Or is it actually the same subject?

[Luke 17:5] Are the Team still chewing over the evil merchandise discussion earlier?

[Luke 17:6] So does the mulberry tree pack its trunk first?

---

my feet up you can dig into your warmed up plate of leftovers.' Would he be gushing his gratitude just because the guy did his job?

10

"Ditto with you guys! When you've scrawled the word 'Done' against all the chores you've been told to do, then all you can say is, 'We're not so special: just doing our job.'"

[Luke 17:10] How many different meanings can you get from the phrase, "just doing my job"?

According to the "Mr Jobsworth" blocking tactic, typically used by someone shaking a rulebook, "just doing my job" is "I ain't shifting".

Then there's the work-to-rule employee who's adamant about doing the absolute minimum for the unpopular new boss: "I'm just doing my job," as in, "and no more!"

Or there's the sense in which Jesus recommends it being used: "I'm just doing my job," as in, "I'm not taking any credit."

Which version would you rather be confronted with?

---

1 **God Reps = Priests.** The "go between" for God and his people — not to be mistaken for the "get-in-between". Years back, this guy named Aaron was the very first God Rep, and since then only his family line was eligible for the post.

Chapter Fourteen

Establishment Wobbles

Ten percent response ratio Luke 17:11-19

11-13

Jesus' targeted destination of Jerusalem takes him south through the border territory between Galilee County and Samaria. He's just striding into a village when ten guys with infectious skin diseases shout over to him, "Oy, Jesus! Boss! Show some heart, eh!?"

14-15

Jesus sees them and says, "Go show your skin to the God Reps[1]".

[Luke 17:11] They're probably coming from outside the village, since these social rejects weren't allowed inside the village limits. See Leviticus 13:45,46 in a proper Bible for how to ensure isolated cases of contagious sores don't spread into an epidemic.

As they make for the village religious HQ[2], their scabs drop off and they get baby-soft skin. One guy, when he realizes he's sorted, comes back shouting his mouth off, saying, "God, you're so worth it!"

16

He bounces up to Jesus and lands flat out on the floor, speaking to the sandal straps, "Thank you, thank you sooooo much!"

It was then that they heard the guy's Samaritan accent.

17-19

Jesus asks, "Hang on! Weren't there ten sets of brand new skin ordered? How come I don't see ten of you whooping up to God? Where are the others? How come they're not joining the 'God, you're so worth it' chorus line with this foreigner?"

He turns to the solo celebrator and says, "Get up and go! It's your taking God at his word[3] that's made you whole."

Apocalypse when? Luke 17:20-37

20-21

The Religious Leaders[4] launch into Jesus with the question on

---

[2] **Local Religious HQ = Synagogue.** Local meeting place for Religious Jews to worship their God. Central point of any Jewish community.

[3] **Taking God at his word = Faith/Belief.** Faith is more than just a Religious Club you belong to. Belief is more than just a vague whim. This big word is an active, gutsy, practical concept. Aka "trust".

[4] **Religious Leaders = Pharisees.** A faction calling themselves literally "the separated ones" – "the exclusives" perhaps. Big into Rules, running a well-oiled propaganda machine which seemed to be fuelled by people's guilt.

[Luke 17:14] Was it the action of moving that clicked on the supernatural power? What would've happened if they didn't move? Would their skin disease not have been sorted? Was it gradual or instantaneous? How far had they moved before they noticed the weirdest feeling of the healing happening? How did people react? This sort of thing only happened in the history books, didn't it? See the famous case of Naaman in 2 Kings 5:14 in a proper Bible.

[Luke 17:15] Does the one guy who comes back think, "stuff the authorities, they can wait"? Or does he go and do the legal necessaries and *then* come back? Either way, how long was the gap?

[Luke 17:16] Check out the early bits of Chapter 12 (see Luke 10:25 – 37, pages 216 – 217) to get inside the skin of this story (pun intended). Basically the "True Jews" couldn't stand these "second class, low-life, half-Jew scum" called Samaritans. Is this a real life version of Jesus' deep-as-you-like Good Samaritan story a couple of chapters back?

[Luke 17:19] So what had made the other nine well? Was it also their trust, their faith? Was it just that they didn't know what had done it, or what? Why can't we just have a tidy formula for all this healing stuff? Hurrumph!

everyone's lips: "When exactly, date and time, is God's New World Order[5] going to arrive?"

Jesus muddies the waters by answering, "God's New World Order isn't the sort of thing you can schedule, chart or tie down! Nor is it the sort of thing where people can say, 'It's over here', 'No, it's there!' 'Cos God's New World Order is out and about already – within arm's reach, within you!"

22–24

Jesus leaves the Religious Suits scratching their brain boxes and lets the Team in on some stuff. "There'll be a time when you're on your toes, straining to see the Big Day of The Man[6], but you'll draw a blank. The papers will run features on The Man candidates; they'll broadcast primetime programmes on The Man wannabes. But, don't go to the gigs, don't line up for autographs. Why? Because The Man will turn up like lightning switching on the sky – a bolt from the blue – and just as unpredictable.

25–27

"But all this is only after major trauma; all this only kicks in once I've swallowed the ultimate rejection from this society. The Man's Big Day will be like an action replay of Noah's 'Waterworld' episode. These were typical, everyday scenes: shopping, cooking, people down at the pub, weekend weddings – it was just like any other day – until Noah entered the big boat (aka 'the zoo ship'). Then the tidal wave hit the shore and swept the oh-so-sure-of-themselves away.

[5] **Heaven on Earth/God's New World Order = The kingdom of God.** Like with monarchies, but with God in charge, so not like with monarchies. There's also a sense of "sort of already/but not yet" paradox. We get to download glimpses now, but the full package would cramp our hard drive's style. **Don't Like This?** [Luke 17:20 – 37] Find all these tricky passages too much?
Alternative A: Don't waste brain space, just skip through this bit and believe what the guy with the microphone tells you it means.
Alternative B: Just make sure you're not on the wrong end of things when whatever it is changes the world as we know it.

[6] **The Man = Son of Man.** Jesus' term for himself – lifted from Daniel 7, where it's a pretty blatant clue that this is no mere mortal: "the Son of Man … surfing in on the clouds … where the Ancient of Days … gives him … all the credit for running the show … and permanent position in the top spot." Nice name badge.

[Luke 17:21] **Is Jesus contradicting himself here? Doesn't he say earlier (see Chapter 9, Matthew 16:4, page 179) that you should be looking for the clues? So how come he's now saying that you shouldn't? Might be 'cos it's a different subject? Back then they were looking for 100 percent proof of Jesus being the One; now they're asking for foolproof clues to the arrival of God's New World Order. A different answer for a totally different question. Sandals maybe. Flip flops, no.**

[Luke 17:26 – 27] **Check out Genesis Chapters 6 to 9 in a proper Bible.**

The Daily Sun

Leper itching to go home!

There's been a spate of returns into society by former Skin Hospital Outpatients. We talked to one of them, Jonathan Hoyland, and found out what it's like to be healed:

DS—Thanks for speaking to us, Jonathan.

JH—It's nice to be here … but then, it's nice to be anywhere!

DS—I imagine. How long were you out in the Enclosure?

JH—About six years.

DS—And no contact with your family throughout this period?

JH—No physical contact. They came to the gate, brought supplies and stuff, but that was it.

DS—And how long did the doctors give you to live?

JH—Well, it depended. If I didn't have any accidents, then probably another five to seven years, max.

DS—I understand the Healer sent you back to the doctors, they confirmed the remission of symptoms and now you're back with your family with the prospect of long life. So how is it?

JH—Well, it's good. Got to sort out a pension scheme, but of course it's good. But it's not easy. The wife's been running things fine without me for six years, the kids are teenagers now – so no idea who they are – and I've got to work out how I fit in.

DS—But they must be thrilled. Do people treat you differently, being a miracle case?

JH—At first, yes. It was all parties and hugs and handshakes – really special things like that – but now people start glazing over whenever I talk about the enclosure years. Like they just want the miracle bit.

DS—Understandable in a way.

JH—But I want them to know how horrific it was and what I went through, while they're all smiles with their "that's all behind you now" type stuff. But that's all I know.

DS—And I believe you've been doing some volunteer work at the Skin Hospital?

JH—Yes, but not sure what good I'm doing there. I keep wondering if because I'm okay now, that disqualifies me.

DS—You mean the patients resent your being healed, given they're still suffering?

JH—No, they're glad to chat, but I'm sure they're thinking, "It's alright for you, you had a lucky escape." See, they're not expecting a visit from Jesus Davidson any moment; they're still facing an early death, so what right do I have to try and cheer them up?

DS—Sounds like survivor guilt to me.

JH—Maybe. It's just not proving a doddle to work out what I'm supposed to be doing. I'm not ungrateful, of course it's amazing to be able to feel my extremities again, but then I've got to relearn all sorts of practical things. Like now, if I cook, I actually feel the pain if I burn myself!

DS—It seems like you've got a lot of adjusting to do.

JH—And people ask me why I've not gone back to thank him. Well it's not all "Halle-blinkin-lujah", you know.

DS—Have you had any counselling from the Hospital?

JH—Well, they're not really geared up for miracles; they don't even use the word, not on duty anyway. They're happy with the unexpected remission in symptoms, but I suppose they've got to go with what normally happens, for the sake of the majority.

DS—Can't you talk to the other guys who got healed?

JH—Most say the same. "Life's moved on" and "So what do we do now?" I mean, what's the point in coming back from death if we don't have a life?

If you're interested in a self help group of similar people, Jonathan Hoyland has set up a public weblog: www.whathappensnow.org.il/share.

28 – 29

"It'll be a rerun of the old 'Lot legging it from Sodom' episode: People were filling their faces, filling their bank accounts, filling their work diaries. But the day Lot exited Sodom City, the lightning bolt and the sulphuric acid rain zapped the rest of them off the planet.

30 – 33

"Take the freeze frame image of Noah, lay it over the enduring image of Lot and let that be your backdrop to the text of The Man's Big Return. On that day a guy will be lying out on his sunroof when the disaster hits and, no, he doesn't go down to grab his family heirlooms. He's out of there! Same deal for anyone out in the yard: No, he doesn't go back for the family photos or whatever. He's gone.

"Mrs Lot – remember her? Like I say, if you fight to keep a grip on life-as-you-know-it, it'll slip out of your hand and hit the deck. But if you open up your palms and give up your life – it'll fly to safety!

34 – 37

"I'll tell you straight, there'll be bedroom scenes: A couple in bed. The 'lightning' strikes, and one will be taken out and the other will be left lying there. There'll be kitchen scenes: two women discussing the new bread making machine – the 'wave' hits, one's taken out and the other's left holding the manual."

[Luke 17:28 – 29] Another epic, this time it's Genesis Chapters 18 and 19. This one has a "Parental Advisory" sticker all over it.

[Luke 17:34 – 37] So is all this Big Return stuff for The Man about Jesus coming back and whisking his people off to heaven, or is it about people being washed away to their doom? Who's being taken out of the picture and where are they going? There're no clues in the text showing it's the "good guys" who get taken; there's no hint that they're off to an idyllic heaven while the rest tough out a disaster!

So is this interpretation by some quarters just escapist wishful thinking? As we look at the earlier bits of the passage – where it talks history – aren't the people there "taken out" in a slightly more negative sense, like "taken out" by a flood or a bolt of lightning? So is this actually talking about being "taken out" by a Roman sword? Is Jesus hinting at the judgement day of Rome, or is he talking about the Judgement Day at the end of time? Or what? Not quite clear enough to build a position on?

"Where, Boss? Where?" the Team ask.

Jesus just says, "Vultures only have a get-together when there's a dead body for snacks!"

Nagging God Luke 18:1-8

1-3

Straight off the back of this, Jesus moves back into storyfying-mode with one about not calling time on your God chats. He goes, "There's this place where a judge does his judging thing and he's not into all this God stuff, nor is he into all this doing-good-for-people stuff. Enter this vulnerable widow with no visible means of support. She just keeps nagging away at him, saying, 'this case, won't you call it my way?' and 'you'll give me a decision, won't you Judge?' and 'I need justice' and so on and so on and so on.

4-5

"For yonks he leaves the woman's case at the bottom of his in-tray, but finally the nagging cracks his defences. 'I don't give a fig about God; I'm even less bothered about people, but this woman's driving me to extraction, I mean distraction – enough already! She'll get her "result"! Or I'll get my ear drums eroded from her constant nag, nag, nag!'"

6-8

Jesus tags on, "D'you get the bent judge's line? And what about those who nag God? Isn't he going to pull some strings for Justice to make personal house calls at their place? Yup! Will he shove their case to the bottom of his in-tray? Nope! He'll make dead sure that they get a personal introduction to Justice, and it'll be quick too! The question isn't, 'Will God come through for you?' The question is, 'Where on earth will The Man find anyone taking God at his word?'"

[Luke 17:37] Why so cryptic? What's all this vulture metaphor talk? Doesn't he normally spell it out clear as day for the Team and keep the cryptic stuff for the hangers-on? Or was it really so cryptic for the Team? Did they spot his deliberate use of the word "vulture" which they'd all been taught in school was in the eagle family? And what bird symbol was pasted on the walls of every town in the Roman Empire? Maybe it was completely clear that the answer to their "where?" question was tightly linked to the tidal wave of Rome?

And who's the dead body? Is this the bankrupt Religious Establishment he's constantly jabbing away at, or is it more autobiographical than that?

Holier than thou sands? Luke 18:9-14

9-10

Then Jesus has a deep-as-you-like-story[7] for some cocky guys in the crowd; noisy, do-gooder types who were so full of themselves they were bursting: "Two guys, right? Both talking to God in the Religious HQ, Jerusalem. First guy, a Religious Leader (aka the 'Holier Than Thou' club chairman) and, second guy, an Outland Revenue[8] official (aka a Roman lackey).

11-12

"The Religious professional has his best voice on and he's booming, 'Oooohhh, God! I thank thee that I'm not like these lower socioeconomic groupings, with their stealing, their adulterating, their general naughtinesses. I'm particularly grateful that I'm not like this dirty Roman lackey person standing disturbingly close to me. Thank thee that I go without food for Religious reasons at least twice a week. Thank thee also that I give thee all of thine ten percent commission. Thank thee that this maketh me such an asset unto thee. Amen.'

13-14

"The Outland Revenue worker stands at the back. He doesn't even feel he can look up, he thinks he's such a sleaze ball. He's pummelling himself with grief, murmuring, 'God, I'm so messed up. Please ... please go easy on me?'"

Jesus says, "I'm telling you, it's the second guy, not the first who walks out in God's good books. Anyone who sets themselves up as something special will come crashing down; and anyone who knows his place, and shows it, will get promotion."

[7] **Deep-as-you-like-stories, riddles and images = Parables.** From the Greek word to "put things side by side" (ie, parallel). An ancient craft where you say things different ways; where an earthly story can take on a heavenly meaning ... if you dig.

[8] **Outland Revenue = Roman Tax Department.** Where the Empire collected its taxes from the minions. Hence Outland Revenue Officers weren't exactly popular.

[Luke 18:13] Who would the despised tax collector morph into for today's audience? What groups of people today get to feel distant and unworthy in the presence of the overly Religious types?

[Luke 18:14] Might there also be a third character in the subplot? Someone who's perhaps given up going into Religious territory altogether because it just makes them feel bad?

Divorce Matthew 19:1-12

1-2

Jesus wraps up the story session and takes the Eastern Avenue to leave Galilee by the Jordan bridge going to Judea. Huge numbers make up an extended convoy and his mobile healing clinic is chockablock with success stories of people striding away whole.

3

A catch of Religious Leaders jump the queue and quiz him with some pre-loaded questions: "What's your interpretation on our divorce laws? To which school of thought do you subscribe? Is it lawful for a man to give his wife the divorce papers for any and every reason? What's your position?"

4-5

Jesus parries their thrust with a question of his own. "So you've obviously never read the Instruction Manuals then?!" Jesus asks, "First off, and I quote, 'the Creator made them male and female'. Then later, ' ... which is why, when people get married, they leave their parents behind and set up their own family unit. Sex makes them one person: you can't tell where one stops and the other starts.'

6-7

"So you should count them as one person, not two. And if God's brought them together, don't let anyone pry them apart."

But they're ready with the (rehearsed) comeback line, "So why then did Moses say all you have to do is fill in the appropriate divorce form

[Matthew19:3] Which schools of thought are they on about? The Shammai School says a man can divorce his wife only for sleeping around, but the Hillel School says a man can divorce his wife for anything he likes: nagging him, burning his toast, or just 'cos he's got options on trading her in for a younger model.

So they're asking, "Are you a Shammaite or of a more Hillelesque persuasion?" Mind jump back to the late John Baptizer and why he lost his head? By challenging King Herod on his marriage to a previously married woman ... hey, juicy trap!

[Matthew 19:4] See Genesis 1:27b in a proper Bible.

[Matthew 19:5] Ditto for Genesis 2:24.

⁹ **Big Ten Rules = Ten Commandments.** Dictated by God to Moses on the top of the Sinai Mountain and the basis of Christo-Judaic law since then. Check out Exodus 20 for the breakdown.

and you can cross the box marked 'single' on the marital status section?"

8 – 9

Jesus hits them with, "Look, Moses allowed for divorce as a Plan B, a compromise law 'cos he knew you had chronic hardening of the heart. But back before all the mess they didn't even have a word for 'divorce' – no need. So don't abuse the loophole. I'm telling you the only legit reason for issuing divorce proceedings on your wife is if she's been sleeping around. Any other reason and you're breaking Big Rule⁹ No. 10."

10 – 12

One of the Team chips in, "If the domestic squabbles are looking this rough, then it's best not to walk up any aisles!"

Jesus replied to his Team, "This is tough stuff! Not everyone can handle what I'm saying: only those with a mission statement that has the word 'celibacy' right up there at bullet point one. Even then, there are different reasons for backing off from sex: some are celibate from birth; some become celibate through disease/damage/deliberate tampering; others choose to become celibate for spiritual reasons like wanting to focus only on making Heaven on Earth happen. Like I say, this is tough – only some can handle it."

Kids holding the keys Mark 10:13 – 16

13 – 14

The crowds are bringing their toddlers and young kids to Jesus, clamouring for Jesus to touch them. But the Team make like border

---

[Matthew 19:8] Is Jesus itching to quote old Ezekiel (36:26 – 27) to them, when God says, "I'm going to operate on you; extract your stone heart and replace it with one with feeling, one with a new attitude. I'll infuse you with my Holy Spirit and motivate you to want to choose life by keeping the Contract"?

[Matthew 19:9½] There is no verse 9½! Sadly, we don't get the Religious Leaders' reaction to Jesus' Moses Quote Fest – probably just random mutterings, or possibly unprintable! No doubt they were well miffed that he didn't give them a twistable sound bite worthy of Herod's attention. Herod's executioner is left still twiddling his thumbscrews.

control police, shooing them off from their "way-too-busy" Boss. Jesus spots their hard-line tactics and is ticked off with them. He calls over, "Let them through! Stop hassling them; stop making me so hard to get. These kids own the keys to God's New World Order.

15-16

"I tell you straight, anyone who's not into accepting God's New World Order like a child accepts a present will never get through the border controls into Heaven on Earth."

Once the kids get to him, he cuddles each of them, calling down God stuff for every one of them.

Affluenza drags you down Mark 10:17-22

17-19

Jesus is just setting off when this Yuppie guy rushes over, lands on his knees and launches into, "Good Coach, this limitless life you chat about: what's a chap got to do to qualify?"

Jesus asks, "Why good Coach? Only God's really good! Anyway, you're well read, you know Moses' Rule Book: 'You won't snuff out a life...'"

The Yuppie goes, "Check."

"You won't sleep around..."

[Mark 10:15] So is this just patronising "they're the leaders of tomorrow" talk; or is this 'cos he's going to get more spiritual awareness from kids than from his Team and the Religious gatekeepers combined?

[Mark 10:19] Jesus lists just a sample of the Big Ten Rules from Exodus 20. Strange order though: why does Jesus list them in the order of Nos. 6, 7, 8, then 9, and then go back to No. 5? Were Jesus' antennae probing for possible dints in his holy armour? More interesting are the ones he leaves out. Why doesn't he challenge the guy on any of the first four commandments that talk about needing 100 percent devotion to God? He also leaves out No. 10 – "you won't drool over other people's stuff" – for now at least.

So why are Moses' Rules so crucial? God downloads to Moses the heavenly press release for the people (see Deuteronomy 30:19b,20a). "See, I set before you today two options: Option (a) life and prosperity; Option (b) death and destruction. Choose life!"

The Yuppie guy says he wants this limitless life, but does he really?

Don't Like This? [Mark 10:17 – 22] Jesus is systematically undermining the big three of our society: money, sex and power. He's showing money doesn't matter, sex isn't everything and kids have more clout than adults!

Options on neutralising this threatening material are as follows: 1. His ideas are pre-dark age and unrealistic for today's civilised society. 2. His ideas are too influenced by his acknowledged suicidal attraction towards Jerusalem. 3. You can't run anything without the leverage of money, sex and power. 4. It's all hyperbole and he doesn't really mean it. After all, the big three of money, sex and power are pretty useful if you want to get things done. 5. The Movement he set up has itself proved beyond doubt that all three are still *very* important if you're going to run an organisation.

Again, "Check."

"You won't thieve. . ."

"Check."

"You won't deceive. . ."

"Check."

"You won't grieve your parents but show them respect. . ."

"And, yah, check!

20

"No problem, Coach" he says, all confident. "Done all that since I was in prep school actually!"

21

Jesus looks at him and feels a surge of love for the guy. "You're missing one thing, though," he says. "Sell up! Everything you own – sell it and donate the money to charity. Your bank balance in heaven will be off the top of the graph. Then, when you've sorted the finances, game on! Come join the posse."

22

The guy's face shifts down through the gears, from excited to hollow. He walks off, body language screaming "depressed". Why? He's seriously loaded.

Smuggling cash into heaven? Mark 10:23-31

23-25

Jesus turns to his Team and asks, "How hard is it for rich people to get into God's New World Order?" The Team are stunned. Jesus tops it off with, "It's so hard to get into

[Mark 10:23 – 25] Just how weird would this brain-shifting stuff have been at the time? Jew or non-Jew, plenty of dosh was proof positive that God/the gods (depending on your theology) liked what you were up to, the things you were into and the ideas you were onto. For Jesus to state that dosh could get between you and God was brand spanking new to most people then...

And now?

Heaven on Earth. How hard is it for a people carrier to squeeze its
bodywork through the tiny hole on your gran's embroidery needle?
You're more likely to see this happen than you are to see any million-
aires in the new Heaven on Earth!"

26-27

Now they're really stunned! Whispering to each other, "So what
chance is there of anyone getting straightened out then?"

Jesus answers them, "No chance! Not humanly speaking. But with
God – every chance. Impossible's possible when God's on the case."

28-31

"We've jacked it all in to be with you," says spokesperson Pete.

"Truth is," Jesus says, "I'm telling you: Everyone who's given up home,
family or wealth for me and my way of life will enjoy a 10,000 percent
increase in homes, families and wealth – plus tyranny and torture – in
this era. And in the next, yes, limitless life. Those at the top of the
ladder will end up at the wrong end when I turn the world on its
head. Those at the bottom will be laughing from above the clouds."

Unfair wages in heaven? Matthew 20:1-16
1-2

Jesus tells the Team, "I'll tell you what Heaven on Earth'll be like.
Download the mental image of a businessman, big in the wine making business. Crack of day – dead early – he's out headhunting some
extra staff for the fieldwork department. He shakes hands with some
guys on paying them the going daily rate. Happy with this, they put
on their Vista Vineyard overalls and make for his fields.

3-5

"Later, round 9 AM, the boss guy sees a group hanging round in
the shopping centre, doing squat except murmuring about the iffy
employment market, so he says, 'Need a job? Get yourselves to my
field and you're hired. I'll pay you the right rate.' They go join the others in overalls. Round noon and then again at three in the afternoon,
he sees more workers kicking their heels, so he takes them on too.

6 - 9

"Then it's action replay at 5 PM – just an hour to go till clocking off!
He asks a gang of guys, 'Why are you killing time here all day?'

" 'No job, nothing to do!' is their come back.

"He tells them, 'You have one now!' He hands them the Vista Vineyard overalls and says, 'Get over to my fields and get working.'

"End of the working day, the boss has a word with his personnel
officer. 'Line up the workers in front of the pay desk; those who came
in last at the front of the queue and the guys from early this morning
at the back. Hand out the pay packets.' The workers who'd only spent
one hour in a Vista Vineyard overall open up their pay packets and
count a full day's cash!

10 - 12

"So, catching onto this, the guys at the back whose overalls are caked
in a full day's sweat are doing their sums, buzzing about what they're
going to spend their bonus on. But when they get to the pay desk they
open up their wage packets and start counting a day's wage, but no
bonus, no windfall, no shopping binge to come ... just a day's wage,
as agreed. They start getting all militant, mumbling about possible
industrial action. 'Those slackers didn't work long enough to raise a
pulse rate! So how come they get treated the same as us lot who've
worked through scorching working conditions – our production figures are way past theirs!'

13 - 16

"The boss comes back to one guy with, 'Am I ripping you off? What
was our verbal contract? Listen mate, I'm paying you exactly what I
said I would. Take your readies and clear off! It's not your business if
I want to pay those other guys the same as you. It's my money! Can't
I spend it as I like? Or has my generous streak kick-started your
greed?' "

Jesus sums up with, "Like I say, the guy at the bottom of the ladder
will end up on top. The guy at the top will end up at the duff end
of things."

Jerusalem calling Mark 10:32-34

32-34

Jesus and Team are still following signs for Jerusalem, and Jesus is striding on ahead. They're stunned that he's so focused on getting to Jerusalem; the other pilgrims on the road are more than stunned, they're downright scared. Again, he calls a huddle with the Team Twelve, out of earshot from the crowd. He's repeating the plotline, "So, Jerusalem here we come! This is how it's going to be: we'll arrive in Jerusalem and The Man will be stitched up and handed over to the Big God Reps[10] and Religious Law Enforcers[11]. They'll pronounce the death sentence and hand him over to the Roman Execution Squad. He'll be dissed, spat on, smacked about and executed. Two days on – the ultimate plot twist – he'll be given a hand up back into life."

Over their heads Luke 18:34

34

Jesus' Team didn't get any of this! Somehow they couldn't get a signal to pick up the message – something blocked them off from connecting with the truth of what Jesus was on about. Not a clue!

[10] **Big God Reps = Chief priests.** If "God Reps" (priests) were the "go between" for God and his people, then *chief* priests were the ones with real clout. This eminent group are the ones who've done their year's stint as Top God Rep (High Priest).

[11] **Religious Law Enforcers = Teachers of the Law/Scribes.** Experts in Moses' law. Academics, who sadly, often became "academic" in the sense of "irrelevant".

[Mark 10:32] Jesus and the Team know Jerusalem is dangerous for him, but they go anyway. The Team knows this from the hassle they've been getting from the Religious Suits. And Jesus knows 'cos he's read The Good Book from a different angle.

Might Jesus be chewing over the lyrics of Isaiah 50:7? "Since the God who runs the show helps me, I'll not be shown up. / So I'm setting my homing device on my destination and nothing's going to get me off track. / And I'm convinced, there's nothing going to embarrass me, nothing."

[Luke 18:34] Is this denial? How much clearer does Jesus have to be to get through? Is this a case of Jesus' talk of Liberator agony and execution stuff just not fitting their theological formulae, so it goes over their heads? Or are there some sort of spiritual cataracts being applied here? If so, by whom – and why? Whichever, just how alone do you think Jesus felt?

Don't Like This? [Matthew 20:20 – 28] All this world-turning stuff is disconcerting. Best just pretend to be at the bottom of the ladder. Even better: don't pretend, but actually be at the bottom. Don't realize your potential, just doss around on the sofa all day, 'cos what's the point of climbing to the top of the ladder when it's all getting turned on its head?

Whatever you do, avoid Solomon's Proverbs about couch potatoes. Ignore Proverbs 6:6; 13:4; 20:4 and especially 26:15.

Playing status games to lose

Matthew 20:20 – 28

20

Zebedee's missus comes to Jesus with her two boys, Jim and Jonno Zebson and makes all respectful, getting down on her knees. She's got a favour to ask of Jesus.

21 – 22

"What d'you want?" asks Jesus.

"See my boys here?" she asks. "Well, give the command that they get the top jobs in your New World Order ... the best offices just down the corridor from yours – one to your left and one to your right, yes?"

"You've got no idea what you're letting yourself in for," answers Jesus. "Are you up for drinking my whole Suffering Cocktail?"

The boys respond, "We're up for it! Bring it on!"

23

Jesus comes back, "Actually, you will have to down the Suffering Cocktail for me. But as for who gets the key positions

---

[Matthew 20:21] Could they have picked a worse moment? Jesus has just bared his soul about the looming agony pulling him toward Jerusalem, and Mrs Silome and two of his best men approach him with this?

But for most Religious Jews, put "Liberator" in the same equation as "Jerusalem" and the end result probably comes out as "Revolution": the Jewish Nation rising up against their Roman oppressors; opposition forces legging it, tails between their togas; The Liberator doling out top jobs for the inner circle.

[Matthew 20:22] What's this Suffering Cocktail Jesus is talking about? Is it God's famous Cup of Punishment? As in Jeremiah 49:12: "If those who do not deserve to drink the cup must drink it, why should you go unpunished? You will not go unpunished, but must drink it."

And what's this "baptism"? It was linked with stuff like Psalm 69:1. "Get me out of here God. I'm up to my neck in filthy water. I'm in a cesspool with no steps, no ropes, no handles." Basically, "I'm a Jew, get me out of here!" Slap the two images in the same statement, and it's no picnic waiting down the road for Jesus.

---

in the new set up, that's not my call. Those roles have already got names written against them; my Dad's already put name plaques up on the doors."

24-27

When the rest of the Team Twelve get reports of this private lobbying of Jesus they're furious. Jesus calls an emergency Team talk, repeating, "You know how the world hierarchy works: people at the top control the pulse of those below them, who control the pulse of those below them.

"But that's not us. No, we run things differently. You want to be a big name in our new system? Start making the drinks! You want to be top dog? Start cleaning out all the bins!

28

"If you need a mentor for this — look and learn. Yours Truly, The Man, turned up and did he click his fingers and start ordering people about? No, he had a three-track mind — serve, serve and serve. He's so locked onto serving others he even hands over his life as a sacrifice to pay the ransom note and buy people back from darkness."

A dinner party Luke 19:1-10

1-2

Jesus is passing through Jericho Town on the Jerusalem Road. One of the town's Outland Revenue Officers is this guy called Zacchaeus. He's the tax boss of the town, creaming off the profits of all the other collectors; he's rolling in it.

3-4

As ever, it's Jesusmania — there's a crowd jostling for position around Jesus. Zach's desperate for a look see, but with him being vertically

---

[Matthew 20:28] Spot the inspiration behind this ransom-paying sacrifice in Isaiah 53:10 – 12.

[Luke 19:1] How far to go now till Jerusalem? A road sign tells him "15 miles/24 km to the Holy Capital".

[Luke 19:3] So is the addiction to celebrities back then pretty much like today? Perhaps even more so. With no cameras, no videos and no TV, the name is better known than the look, so when you get a chance to see "the face", you drop everything to get there. No wonder there's Jesusmania.

challenged — about five-foot-nothing when he stands on a box — he's got no chance of getting an eyeful of courier. But the guy's nothing if not adaptable: his little legs get blurring, he gets himself way ahead of the crowd, spots a sycamore-fig tree, climbs it and waits for Jesus and Co. to stride into view.

5-6

Jesus gets there, stops, looks up and says, "Grandstand view, eh? Good plan, Zach! You want an even better view?" asks Jesus. "Come on down; you've got guests!" Zach climbs down and is chuffed at the prospect of an open house with Jesus.

7-8

All the crowds start griping about Jesus having a dinner party with the most corrupt guy in town. Zach, though, is a changed man. He puts on his public-speaking voice, eyeballs Jesus and makes the shocking announcement: "Boss, to commemorate this occasion, I'm donating half my estate to those in the poverty trap. In addition to this, I hereby declare that if I have defrauded anyone out of anything, they just have to submit the paperwork and I'll reimburse them to a multiple of four."

9-10

Jesus, in his excitement, says, "Liberation makes house calls! Whatever you lot think, this guy's also a distant relative of Abraham. This is why The Man has shown: to track down the missing persons, straighten them out and reintroduce them to life."

Kingly come back Luke 19:11-28

11

While Jesus has the Jericho punters' undivided attention, he pulls another deep-as-you-like story from his repertoire rucksack. It's sparked by being so close to Jerusalem and all the rumours bouncing

[Luke 19:5] Does the crowd think Jesus is talking to the branches? At what point do they recognise the guy they love to hate?

[Luke 19:6] "Zach climbs down"? That's got to be a first!

off the houses about God's New World Order coming into play pretty soon.

12-13

So he tells them, "This guy of aristocratic birth goes abroad with plans to be made King and to come back with a crown on his head. Before he goes, he calls a meeting with ten of his staff and gives them each funds worth about three months' salary.

"'Invest this,' he says. 'And make sure you get a good rate of return. I'll expect to see the accounts when I come back.'

14-15

"But his staff turn against him and constantly vote against him being their King; they send a delegation with petitions and placards stating 'we don't want you', and 'you're not our King'. Despite this opposition, the coronation goes ahead and the royal vehicle brings him home. He sends for the same ten staff members, the ones who'd been delegated the funds, and asks, 'So, what sort of profit have you made with my money?'

16-17

"The first guy proudly announces, 'Well, I've achieved a tenfold increase, sir. Nearly three years' salary currently in the coffers, your highness.'

[Luke 19:11 – 28] Jesus doesn't stay with the Zach subplot long; he's back thinking about the Big Story. So do you think he sees himself as the King in this story? In what sense is he returning to people who don't want him as their King?

So why does he tell a fictional story which has a King in it, if he knows he's not going to be treated as a King when he finally hits Jerusalem? Or is he just going with the urban myth of what's going to happen when The Liberator shows up and then launching from that?

Or is it all about much, much later when he finally does come back as King and has to deal with those who got results and those who'd campaigned against him? What if both interpretations of the story – a week off and ages off – turn out to be true?

New Roman Times

Tax man Zach in public relations shift

Infamous "Zach the Tax Man" has recently undergone a major image makeover. We talk to him about whether this is just a PR exercise or something deeper:

NRT—So, Zach, no more "Mr Bad Guy"? Why the change?

Zach—This is more than just a PR exercise. I tell you, meeting Jesus Davidson is like a total body, mind and spirit overhaul.

NRT—The reports coming in are all positive.

Zach—And I'd agree. *I* like me more now!

NRT—So why the big turnaround? Did Jesus threaten to blackmail you?

Zach—No, he just sparked my imagination. I got a sense of the impact I was having on the community.

NRT—You mean like mothers not being able to feed their toddlers because of crippling debts.

Zach—Precisely.

NRT—And you'd never thought about that before?

Zach—Well, I was so busy, and I only ever socialized with work colleagues, so I didn't really know the effects.

NRT—And now you're out there mixing with all sorts?

Zach—Well not yet – I'm inundated with all the paper work right now.

NRT—From the Big Payback?

Zach—Yes. I don't want to shortchange anyone. But once the financial restructuring is complete, I'm sure I'd enjoy, uh … "hanging out" with some of these people. They seem fun.

If you know that you've been unfairly invoiced by Zach the Tax Man, and can prove it, contact us at www.newromantimes.gos/taxrebate.

" 'Impressive!' says the new King. 'You're a good worker: you can obviously handle small projects, so you get a promotion to the big league – Governor of ten cities!'

18 – 19

"Another worker shows his spreadsheets and says, 'Look, sir, you gave me three months' salary; I've turned it round into fifteen months worth! Five times the original figure, uh, your highness!'

" 'Also impressive!' says the new King. 'You're the Governor for five cities.'

20 – 21

"Then another staff member bites the bullet and says, 'Here's the dividend you gave me. Still in pristine condition – untouched. Not lost a penny of it! It's been wrapped up safely in a special towel 'cos I knew your reputation that you played pretty ruthless on the old Monopoly Board of life; that with you, give and take mean, we give and you take. So I kept it safe. Nothing missing, uh, your Royal Highness, sir.'

22 – 23

"The new King fumes, 'You are an evil waste of an excuse for a worker. And yes, like you say, I'll take and you'll give. Why didn't you even just put it in a savings account? Then I'd at least have some compound interest stacking up!'

24 – 25

"The King swivels the office chair round to the others in the meeting and says, 'Take the money off him. Let the first guy with the times ten track record manage the funds for me instead.'

" 'But your majesty,' they counter, 'he already has amazing results! I mean, times ten!'

26 – 28

"The King says, 'Exactly! Those who've got plenty, get given even more; and those who've got a pittance, even what they've scraped together will be given to those with ample sample. That's how it works! And where are those guys who lobbied for me not to be King? Drag them in and execute them right here, right now!'"

Jesus leaves Zach's open house party with everyone chewing over the not-such-a-happy-ending story. He's off out of there ... up the steep hill to Jerusalem.

Blind belief Mark 10:46-52

46-48

Jesus, the Team and, of course, a troupe of groupies are travelling on the Jerusalem Road out of Jericho City. As they're leaving, they pass this homeless blind guy, surname Timaeusson. He's sitting just off the road begging for some loose change, "You give – I live!"

The blind guy picks up that the reason he's in danger of being trampled on is 'cos Jesus of Nazareth's entourage is trucking down the road. He yells out, "Liberator Davidson! Jesus! Give me a break! Please!"

Most of the crowd within spitting distance tell him to zip his lip. But this just fuels his yelling with even more grit. "Liberator Davidson, give me a break, eh, please!"

49-50

Jesus slams the brakes on, says, "Call him over."

The crowd switch faces and turn all friendly to the homeless guy, telling him, "Brighten up, get off your backside – he's calling you over."

Timaeusson flings his cloak to one side, jumps up and fumbles his way over to Jesus.

[Mark 10:46] This Mr Timaeusson is only known by his family name – the "Bar" bit being a standard add-on to say "son of", like son of Timaeus might be Timaeusson now. So has his family now abandoned him, leaving him as a homeless beggar? How sad is this that no one knew his first name? Just which family had he been rejected from?

[Mark 10:50] In the process of chucking his coat, does the blind guy lose some of his pathetic takings for the day?

51 – 52

Jesus pulls him in with his voice and asks, "What d'you want me to do for you?"

"Coach," the blind guy says, "let me see, please, I want to see!"

"Go!" Jesus says, "You taking God at his word is what's made you whole."

Straight off, the guy gets his sight. But he doesn't "go", he "stays", hooking up with the Team and joining Jesus on the hill up to Jerusalem.

[Mark 10:52½] There is no verse 52½, but just press pause to mull: Only one day to go before Jesus gets to Jerusalem. This long journey south is about done. Does he have a big entrance planned? What's the reception going to be like?

So if he knows the ending's going to be in Jerusalem territory, then how come there's still about a third of the book to go? Is the story going to extend out for years yet with twist after twist delaying the inevitable? Or is the pace going to slow down, like a skimming stone that only lands on certain bits, skipping others, and then finally landing on the story of the final week and going deep?

Chapter Fifteen

What an Entrance

Donkey ride Mark 11:1-7

1-3

Jesus and the Team draw Jerusalem slowly in towards them: trudging up through Bethany; slogging away past Bethphage; looking up at the Olive Mountain ahead of them and knowing that Jerusalem's behind it. Jesus sends two of the Team on ahead and tells them, "Change gear, go up in front, you'll see Bethphage and just on the outskirts you'll find a baby donkey tied up – untamed, not yet ridden! Untie it and

---

[Mark 11:v½] There is no verse ½ but let's have a quick time check: Sunday, a week before Flyby Festival, aka Passover. This is a major Jewish Religious festival which celebrates God liberating their ancestors from the sweatshops of Egypt. The name derives from when the angel of death passed over/flew by Jewish homes. Also, quick geography briefing: To walk from Jericho, "Lowest City on Earth", to Jerusalem is uphill all the way – for Jesus, in every sense. You're climbing from about 800 ft/245 metres below sea level to about 3,000 ft/1000 metres above sea level in just 12 miles/20 km, which makes it a pretty steep gradient. We're talking perfect triathlon training conditions, especially in the heat of the Middle East, but it's doable when there's a Flyby Festival at the end of it.

---

[1] God's Courier = Prophet. Personal message delivery service direct from God. Think any package delivery corporation, but think "quick". Although, thinking about it, with their record, the depot for uncollected packages would've been pretty chocka by the end of the Old Testament.

bring it to me. If you get any 'Oys' or 'what'ja think you're doings', your line is, 'The Boss needs it, and he'll have it sent right back.'"

4 – 6

Sure enough, they find the baby donkey in the street tied up near a doorway. They start untying the knot and, as warned, they hear the objection, "Oy, what'ja think you're doing?"

They deliver their rehearsed line, "The Boss needs it..." and the neighbours are fine with it.

7

They bring Jesus the baby donkey and fling their coats on it as a makeshift saddle. Jesus gets on.

Old clues Matthew 21:4 – 5

4 – 5

All this slots in nicely with clues the old courier[1] gave:

"Get through to Jerusalem, girl!
'Look up, your King's doing his Big Entrance thing.
But it's Big Entrance alternative style:
A gentle man, no hype, no pose.
Riding on a donkey, a baby donkey!
The gentle man shows.'"

[Mark 11:6] So did the people recognise the two Team members – and who their Boss was – who were delegated to sort the transport issue? Probably, Jesus was a known celebrity figure; people would've backed off once they knew it was for him.

[Matthew 21:5] What King comes in on a baby donkey? In today's terms, what world leader drives into a capital city on a 50cc scooter? How many people would have spotted the reference to The Good Book (see Isaiah 62:11 and Zech 9:9 in a proper Bible) that Matthew points up?

The Religious Leaders probably clicked their mental search facility and came up with the Isaiah and Zechariah bits. Question is, were the hardened cynics saying stuff like, "He's staged this deliberately! It's a gimmick, just a publicity stunt to set him up as something special!" You just can't win with some people.

Welcome party Luke 19:36-38

36-38

Jesus shudders along on his tiny taxi towards the Big City. The
crowds are going crazy: throwing their coats into the road for
him as makeshift suspension softeners. He's plodding through
the Kidron Valley where the road dips down from the Olive
Mountain. Whole crowds of crew are busting a gut with exhilaration; piles of fans getting off on how amazing God is, buzzing
with all the supernatural stuff they'd seen Jesus kicking off.
They're blasting out the lines,

> "Welcome, well happy, is the one who comes in here for God.
> Serenity oozing out of heaven,
> Dazzling power pouring over the balcony
> and dripping down our way."

Confirm or deny Luke 19:39-44

39-41

Some of the Religious Leaders[2] in the crowd shout over the
chanting, "Coach! Calm the frenzy; tell your fans to shut it."

Jesus calls back, "If they button it, the stones would have to
scream out instead!" Jesus climbs to the brow of the hill and
locks his sights on the urban sprawl that is Jerusalem City. He's
overwhelmed. He's weeping.

Don't Like This? [Luke 9:39-44] Not into the radical nature of what's looming; not up for the status quo being threatened? Join with the Religious Leaders of the time as they sing, "Lord won't ya keep things broadly the same. / Frankly revival would drive me insane. / If it ain't broke don't fix it, so I'll ask you again. / Oh, Lord won't ya keep things broadly the same."

[2] Religious Leaders = Pharisees. A faction calling themselves literally "the separated ones" – "the exclusives" perhaps. Big into Rules, running a well-oiled propaganda machine which seemed to be fuelled by people's guilt.

[Luke 19:36] Why the road padding? You don't turn your coat into a carpet for "just a friend", not in dusty Palestine. You only act this crazy for top royalty. What did the people think was going to happen? Was this the Revolution they'd been on the edge of their seats waiting for?

[Luke 19:38] They're shouting their traditional hymn with extra oomph this year. It's lifted from Psalm 118 – this bit's verse 26   check it out.

[Luke 19:39] Why are the Religious Leaders fretting with their "keep your voices down" routine? Are they worried that the Roman authorities will get a sniff that this is some sort of anti-Rome demonstration?

Are they scared spitless they'll lose their Roman license to practise their Religion? How desperate are they to keep the status quo going?

³ **Religious HQ = Temple.** Jerusalem's focal point of the Jewish Religion. Literally a house for God. Question is, how much does God get let out?
⁴ **Big God Reps = Chief priests.** If "God Reps" (priests) were the "go between" for God and his people, then *chief* priests were the ones with real clout. This eminent group are the ones who've done their year's stint as Top God Rep (High Priest).
⁵ **Religious Law Enforcers = Teachers of the Law/Scribes.** Experts in Moses' law. Academics, who sadly, often became "academic" in the sense of "irrelevant".

42 – 44

Between the sobs he says, "If only you, yes, even you had only caught on – what's the date? Mark it down as the day you get your serenity, personal delivery. But you won't! Not now, you've been registered Spiritually Blind. So now there's a different Red Letter Day inked into your forward planner: the day enemy troops will build a barricade and activate 'Operation Obliteration'. They'll surround you and pummel you into the ground; your kids' fine facial bone structures will be smashed against local stones. Your brick buildings will be flattened to rubble. Why? 'Cos you didn't wake up when God showed up for you."

Matthew 21:10 – 11

10 – 11

Jesus hits Jerusalem and the whole city's buzzing with, "Who is this guy?" The crowds shout back their answer, "It's the God courier Jesus, from Nazareth, Galilee!"

Kids! What do they know? Matthew 21:14 – 17

14 – 15

The visually impaired and the physically disabled fumble and limp their way over to him at the Religious HQ³, and he sorts their medical problems … completely. The Big God Reps⁴ and the Religious Law Enforcers⁵ check the CCTV footage of all the awesome stuff he's pulling off and the loops of audio tape with local kids chanting,

"Liberation – it's got the Davidson logo all over it."

'Course the Religious Big Cheeses are curdling with disgust.

16 – 17

They confront him and ask, "Do you need a hearing aid or what? These children are talking you up like you're The Liberator."

[Matthew 21:16] Check out King David's full song lyrics of Track 8 from the Greatest Hits Compilation of Songs, aka Psalm 8. It's talking about the kids singing, but look who's not singing! How often is it that kids spot what goes over the heads of so-called sophisticated adults?

"Yeah," Jesus smiles, "don't you recognise the source? 'And you get kids to sing you songs. Unqualified praise from the amazed.'" Jesus walks off and goes back to the suburbs – Bethany – where he can crash out for the night.

Figging curse words Mark 11:12-14

12-13

Next morning, the Monday, they leave their digs in Bethany Town and Jesus is getting hunger pangs. Just up ahead Jesus spots a leafy fig tree. He's salivating for a juicy fig breakfast but pulls up leaf after leaf and no figs! Fair enough, it's not fig season yet.

14

But Jesus confronts the tree, loud enough for the whole Team to hear and says, "That's it! No one, ever, is going to get breakfast, dinner, tea, supper or snacks from your branches. Ever!"

[Mark 11:12] How well had Jesus slept – knowing what wasn't far off in Jerusalem; knowing how the Religious Board of Directors would probably be up all night planning to take him out of the equation? But then if Jesus could sleep through an actual storm (see Chapter 8, Luke 8:24, page 141), maybe he could sleep through a mental storm too.

[Mark 11:14] What's with this? Is the whole thing a piece of symbolism that the Team would've got? Depends what word association you have for "fig tree". Most Jews would've triggered the word "Israel" when thinking laterally around "figs" because of chunks from the Courier Files such as Hosea 9:10 or Micah 7:1.

[Mark 11:14 1/2] Again, there is no verse 14 ½ but hit the pause button for a sec. Swot up on your Malachi before you (even remote-ly) press play. I'd prod you to look it up yourself, but would you? Here it is: Some of the last lines of the Old Instruction Manual (see Malachi 3:1 – 3) have God going,

> "Watch, I'll send my personalized memo, my walking billboard to do the prep. Watch, no warning, the One you're on you toes to see will stride into his HQ. My living contract, my walking promise – the one you're desperate for will show.

> "But who can cope with the impact of his arrival day? Who can stay on their feet when he shows? The heat will be like a refiner's oven, the purity like a launderer's soap. He'll clean up the act of the HQ workers, burn off all the corruption – like a skilled gold or silversmith.

> "The end result: God will have people who bring sacrifices made sacred by right lifestyle; God will get offerings not polluted with crime." Now, ready to play the next episode? Lift the pause button...

Dead Man Walking

Dead man walking tall and strong to his dangerous appointment.
Still patient when the Team go blank and stoke his disappointment.
Representing us up there if we don't disown him down here.
Reversing the roles, speaking up for us so God will hear.
Control-free enough to send them off to learn life's lessons.
Radical enough to host unisex coaching sessions.
Admitting that life is rough and celibacy is tough,
But we won't be owed a thing by God if we give up stuff.
Not holding back on the realities and strife,
Highlighting the payoffs of a sacrificial life.
Wants us to lose the "me, me, me".
Aims to be our only priority.
The cost needs counting,
Emotional accounting,
And the pressure
Mounting.   Nailed up high?

Dead man talking away about the one percent of the flock, the ten percent of the pay,
Searching for the extravagant younger son who upped and wandered away.
Frustrating the activists with a more dangerous form of Revolution.
Handing down the where, the how and the why on conflict resolution,
Promising if we help the poor that he'll pay us back in kind.
Warning us that we won't know when his Big Return is timed.
Pointing out history's eating habits — how she repeats herself,
Waiting for more key workers to step down off the shelf.
Yearning for the vulnerable who'd hide under his wings,
Longing for the freedom that abandonment brings.
Wanting everyone to join but not on their terms,
Avoiding the risk of materialistic germs.
Stressing even Samaritan half-Jews
Can bring good news
And the pressure
Accrues.   Nailed up high?
                                                                  Crucify?

Dead man zoning in on the unpopular guy; drawing the lavish from the miser,
Opening up the eyes of the blind, leaving the sighted none the wiser.
Reversing the status games of the "have nots" and the "have yachts".
Big on women getting heard; the mic being handed to tiny tots,
Rocking the boat for the stay-at-home, status quo fans.
Steadying the boat by tipping the Team off on future plans.
Stamping on the snakes and spinning ladders till injustice stops,
From mending tables to sending tables turning on their tops.
Insisting on an open door for kids who can't help him any,
Pointing out the blockage of a life lived to the penny.
Ensuring the late comers get more than they deserve.
Sliding early adopters back down their learning curve.
A three track mind of "serve, serve, serve".
Allowing them all to observe.
Will the pressure
Unnerve?

                              Nailed up high?
                                    Crucify?
                                       Purify?

Dead man ranting at the vultures who are keeping their manicured claws clean,
While they blame and blast and block the good news off the screen.
Determined to pop the pomp and circumvent the circumstance.
Not puffed up by being famous, not milking every promo chance,
Opening up the party table for those who could never have paid.
Banishing the arrogance of the Religious tutting brigade,
Proposing the promotion of those who know their place.
Outing the holier-than-thou's as a total waste of space,
Ignoring passports for proof of team identity.
Accepting his crew based simply on integrity.
Freeing the guilt glands of the normal Joes,
Exposing those who just suppose
It's about putting on shows:
Religion's one big pose.
And the pressure
Grows.

                              Nailed up high?
                                    Crucify?
                                       Purify?
                                         Why?

Part 3

(Com)passion Week

[1] **Religious HQ = Temple.** Jerusalem's focal point of the Jewish Religion. Literally a house for God. Question is, how much does God get let out?

Chapter Sixteen

Confrontation

Vandal with a cause Mark 11:15-19

15-16

Jesus moves on into Jerusalem and makes straight for the main Religious HQ[1] courtyard. He strides into the Non-Jew Prayer Zone and starts stampeding the dodgy traders from their stalls. He's trashing the trestle tables of the Cash Converters; he's smashing the pens of the dove salesmen; he's barricading the thoroughfare for those wheeling boxes of merchandise through the HQ complex.

[Mark 11:15 – 17] Why suddenly Mr Angry? We know Jesus checked the HQ out the night before, so no way is this a "spur of the moment" tantrum. Is this a rare example of pure anger ... literally? Why so livid? Bit of background: The Cash Converters kiosk was a Bureau De Change for pilgrims swapping dirty Roman lucre into proper Jewish Tyrian currency – at the rip-off prices laid down by Exchange R Us.

The dove dealers get vandalised for making a killing off people killing doves for Religious sacrifices – mostly poor people – with their Animals Ready 4 Sacrifice programme, courtesy of Easy-Life, Inc, which knew weary pilgrims would rather travel light.

---

[2] **Big God Reps = Chief priests.** If "God Reps" (priests) were the "go between" for God and his people, then *chief priests* were the ones with real clout. This eminent group are the ones who've done their year's stint as Top God Rep (High Priest).

[3] **Religious Law Enforcers = Teachers of the Law/Scribes.** Experts in Moses' law. Academics, who sadly, often became "academic" in the sense of "irrelevant".

17

All this while he's re-educating the people. "What's it say in the Courier Files? Isn't there a line where it goes, 'My house will be a station for every nation; a place for every race to connect with God.' And what do you lot make it? Quick Buck Quarters, Rip-Offville, Crime County."

18-19

The Big God Reps[2] and the Religious Law Enforcers[3] adjourn their meetings and hang out their office windows to hear Jesus' rant. They scribble "kill Jesus" in angry lettering to the "any other business" section at the bottom of their agenda pages. They're seriously rattled by this Jesus phenomenon, but more scared by the amazing reviews he's getting from his public coaching sessions.

The day ends with Jesus and Co. exiting the City for their digs in the suburbs.

Mountain sculpting Mark 11:20-25

20-21

The next morning, the Tuesday, they're on the Jerusalem Road again and they clock yesterday's fig tree, but it's shrivelled up, roots to tips. Pete points it out to Jesus, "Coach, get an eyeful of that! Your fig tree from yesterday is, like, history."

[Mark 11:15 – 19] But maybe it's not just about corruption; not just about making fast pounds on Religious grounds. Maybe it's also about the mistreatment of non-Jews. All this manic haggling over stinking animals is set up where exactly? In the Non-Jew Prayer Zone – the place designated for foreigners to have some quiet to connect with God! Fat chance of that happening with all that "roll up, roll up, you'll go coo at our dove deals" going on!

And what was the Religious HQ in Jerusalem for anyway? Let's hear from the guy who built it, King Solomon (1 Kings 8:27 in a proper Bible). He's talking to God, asking, "So, you're serious?! God living down here on earth? But you scratch your elbows on the sides of this cosy cosmos of ours; you have to breathe in to squeeze yourself into it. So how come this building, this HQ I've made, is now going to be your home?"

So how does God feel about the HQ he squeezed himself into becoming a focus for exploitation?

---

22 – 23

"Take God at his word[4]," Jesus comes back. "Truth is, if anyone says to this Olive Mountain, 'out of here, land yourself in the Dead Sea', and if they've got no reservations about it – but trusts it'll happen – sure enough, wait for the almighty splash!

24

"So, whatever you lobby God for, be convinced it's already in your in-tray of God gifts, and sure enough, it'll be yours.

25

"Plus, when you're standing there asking God for stuff, and you're still riled by what someone did to you last night, wipe their slate clean and file it under 'D' for 'Dealt With', and then your Dad in heaven can sort your mess out too."

Handling the hecklers

Matthew 21:23 – 27

23

Jesus returns to the Religious HQ Courtyard. He's mid-flow in his lifestyle coaching talk when the Big Reps and Councillors[5] start heckling, asking, "So, who's backing you? Who gave you any right to lift a finger against the Religious HQ system?"

Don't Like This? This verse 25 causing you some frowns? There's a whole raft of possible ways out of this direct instruction:

Focus on just how bad a thing it was that this person did to you.

Focus on how it's really damaged you for life and how much they need to realise how they've damaged you for life.

Focus on just how focused you are on how much they need to realise.

But don't lose your focus and look up the story of the unforgiving servant in Chapter 11 (see Matthew 18:21 – 35, pages 206 – 207).

[4] **Taking God at his word = Faith/Belief.** Faith is more than just a Religious Club you belong to. Belief is more than just a vague whim. This big word is an active, gutsy, practical concept. Aka "trust".

[5] **Councillors = Elders.** The non-Religious element of the ruling of the people. Sort of civil servants.

[Mark 11:21] All power, even supernatural power, can be used for creating or destroying. This is the only record of Jesus using the supernatural to destroy. And for good reason? Yes, if the Team get the right end of the stick.

[Matthew 21:23] Bureaucracy jargon buster: The Big God Reps, the Religious Law Enforcers and the City Councillors made up the Sanhedrin, which was the high court of the Jews, who ran the temple police. They'd no doubt been up half the night filing their angry report on the vandalism when Jesus overturned the tables in the main Religious HQ.

⁶ **God's Courier = Prophet.** Personal message service delivery direct from God. Think any package delivery corporation, but think "quick". Although, thinking about it, with their record, the depot for uncollected packages would've been pretty chocka by the end of the Old Testament.

24 – 26

Jesus hits back with, "I've got a teaser for you too! Here's the deal: You answer mine and I'll answer yours. Fair? Here goes: Who was backing John? Where'd he get the right to baptize people, from (a) heaven or (b) earth? Was he tapped into heaven power, or just human power?"

They huddle for an impromptu powwow.

Some say, "Play the (a) 'from heaven' card." But others are thinking ahead with, "No, he'll trump it with 'why weren't you into him then.' So we play the (b) 'just plain old human' card then?" But others point out, "Then we'll have the public at our throats, 'cos they're still paid up members of the late God courier's⁶ fan club."

27

Their considered response is, "Uh, we're not sure."

Jesus keeps his side of the bargain and says, "And I'll stick with a 'no comment' on your question about my power sources."

Young people of today! Matthew 21:28 – 32

28 – 30

Jesus shifts into story-and-question mode. "Mull this question over and let me know what you reckon: This guy's got two sons. He goes to the big brother's bedroom and says, 'Son, go work in the wine factory today for me, yeah?'

" 'Oh, you're soooo unfair! I'm busy,' whines the son. But then he has second thoughts and goes grape picking for his old man anyway.

"Then the dad goes down to the kid brother's room, same ask. The younger boy says, all keen, 'I'm there! No worries, dad.' But he never quite breaks out of his bedroom door.

[Matthew 21:24] Jesus' answer, or rather question, was not the response they wanted. What they wanted to hear was something like, "I had no right. I'm sorry, it won't happen again, ever."

[Matthew 21:27] They must've been in trouble if their best option was to look stupid! Up there at the top of the list of Things Religious Power Players Never Say has to be "we're not sure".

[7] **Outland Revenue = Roman Tax Department.** Where the Empire collected its taxes from the minions. Hence Outland Revenue Officers weren't exactly popular.

[8] **Heaven on Earth/God's New World Order = The kingdom of God.** Like with monarchies, but with God in charge, so not like with monarchies. There's also a sense of "sort of already/but not yet" paradox. We get to download glimpses now, but the full package would cramp our hard drive's style.

31 – 32

"The question's this: 'which of the two did what his father asked?'"

"The first!" the Religious Suits answer.

Jesus then unleashes his point and says, "I tell you straight, the corrupt Outland Revenue[7] workers and the prostitutes are getting their citizenship papers to God's New World Order[8] while you guys are way back in the queue. Why? 'Cos John B turns up with a guided tour down Right Lifestyle Road, but you meander off down Do It Yourself Drive. But the crooks in the tax office and the women from the brothels went for it. And even after you see their change of attitude, you still don't do a U-ey, you still don't trust him."

Workers' uncooperative Matthew 21:33 – 46

33 – 34

Jesus is still prodding the Religious Suits with his stories. "Time for another yarn? A big businessman decides to diversify into wine production. He builds a big wall, buys the machinery, installs the state-of-the-art CCTV cameras. Then he headhunts his workforce and leaves them to it. He's off. Come end of season, he sends his staff to pick up his percentage of the revenue.

35 – 37

"But the workforce get physical with the staff from out of town – beating them all, killing some. So the absentee businessman sends a bigger team, a whole department! But they suffer

---

[Matthew 21:33 – 41] This time Jesus lays an allegory on them. With allegory you know it's fictitious, but the comparisons with real life are fully intended. So what does a Jew tend to think of when hit with a story about a vineyard? Answer: The Nation of Israel. Check out Isaiah 5:1,2 in a proper Bible, for example. And why did the owner guy leave in the first place? Well, it happened all the time. The listeners would've all known of rich absentee landowners contracting with local tenants on a crop-sharing basis.

Is this why the Religious Leaders got carried away with their rather aggressive suggested ending? Were they so into the story they'd not spotted the self-condemning parallels?

---

heavy collateral damage too. He realises the only thing to do is send his son, thinking, 'Surely they'll show him some respect!'

38–39

"Unlikely! The workforce see the son and hatch a scam: 'This is the heir, just one more life on our consciences; if we get rid of him then we'll inherit the whole caboodle!' So they grab him, walk him off the premises and do him in ... permanent."

40–41

Jesus goes interactive and tells them, "So you finish off the story. The business owner turns up and ... what happens next?"

The Suits are really getting stuck into it, going, "He'd sort the scum out good and proper; they'd get what's coming to them! Then he'd rent the business out to some reliable group who could be trusted to distribute the profits as agreed at the end of the financial year."

42–43

Jesus comes in from left field and says, "Have you ever stumbled across the bit in the Instruction Manuals where it says,

> 'The foundation stone the workers chucked out
>   Is the very same one God picks out
>   And builds everything else on top.
> God's the architect, and it's awesome to watch him work.'

"So you're spot on: God's New World Order will be forcibly removed from you lot and handed over to people who'll come up with the goods.

44–46

"It'll be bad enough to trip over this foundation stone — we're talking broken bones. But worse still to have it land on top of you — we're talking crushed bone dust."

[Matthew 21:42] Jesus is quoting a famous lyric, a regular song in Jewish Religious sing-alongs (see Psalm 118:22,23 in a proper Bible). They could've all sung along as Jesus quoted it, but would the volume have dipped toward the final line as they see an old song getting a total meaning overhaul?

The Big God Reps and the Religious Leaders[9] totally GET the point that they are the unsavory courier killers in the story! So they go through scores of options on getting the subversive storyteller out of the public eye. But they are stopped short by the potential public backlash. They're scared stupid of arresting him and having public opinion turning against them, 'cos the word on the street about Jesus usually included the term, "God's Courier", capital "G", capital "C".

Some reception! Matthew 22:1-14

1-3

Same audience, same approach: "storyfying" God's New World Order. Jesus goes, "Tell you what Heaven on Earth's like ... it's like a King who's got a royal wedding in the pipeline. His son's getting married and he's sent out all the invites to their Poshnesses from the very highest circles of society. Thing is, no one's confirmed they're coming! So the King gets his staff to follow up personally with the designer set. But it's like the worst type of cold calling job – no one's interested, and his people are all having the front doors slammed in their faces.

4

"So he sends another department of the Royal Staff with a rehearsed speech for those on the invite list, direct from the King: 'The King wishes to inform his honoured guests that the menu is set, the best beef is simmering away nicely, and we simply require your esteemed company to complete the festivities. The wedding reception awaits you, now!'

5-7

"But the great and the good just give the royal staff the cold shoulder and leg it – some off to the countryside; some to the office. Some of them just stick around long enough to bundle their royal messengers

[9] **Religious Leaders = Pharisees.** A faction calling themselves literally "the separated ones" – "the exclusives" perhaps. Big into Rules, running a well-oiled propaganda machine which seemed to be fuelled by people's guilt.

[Matthew 22:1 – 14] Hasn't Jesus done this story before? Yup, to a similar crowd back in Chapter 13 (Luke 14:15 – 24, pages 239 – 240). But this isn't just a repeat; it's a variation on a theme. How is Jesus adapting the story as he tells it again this close to his deadline? Is this why there's a heavier last scene in this version (v13)?

into a corner, thrash the life out of them and discard their dead bodies. The King's in a right royal rage. He calls in his Army Chief and gives him his orders for Operation Comeuppance – to take out those murderers and trash their command and control centres.

8–9

"Then the King tells the remaining staff members, 'The wedding reception is ready. But those on the original list aren't worth the stamp on the invitation envelope. Go find some new people. I've got some new invites printed – go hand them out to whoever you see hanging out on the streets.'

10–12

"So the royal staff go looking for some guests. They collect all sorts – salt of the earth, dodgy characters, others. The palace banquet hall is buzzing. But when the King makes his big entrance, straight off he spots a guy not wearing his made-to-measure wedding kit. He goes right to him and asks, 'Friend, how is it that you were permitted to take your seat in your torn T-shirt and cutoffs?' But the guy says diddly-squat.

13–14

"The King has stern words with the waiters, telling them, 'Handcuff him, kick him out the back into the dark alley where the walls echo with shrieks of grief and the silence is scared off by the sound of teeth grinding against the pain.'

"Why? 'Cos there are loads on the invite list. But not many are picked out."

[Matthew 22:12 – 13] Does this seem a bit harsh? Some running commentaries reckon the guests were given the posh garb – their equivalent of a tux and tie – by the King himself. If so, then this guy's got such an attitude problem that he's refusing to don the three-piece suit, let alone shower, shave and shine his shoes.

Poll tax trick questions Mark 12:13-17

13-15

After a back-to-the-drawing-board meeting or ten, the Religious
Leaders hook up with the cronies of Herod Antipas to try and twist
Jesus' own words against him. They slide up to him, all smarmy.
"Coach," they crawl, "we're aware of your standing, your integrity, your
authenticity. We know that you aren't easily influenced, that you rise
above labels, status games and opinion polls. We're ever so aware that
you coach God's ways in line with the truth. So, are you in agreement
with the paying of the poll tax to Caesar? Or is it unacceptable?"

Jesus spots their two-faced-shifty-trick-of-a-question and asks, "Why
the trip wire? Why the trap? Got a denarius on you? Throw me the
coin you were thinking about sending off with your tax return. Let's
have a look, shall we?"

16-17

They fumble around, rustle up the coin and hand it to Jesus, who says,
"So who's fine Roman profile is this? And who's the writing round the
edge about then?"

"Caesar's," they admit. "That's his image in the middle and his
inscription on the side."

[Mark 12:13 – 15] Just how desperate is the Religious Establishment to have to send a delegation of some of their top Jewish Nationalists with some of King Herod's Roman sympathizers? These people would probably not even be seen in the same room together let alone "join forces".

Brilliant! If he boycotts Roman taxes, they'll quote him in front of Pilate, the Roman Governor, labeling him as an insurgent/terrorist. If he plays it all loyal to Rome, they'll spin this for maximum effect with the people and puncture his public rating by labeling him a Roman puppet.

[Mark 12:16] Ever seen a Roman coin in a museum? The front side has the inscription, eg, "Tiberius Caesar Augustus, son of the divine [yes, as in deity/God] Augustus". Perhaps designed to rile the Jewish Religious Leaders?

Bit of background: The typical Galilean had to pay four separate lots of taxes – local taxes, Religious HQ taxes, Herod's taxes and, worst of all, Roman taxes. And do you think that any of the taxes got siphoned off? Why else were the tax collectors such natural hate figures in society?

[Mark 12:17] So is it that they've already bought into the system and Jesus is provoking them to consider that there's another paradigm, which has its own currency?

[10] **Religious Traditionalists = Sadducees.** These guys were only into Moses' first five books of the Instruction Manuals; anything later was to them liberal hoo-hah to be sniffed at. One of their big things was that all this rising from the dead malarkey was indulgent hogwash, brought in by liberal lightweights like Daniel, among others. Not natural partners for the Religious Leaders.

Jesus tells them, "Well, if it's his image and his words, it must be his coin: fine, give it back to him. But if you find a currency with God's image and God's words: even finer, make sure you give that back to God."

And? Their comeback? Zip. Just too stunned by him to respond.

No confetti in heaven! Mark 12:18-27

18-19

Then the Religious Traditionalist[10] Party – whose official line is clear about there being no physical resurrection – approach Jesus with plans for some more verbal arm wrestling.

"Coach," they say, "Moses laid it down in black and white that if a guy's brother dies leaving his wife without kids, then the brother-in-law should marry his brother's widow to make babies with her to carry on the family line.

20-22

"Well, there's this family of seven brothers. The first brother marries this woman but dies, leaving her with no baby. The brother-in-law does the right thing, marries her, but then he dies, leaving her with no baby. The next brother comes

---

[Mark 12:18 – 27] In addition to making a big deal out of their main man Moses writing about the surviving brothers' duties (it's there large and clear in Deuteronomy 25:5), these Traditionalist lads also have a Not Budging Party position on the whole "no physical resurrection" thing. As far as they were concerned, the afterlife was indulgent hogwash, brought in by liberal lightweights like Daniel. So how ironic is it that Moses himself has just been spotted by Jesus' Team chatting away with Jesus around 1,400 years after his untimely death up another local mountain?

But was their question also political? If you don't believe in the physical resurrection after death, then being martyred for your political beliefs really is final. So by pushing this conservative line theologically they also maintained the status quo politically by reducing enrollment for potential terrorist suicide killers.

[Mark 12:20 – 22] Is this a hypothetical situation? You'd hope so for the sake of the poor woman. Otherwise, let's hope she got on with her in-laws.

[11] **The Good Book = Old Testament.** The bit of the Bible they had in first century Judah. Aka God's Instruction Manual.

along and does the right thing, marries her, but dies, still no kids. This happens four more times, all four brothers do the right thing, then die on her, and she's still got no baby. And then, the woman dies!

23 – 25

"So, in this replay of 'Just the One Bride for Seven Brothers', at the physical resurrection, which one of the ex-hubbies gets the girl?"

Jesus shoots from the hip and says, "Isn't the reason you're way off-line is 'cos you don't know The Good Book[11] and you don't know God? When people rise to new life, there's not going to be vows and 'getting the girl' and all that marriage stuff – people will be like the community of angels."

26 – 27

Jesus ploughs on, "And on the dead-coming-back thing: let's look at your specialist subject – Moses himself – the famous bit when the desert bush combusts, but doesn't burn up. What's God's line to Moses? Isn't it, 'I am the God of Abraham, I am the God of Isaac and I am the God of Jacob'?

"If he is still, present tense, the God of these father figures, then they're still living in some form, no? Or is he just God to some dead guys? You really are way off on this stuff!"

Matthew 22:33

33

The reaction of the general public?

Wowed. Totally gobsmacked by this level of life coaching.

[Mark 12:25] Even mentioning "angels" rubs these Traditionalists the wrong way. They don't believe in those either, which is just getting weird, since Moses himself wrote about Jacob seeing an industrial scale escalator with angel workers moving up and down at will between the floor marked heaven and the floor marked earth. (See Genesis 28 in a proper Bible.)

[Mark 12:26] It's Exodus 3:6, if you're checking.

Luke 20:39

39

The reaction of the Religious Law Enforcers?

"Here, here! Well said, that man!"

At last, someone gets it! Mark 12:28-34

28

One of these Religious Law Enforcers is listening to the whole to and fro argument. He's impressed with Jesus' answer and he chips in, "Of all our shelves of Rule Books – which Rule is The Big One?"

29-30

"No. 1," Jesus says, "is this beauty: 'Listen up, Israel, your God is one. Love this God with everything you've got – your emotions, your decisions, your imagination, your physicality.' This is the No. 1, top priority, The Big One.

31

"And No. 2 is this: 'Love the people round you as you love yourself.' A thousand column inches of writing by Moses and the couriers boil down to these two Rules."

32-33

"Bravo, Coach! Great answer!" the man buzzes. "You're spot on in saying that God's one and there's nothing else that gets close. To love him with all your emotions, all your imagination, all your physicality and to love others as you love yourself is the best. These are the things

---

[Luke 20:39] The reaction of the Religious Traditionalist Party? Obviously unprintable! Even though the Religious Law Enforcers were anti-Jesus, they couldn't resist cheering when he backs their theology against that of the opposition party.

[Mark 12:28] Just how many Rules are there? The answer is 613. There are 365 "don'ts" – one for every day of the year. And 248 "do's" – one for every weekday of the year, less one off for every month. Not sure what that means . . . you work it out!

[Mark 12:29] Flick a proper Bible open to Deuteronomy 6:4 – 5 for the original appearance. Just after Moses does a rerun of the Big Ten Rules for the Jews, he sums them all up with this biggie.

that hit you first, looking at the big picture. All these other Religious practices are just the frame the picture sits in."

34

Jesus sees that the guy really does get it, and says to him, "You're sooooo close to God's New World Order; within touching distance of Heaven on Earth, believe me!"

And from here on in, no one has the guts to quiz Jesus on anything.

Just a Davidson? Matthew 22:41-45

41-42

While the Religious Leaders were all together, Jesus turns the tables and asks them a question: "What's your take on The Liberator? What family line's he from?"

"Well, he'll be a Davidson for sure," they come back.

43-44

Jesus pushes his point home and says, "Then how come David, inspired by the Spirit, calls The Liberator his 'Boss' in this song lyric:

> Backing vocals: 'The Boss says to my Boss:'
>
> Lead singer: 'Sit next to me, in the top seat.'
>
> Backing vocals: 'The Boss says to my Boss:'
>
> Lead singer: 'Sit next to me till your enemies are kissing your feet.'

45

"So, logically, if David Senior calls David Junior 'Boss', how can he be just a junior descendant?"

[Mark 12:33] Would Samuel have been whooping it up in heaven? He once said, "Does God thrill at burnt animal flesh sacrificed to him, / or is he really into people doing what he says? / To obey is way better than sacrifice, / To listen is way better than the fat of some dead ram!" (See 1 Samuel 15:22 in a proper Bible.)

Would the God courier Hosea soon have joined in? He once quoted God as saying: "What I really long for is giving others some slack, / not the sacrificial killing of some poor animal; people admitting I'm around means so much more / than burnt offerings on some ceremonial BBQ." (See Hosea 6:6 in a proper Bible.)

[Matthew 22:44] Track 110, verse 1 in The Greatest Hits Compilation known as the Psalms.

Jew News Letters Page

Unity in the face of heresy

Dear Sir,

It doesn't matter how cleverly this Jesus Davidson twists the words of Moses; it doesn't matter how he uses his personal charisma to silence our best academics—the whole constitution of the Religious Traditionalist Party is not about to be shredded. This important tradition has served the Nation well for centuries, providing a crucial counter balance to the dual heresies of Greco-Roman secularism and Jewish Pharisaism.

However, despite our deep-founded theological and political disputes with both these influential worldviews, it may be time to put our differences behind us and unify in the interests of the Nation. The essential and pressing need today is to join together in ridding ourselves of the dangerous anti-establishment figure that is Jesus Davidson. If we continue to fight amongst ourselves, then history may indeed judge us to have erred in our handling of this threat to the stability and traditions of God's chosen Nation.

Sincerely ,
Dr Boaz Fadstein
Religious Traditionalist Party Headquarters, Jerusalem.
www.traditionistruth.com.gos/unitedfront

My mentor's a younger man

Sir,

I'd always thought I wasn't merely *in* God's New World Order but that, as a Religious Law Enforcer, I was a major pillar holding it up. Then this new life coach on the block, Jesus Davidson, tells me I'm "close" to it, as if I was doing really well! What stunned me was that I wasn't annoyed. Any other young upstart of a Rabbi saying that to someone in my position and I'd have torn him off a strip for his generational arrogance. But instead of feeling patronized, he made me realize I was both miles off and almost there. A curious combination—simultaneously feeling deflated at having been off the mark for so long while feeling elated at actually being quite close despite my failure. Now I and others within the Religious Establishment will have to seriously consider our future direction.

Sincerely,
Rabbi Jacob Cronenberg. Address withheld.
J.Cronenberg@religiouslawenforcement.rel.il.gos

Do not be deceived

To all Jews,
In my position as current Top God Rep, I must call upon all the people of Israel to resist the fine-sounding teachings of this would-be Liberator, Jesus Davidson. We must stand firm in the face of his supernatural trickery; we must not be duped by his charisma when arguing his outrageous theology. I can assure you, there are many of us working within the Religious System who have felt the sharp side of his silky tongue. I can vouch to the Nation that his charm certainly leaves him when he is threatened by authority. If he were to be voted into any sort of public leadership position, this disregard for authority would certainly be counterproductive with those walking the corridors of power in Rome. It is essential to maintain what we have secured in our coexistence pact with Rome; we cannot allow this naïve upstart to catapult the fine people of this Nation back into the dark ages of Religious oppression. To quote his own words, he is a wolf in sheep's clothing and should not be trusted with any sort of position of influence.

Sincerely,
My Eminence Caiaphas, Top God Rep,
Religious HQ, Jerusalem
www.religiouslead.com.gos/caiaphas

Not my kind of people Matthew 23:1-12

1-4

Then Jesus shifts his focus off the Religious Leaders and talks direct to the general public and the Team Twelve. "The Religious Law Enforcers and Leaders sit where Moses sat – so make sure you listen and do what they say. But don't do what they do! 'Cos they're two-faced! They weigh people down with their 'shoulds', their 'musts' and their 'have to's', but they don't risk breaking a precious nail to help get people standing strong again.

5-7

"They're performers! Sporting their spirituality for the applause of the crowd, for the celebrity ratings. They wear their Moses quotes on their sleeves, below their fringes – fine, but it's extra large and full-on loud. They sew logos from The Good Book into their gear; they've got the labels and they want you to know it! They just love sitting at the top table at dinner functions; they take the best pew in the Religious HQ. They get off on the plebs stepping aside in the shopping malls, saying, 'After you, coach.'

8-10

"Don't use the title 'Chief Religious Consultant' on your business cards – 'cos you've only got one Chief and you're all brothers. Don't write 'Dear Father' in your terrestrial e-mails – 'cos there's only one Father and his address is God@heaven.org.uni. Don't sign off your circulars as 'life coach' – 'cos there's only one Coach and he's The

[Matthew 22:45] So what? Yes, of course The Liberator's a Davidson; wouldn't most of them have known that? Yes, but what's new here is that The Liberator's not just a junior descendant way down some branch of the Davidson Dynasty. No, The Liberator's actually David's senior. But how much more senior? As in Boss? As in Divine? Is Jesus saying here that Jesus "Liberator" Davidson has also got the last name Godson – double barrelled, if you like: "Davidson-Godson"?

Liberator. The ones who get tagged with words like 'Greatness' will be those who live for serving other people's agendas.

11-12

"Those who set themselves up will be brought crashing down. And vice versa: those who aren't into self-promotion will get all the breaks, fast tracking their way up through the ranks to great things."

Bad news coming Matthew 23:13-36

13

"You're looking down the barrel of bad news, you Religious Leaders and Law Enforcers. Two-faced, smarmy actor-types the lot of you; you're standing idle and you're blocking the path up to God's New World Order. Okay, maybe you're not about to shift, but how dare you wedge yourself in the way of others making their entrance!

15-16

"You're riding for a fall, you top brass, you Religious HQ hypocrites! You travel the world on your company card to win your trophy converts, but then you indoctrinate them so they're twice as clueless as you, like the worst sequel to your own biographies: 'Hell Spawn 2'. You're facing your own extinction, you blind tour guides; you dumb advisors. You give it, saying, 'If someone swears by the Religious HQ, we won't count it. But if someone swears by the gold in the Religious HQ, then, oh yes, we'll keep him to that.'

[Matthew 23:5] So is Jesus against these theological clothing statements from Numbers 15:38? Or is it that they were designed to remind the wearer of their faith and not as a "look how spiritual I am" fashion statement?

[Matthew 23:13 – 36] Question is, are the Religious Suits still listening in on Jesus' rant or have the Religious Quizmasters shuffled off with their question cards?

He's going "you", so if they're sticking it out, hearing him slagging them off while the people listen in, then just how dangerous is this? Why's he pouring fuel on the smoldering anger of very powerful people? Is this deliberate provocation, knowing that they'll call for the Death Penalty?

17-18

"You blind-from-birth plonkers! What makes something sacred? Is it its chemical makeup or its use in the Religious centre? Then you regurgitate the same formula: 'If someone swears by the altar, we won't count it. But if someone swears by the gift they've just put on the altar, then, oh yes, we'll keep him to that.'

19-22

"You visually disabled! What makes something sacred – the price tag on the gift or who you give it to? So, if you're swearing by the altar, that includes whatever's on the altar. If you're swearing by the Religious HQ, that incorporates the Religious HQ and the One whose Religious HQ it is. If you're swearing by heaven, that includes God's throne and the One keeping the seat warm!

23-24

"You're washed up, you Religious fraudsters, you phoneys! You give God his ten percent to the fifth decimal point, but you forget that rules exist to breed fairness, love, loyalty. Okay, so do the pedantic calculations on the quantities of mint, dill and cumin owing, but don't let the aroma distract you from what it's all about. You blind guide dogs! You use sterilized tweezers to fish out the hair from your first-course soup; then you chomp into your mad-cow-diseased steak for the main course!

25-26

"You're down the tubes, you ringers for 'real' Religion! You scrub the bowls and cups so they're sparkling on the outside, but on the inside you leave the bacteria of greed and selfishness to fester. You Religious Leaders are groping round in the dark! Here's the plan: Stage One – get some detergent on the inside, then Stage Two will see to the outside being hygienic too.

27-28

"You're up the creek without a paddle, you back-stabbing blaggers, you garden-path tour guides! You're like marble-paved graves – all

suave on the surface — but six feet under? Just decomposing bodies giving off the stench of death and decay. Same story with your
lifestyle: it's all doing the right thing on the surface, but behind closed
doors you're leading your evil double lives.

29 – 32

"You're in double jeopardy you fakes, you conmen! You put flowers
on the graves of God's couriers. You make your speeches, saying, 'Fly
us back in time and we'd not repeat the mistakes of history, no, we'd
never have murdered these fine couriers for God.' But anything you
say can be used in evidence against you, and this proves that you're
just a chip off the old blockheads that came before you — stamping
out anyone that threatens the status quo. You're bad history, stuck on
repeat.

33 – 34

"You've hell to pay, you snakes, you colony of cobras! You've got a one-
way ticket down. Express. Next stop: hell. You're the reason God has
to send so many of his wise couriers and life coaches, 'cos your lot keep
lynching them, bumping them off or running them out of town.

35 – 36

"Your generation is going to take the heat for all the good blood wasted
right from the start. We're talking as far back as the first recorded
homicide — Abel Adamson. We're talking right through all the murder
records — and those that went unreported — right up to Zechariah Berekiahson, virtually the last pages of your Instruction Manuals."

[Matthew 23:35 – 36] This running theme of murdered couriers in the Bible kicks off at Genesis 4:8 when Abel
is Cain-ed to death for going about his work. The killing spree goes right through to 2 Chronicles 24:20 – 22
when Zechariah gets stoned to death for challenging their drifting off from God.

So since the layout of the Hebrew Scriptures placed Genesis first and Chronicles last, is Jesus cataloguing a true
"A to Z" of courier killings from virtually page one to right to the end of the book?

Don't Like This? [Mark 12:41 – 44] Disagree with Jesus rounding up the old girl's donation? Feel that no church project would get off the ground without the bigger donors feeling good about themselves? Just remind yourself that things have moved on and very little works these days without money.

Collection box techniques Mark 12:41-44

41-42

Jesus takes a break. He sits down opposite the Religious HQ collection boxes and watches the loaded waving their big wedges of money around so everyone can see how much they're giving to God's charity. He doesn't miss the cash-strapped widow who sneaks up and puts two measly little copper pennies into the box.

43-44

Nudging his Team, Jesus points her out and says, "Truth is, this woman's put in more than the rest put together! If we're talking percentages, they give a tiny fraction of their vast disposable income; she's giving all of it, 100 percent."

[Mark 12:42] What was it Jesus said in the "money drags you down" coaching sessions? How many times has Jesus talked about those at the top of the ladder ending up at the wrong end? How many times has he longed out loud for the time when those at the bottom will be laughing from above the clouds? Is this what asking God to bring Heaven on Earth is all about?

[Mark 12:44] Just how inspirational must this have been for Jesus? Pretty soon he's going to have to go through with pouring his lifeblood into God's collection box. Does this anonymous old woman become a great mental image for him for the next few days?

1 **Religious HQ = Temple.** Jerusalem's focal point of the Jewish Religion. Literally a house for God. Question is, how much does God get let out?

Chapter Seventeen

Times Change

Alarm bells of disaster Mark 13:1-23

1-2

Jesus and the Team are leaving the main Religious HQ[1] when one of the more aesthetic Team members looks up and says, "Coach! Humungous stones! Awesome architecture! Beautiful or what!?"

Jesus' comeback: "I tell you, all this'll be like a tower of toy blocks with a toddler – flat, not one stone left on another."

[Mark 13:1 – 23] So here's Jesus facing what he knows will be his own gruesome end, and he seems more preoccupied with the end of God's Religious HQ – an apocalypse wiping out the old corrupt systems.

But is it just about the Romans trashing the place in about 37 years' time (AD 70)? Or is it also about the Big Return of Jesus (date as yet unconfirmed) and The End Of The World As We Know It? Mmm, it's tricky, since figurative language can often mean multiple things at once. So it's possibly not "either/or" but "both/and". The biggie isn't "what's going to happen and when?" but "what prep can we do for when nasty things hit?"

---

3 – 6

Later Jesus parks himself on the slopes of the Olive Mountain and looks down across the Kidron valley at the Religious HQ. The original four – Pete, Jim, Jonno and Drew – have a quiet word: "When? When's all this tower-toppling grief going to happen? Will there be clues/signs/rumblings that the end's closing in?"

Jesus tells them, "Keep sharp, don't get duped! You're going to see the headlines, the newsflashes, the circular e-mails about this guy or the other guy who's flashing about his 'I'm the One' logo. And loads will buy into it; signing up like there's no tomorrow. But ignore these sad wannabes – there will be a tomorrow!

7 – 8

"You're going to have your regular soap ruined by the announcement, 'We interrupt this programme with news of war and rumours of wars,' but don't be fazed! It's not the end of the world! The wars, the atrocities, the grief-stricken cities all have to happen, but don't panic. That's not the end ... that's just 'the fat lady' warming up her voice! Countries will flex their pecs at each other; nations will beat the heaven out of each other. Earthquakes are going to rip places apart, whether they're shanty towns or skyscrapers – ripped apart! All this breaking news will reduce the ongoing famine reports to the scrolling panel on the bottom of your screens. But this is just for starters – the painful contractions are just kicking in.

[Mark 13:7 – 8] So all these painful events are contractions before God's New World Order is born. But how can you know which contraction will cause the baby's head to crown?

[2] **Victimisation/Religious intolerance = Persecution.** In our PC world you can't be racist, sexist, ageist or any other "-ist" (and rightly so), but you can be Christian-ist, only it's not called that, it's called "freedom of speech".

9

"On your toes! It'll be a time of Religious intolerance[2] and you're the ones they're after. They'll come for you in their security vans, give you a practical workshop in assault, with you at the sharp end of the learning curve. All because they've got sightings of you sporting my badge or bracelet; recordings of you with my phrases on your lips. You'll get hauled up in front of judges and politicians and you'll have to tell it like it is.

10-11

"And the great news of God's Liberation will be pumped out onto the airwaves; it'll spread through cyberspace like the ultimate virus – I'm talking global broadcasts by the crew. So when they round you up and stick you in the dock, don't wobble about what to say to the councillor, for my counsellor, God's Holy Spirit, will cue you the right words at the right time. Just open your mouth and hear his poetry pour out.

12-13

"Brothers are going to grass each other up. Dads are going to slam up their own kids. Sons and daughters are going to report their own parents and stick them on death row! Everyone's going to hate you because of me. But if you stand there and take what they throw at you,

---

[Mark 13:10] **Did the victimization of the Jesus Liberation Movement (aka the church – the institution, not the building) help spread the great news?** Probably, yes. This was a boom period for the early JLM, spreading across the infrastructure that Alexander the Great had set up; getting the great news stories about Jesus The "Liberator" Davidson out onto the street and spreading like a particularly wild and crazy fire. Check out the book of Acts in a proper Bible.

So what goes through the minds of the first Christians in Jerusalem (who were Jewish) when, in about 37 years time, they see the Roman legions hovering outside their city with violence on the agenda? History, that's what.

- 722 BC – Samaria, Capital of Israel, smashed by Assyria.
- 586 BC – Jerusalem, Capital of Judah, trashed by Babylon.
- 167 BC – More smashing and trashing of Jerusalem by the Syrians.
- AD 66 – 70 – A Roman-Jewish war ending with the Jerusalem Religious HQ getting a bashing by General Vespasian and his boy Titus.

even if it's bricks – and I'm not talking toy blocks now – you'll be cast in a key role in the ultimate sequel.

14-17

"When you see 'the bedlam that makes God vomit; the sacrilege that totals everything; the contempt that pulls the plug on the whole deal; the insolence that gets everything written off,' and when you see it setting up where it has no right: Don't hang around. Hit the road! You're on the sunroof, don't go back for the family photos. Slide down the drainpipe and leave Judah shrinking in your rearview mirror. You're down the park; don't even think of going back home for your wallet. Get out of there! How horrific will it be for pregnant women; how hideous for breastfeeding mums!

18-20

"Beg God that it won't happen in winter, because this is as bad as it's been and as bad as it gets. This'll be a first. It'll be declared a National Disaster Day and the calendar date will become code for everything terrible. If God didn't step in for the sake of the Selected, if he didn't clap his hands and call out, 'Enough already; hold it right there,' no one would even survive.

21-23

"Don't get hoodwinked; you won't be able to move for iffy life coaches, self-proclaimed couriers of God[3]. You'll hear people raving about this or that liberator, with their how-do-they-do-that magic shows; supernatural spectaculars that might even sucker the Selected – if that was possible. Don't buy into their scams; don't get hypnotized by their charm. Keep on your toes. I've told you the plot ahead of the game."

[Mark 13:14] What's Jesus quoting? See the prophet Daniel's book in a proper Bible. The guy famous for his "sleepy lions" episode went on to talk about this "bedlam" and "sacrilege" three times. (See Daniel 9:27; 11:31 and 12:11.)

4 **The Man = Son of man.** Jesus' term for himself — lifted from Daniel 7, where it's a pretty blatant clue that this is no mere mortal: "the Son of Man . . . surfing in on the clouds . . . where the Ancient of Days . . . gives him . . . all the credit for running the show . . . and permanent position in the top spot." Nice name badge.

Enter The Man[4] Matthew 24:26-31

26-28

"So if anyone tells you, there he is, some wannabe liberator — out in the middle of nowhere — don't waste your petrol in the gridlock. Or say there's a sighting of some liberator impressionist behind closed doors, don't even try the handle. Lightning — it cracks in the eastern sky and it's seen from way out west. Ditto with the arrival of Yours Truly, The Man — totally unmissable. Anyone who watches the nature channels knows: dead body equals vultures overhead, every time.

29

"Smack bang on the tail of these disasters of those days, I tell you:

'The sun'll go pitch black;
The moon will have nothing to reflect;
The stars'll go into free fall;
The spiritual forces of the cosmos will curl up and quiver.'

30-31

"All this is the entrance cue; The Man will show up and every nationality will watch the event live and connect with their grief. They'll see The Man surfing in on the clouds; he's glowing with all the kudos; he's taking all the credit for running the whole show his way. He's giving the nod to the angels, and their trumpet chorus will kick off the collection of those picked out; they'll be scooped up from every grid reference point on the planet."

Mark 13:28-32

28-29

"Okay, back down to earth: It's like with a fig tree — locals learn the signs that summer's on its way. First clue: soft twigs. Second clue: leaves. Conclusion? Exactly: summer's round the corner. Change the

---

[Matthew 24:29] Jesus is deliberately paraphrasing lyrics from Isaiah 13:10 here. Would his audience be hearing the tune in their heads since it's a regular at their hymn singing sessions?

[Mark 13:28 – 32] Why's Jesus going over stuff he'd just said on the road down to Jerusalem? How much more do the similar lines resonate when the heat is really turned up? When Jesus was still on the road, he could still have done a U-ey and bottled out of going to Jerusalem, but now he's right in the thick of it. So how hard is it to do a one-eighty out of there?

picture back to cosmic scale and these events will be the clues that the day is not far off – waiting in the wings, warming up.

30 – 32

"And the truth is, this generation will still be around when all these events start clicking into place. The stars may go all supernova on us and devour the planets before they totally burn out. But the truth of what I'm saying here will still be echoing round the solar system; my words won't fizzle out – they'll be burning bright and true for eternity, and some! As for when – time/date/year? Top secret, sorry! The angels don't know; I don't know. Only Dad knows … and he's not telling."

Top secret Matthew 24:37 – 41

37 – 39

"The days before the Big Entrance of The Man will be like an action replay of Noah's 'Waterworld' episode, only in full colour. Normal everyday life for normal everyday people – births, weddings, funerals – until Noah stepped onto the zoo ship. They had no clue about the disaster movie about to play out in real life, sweeping them off. And that's how The Man's Big Arrival will be.

40 – 41

"Typical working day for your typical working guys – clock on, work away, clock off – except one guy will be swept off his feet, the other guy left gawping at the gap where his mate was. Two cafeteria ladies sloshing out the school lunch: one will be whisked out of there while the other is left with some solo washing up.

Luke 21:34 – 36

34 – 36

"Keep on the ball!" Jesus tells them. "D'you want your heart deadened and dragged down by liquid lunches? D'you want your mind shot

[Mark 13:32] Hey, here's an idea: if it's going to be as unpredictable as Jesus predicts, then let's not bust a gut trying to predict it!

[Matthew 24:38] Again, more stuff being repeated from before (see Chapter 14, Luke 17:26 – 27, page 257). Is that 'cos not everyone was there? Or 'cos not everyone got it?

from lost nights of sleep with worries whirling about your brain? The day's going to arrive like the snap of a rat trap. It'll hit everyone, so quit playing the slouch-on-the-couch and lobby God that you might yet escape the bad news ahead, that you might still be standing when The Man turns up."

Mark 13:33-37

33-37

"Don't drift off! On your toes! You don't know the time/date/year when it'll happen. It's like a homeowner leaving his property, employing a professional security firm – the guy on front door duty does not nod off! So, keep your eyelids open for business, 'cos you've got no clue when the Boss might be back, what the clock face will be looking like, which direction the little hand will be pointing. Whenever it is, you do not want to be mid-power nap. My advice? Like I said to you at the start, now I'm saying to the crowd, 'Keep sharp!'"

Good management Matthew 24:43-51

43-44

"But get this: if some homeowners get tipped off about a planned heist at their place, then they organise a reception party with plenty of police. No one's breaking and entering that place! Same with you lot, 'cos The Man will make an appearance, and there's no news on his ETA.

45-47

"What's loyalty to the boss look like? What's wisdom in the workplace? A manager's put in charge of the workforce, special duties in the catering department. How good a career move would it be for him if the workers are mid-mouthful when the Boss turns up unexpectedly? He'll be looking at a huge promotion, bonuses, bigger office, more interesting work. The days of him just heating up oven-ready meals for grumbling workers will be long gone   he'll have a say in major responsibilities.

48-51

"Or switch to an alternative universe where the same middle management guy gets to thinking, 'The boss has been off jet-setting for yonks

5 **Heaven on Earth/God's New World Order = The kingdom of God.** Like with monarchies, but with God in charge, so not like with monarchies. There's also a sense of "sort of already/but not yet" paradox. We get to download glimpses now, but the full package would cramp our hard drive's style.

now.' The stand-in manager starts harassing the personnel, dishing out some physical abuse and using the office space for drunken binges with his mates. Sure enough, the boss opens the door and says, 'Gotcha!' The manager gets cut to shreds; his career path hits a stone wall at terminal velocity. The only self-help book he's likely to write is *Teeth Grinding for the Tormented*."

Ten teenage girls and a wedding Matthew 25:1-13

1-4

"Same thing, different way of looking at it: Heaven on Earth[5] will kick off with a big wedding. Picture it: it's dusk and ten teenage girls in their posh frocks are ready to join the torchlight procession to the wedding feast – they're providing the lighting special FX. See, five of them have common sense, they've come prepared with spare batteries in their handbags. The other five are, well, airheads; it just doesn't occur to them to have back-up power supplies.

5-8

"Transition of time ... no bridegroom, girls giggling ... more time ... still no bridegroom ... girls chatting ... more time ... what's the guy doing?! ... girls drooping. They peaked way too early and now they're slumped together on the sofa, nodding off. Close up of the clock striking midnight and a voice from off yells, 'He's here! The bridegroom's here. Let's go hook up with him!' The teenage girls wake up and start sorting their flashlights for the parade. 'Course the airheads are more or less out of juice, so they go to the ever-so-wise-ones and ask, 'We're nearly out! Give us some of your batteries?'

9-13

"The smart ones reply, 'No way! There's not enough for you gals and us. Get to the 24/7 shop, sharpish, and buy your own!' So they make for the battery shop and while they're there the bridegroom turns up and he's ready to party! The five wise-beyond-their-years teenagers provide great lighting for the procession and get to dance/eat/drink at the wedding reception.

"There's a big slam of heavy doors into the party. The others come back from their battery reconnaissance trip. They make straight for the venue, bang their now grubby stilettos on the front door and demand, 'Sir, sir, open up. We're here now. Open up.'

"The bridegroom's voice from behind the door asks, 'And you are?' He has no clue who they are through the spy hole. And the moral is? Be prepared. Why? 'Cos you never know the exact timing."

Investment trust Matthew 25:14-30

14-15

"Or put it this way," Jesus goes, "a wealthy businessman is about to go off on a long work trip. He sends a memo round to three of his staff calling them into his office. They arrive and he drops the bombshell and tells them, 'I'm out of here! And I need you guys to look after the proceeds while I'm away.' He pulls out three briefcases and starts handing them out. The first guy (a real talent) gets a case stuffed with five hundred grand worth of crisp notes; the second guy (good, but nothing stunning) gets two hundred grand, and the last guy (steady) gets 'just' a hundred grand. Then the boss says, 'I'm off!' and leaves them staring at each other in shock.

16-18

"The first guy goes off to read up on his investment mags; he picks the brains of some financial advisors and eventually comes up with a detailed investment portfolio. After a while he's doubled the money and hits the million mark. He's well happy. The second guy also goes off and puts together a strategy. And likewise, doubles his money to four hundred grand. Again, well happy. The third guy, mmm, he goes off and buys a safe, stuffs the money inside and stashes it away two feet under his back garden.

19-20

"Ages later, like, really ages later, the boss comes back and rings round the three. 'I'm back; let's meet, usual place.' The first guy sits in the

---

[Matthew 25:15] Why doesn't the boss give any tips as to what they're to do with it? Is he testing them, or did he just assume it was obvious they had to invest it?

[Matthew 25:18] Does he think, "What if the market crashes? What if there's a run on the banks? What if I invest in gold and they discover an enormous gold mine lying under every garden in the city and the gold price plummets?" What if he's so busy worrying about then that he does diddly-squat now?

meeting, looking smug, and says, 'You gave me five hundred grand and I've done a bit of wheeling and dealing, ducking and diving – all legal of course – and I've doubled your money!' He hands over two briefcases, stuffed full with a cool million.

21–23

"His boss says, 'Well done; done good! You've proved yourself, shown your commitment. Now you get to manage bigger projects for me. You and me, we've got good times lined up!' The second guy, also looking pretty pleased with himself, says, 'You gave me two hundred grand, and I've doubled your money as well!' Handing the boss the case, he grins, 'There's four hundred grand in there.'

"Likewise, his boss is impressed, 'Well done; done good! Great commitment. I've got some good projects for you too. You'll have nothing to worry about from now on. Contentment, here you come!'

24–27

"The third guy is twitching by now. The boss turns to him and says, 'And?'

" 'And you gave me only one hundred grand,' he mumbles.

" 'And what did you do with it?' asks the boss.

" 'Well, I've heard the rumours about your middle name being "Ruthless" and how you can't be doing with losers. I didn't want to risk losing the cash, so I buried it in a safe place. It's all here, not a fiver missing.'

"The boss is fuming and says, 'You evil, lily-livered, useless, gutless, spineless excuse for a half-life! You're pathetic. If you knew I was so

---

[Matthew 25:28] So does Jesus agree with the principle of the rich getting richer and the poor getting poorer? Or is this just his observation of how things work? Which fits best with the rest of Jesus' coaching? Whose corner does Jesus usually fight from?

"ruthless", then why didn't you get your act together and at least put the money into an interest account? Is that really so tricky?'

28-30

"So the boss takes the briefcase from him and gives it to the first guy, saying, 'You have it, 'cos those who've got loads, get given even more; and those who've got zilch, even the little they've got will get transferred over to those with loads. Get this loser out of my sight! Throw him out on to the streets where he belongs; where the whimpering drives you crazy and the teeth grinding takes you beyond.'"

Global court of justice Matthew 25:31-46

31-33

"Imagine the special FX when The Man comes back to dazzle the planet with his laser light show and angel chorus. He'll sit on his throne looking out over the world population and he'll start separating people out, like he's got his Sheep Security Officer hat on. It'll be 'sheep' on the right side, 'goats' on the left.

34-36

"He'll say to the 'sheep', 'You're in God's good books. Come forward, collect what's been waiting for you since before I juggled the planets into place. All this 'cos I owe you – when I was starving, you made me meals. When I was thirsty, you poured me a drink. I was a loner in the corner, you opened the circle and brought me in. When my clothes

Don't Like This? [Matthew 25:31–46] Find this social action stuff a little uncomfortable? Prefer just to sign a Statement of Faith and have your Sheep Club badge to prove you're in? Spent your whole life telling people they can't "work" their way to heaven, and you're determined not to lift a finger to prove it? Tricky. Best stick these pages together with superglue.

[Matthew 25:31] Isn't it pretty clear by now that Jesus is talking about himself? This gives a different angle on the question "Who's The Man?"

[Matthew 25:32–33] Not a land lad/lass? Here's an urbanite's "Rural Guide":

Back then, over there, sheep and goats generally had a "joint tenancy" agreement on grazing rights during the day. But at night, the goats got extra warm sleeping quarters because they didn't have the wooly jumpers that the sheep had to keep them warm. Does that help as you read this deep-as-you-like story?

And for another level of meaning, remember that Jews had a long-standing sense of being God's sheep and of him being the Sheep Security Officer. To what extent has the church taken this sheep metaphor a tad too far and just ended up aimlessly following the crowd!? Discuss!

---

weren't up to the job, you took me shopping – on your card. When my health was bad, you nursed me back to strength. When I was in my prison cell, you swallowed your pride, you made the visiting hours.'

37–40

"Those will do the right thing scratch their heads and ask, 'When, Boss? When did we make you meals, or pour you a drink, or bring you into the circle? When did we give you new clothes, or nurse you, or visit you?'

"The King will lay it down for them, explaining, 'Truth is, every good thing you've done for the lowest of the low – my sisters, my brothers – it's like you did it for me!'

41–43

"But the 'goats' on the left will get the opposite treatment: 'Get out of my sight. You're in the biggest hole you could imagine, and the hole is like a huge barbeque that's heating up to grill the Devil and his rebel angels later. 'Cos I was starving and you moaned about you being overweight. I was thirsty, you complained about the cheap wine being served. I was a loner, you laughed at me and told me to "get a life". I was freezing cold, you told me to "jump up and down". I was ill, you told me to "snap out of it". I was locked up, you would've told me I deserved it, but you couldn't even be bothered to make the trip to rub my nose in it!'

44–46

" 'Whoa! Hang on,' say the 'goats'. 'We wouldn't be like that with you, Boss! With someone like you we'd be thoughtful, sensitive, inclusive, generous, caring. With someone like you we'd never make you feel forgotten.'

"He'll say, 'Truth is, the lowest of the low is someone like me! So whatever you didn't do for them, you didn't do for me.' They'll get taken away to permanent punishment. Those who did the right thing, they'll enjoy limitless life."

[1] **Deep-as-you-like stories, riddles and images = Parables.** From the Greek word to "put things side by side" (ie, parallel). An ancient craft where you say things different ways; where an earthly story can take on a heavenly meaning ... if you dig.

[2] **Flyby Festival = Passover.** A major Jewish Religious festival, like our Easter/Christmas. It celebrates God liberating their ancestors from the sweatshops of Egypt. The name derives from when the angel of death passed over/flew by Jewish homes.

Chapter Eighteen

Mutiny

Ticking clock Matthew 26:1-5

1-2

Jesus wraps up his deep-as-you-like stories[1], turns to his Team and says, "You don't need me to tell you that the Flyby Festival[2] is just two days off and counting. You don't need

---

[Matthew 26:1–5] If it's just a couple days before the Flyby Festival Eve, isn't that a busy time for the Top Religious Suits? So how do they manage to "squeeze in time" to brainstorm on the challenges of arresting and RIPing Jesus?

Not long back all the Suits wanted to do was to get him "out of the public eye". This could've just meant threats/deportation/prison/attempted blackmail/beatings. Now they're talking assassination. So what's changed? Have Jesus' recent batch of subversive stories and public verbal assaults on the Religious Leaders really upped the ante? Are the stakes higher now that Jesus has hit the Big City? The Roman authorities are especially twitchy with the city heaving at Festival time.

Does the inevitable increase in soldiers on the street intimidate or inflame? No wonder the Suits are losing sleep.

---

me to tell you that Yours Truly, The Man, will be betrayed and executed Roman style."

3–5

Scene change to the Palace of Caiaphas, Top God Rep[3] of the Year, no less. Secret meeting for the other Big God Reps[4] plus City Councillors[5]. Only one item on the agenda – how to kidnap Jesus and kill him.

"But not during the Festival," some shaky voices chip in. "No, there'll be a riot".

Burial prep Mark 14:3–9

3

Jesus is hanging out in the Bethany suburbs, near Jerusalem. Simon the ex-Skin Disease Sufferer is playing host to Jesus and the Team. Middle of the main course, this woman wafts up to Jesus and gets out her top-of-the-range Parfume de Nard in a marble presentation pack. She breaks the jar and starts pouring the eau-de-posh all over Jesus' hair.

4–5

But some of the dinner party guests are really ticked off at her, griping to each other, "Why, oh why, oh why! What a terrible waste of quality perfume! Even allowing for haggling reductions we could've got at least a year's wages . . . for the Poverty Project, obviously!"

3 **Top God Rep = High Priest.** The main man, the head honcho responsible for all the people's spiritual health. His job description states he's the middleman between God and the people; a "go between" for all negotiations . . . in both directions. No pressure then?!

4 **Big God Reps = Chief priests.** If "God Reps" (priests) were the "go between" for God and his people, then *chief* priests were the ones with real clout. This eminent group are the ones who've done their year's stint as Top God Rep (High Priest).

5 **Councillors = Elders.** The non-Religious element of the ruling of the people. Sort of civil servants.

[Mark 14:3] **Just how much does the former Outcast label wearer, Simon, love playing the host now that he's kosher again? Was he always the gregarious type before his skin condition made a mockery of his social life?**

They reckon it's this nard stuff that's hinted at in the love poetry of Solomon (see Song of Songs 1:12 in a proper Bible). Solomon's lover says, "While the King was at his table, chilling – my Parfume de Nard was spilling into the room, filling the room, instilling the room with romance. . ." No record of Jesus reciprocating. In fact, he just talks more about his death.

[6] **Religious Leaders = Pharisees.** A faction calling themselves literally "the separated ones" – "the exclusives" perhaps. Big into Rules, running a well-oiled propaganda machine which seemed to be fuelled by people's guilt.

6 – 9

"Whoa, back off!" says Jesus. "Stop hassling her. She's just done something exquisite, something beautiful. The poor are not all suddenly going to get rich; there will always be those for you to give a hand up and out of the poverty trap – long term. But you won't always have me. She did the best thing she could've done: it's like she's prepared me for my burial ahead of time. Truth is, wherever God's good news gets airplay, and I'm talking global, you'll always be able to look up 'perfume' and find this fine lady's episode. Her story will become a classic."

Judas The Bounty Hunter Luke 22:3 – 6

3 – 4

At that point, Satan makes his break through and skulks his way inside the head of Judas Iscariot, one of the Team Twelve. Judas then gatecrashes the Religious Leaders'[6] meeting and discusses terms on handing Jesus over to them.

5 – 6

Once the Religious Leaders pick themselves off the floor, they're cock-a-hoop, in danger of embarrassing themselves with excitement. The solution to their when-to-do-the-ugly-deed has landed slap-bang in their lap – Jesus will be delivered in person! They give Judas The Bounty Hunter a cash reward up front for bringing in the man with a price on his head. Judas shakes on the deal and is extra twitchy from now on; looking over (the chip on) his shoulder for a quiet moment to hand Jesus in.

[Luke 22:3] How long had Satan been drilling through the defences of the Team? What lines does Satan feed to Judas? How would Judas' temptation scene contrast with Jesus' own face-off with Satan back in Chapter 3 (see Matthew 4:1 – 11, pages 64 – 66). Does Judas think Jesus was betraying him? Was Judas expecting The Liberator to bring about a political solution to the Roman Occupation problem? And did Judas ever feel fully part of the Team being the only one with a distinctive southern Judah accent? What combinations of fault lines led to the eventual crack?

The Morning Sun

Ex-Leper hosts controversial "King In The Wings"

Just yesterday an ex-Skin Disease Sufferer played host to Jesus Davidson who only last weekend was being hailed as the "King to Be" by an overwhelming majority of Festival goers. Our letters page has been inundated with your ideas about what Davidson's next steps might be. Now we get the chance to hear from his host for the last couple of nights – one of Jesus' many medical success stories – Simon Johnson.

MS—Simon, what was it like hosting the Jewish King-Elect?

SJ—Awesome! I'm up for playing the "host with the most to toast" to *anyone*. I've not stopped having people round since Jesus sorted my skin problem and got me back on the scene, so I was well up for doing it large when he showed up looking for bed and full board for the Festival.

MS—And was he pretty upbeat coming off the back of wowing the crowds with his front page donkey ride entrance?

SJ—Like, totally not! The opposite! He just seemed obsessed by the flak he was getting from a handful of no-life Religious Big Wigs. As if the Suits were capable of going against "the clear voice of the people"! Even the HQ's huge propaganda machine couldn't turn public opinion round that quickly. But Jesus didn't seem to get it. Public ratings all say he's "King In The Wings", a real star!

ers.

MS—And he got the star treatment. Tell us about this-lady-of-the-perfume?

SJ—Yeah, this groupie turns up and she's pouring Parfume de Nard over his head...

MS—And you're sure it was genuine nard?

SJ—Yeah. Not just "spirit of nard" or "essence of impression of nard" – nard! Imported direct from India itself. Pricey or what?!

MS—About a year's salary, our research tells us. He must've been boosted by this almost royal anointing, like it was preparation for an imminent coronation?

SJ—Nope, he was so locked onto the negative. He just saw it as his pre-death embalming, as preparation for his burial.

MS—Well, he's never been predictable. What's next, eh?

Don't miss our Festival Sunday special pull out section: "Jesus – King In The Wings." This weekend!

Your thoughts on Jesus' next move to:
www.themorningsun.news.gos/kinginthewings/nextsteps.

Final Festival meal Mark 14:12-16

12

Thursday is day one of the Yeast-Free Bread Feast, the big meal where they eat the ritually sacrificed lamb. Jesus' Team are getting twitchy about the arrangements and ask him, "We're up for doing the prep, you got anywhere in mind to eat the Flyby roast dinner?"

13

So Jesus sends off two of the Team and tells them, "Hit the city and straight off you'll meet a guy carrying a water jug. He'll come over to you and walk you to the place.

14-16

"As you go in, say to the house owner, 'The Coach is asking where the room is for the Flyby Team meal.' He'll take you up the stairs to a sizeable room, all laid out and ready to go. Do the prep for us there."

The two make for Jerusalem and it all pans out like Jesus said. Pretty soon they're making bread and mixing herbs for Flyby Fest.

Bread breaking Luke 22:14-16

14-16

Candlelight replaces sunlight, and right on time Jesus and the Team Twelve are sitting round the table for the traditional meal to kick

[Mark 14:12] Were the organised, "always plan ahead" types in the Team finding this last minute attitude a tad stressful? 'Cos there were rules about the Flyby meal: It had to be eaten with a view to the inside of the city walls (and they were miles off in the 'burbs of Bethany), on the Thursday pre-Festival (and that's, like, today), between sundown and midnight (and it's afternoon already!). Plus none of them are locals and the restaurants are probably already booked up for Flyby celebrations for the organised! Is it any surprise they were asking where it was going to happen?

[Mark 14:13] "Guy", mind you, not woman. Men didn't do much water carrying back then. It'd be like us saying something like, "You'll see an alien playing hopscotch."

[Mark 14:14] So had Jesus already sorted the table booking? Or was this another supernatural solution?

[Mark 14:16] The main course includes: "Roast lamb with bitter herbs and side dish of fruit-and-nut puree served with flatbread and wine".

off the Flyby Festival. Jesus makes a speech: "I've lost sleep thinking
about having this great meal with you guys. It'll be my last morsel
before the torment starts; my last till God's New World Order[7] arrives
for good."

Status games Luke 22:24-30

24-27

An argument triggers off round the table – basically which one of
them is Numero Uno. Jesus weighs in, saying, "Whoa! Kings in
Egypt/Syria/anywhere pull rank on their minions; those who run the
lives of their subjects have the nerve to call themselves 'the people's
friend'. But that's not you. No! You want to be a big name? Start
making like the junior temp! You want to be top dog? Start serving at
tables! Who's higher in the status game: the waiter or the waited on?
Isn't it the waited on? But get this: I'm the one serving you!

28-30

"You've stuck with me – thick and thin – and just as my Dad doled
out a New World Order to me, so I'm doling out invitations for you
to join me round a different table in God's New World Order. In fact,
you'll each get a throne and make big decisions for the dozen family
lines of Israel."

Sold out Mark 14:18-21

18-21

Jesus and his Team are still round the table, tucking into the tastes,
when Jesus blows the party atmosphere by coming out with, "Truth is,
one of you guys sitting here, noshing away, will stitch me up and sell
me out."

Hands freeze mid-move. Mouths drop open mid-mouthful. All of
them ask, "It isn't me is it?" "Jesus, you don't mean me?"

"It's one of you," says Jesus. "One of you guys dipping a chunk of Flyby
bread in the Flyby bowl on Flyby Festival weekend! The Man will exit

[7] **Heaven on Earth/God's New World Order = The kingdom of God.** Like with monarchies, but with God in charge, so not like with monarchies. There's also a sense of 'sort of already/but not yet' paradox. We get to download glimpses now, but the full package would cramp our hard drive's style.

[Mark 14:18–21] We're talking pretty much the worst version of treachery in Middle Eastern culture: to
betray a friend after eating a meal with him was, and still is, about the lowest you can go.

---

just like The Good Book[8] says he will, but I tell you it's bad news for the guy who plays the role of Defector. He's going to wish he'd never been born!"

Matthew 26:25

25

Then Judas, Mr Defector himself, says, "Me? Surely not me, Coach?!"

"Your words!" confirms Jesus.

All words! Mark 14:27 – 31

27 – 28

Then Jesus says, "You'll all bottle out and run off. Like The Good Book says:

> 'I'll smack the shepherd; broadsword
> And the flock will go bleating off abroad.'

"But when I come back from death," Jesus says, "I'll be ahead of you, back up in base camp, Galilee County."

29 – 31

Pete swears blind, "I'll stick with you through thick and thin. Even if I'm the only one, I'll stick with you."

"Sad truth is," Jesus tells Pete, "within twenty-four hours, by the second time the rooster does his alarm clock impression, you'll have sworn blind that you don't even know me. Not once, not twice, but three times!"

But Pete's not having it and says, "I'd die before disowning you."

[Matthew 26:25] Has Judas got an overactive gall gland or what? Is he bluffing for the benefit of the other 11? Or is he genuine when he asks if it's him? Does anyone else hear this? Or is it on the sly, just Judas and Jesus?

[Mark 14:27] The quote's from Zechariah 13:7 in a proper Bible.

[Mark 14:29 – 31] What did the others make of Pete's vote of no confidence in them? Were they miffed? Is this a carry forward from the "who's Numero Uno" discussion before? What insight does this give into team dynamics under pressure? Is this what fuels their macho posturing in verse 31? Was all this bluff or were they all intending to be heroic? Pete and Jonno get some bravery points, but what happened to the others; what changes between "real words" and "real world"? Why does resolve dissolve?

The others are nodding, clenching their fists and spouting the same bravado.

Luke 22:35-38

35-36

Jesus presses rewind. "Think back. When I threw you in the deep end with no backpack stuffed full of supplies, did you go without?"

"Nope!" they answer.

He continues, "Well ... now it's all changed. If you've got a wallet, take it with you. And you'll need a backpack this time. And if you've not got a weapon, trade in your coat at an armoury shop.

37-38

"Like The Good Book says, 'He was labelled a criminal; associated with the lowest of the low.' And this is going to be my story! What was just words is going to become real life! Poetry in person. Black and white gets a colour tint. In 3-D. Me!"

Someone in the Team says, "Boss, look: two swords at your service!"

"That's enough!" Jesus tells them.

Breaking bread Matthew 26:26-30

26-28

Mid-meal, Jesus takes some bread, sends a "thanks" upward, then snaps the bread and hands it round the Team.

He says, "Here, eat this. It's my body!" Then he reaches for the cup, sends up a "thanks" again, passes it round and says, "Drink it down

---

[Luke 22:36] Why the different Tour Rules? Is there going to be such a paradigm shift that there'll be no welcome mats out for the Heaven on Earth Tour Team after this? And what's with the weapon thing?

[Luke 22:37] See Isaiah 53:12 in a proper Bible.

[Luke 22:38] Have they taken Jesus too literally on the weapon thing? Was he talking poetically, or does he endorse the use of weapons to convert people? What fits with the rest of what he's about? See later in this Chapter (Matthew 26:52b-54, page 333) when he slams into Pete for trying to use possibly one of these very swords to give Jesus his getaway chance.

---

you, all of you. It's the blood that makes the New Contract possible. When it pours out it'll sort the mess of so many.

29-30

"I tell you, this'll be the last time wine hits my taste buds till I drink it with you guys at the inaugural party in God's New World Order; the last till Heaven on Earth is here to stay."

Meal over, they sing a closing hymn. Then they go down the stairs and get themselves some fresh air up the Olive Mountain.

Whose plan? Mark 14:32-42

32

They come to Gethsemane Park. Jesus tells the Team, "Pull up a boulder; take a break here while I go thrash things out with God."

33-34

Jesus takes the inner Team with him: Pete and the Zebson boys, Jim and Jonno. Jesus hits a wave of despair and starts getting sucked down into a black hole of mental torture. "My soul's suffocating ... all this grief ... feels like, feels like it's killing me!" He tells the inner three, "Stay here; stay alert for me, yeah?"

[Matthew 26:26 – 28] Why "snaps the bread"? Well, Flyby Festival bread was a millennia-old traditional recipe for yeast-free bread. It's symbolic – they were remembering the Israelites escaping from the sweat-shops of Egypt and not having time to wait for the bread to rise. They grabbed the flatbread off the table while legging it, even if it is bland and brittle. Jesus keeps the tradition, but then goes off script and improvises some new lines.

[Matthew 26:30] Just how brain frazzled were the Team during this singing of the traditional closing hymn? The Team knew the words well enough – they sing the Hallel Psalms 115 to 118 every year (check out the lyrics in a proper Bible, spot the extra poignant lines given what's going down this year). Good job they knew them by heart, since they were probably reeling them off while still trying to get their heads round the new twist Jesus had just put on the age-old ritual.

[Mark 14:32] Gethsemane Park, on the lower slopes of the Olive Mountain (aka "Oil Press Olive Grove"). A regular refocus site for the Team.

---

35 – 36

Jesus goes off alone to get face-to-face with his despair, but he can't walk. His angst is hacking into the depths of his soul, and he hits the ground, begging God to cancel the plans for the next day.

"Dad," he cries, "with you everything's possible. But do I have to drink the whole cup dry? Can't you find a way round it? Please ... please! But if there's no other ending, no other way, then ignore what I want and carry on with the plan. I'll do it!"

37 – 38

Jesus struggles back to the inner Team and finds Pete, Jim and Jonno having a kip.

"Simon," he says, using Pete's pre-tour handle, "you sleeping on the job? Couldn't you just prop up your eyelids for one hour? Keep alert

---

[Mark 14:33 – 34] Why take the ex-fishing boys? Was he wanting to give them insight into the other end of the spectrum; a contrast with the high point they'd been allowed in on a year or so back? See Chapter 10 (see Luke 9:28 – 36a, page 186 – 187) when he got heavened-up and Moses and Elijah dropped in for a brief briefing.

Why "stay alert"? Only he could go through this, so what help were they? To lobby God for him? For moral support? To keep watch for security guards? To observe his horror?

[Mark 14:36] No Religious Jew would dare call God, "Dad". Most of them didn't even call God by his full Hebrew name, "Yahweh" – or actually "YHWH" since the Hebrew alphabet wasn't into vowels. When they read "YHWH", they said "Adonai" or "Lord/Boss" out of respect, so as to be sure not to mess up on Rule No. 3 in the Big Ten. Some Jews might say "Father", but Jesus says "Dad"! A bit presumptuous? Or is something else going on?

What cup? Don't think "cup" as in "a nice cup of Earl Grey". No, to most Jews, "cup" meant something a bit heavier. Check out Isaiah 51:17 in a proper Bible for an idea.

So was Jesus really wanting to find some way of sidestepping this? Were these second thoughts? If so, why? Did Satan know Jesus' whole mission was about dying a sacrificial death? If so, was he trying to scupper the plan and get Jesus free? Or was Satan ignorant of the twist and just focused on trying to orchestrate the whole Jesus execution as his Big Victory?

[Mark 14:37] Why were the boys asleep? Well, pretty easy answer – they've just had a big Festival feast, with wine! Why does Jesus use Pete's old name? Is Jesus making like Pete's made no progress in nearly three years?

and keep online to God, then you won't get sucked into the mess. Your spirit's up for it, but your body's drooping."

39 – 42

Jesus goes back and wrestles some more with his Father. Next time he comes back they're snoring away again – eyelids clammed shut. He wakes them up and they're speechless.

Third time, same story: Jesus comes back and says, "You lot still getting some shut-eye? Enough already! Time's crept up on us. You're seeing it happen, live and unedited. Look, The Man, is stitched up and sold over to the messed up. On your feet! We're off! Here's the sell-out specialist, my very own Mr Defector..."

Some treasurer! Matthew 26:47–52a

47 – 48

Jesus is mid-sentence when Judas, Team Twelve member, shows up with a mob courtesy of the Big God Reps and Councillors. They're charged for a scuffle, looking threatening while wielding their bats and knives.

Flashback scene: Just yesterday, Judas and the Religious Bounty Hunters were scheming, and Judas said, "The guy I kiss is 'the one'. Arrest him and take him away under guard."

49 – 50

Judas walks right up to Jesus and says, "Hi, Coach," and seals the deal with a kiss.

Jesus responds, "Mate, just do it."

[Matthew 26:47] Time check: By now it's probably the early hours of Friday morning on Flyby Festival weekend.

[Matthew 26:47 – 50] Who were these guys in the mob? Jonno in his bio says they're soldiers, but bats wouldn't have been standard issue for official Religious HQ guards. So were these guys drafted in the last minute to do the dirty deed? Or were these guards working undercover? All seems a bit iffy, really.

[Matthew 26:49] Why the kiss? Nothing weird about that – it's standard practice for an apprentice to meet his life coach with a kiss.

The braver ones from the mob take their cue, move forward, get Jesus into a hold and arrest him.

51 – 52a

Seconds later there's a, flash of a knife, some frantic action and next thing, one of Caiaphas' crew has a work injury to report – a missing ear.

"Put it away, now!" barks Jesus.

Luke 22:51

51

Jesus touches the guy's mutilated ear and makes it good as new.

Matthew 26:52b – 56

52b – 54

Jesus slams into the aggressor and says, "Weapons don't win you battles, they lose you people. Anyway, one word from me and my Dad would give the green light to a dozen squadrons of action angels. They're already on alert and I just have to give the nod and it's 'go, go, go!' But that would be going off the script; it wouldn't sync with what God's couriers[9] said would happen, would it?"

55 – 56

Then he turns to the mob and asks, "What? Am I some violent terrorist? Do I act like a dangerous revolutionary? Why d'you creep in here armed to the teeth? Day in and day out I'm doing my coaching slot there at Religious HQ[10]. How come you didn't arrest me there? I'll tell you 'how come': 'Cos, again, it wouldn't have lined up with the lines God's couriers published way back. This way The Good Book is all coming true."

And vamoosh! The Team leg it while they still can.

[9] **God's Courier.** Personal message delivery service direct from God. Think any package delivery corporation, but think "quick". Although, thinking about it, with their record, the depot for uncollected packages would've been pretty chocka by the end of the Old Testament.

[10] **Religious HQ = Temple.** Jerusalem's focal point of the Jewish Religion. Literally a house for God. Question is, how much does God get let out?

[Matthew 26:51] Matt's not naming names, or may not have been close enough to see, but check out Jonno's version (see John 18:1 – 14 in a proper Bible). He says it was Pete who did the damage! Jonno also names the victim of the assault as Malchus.

[Matthew 26:56b] So much for all their brave words at the meal table. All their clenched fists, all their "I'd die before disowning you" talk! Resolve dissolves – just add some fear-stoked sweat.

Eyewitness Mark 14:51-52

51-52

One young guy – a Jesus crew member – is watching all this just in
his linen pajamas. The guards grab him and he wriggles free, leaving
an empty pair of pajamas while the youth runs off through the park,
wearing only his own sweat and a freaked-out expression on his face.

[Mark 14:51] Who's this "young guy"? Urban myths reckon this was the biographer himself, Mark. Is this
Mark's way of hinting, "I was there"? And "Yup, sorry, but I legged it too"!

Caesar's News Network Interview

Davidson's heavies in night brawl

Pete Jonahson, one of Jesus Davidson's Team, is a wanted man after a violent attack on one of the Religious HQ guards. Here's the victim's version of events. Soldier Malchus Berstein talks to CNN:

CNN—So, a close shave then, Malchus?

MB—Yes, that Pete guy took my ear off! And I tell you this much, he wasn't aiming at my ear! This was no "shoot to stun" warning shot! It's only after the incident that you realize the years of training are there to draw on; years of combat training focused in on a split second that saved my life. Though, if I'm honest, the northern yob shouldn't have even hit my ear. I'm obviously a bit rusty, or he was especially pumped up.

CNN— Have you considered bringing charges against this Mr Jonahson?

MB—I was thinking of it – I mean it was attempted murder – but even if I tracked him down it'd be tricky to sue him since Jesus sorted the gash out and, effectively, tampered with the evidence. Even if I went for an "emotional trauma" charge, I'm still getting night sweats and bad dreams in the barracks. The only witnesses are my own colleagues and a bunch of Davidson's guys who are probably halfway back up to Galilee by now! Plus it was pre-dawn, in a dark olive grove. Odds of making the charges stick are somewhere past "pretty hopeless".

CNN—So how did you feel about being healed by a "dangerous revolutionary"?

MB—The whole thing is weird, but just 'cos he's got a human side doesn't mean he's not dangerous. All I know is that I've had a near death experience, but I've got nothing to show for it. Weird.

Send your views on this "dangerous or dangerless" debate to: www.caesarsnewsnetwork.rom.gos/dangerousorno.

* See Appendix at back of book for definition.

1 **Big God Reps = Chief priests.** If "God Reps" (priests) were the "go between" for God and his people, then *chief* priests were the ones with real clout. This eminent group are the ones who've done their year's stint as Top God Rep (High Priest).

2 **Councillors = Elders.** The non-Religious element of the ruling of the people. Sort of civil servants.

3 **Religious Law Enforcers = Teachers of the Law/Scribes.** Experts in Moses' law. Academics, who sadly, often became "academic" in the sense of "irrelevant".

Chapter Nineteen

Trial Times

Tried Religiously Mark 14:53-65

53-54

The lynch mob of guards "escort" Jesus to the Jewish Supreme Court*: a scary combination of Big God Reps[1], Councillors[2] and Religious Law Enforcers[3].

Switch scenes to Pete tracking Jesus from a safe distance; sidling his way into the Top God Rep's courtyard. He's sitting there with the guards, warming himself by the charcoal fire.

55-56

Upstairs, the Big God Reps and the whole Supreme/Kangaroo (depending) Court are scraping through the records looking for creative ways of generating evidence to be sure of the crucial death

[Mark 14:54] What range of emotions has Pete just been through? He's rebounding off anger (at Judas' betrayal); aggression (the assault on Malchus); frustration (at Jesus stopping him); fear (legging it with the others) and now . . . guilt.

⁴ **Religious HQ = Temple.** Jerusalem's focal point of the Jewish Religion. Literally a house for God. Question is, how much does God get let out?

sentence for Jesus. And? Nothing that quite clinches it, even though they bring in the best "witnesses" money can buy. Not even the most convincing liars get anything to stick on the accused. Put all the flannel together and it just doesn't hold water.

57 – 59

Then some guys take to the witness box, lying through their teeth that, "We're pretty sure we heard Jesus say, 'I'll wreck this man-made Religious HQ⁴ and two days later I'll have another one made, only this time there won't be a man-made sign in sight.'" But even now, the cross-examination shows the different witnesses can't agree.

60 – 61

It's not going according to script(s), so the Top God Rep decides to step into the interrogation personally and asks Jesus, "You not going to speak up for yourself? What are they saying about you?"

But Jesus stays mute; no response. So the Top God Rep cuts across the waffle and confronts him, asking, "Are you or are you not the sent Liberator? Are you the Son of the Awesome and Sacred God?"

[Mark 14:55] Seventy senior guys scratching their skulls on how to reach a verdict that will work for both them and the Romans since, in Occupied Territory, only their Roman overlords can inflict capital punishment.

[Mark 14:58] How long did it take before they worked out that Jesus' quote didn't refer to the Religious HQ building, but his own body? Hindsight spells it out – Friday: execution/demolition. Two days later – Sunday AM: back from the dead/reconstruction. It all fits, but only when you know the ending, which Jesus did, but the others didn't.

[Mark 14:60] Yep, this year it's Caiaphas in the Chief Chair.

[Mark 14:60 – 61] Why is Jesus so silent? Is he:

    (a) frozen with fear?
    (b) on a death-wish mission?
    (c) resigned to Caiaphas never understanding?
    (d) not needing to prove himself, especially to people with no ears to hear?
    (e) other?

62

Finally Jesus breaks his silence, "Yes … I am! And what's more, you'll get proof of it when you see Yours Truly, The Man,[5] sitting in the place of total authority, right next to The Source of all authority – Awesome God himself. You'll get proof when you see The Man step down onto the clouds and ride them between heaven and earth itself."

63 – 64

The Top God rep goes ballistic, ripping his top-of-the-range Religious robe in rage. "Outrageous! Sack the Witness Guidance Programme; they're a waste of space!"

He rounds on the Court "jury" and says, "You heard him – now he reckons he's God! Gentlemen of the Council, you've heard the heretic. Will you do your duty, or not?"

They come back, "There's only one verdict – the Death Penalty." Unanimous decision – capital punishment.

No question; no debate.

65

Those who can get close enough start gobbing at him; others improvise a blindfold; still others lay into him with their fists, sneering, "Guess, go on, guess whose fist!" Then the Religious HQ guards frog-march Jesus off and fill in the gaps in his growing bruise collection.

[5] **The Man = Son of Man.** Jesus' term for himself – lifted from Daniel 7, where it's a pretty blatant clue that this is no mere mortal: "the Son of Man … surfing in on the clouds … where the Ancient of Days … gives him … all the credit for running the show … and permanent position in the top spot." Nice name badge.

[Mark 14:62 – 64] Why does Caiaphas take Jesus' final answer as blasphemy? Apart from using God's own phrase for himself – "I AM" – Jesus also delivers an "outrageous" quote from The Good Book. These Religious boffins would have all picked up Jesus' paraphrase of Daniel 7:13 and the references of God saying to his Liberator (from Psalm 110:1): "Sit in the place of total authority till I make your enemies bow in front of you, so you can use their neck as a footrest."

[Mark 14:63] Why rip the linen robe? It's a time-honoured way of expressing grief and outrage … except that this was probably a calculated display. The Top God Rep was most likely feeling the opposite: a combination of excitement and relief at finally having something to nail Jesus on (figuratively … at first).

[Mark 14:64] Check Leviticus 24:14 for the details on the verdict for bad-mouthing God. (Getting stoned meant something different back then.)

[Mark 14:65] What was going through Jesus' mind as they lay into him? Were his covered eyes scrolling his memory for the lines from Isaiah 50:6 – 8?

You want to beat me? Here's my body. / You want to tear out my beard? Here's my chin. / You want to gob in my eyes? Here's my face. / You want to mock me? Here's my heart. / No way am I dying of shame. / Why? 'Cos the God in charge helps me, of course. / So I'll lock my sights on the target and aim, / No way am I shifting off course.

Right on cue Mark 14:66-72

66-68

Cross back over to Pete, still crouching by the courtyard fire. One of Caiaphas' cleaning girls gets up close and has a good view of Pete's fire-lit face and bursts out with, "You're one of the Galilee Gang with that Jesus of Nazareth!"

Pete blanks her out with, "Haven't got the first clue what you're talking about!" He backs off to the courtyard exit sign.

69-70

But the girl's not backing down; she spouts her mouth off to anyone and everyone, saying, "This guy's one of that Jesus lot!"

Again, Pete bluffs his way out, denying all knowledge. But within minutes the guys next to him are hitting the same conclusion. "You must be one of Jesus' Team, your accent's a dead giveaway."

71-72

Pete swears blind, "On my life, I've never even met this Jesus guy you're banging on about!"

On cue, there's a repeat call from the local rooster. Pete plays back Jesus' line in his head: *Within 24 hours, by the second time the rooster does his alarm clock impression, you'll have sworn blind that you don't even know me. Not once, not twice, but three times!* Pete loses it completely, weeping enough tears to sink a fishing boat.

[Mark 14:68] Why can't Pete quite leg it completely? What's keeping him hanging around just under the courtyard exit sign?

[Mark 14:70] Galileans were known for their northern accent – Jewish Aram (aka Irritable Vowel Syndrome to the snobby southerners).

[Mark 14:71] You can imagine the vocab. Pete had available to upload from his fishing days back up north. Who's to say it wasn't more colourful language?

Death sentence Matthew 27:1-2

1-2

It's sun up on Flyby Festival[6] Friday when the Religious Suits make the momentous decision to have Jesus executed/murdered/assassinated. They handcuff Jesus and frog-march him off to Pilate, the Roman Governor.

Bloody money Matthew 27:3-10

3-5

Scene change to Mr Defector, Judas, who's kept himself fully up to speed on developments. Jesus' Death Penalty stuns Judas into a guilt-ridden mental replay of what he's done. All he can do is take the 30 silver coins back to the Suits.

"I've messed up. Big time. His innocent blood's screaming at me!" Judas blurts out.

"Deal with it!" the Suits sneer. "Not our problem." Judas hurls the coins at the sacred HQ porch. Runs off. Hangs himself.

[6] **Flyby Festival = Passover.** A major Jewish Religious festival, like our Easter/Christmas. It celebrates God liberating their ancestors from the sweatshops of Egypt. The name derives from when the angel of death passed over/flew by Jewish homes.

[Matthew 27:2] Stage One complete: Jewish verdict in the bag. Now moving swiftly on to Stage Two: the big one. Getting the Jewish death sentence won't mean much until it's ratified by the people who really run the joint – the Roman Occupation Forces, specifically Pilate. His recent track record doesn't make him a popular public figure in Jewish folklore.

Quick bio: Pontius Pilate scrapes his way up to middle management in the backwater of the Roman Empire known as Judah. Once in office, a long list of bungled decisions, including: (1) laundering funds from the Jews' Religious HQ coffers to build a White Elephant of an Aqueduct; and (2) giving his Army Officers the "fire at will" command to murder Jewish civilians. So just how galling was it for the Religious Big Wigs to have to crawl to this guy for the decision they were desperate for?

6-8

The Big God Reps pick up the coins but hold them at arm's length. One of the sticklers points out chapter and verse, "The Religious HQ Rule Book doesn't allow us to put this cash back in HQ Funds, as, technically, it qualifies as 'blood money'."

Some quick thinker comes up with an idea. "Buy something with it." Another chips in, "Yeah, buy a field with it." Another adds, "Hey, Potter's field is up for sale, and cheap!" "We could use it as a cemetery." "No, not for Jews!"

Finally, a compromise hits them and they land on a plan, "Yes, a cemetery, but only for foreigners!" They all agree. Top idea! It's still there; you'd find it in the yellow pages under "Potter's Place of Rest", but locals all know it as "Bloody Burial Field".

9-10

All of which fits with God's old courier[7] Jeremiah:

"They took the proceeds of the human trading – the recommended retail price set for his life by the Jews. They bundled up the thirty silver coins and went shopping for a Potter's Field, as directed by God."

Criminal delivery service Luke 23:1-4

1-2

The whole of the Jewish Supreme Court drives Jesus up the road to Governor Pilate's pad. They reel off the charges against him, spin-

---

[Matthew 27:9] This is a fusion of bits from Jeremiah 18,19 and 32 ... and Zechariah 11 as well.

[Luke 23:1–2] Did Jesus oppose people paying their dues? Nope, but spin can get terribly creative when the stakes are this high. And why's there no mention of the Religious crime of bad-mouthing God? Why's the charge been changed to the political crime of high treason? Because the Religious Leaders know which tactic is likely to get their Roman Governor's adrenalin pumping. To Pilate, "Jewish King" meant "Terrorist", "Rebel" and "Coup Leader". And yet Pilate pronounces the innocent verdict so quickly! How much background info did Pilate already have on Jesus? Or was it just that he knew the track record of the current Sanhedrin?

Just how ironic is it that Jesus gets put on trial for trying to lead a political revolution since his refusal to move into rebel politics was probably reason Numero Uno why much of the public – maybe even including Judas – had become disillusioned with him!

ning it to prick up Pilate's paranoid ears. They're claiming, "This man's been found guilty of subversive crimes against the Nation. Oh, and he's anti-Rome – barring people from paying their taxes. And he swans around making out he's a National Liberator – a King, a Jewish King no less!"

3 – 4

Pilate asks the straight question to Jesus, "So, Jewish King or not?"

"Yup, if you say so," answers Jesus. Pilate's not having it. He makes his announcement to the Big God Reps, and he makes it loud enough for the crowds to catch too: "The guy's innocent! No charge to answer."

Poor self-defence Matthew 27:12 – 14

12 – 14

With the Big God Reps and Councillors sticking their oars in, stirring up Pilate, Jesus shifts back into mute mode.

Pilate goes to Jesus, "You deaf or what? Can't you hear the load of charges they're chucking your way!"

But Jesus stuns the Governor by refusing to act as his own defence – he's silent. Not one single comeback.

Pass the buck Luke 23:5 – 12

5 – 7

The Religious Heavies are desperate and pile the pressure on Pilate. "But he's causing riots all over the place – from his old stomping ground, Galilee, down to the capital."

Pilate hears the word "Galilee" and asks, "So this Jesus is a Galilean, eh?" *King Herod's patch*, he thinks. *So Jesus is, technically, Herod's problem – perfect!* Plus he knows that Herod's in Jerusalem for the Festival.

[Luke 23:6] Galilee? Pilate's ultimate cop-out strategy: why deal with a problem when you can delegate?

[Luke 23:7– 8] So we're back to the family line of Herod locked onto destroying Jesus. Back about 30 or so years ago Herod Antipas' old man, Herod the Great, issued the Infanticide Order for his troops to top any boy toddlers with a Bethlehem address on their birth certificate, and now these Herods are at it again.

8 - 9

Herod Antipas is happy to help; he's been itching to meet Jesus for ages. He's read the reviews, and he's on the edge of his seat waiting for something spectacular from the miracle man. But Jesus is exercising his "right to remain silent" and it's not much of a conversation – question after question from Herod, deafening silence coming back from Jesus.

10 - 12

The Big God Reps and the Religious Law Enforcers are still on the case, throwing the book at Jesus. Herod gives up asking questions and decides to have a laugh. He signals to his soldiers that it's a free-for-all. They dress Jesus up as a King; they lay into him with their dark sarcasm, role-playing groveling citizens. When the novelty of this wears off, Herod passes Jesus back to Pilate, fully dressed in the robe of his black humour. This turns the corner for Roman/Galilean relations. Pilate and Herod bury the hatchet of recent history and become good mates from here on in.

Amnesty for terrorists Matthew 27:15-16

15 - 16

Bit of background: The Governor's got this keeping-the-Jews-in-line tradition called Flyby Amnesty. Basically every Flyby Festival, Pilate unlocks one of their "political prisoners" as a goodwill gesture to their Religion. They just have to name the guy. One possible walker this year is another guy with the first name Jesus: the infamous prisoner Jesus Abbason, aka Barabbas.

Mark 15:7b - 8

7b - 8

Quick bio on Abbason/Barabbas: Member of the rebel group of the Judah Liberation Army. Locked up for murder after the recent people's uprising against the Roman Occupying forces.

[Luke 23:12] Old enemies finding a uniting cause in thrashing the life out of Jesus.

[Matthew 27:16] "Abbason" is a variation on his more familiar name, Barabbas. The interesting thing is, if you've got a bit of Hebrew vocab., you get the "aha" moment when you realize his name literally means "son of a dad". How's this sit against Jesus' term for himself of "Son of Man"?

The baying crowd is asking Pilate to activate the Flyby Amnesty, like every year.

Off the hook Matthew 27:17-21

17-18

So Pilate offers the crowd a simple choice, "Which Jesus is going to get lucky? Abbason of the Judah Liberation Army or Davidson, aka The Liberator? Which one am I going to have the pleasure of liberating?"

Pilate, ever the politician, is probing public opinion. He already knows where the Religious Suits' block vote is landing – it's obvious from the fog of envious green mist above their heads – but what do the people think?

19-20

Just then, as Pilate's sitting in his Big Judge Chair, he gets a message from his missus, saying, "I've just had a horrific nightmare about this Jesus, the Galilean – he's innocent! Don't touch him with a javelin pole."

Meanwhile, the Religious lynch mob of Big God Reps and Councillors are hyping up the crowd, using all they know to swing the vote to, "Free Abbasson" and "Execute Davidson".

21

Governor Pilate asks the big question again: "Which Jesus is going to get lucky?"

The crowd shout their vote out, "Abbason! Abbason! Abbason!"

Nothing doing Luke 23:13-16

13-16

Pilate gets the Big God Reps, the Jewish Leaders and the crowd to shut up and listen, arguing, "You drag this Jesus Davidson guy in here

---

[Matthew 27:19] Is this women's intuition or something (even) more spiritual?

[Matthew 27:20] Will we ever know what the bulk of the people actually thought? How guilty is a mob when they're swept along on the hype of their influential leaders? How hard was it to untangle the spin from the Big God Reps? How could they block out the pro-Abbason argument of "he's not a terrorist; he's a freedom fighter"?

saying he's pumping the people up to revolt. I've checked it out and the case is full of holes. He's done nothing! Plus now Herod's talked to him, but again, nothing. He's been sent back from Herod a free man. It's obvious, he's done nothing to get him even close to the Death Penalty. I'll have my men flog him and let him go. End of story."

Public demand Luke 23:20-22

20-21

But Pilate doesn't like the way they're voting. He's scraping his brain for a way to let Jesus Davidson walk free. He keeps pushing back against public opinion, but his argument is drowned out by the waves of hate shouting, "Execute him, Roman style! Execute him, Roman style!"

22

Pilate pushes it a third time, upping the volume to make his point with the crowd. "Why? What's the guy done? Nothing worth dying for! Like I say, I'll have my men flog him – should teach him a lesson – then let him go. End of story."

Blood on whose hands? Matthew 27:24-26

24

Pilate knows he's getting nowhere. Worse, this is threatening to escalate into a full-scale riot. So he crumbles, sends for a bowl of water and starts making some big gestures. The noise dies down and he

---

[Luke 23:16] Was Pilate thinking this would sort it? One quick compromise punishment beating and the Jewish Suits' blood lust for Jesus would be satisfied? How evil is this? Even though he finds Jesus innocent as charged, he still has him whipped ... and how?

[Luke 23:21] Execution "Roman style" meant crucifixion, the gruesome tactic of an Empire which spouted sound bites about bringing justice and peace to the known world. But this "peace" was maintained by the barbaric and highly uncivilized act of crucifixion. The cross was never the last gasping place of a Roman citizen, so it was symbolic of, "You mess with us, you die the worst possible way".

[Matthew 27:24] Why wash his hands? It's an old Jewish custom based on Deuteronomy 21:6,7. Pilate's been around the place long enough to know the whole bowl deal will make the point visual and therefore memorable. Especially with the noise levels cranked up like this.

says, "I've tried! My hands are clean. None of his blood's on my hands alright? You want it; you take the weight of it!"

25 – 26

The whole crowd screams back, "No problem. We'll have his blood on our hands. Us and our kids."

So Pilate gives the signal for Abbason's cell to be unlocked and for the prisoner to be escorted to the open prison gates and to walk. Pilate has Davidson whipped with lead-tipped whips and then handed over to the Duty Death Squad to be executed, Roman style.

[Matthew 27:25 – 26] So what does this mean? Is it legit to lay the blame for the crucifixion of Jesus at the door of the Jews? Or is this absurd given Jesus' coaching, not to mention his final act of forgiveness before dying: "Dad! Don't hold this against these people – wipe their slate clean. They've got no idea what's going on here!" (See Chapter 20, Luke 23:34, page 356.)

[Matthew 27:26] So Pilate backs off his original plans to flog then release Jesus and releases a convicted rioter instead.

Victims of Roman punishment beatings often didn't "graduate" to the actual crucifixion – the pummelling they got was so horrific that they were often dead already. The flogging instrument? A sadistic torture tool with several leather strips, each of which had pieces of bone and lead worked into it. Two soldiers stood on either side of the victim and let loose on their naked body.

Revolutionary Times: Main Man Interview

The Revolution's back on!

The release yesterday of Jesus Abbason has given new hope to many that Revolution is in the air again. We have a transcription of an exclusive interview given from the confines of his safe house where he talks openly of death row, The Movement and, of course, the other Jesus:

RT—Good to have you back, Jesus. So, what's it like "coming back from the dead" then?! Being a free man again!

JA—I'd love to know. We won't be free men till we see the back end of the Roman Occupation, but I'll take this fresh air as an unexpected bonus!

RT—Were conditions pretty harsh in the prison?

JA—Barbaric, by design. But then we'd treat them the same given the chance. You just have to tough it out and stay sane. The main thing is keeping your focus sharp on why you're there: hatred for the enemy.

RT—Tell us about the Davidson trial. Pretty weird, no?

JA—Yes, weird, but sometimes all you need is a bit of luck and it can turn the course of history. It could be a new lease on life, not just for me, but for The Movement.

RT—So you won't be taking a holiday and enjoying life then?

JA—I've sat long enough on my backside. No, I'm back and this time there's no fear – what can they do to me? How can they kill a dead man walking?!

RT—You didn't exactly have the reputation of being timid before the riots and your arrest.

JA—These are not times for the timid! As my namesake, Mr Davidson, has found out ... to his cost. I'd always had my doubts – loads of people talked of him being "the face of the Revolution" – but he never had the stomach for it, never had the head for heights that you need at that level of celebrity or notoriety.

RT—So why wasn't he defending himself at his trial? Couldn't he think of answers? Everyone knows that it was an appalling miscarriage of justice. Why wouldn't he fight his corner, argue his case?

JA—I'm still trying to get my head round that one. There was something of a death wish about him, a resignation. Like he wanted to take what was coming to me.

RT—Was he just too weak?

JA—And maybe we'll be stronger, come The Day, because of his weakness.

RT—And this will be something you'll be driving home on your new Basics of Revolt course?

JA—Yes, it'll be much more hands-on. Prison hours go slowly, but they give you more time to think. Got some nice ideas brewing.

RT—Power to you.

JA—And to us!

Anyone wishing to sign up for Jesus Abbason's Basics of Revolt class, click on www.revolutionarytimes.org.gos.il/judahliberationarmy/basicsofrevolt.

Chapter Twenty

Execution

Gratuitous violence Matthew 27:27-30

27-28

Pilate's personal militias get their Dead Man Walking behind the closed doors of the Military HQ[1]. The full complement of army personnel put down their playing cards and mags – everyone's up for a piece of the action. They upstage each other, different soldiers taking the gratuitous violence – mental and physical – up a gear. First, they strip him naked, then they grab a scarlet army cloak and dress him up in a spoof King costume.

[Matthew 27:27 – 30] Jesus has zigzagged about the city in the last 12 hours. From eating the Flyby Festival meal in the southwest of the city, to his soul searching in the park outside the northeast city wall; then he's arrested and taken back down to the southeast for his trial by the Religiously Outraged; then up to the north of the city to the Antonia Fortress to see Pilate; then down into the City Centre to block out Herod Antipas' questions before going back up to the Antonia Fortress and the military barracks.

Don't Like This? [Mark 15:20 – 21] If this is what Jesus meant back in Chapter 8 (see Matthew 10:38, page 157) about taking "the strain under the weight of your own execution equipment", then you might have second thoughts about signing up as his crew.

Just focus on the storytelling Jesus – but not on the stories he told about seeds falling into the ground and dying, or any of the waiting for Judgement Day stories.

29 – 30

They get creative: plaiting a mock crown out of some thorn spines and slamming it down into Jesus' skull. The "King effect" is finished off with a staff made of reeds standing in as a royal sceptre. The soldiers are laying into him with their biting satire, playing the ever-so-humble-servants, saying, "Hail Jewish King, we salute you!"

They keep the sadism stuck on max: building the humiliation by going for the best shot of phlegm in the face; building the dehumanization with more whackings across the head as they smack him with the staff again, again, again, again.

Semi-dead already Mark 15:20-21

20 – 21

Eventually they quit the gratuitous violence. They tear the officer's rich-coloured cloak off his back (opening up the semi-clotted wounds again). They dress him in his own clothes and lead him out to his execution.

There's this bloke in the crowd – Simon Cyreneton, a family man and father of two, Alexander and Rufus – who has made it into Jerusalem after a long trip through the countryside. The Roman soldiers press-gang him into service. The temporary enrollment form reads: "crossbar carrying for too-far-gone execution candidate".

[Matthew 27:30] How weird was it for the Roman soldiers to punish a healer, to punch a peacemaker? Would they have much preferred to get under the skin of an insurgent? Were they even aware of Jesus' coaching on "turning the other cheek"? Did it matter if they weren't?

[Mark 15:20 – 21] Where did Jesus get the strength from? How did he manage – so sleep deprived, so beaten up – to lug the crossbar of his own tool of execution out toward the city gates? It's amazing that he got as far as he did.

[Mark 15:21] Who was Simon Cyreneton? Quick bio: probably a Religious tourist from Cyrene on the North African coast, in town for the Flyby Festival.

Public spectacle Luke 23:27-32

27-29

Huge crowds jostle to gawk at the Gore Fest, staring at the spectacle passing through their streets. The women are in top grieving gear, screaming the morning skies apart with their raw emotion. Jesus engages them with, "Jerusalem girls! Don't go shedding your tears for me; break the flood banks with tears for yourselves, with tears for your kids. Not long now, the time when you'll count the childless women as well happy; the time you'll say wombs that have never moulded babies are happy wombs, breasts that have never produced milk are happy breasts.

30-31

"You'll be quoting, 'Hey mountains – over here! Crush us! Oy, you granite hills – fall on us, us, us!' If people get this barbaric when the tree's a lush green colour, just how ugly do they get when the tree's dry and dead?"

32

But Jesus isn't the only one on today's Death Rota. Two other guys – both convicted terrorists – are taking their final steps toward Skull Hill[2].

Drink the cup? Dry? Matthew 27:33-34

33-34

The macabre scene moves slowly up Skull Hill. They get there and the Roman Death Squad shove a cocktail made of wine with myrrh

[2] **Skull Hill = Golgotha (Aramaic)/Calvary (Latin).** Outside the Jerusalem City Limits, either to the west or northwest of the Religious HQ, depending on which archaeologist you ask for directions.

[Luke 23:30] See Hosea 10:8 in a proper Bible.

[Luke 23:31] What's Jesus getting at? Is he the green tree who brings life? And is the dry tree an image of him dead? What do the crowd make of it? Do they get it, or do they just write it off as the demented ramblings of a half-dead, blood-light man?

[Luke 23:32] Terrorists or criminals/thieves? Not even Rome (in all its gory) would crucify people for just a bit of stealing. It's likely that these "criminals" were insurrectionists who'd been caught red-handed; insurgents with a blood debt to pay.

---

into Jesus' face. He takes a sip but spits it out, flat refusing to drink the stuff.

Roman execution Luke 23:33b – 34

33b – 34

They pin Jesus to the rough crossbar leaving him to die. Him and the two hardened criminals – one on either side. Jesus says, "Dad! Don't hold this against these people – wipe their slates clean. They've got no idea what's going on here!"

The Death Squad rip his clothes off and start playing gambling games to see who "inherits" the clothing mementos.

Jewish King? Mark 15:25 – 27

25 – 26

Time check: Friday 9 AM. One of the soldiers grabs the multi-use Offence Placard, writes up Jesus' "crime" and then pins it just above his head. It reads, "Jesus: King of the Jews".

[Matthew 27:33 – 34] Why does Jesus not drink the cup? Was it just the disgusting bitter taste? Or does he spot the myrrh in the recipe and reject its anaesthetic qualities? Is he determined to face this fully conscious?

Or is he replaying his lines at yesterday's Flyby Festival Team meal about not drinking any wine until the inaugural party in God's New World Order? So Jesus is offered two "cups" – one from his Father, which he drinks; one from the soldiers, which he refuses.

[Luke 23:33b] The Romans had "perfected" crucifixion: Driving dirty, six-inch nails through the hands, stapling the feet onto the upright stake, lifting it upright and leaving the victim to hang from their broken hands and feet while the cumulative effect of asphyxiation, gradual blood loss and, finally – sometimes after two or three days – the collapse of vital organs lead to the eventual death.

[Luke 23:34] Totally naked? Yes, forget the fake modesty of Western art that has material draped over the unmentionables. No, Jesus – and every other victim – was executed naked, all part of the World Super Power's Total Humiliation Programme.

[Mark 15:26] Why display the offence? The whole thing wasn't just about executing offenders, it was as much about providing a visual deterrent to other would-be revolutionaries.

27

The other two victims with him – the terrorists – one on either side of the central focus point, Jesus.

Verbal assassination Matthew 27:39-44

39-40

The crowds going past are slowing down to have a go at the (not quite) dead meat stapled up there. They're tutting and frowning and throwing out cruel one-liners; acidic libel propelled with venom.

"Whose line was this then: 'I'll demolish the Religious HQ[3] and have it back up again in two days'? Where's your bull-dozer now?!"

And, "Who said he was the Son of God? Well, who's your 'daddy' now, Jesus?!"

Still more: "Can't you use your Son of Awesome God Power to bite your way through those Roman nails? If you're the Son of God, come on down!"

41-42

The Big God Reps[4], the Religious Law Enforcers[5] and the Councillors[6] are getting stuck in too. "He straightened out so many, sorted so many, but now he's lost his supernatural pow-ers. Bad timing! He can't even sort things for himself!" "But he's the Jewish King, isn't he?" "Well, that's what the sign says! Hey, can't you come on down? Are we ready to see it?! Are we just so pumped up to sign our lives over to him?!"

[3] **Religious HQ = Temple.** Jerusalem's focal point of the Jewish Religion. Literally a house for God. Question is, how much does God get let out?

[4] **Big God Reps = Chief priests.** If "God Reps" (priests) were the "go between" for God and his people, then *chief* priests were the ones with real clout. This eminent group are the ones who've done their year's stint as Top God Rep (High Priest).

[5] **Religious Law Enforcers = Teachers of the Law/Scribes.** Experts in Moses' law. Academics, who sadly, often became "academic" in the sense of "irrelevant".

[6] **Councillors = Elders.** The non-Religious element of the ruling of the people. Sort of civil servants.

[Matthew 27:40] **"Come on down"?** As is so often, the Religious Boys are all at once dead on and way off the mark. He could've liberated himself, but not if he was going to fulfil his mission. How torturous is this?

[Matthew 27:42] Are the Religious Suits just loving this or what? After months and years of never being able to outwit Jesus, with all the growing fears about the people going for this table-turning hooligan, finally they've got him where they want him and they're busting a spleen with their outburst of pent-up aggression.

Deuteronomy 21:23 surely came to their minds: "Anyone executed and left hanging on a tree is written off. It's total humiliation, reputation suicide."

Don't Like This? [Luke 23:39 – 43] Not happy with this iffy character getting his entry ticket into paradise without completing a member's course or even signing a Declaration of Faith? Mmm. Best not think back to Jesus' deep-as-you-like story of Chapter 14 (Matthew 20:1 – 16) about the guys who join the workforce at the last minute and get the full salary package. It's on pages 267 – 268, but don't go there.

43 – 44

Others are spouting, "He's oh-so-cosy with God, but we don't see the Almighty stepping in!" "Yeah, didn't he make claims about being God's Son?" "Well, surely God wouldn't leave his own boy, would he?!"

Everyone else seems to be having a go, so the hardened criminals bite back their excruciating pain and add their jibes to the mix...

Beam me up to paradise Luke 23:39-43

39 – 43

One of the professional criminals hanging next to Jesus gets a second wind: "Aren't you supposed to be The Liberator? Get liberating, won't you? You need it and we need it!"

But the other guy calls across, "Don't you have no respect for God? You're getting what you had coming to you, but this guy's done nothing wrong. So shut it!"

This second career criminal turns to Jesus and says, "Jesus, don't forget me when you get to sit on your throne, okay?"

Jesus answers him, "I'll tell you today – no lie – you and me, we'll be in paradise together!"

Dying Matthew 27:45-49

45 – 46

Time check: 12 midday. It goes dark, totally dark, for three full hours right across Judah. Nothing except the chilling sound track of three men inching toward Death. Later, about three in the afternoon, Jesus freaks those still left there by shouting, "Eli, Eli, lema sabach-thani?" Translation: "My God, my God, why've you abandoned me?"

[Matthew 27:45] So was the lights out effect an eclipse of the sun? Nope. Flyby Festival always landed on a full moon! The next two possible explanations are "dark clouds" or "black sirocco wind" – possible climatological phenomena in Jerusalem in the month of April. Or it could be a God-thing? What's not up for debate is what they all read into it: sinister supernatural atmosphere.

[Matthew 27:46] Quoting Psalm 22:1.

47–49

Some of those within earshot hear the "Eli, Eli" bit and get the wrong end of the stick, saying, "Listen, he's trying to connect with Elijah!"

Knee-jerk reaction for one guy was to offer some soured wine to the sufferer, hoisting a soaked sponge of the stuff up to Jesus on a stick. Others are going, "Whoa! Hang on. Wait to see if Elijah's going to turn up like a one-man SWAT team and rescue him."

Dead Matthew 27:50

50

Jesus shouts out one more time and finally allows his spirit to be torn out of his broken body.

Dead Luke 23:46

46

He cries out, "Dad, I trust you with my spirit!"

His last words.

He dies.

Out from behind the curtain Matthew 27:51–54

51–53

Eyewitnesses record absolute precision timing: it's exactly that second, back in the Jerusalem Religious HQ, that the big back-off curtain gets ripped in two – split down the middle – top to bottom!

Same time, there's an earthquake, rocks rip apart, graves open up and the corpses of spiritual people climb back up and out of them, alive and clicking on "restart".

Later, when Jesus gets back from sorting death, these ex-dead crew go out on the town, making guest appearances. Many people see one of The Returned, "live and in a venue near you!"

[Matthew 27:51] Is this God's supernatural way of saying, loud and large, "My presence has left the building"? Or is it his way of saying that Jesus' death has blown away the barrier of mess between us and God? Check out Exodus 26:31 – 33 for Moses' now defunct curtain-hanging instructions. And Hebrews 4:14 — 5:10 and 9:11 – 15 for how Jesus steps up to the role of Top God Rep in the "No Curtain" era.

Three Long Hours

Where was Jesus' head through all this? Maybe the quote from Psalm 22:1 in Matthew 27:46 gives us a clue. We know from his spates with the Religious Leaders that he really knew his Scriptures; we know from three years earlier in the wasteland encounter (see Chapter 3, Matthew 4:1–11, pages 64–66) that he quotes from The Good Book to defend against Satan's misquotes. Is he scrolling through The Good Book, searching for verse injections to get him through this? It looks like Jesus is quoting a rough version of his ancestor David's song lyric from 1,000 years back:

> My God, my God, why've you abandoned me?
> Why'd you turn your army round and march them off like that?
> You walked out of earshot of my groans, my agony.
> Why d'you abandon me?

What's going on in Jesus' head? Is he scrolling through the rest of the Psalm in his derelict state, picking out the lines that get close to expressing the horror of this victimisation, like Psalm 22:6,7?

> I'm a slug, they take the rip out of me … they slander me …
> Enemies on every border, can't you order them away…

Off God's radar for the first time ever, is he drawing on David's lines from Psalm 22:14,15?

> I'm written off, trashed…
> A dislocated skeletal form of the former me…
> My heart's pulped, mashed, smashed, shredded.
> Drowning in the dreaded dust of death. Hung out to dry.
> As the blood leaves me and I'm struggling to hold on to "why?"

Is there any part of Jesus' mind still back in Gethsemane Park? Is any part of him getting flashbacks to the verses Satan twisted before? (Matthew 4:6 and Psalm 91:11,12):

If you're God's Son, jump! 'Cos The Good Book states categorically,
"The angels have their orders, orders straight down from the top.
They'll catch you. Carry you. Set you down gentle.
You won't even get to land on all fours,
'cos these out here are uneven floors,
you won't even turn an ankle.
So jump! Get yourself some proof!"

Or is Jesus only locked into his Davidson namesake's angst-ridden track?
(Psalm 22:16,18):

They've surrounded me, mugged me.
They've driven holes through my hands,
holes though my feet.
They're gambling for the shirt off my back . . .
Why d'you abandon me?
Stay! Stay! Stay! Stay!
Stay! Stay! Stay! STAY!

Could there be more flashbacks? Was Jesus able to see the city skyline from up
here? Was he ever even aware of Satan's past offer to wow the "powers that be"?
(Matthew 4:9):

All these networks, all these mobilizers and empire builders —
they're on my payroll, and I'll lease them out to you at very reasonable rates.
They're at your disposal. They'll jump to your text messages.
They'll make it all happen for you.
All I ask is . . . you work on my terms.

Is Jesus downloading the strength of Liberator passages he's read and read? Is he
toughing out the pain with the Big Picture of it all with lyrics from Isaiah?
(Isaiah 53:3–6):

He was dissed by most, given the cold shoulder by many.
There was a sadness about him.
You could see in his face he was on personal terms with grief.
People blocked him out, verbally abused him, didn't rate him.
But whoa! Step back a sec!
Weren't those our weaknesses he took on?
Wasn't that our damage he carried?
But we were convinced he'd been rubbed out of God's good books,
punished by him, held down by him.
How wrong can you be?!
He was messed up for our mess.
He was knocked down for our slip-ups.
The slapping we should've got — he got.
And we got serenity instead.
His punishment beating left him half-human
and us whole and fully human.
We've all wandered off like lost kids,
all followed our own directions.
And God's punished him
for everything we've done wrong.

Did Satan want him to stay on the cross? Did Satan think this was his Evil
Empire's finest hour? Was Jesus blocking out the agony with more from The
Good Book? (Isaiah 53:7 – 9):

Victimized and tortured,
but did he rant against this injustice?
No, he shut his mouth,
like a lamb entering an abattoir — eerily silent.
Terminated by the oppression of a corrupt legal system.
Leaving no kids — cut down in his prime.

Silenced for the foul-ups of my people.
My people who'd been pushing God's patience for years.
Killed like a common criminal (but buried by a rich man)
even though he was totally in the clear.
No blood on his hands. No hint of a half-truth in his mouth.

Is Jesus still leaning on Isaiah's shoulder? Is Isaiah willing him on from
heaven's balcony? (Isaiah 53:10,11a and Hebrews 12:1):

But God had planned all this way before.
God knew he'd be ripped apart and killed as a sacrifice,
a ceremonial offering to write "cancelled" across our guilt.
And he'll see the final score, how he won generations of "children".
And God will give him his life back
because the plans were completed to the letter.

Is Jesus tasting Scripture? Locking onto the future? Is Isaiah looking over heav-
en's balcony, somehow projecting them into Jesus' resolve? (Isaiah 53:11b,12):

He'll remember his agony,
he'll look at the results and be completely satisfied.
Knowing him, being connected with him
will lead to the acquittal of many in God's court.
He's already been punished for their mess.
So God will reward him big time!
A king-size jackpot of a reward.
'Cos he poured out his life till he was empty.
In his death he's associated with the lowest of the low.
He takes on the blame for the mess of so many.
He stands up for our falling downs.
He steps in for our leaving outs.
For all of it,
he takes the hit.

54

Close in on the soldiers guarding Jesus' corpse: The Roman Army Officer and his men get a close-up view of all this – the earthquake, the crumbling rocks, the returning corpses – and they're scared witless! Seen-it-all-soldiers, hardened Roman executioners, freaking out, giving God the credit and swearing, "This guy had to be God's Son!"

Luke 23:48-49

48-49

The crowd at Skull Hill see it all too. They connect with what they've just seen and drop into depression, trudging back to their homes. Those who knew him, including the women who'd come down from Galilee, stand way back, trying to take it all in.

Mark 15:40-41

40-41

This group of eyewitness women included Mary Magdalene, the other Mary – James Junior and Joses' mum – and Salome. They'd been part of Jesus' squad up in Galilee County, heading up the on-tour catering and management. A load of other women who'd travelled down to Jerusalem with him had also seen it through to the bitter end.

[Matthew 27:54] So how come it's so often the foreigners who get it? From right back in Elijah's day (1 Kings 17), Elisha's day (2 Kings 5), Jonah's day (Jonah 3) to the Eastern Astrologers who showed up after Jesus' birth (Matthew 2). Not to mention, the Roman Officer with the dying servant (Luke 7), the woman in Phoenicia (Matthew 15), and now this Roman Death Squad Officer sussing out who Jesus really is.

[Mark 15:40 – 41] Salome is Jim and Jonno's mum.

[Mark 15:41] Who were these other women? We want names! We know from Jonno's bio that Mary Davidson, Jesus' mum, was there. Probably the rest were the same crew mentioned at the top of Chapter 6 (see Luke 8:2 – 3, pages 120 – 121) including Joanna, Susanna and loads more.

He's buried Mark 15:42-47

42-43

Time check: getting on towards evening on the Friday, (that is Prep Day before Rest Day[7] Saturday).

A role for Councillor Joseph from the town of Arimathea – one of the big noises on the Jewish Supreme Court* and on the alert for God's New World Order[8]. He bites the bullet, gets an appointment with Pilate and asks, "Would it be okay for you to sign over Jesus' body for me to bury, your governorship?"

44-46

Pilate can't believe Jesus is dead already. He keeps Joseph waiting while he checks with the Duty Roman Officer and, once he gets the "confirmed dead" signal, signs the burial rights over to Joseph. So Joseph gets to the market and buys a job lot of linen strips. He takes Jesus' corpse down, uses the strips as a shroud and places the body in a new tomb cave. He has a huge stone shunted across the entrance.

47

Mary Mag and Mary, Joses' mum, have both eyes peeled watching the burial. They see the exact spot where Jesus' lifeless body is laid out.

Luke 23:56

56

The women trudge back to their digs and do the prep on the burial spices and perfumes. But they leave everything where it

[7] **Rest Day = Sabbath.** Rule No. 5 in Moses' Big Ten: "You'll keep my rest day special." By now this "special" had been defined down to the nth degree. There were plenty of things you shouldn't do.

* See Appendix at back of book for definition.

[8] **Heaven on Earth/God's New World Order = The kingdom of God.** Like with monarchies, but with God in charge, so not like with monarchies. There's also a sense of "sort of already/but not yet" paradox. We get to download glimpses now, but the full package would cramp our hard drive's style.

[Mark 15:46] How much of a panic rush was this for Joseph? He knew his Rule Book where Moses lays down the law (Deuteronomy 21:22 – 23): "If a guy gets the Death Penalty, and is hung up on a tree, do not leave his body on the tree overnight. Bury him that same day."

The Roman Execution Manual, however, showed no such scruples. The Romans are big into visual deterrents, leaving the bodies of crucified criminals hanging for days, in full view until the flesh rots away. If they got any sort of burial, it's only by express permission of the imperial magistrate   Pilate. And then only if friends or relatives have the guts to apply, but never in the case of high treason.

[9] **Religious Leaders = Pharisees.** A faction calling themselves literally "the separated ones" – "the exclusives" perhaps. Big into Rules, running a well-oiled propaganda machine which seemed to be fuelled by people's guilt.

[10] **Flyby Festival = Passover.** A major Jewish Religious festival, like our Easter/Christmas. It celebrates God liberating their ancestors from the sweatshops of Egypt. The name derives from when the angel of death passed over/flew by Jewish homes.

is for the Saturday Rest Day – out of respect for No. 5 of the Big Ten Rules.

Cover version Matthew 27:62-66

62-63

Meanwhile, the Big God Reps and Religious Leaders[9] are getting overactive paranoia glands. So they go to see Pilate the next day, even though it's a Rest Day, Flyby[10] Rest Day no less!

"Sir" they creep, "it occurs to us that this compulsive liar made some absurd claims about returning from death after two days. By our calculations, that's tomorrow, Sunday.

64-66

"So, we humbly suggest that you place some of your guards until tomorrow to stop Jesus' old Team from exhuming the body and spinning some hype about his 'restored in two days' claims coming true. This would even outdo his most outrageous lies."

"You've got your own Religious HQ Security Team," grumbles Pilate, "So go make it as thief-proof as you know how!"

Which they do: sealing the boulder and setting a round-the-clock guard so no one's breaking in there!

[Luke 23:56] The Burial Kit items weren't to preserve the body – Jews didn't do embalming. No, it seems it was more an act of love and devotion, probably partly meant to reduce the stench of the decomposing body in Palestine's hot climate. But it's too late now, sun's sinking. It'll have to wait till after Flyby Rest Day.

The perfumes included myrrh ointment – the same stuff the Eastern Astrologers brought to celebrate Jesus' birth day, way back some 400 months ago.

[Matthew 27:62] Just how serious did they think the risk was to ignore their precious Rest Day Rules and make this visit? The same rules they were so persnickety about Jesus flouting. Or were they actually just using them in a dirty tricks campaign against Jesus?

[Matthew 27:63] How is it that Jesus' sworn enemies remember his threat/promise to come back from death after two days, but his Team don't?

Councillor Joseph
makes grave protest

Yesterday a pillar of the Religious Establishment came clean on his long suspected pro-Davidson position. Joseph, an Arimathean member of the Jewish Supreme Court, was spotted yesterday burying the mutilated corpse of the discredited courier Jesus Davidson. We ask him why he did it and what are the prospects for his public service career now:

NJ—Councillor Joseph, that was a brave step – though some might say a bit foolish, perhaps – personally placing a would-be Jewish King in your own tomb cave.

JA—Yes, it's probably not going to go down well with my colleagues come Monday morning.

NJ—The obvious question, though, is why come out as a supporter of Jesus Davidson now, when it's all over – bar the grieving?

JA—I couldn't handle Jesus' body being chucked into an open grave to rot. I knew his mum, Mrs Davidson, was in no fit state to do anything. She was murmuring something about "a sniper's bullet through the soul" time and again, and I'd lost track of where the rest of his Team were. Jonno was off trying to console Jesus' mum I think, but the rest of them … no idea. Basically, if I didn't step up, they'd discard his corpse into a mass grave without even as much as a linen body bag.

NJ—But going to Pilate and making your own tomb cave available – isn't that considered to be career suicide?

JA—There comes a time when you just have to do the right thing. Admit to the world, and maybe even to yourself, that his way was right. Like a lot of people, I've followed the whole project from a distance. It was just time to stand up and be counted.

NJ—You must have strong powers of persuasion because Pilate wouldn't normally give a corpse to a non-family member.

JA—Unless he thinks he killed an innocent man.

NJ—Which you obviously do?

JA—Yes.

NJ—And how will your colleagues in the Supreme Court react to such a view? Won't they see it as a serious error of judgement?

JA—Maybe they will. But, like I say, I'm not the only one. There's plenty more people who felt strongly about Jesus, who'd been intrigued with him for years, even argued his corner at the drinks machine in many a public building.

NJ—But the difference is, they've not gone public about it, they've not gone out on a limb for him.

JA—True, they haven't, and they might well close ranks now and deny any former interest.

NJ—If they know what's good for them they will.

JA—It's so tragic! It was building up to quite a critical mass of people. Sooner or later it would've sparked into quite a movement, if only he'd managed to keep out of trouble.

NJ—You really think the movers and shakers would've come round?

JA—Not so many at the Religious end of the spectrum – some, but not many. But enough other people were asking the right questions. Fewer people were paranoid about being reported to the Religious Big Boys; there was less fear about getting your career blocked for having the wrong membership cards in your wallets.

NJ—So now you're left high and dry. Do you think you'll ever get any further promotions now?

JA—Not unless I change my name! I've got plenty of contacts; I know lots of people who hold, or held, the same views. Plenty of people who might still quote Jesus' ideas – off the record. But they're not likely to put their judgement under scrutiny by backing me for more responsibility. Why would they? Now it's all over.

NJ—I imagine they'll be pretty relieved they didn't blow their cover earlier.

JA—Only they will know how close they came to losing their prospects for him.

NJ—And rather grateful that their sensible side won the day.

Don't forget, if you feel your career's in a rut, you can always see if there's a new start for you at: www.newjews.com.gos/jobsearch.

ers.

Mary Magdalene Diary Page, Flyby Saturday:

What a pitiful bunch we are! Huddled together, doors locked, scared stiff ... wondering when they'll knock the doors down and it'll be our turn. Jonno, sad-eyed Jonno, totally disillusioned, depressed beyond words. Just focused on his "new mum" Mary. How's he to look after her when he's almost lost the will to live? And Mary! Oh, all she's been through — from the village gossips through her pregnancy, to losing Joe before all the family grew up, to her own sons laying into their big brother. Then there's the Big God Reps' bile, the soldiers getting off on her son's blood, the blood-thirsty crowds.

Pete looks the most morose! Is he replaying Friday morning in his mind, muttering "cock-a-doodle-don't" over, over, over. Is he losing it? Some rock-solid foundation for the Jesus Liberation Movement to build on, not! At least he got there; where were the rest? Which is probably what the other ten are locked onto; where were they when it mattered? They didn't even get close enough to blow it. Joanna's in a mess too. How can she go back to Cuza and live in Herod's staff quarters again knowing what ugly stuff Herod dealt out in the early hours of "Bad Friday" morning?

Salome's in a right state. Susanna's traumatised. What prospect is there for any of us? Can Matt go back to his desk and collect Pilate's taxes now that he's seen the guy's dark side? Can Pete or Drew or the Zebson boys ever go fishing again? How can Pete get back into a boat now that he's walked on water?

And what if they round us up? What if we really have to follow through on Jesus' talk of carrying our own execution equipment — literally — now that we've seen such gore? Looking round the room, who's churning over the ultimate cop out — Judas Iscariot's final solution?

What about me? I'm just as messed up, maybe more! Are my demons coming back? Are some of my pre-Jesus issues raising their ugly foreheads again? But he'd cleared them out! Evicted them! It was permanent, wasn't it? Do they know he's off the scene? But they're coming back. Not sure it's all seven, but I know they're creeping round the place again. Do they still have the keys after almost three years clean? No! Not after three years of virtual Heaven on Earth. Me and the girls touring round with Jesus and the guys; Jesus delegating the running of things to his female sponsors. Amazing stuff! But now it's all down the pan; and already, just a day later, my demons are flexing their muscles. No! Please God, no!! Got to get to the tomb. How long till sun up? Hours! Got to tough out the night. First thing, got to get there. Sense his presence, somehow. Prep's all done. The guys aren't up to it, but maybe ... by touching him, I might just ... oh, I don't know ... just got to get there. Got to!

Chapter Twenty-One

And Initially...

Unfinished work Matthew 28:1-4

1

First hint of sun, Sunday morning: Mary Mag and Jesus' Aunt Mary (James Jnr and Joses' mum) leave their digs and set off to go and brave a look at Jesus' body in the tomb cave.

2-4

What they don't know is there's been a full-on earthquake, courtesy of one of God's angels. Mr Wondrous Wings himself has shifted the boulder which had been blocking the tomb entrance and now he's sitting there, calm as you like, on top of the thing. What's an angel look like? Imagine a body giving off lightning, reflecting off an outfit white as snow — we're talking headache-inducing dazzle! This has the desired

---

[Matthew 28:2] The usual opening line of any angel visitation is "Don't panic", but obviously this visitation is meant for maximum effect on the already twitchy guards. "Actually, do panic!"

Or was the earthquake to crack open the sealed tomb so the women could get a look in?

---

[1] **Religious HQ = Temple.** Jerusalem's focal point of the Jewish Religion. Literally a house for God. Question is, how much does God get let out?

effect on the Religious HQ[1] Security Guards on duty: Uncontrollable shakes followed by frozen fear. You'd have sworn they were dead.

Ground shift Mark 16:2–4

2–4

So it's early morning, Sunday, and the women are making for the tomb cave. Just before getting there they clock the problem. "Whoa! Who's going to shift the huge boulder from the entrance?" "Yeah, we're going to need some serious muscle!" They look up and their eyes are popping out of their heads struggling to spot where the ginormous boulder's been shunted to. The tomb cave entrance is wide open; there's nothing to shift.

Ring any bells? Luke 24:4–8

4

They're trying to get their brains to behave; trying to work out where Jesus' body is. Next thing, these two strange figures are brightening up the whole cave with their clothes plugged into some sort of lightning connection.

5–8

The women hit the deck, petrified. But the two strangers ask them straight up, "Why you looking in a grave for someone who's alive and well? D'you think he'd hang around in a tomb? He's out of here. He's back from the dead! Remember what he said up in Galilee? *He'd be handed over, executed and then come back after two days.* Doesn't this ring any bells?"

Suddenly it does! It all comes back: *Of course! Dying . . . coming back from death . . . he told us, and he meant it literally! Whoa!*

Mark 16:7

7

The shining man gives the women their game plan, telling them, "Now go back to the rest of them, including Pete. Tell the Team, 'Jesus is going up to Galilee. You'll see him there, just like he said.'"

[Mark 16:7] How sweet are these two words – "including Pete"? Pete had messed up and the angel memo was clear: he's back in.

First sight Matthew 28:8-10

8-9

The women run! Weird combination of scared stupid and ecstatic. They're locked onto their target – to tell the rest of them the news.

Suddenly from nowhere, Jesus turns up and says to the women, "Morning!"

They hurl themselves and land flat out in front of him, grabbing his feet and hitting full-on worship mode, going, "You're so amazing – incredible!"

10

Jesus gives them the plan: "Don't freak, go tell the guys to head back to Galilee; they'll get to see me up there – proof, if they still need it."

The guys catch on ... nearly Luke 24:9-12

9-10

The girls get back from the tomb cave and blurt out the whole story to the Team Eleven and the other crew in hiding. Mary Mag is bursting with it; Joanna is blasting it out over the top of Mary Mag; and Mary, James' mum, is filling in the gaps with her own stream of superlatives. The others pile on the volume as they gush the great news to the Team.

11-12

But the guys can't process this avalanche of words/sights/emotions; they slap the label "raving mad" over the whole idea and write it off to stress. But Pete gets his running feet going and flies to the tomb on pure adrenaline. He gets there and bends down to inspect the linen body bag that Jesus had been laid out in. Just the linen; no body.

Don't Like This? [Luke 24:9 – 12] Find this an unbelievable end twist? Counter with claims of hallucinations and ravings. Just don't consider that this was the Team's first conclusion and pretty soon they were convinced otherwise. Or you could always persuade yourself that all four biographers had a severe case of Hollywood-itis – getting sucked into the classic storytelling formula that finds a way for "the worst thing imaginable to become the best thing possible". Don't even consider the fact that what happened to Jesus is probably the reason why classic storytelling exists.

[Matthew 28:9] What's going on here? Are human beings worshipping another human being? But they're not getting burnt to a crisp and the ex-dead Jesus isn't stopping them on the grounds of health and safety. Is this confirmation that he's God, Divine, the Deity for the laity??

Just linen. On it's own. No body. He goes off, trying to get his head round what's happened.

The cover story Matthew 28:11-15

11-12

While the women were racing to give the Team Eleven the good news — or trying to, anyway — some of the runaway guards were giving the Big God Reps[2] the bad news. So the Religious Suits do what they do best — they call a meeting. The Big God Reps and the Councillors[3] agree on the party position and create a sizeable budget to be sure the guards toe the line — they get a financial incentive if they remember their lines.

[2] **Big God Reps = Chief priests.** If "God Reps" (priests) were the "go between" for God and his people, then *chief* priests were the ones with real clout. This eminent group are the ones who've done their year's stint as Top God Rep (High Priest).

[3] **Councillors = Elders.** The non-Religious element of the ruling of the people. Sort of civil servants.

[Luke 24:12] So what's going on in Pete's head? Does he dare even consider the chances of Jesus coming back from death?

Could "The End Of The World As He Knew It" really morph into "Day One Of God's New World Order"? Is he trying to work out who would want to remove the body and start the come back conspiracy theories? Does he run through the different options one by one:

(a) Not Herod — he'd be shunted off his throne in a day; he'd want Jesus to stay dead.
(b) Not the Religious Leaders — they lobbied to get Jesus eliminated.
(c) Not the Religious Traditionalists — they don't believe in life after death so they'd want Jesus to stay well and truly dead.
(d) Not the Romans — they wouldn't want people thinking Jesus is alive and no way do they want a people's uprising on their hands.
(e) Not the Jewish Revolutionaries, Abbason's lot — as Jesus' methods are too indirect for them.
(f) Not any of the Team — they've not shifted from the hideout all weekend and certainly aren't up for any heroics.

And who else is there?

Having thought it through, is Pete still wondering who tampered with the grave? Or is he daring to think, "Well, he did raise people like the widow's son back in Nain Village"? And even, "He also did a 'come back' job on Jairus' little girl, so maybe it really is possible that..."

[Matthew 28:12] Is it a unanimous decision? Or are there some who are having second thoughts?

13 - 15

The minutes of the meeting read: "It was agreed that, when challenged, the loyal Security Guards are to state the following: 'Jesus'
Team hid in the bushes, waited for us to drop off, and then stole his
body while we slept.'"

They're promised full back-up. "If Governor Pilate hears about this,
we'll keep him happy and keep you out of trouble, if you remember
your part!"

This sizeable wad of cash is a great memory aid; the Guards recite
their lines word perfect any time they're asked. The story's still doing
the rounds in cynic clubs even as we eyewitnesses are working to
publish the facts.

More sightings Luke 24:13-32

13 - 17

Same Sunday, two of Jesus' squad members are getting Jerusalem
behind them and making for the village of Emmaus, seven miles
(about 10 km) west of their worst memories. They're batting the
whole episode around, trying to make sense of it. Then someone
else joins them in the slow lane — Jesus, in person. But something
keeps the guys from realizing who's just hit the road with them.
Jesus makes all naïve and asks, "What's the hot topic? What are you
thrashing out?"

They stop in their sandal tracks, their faces somewhere between
depressed and confused.

18 - 20

The guy called Cleopas comes back with, "You must be the only
tourist in Jerusalem who's not up on what's happened back there this
weekend."

[Matthew 28:13] What else are the Guards going to come out with? "We saw the whole thing – the Team took
the body while we were getting some shut-eye . . . we saw it all"!

[Matthew 28:15] How much were they paid off? It'd have to be a decent packet for a soldier to own up to
sleeping on duty. More than the 30 pieces of silver Judas got?

"Get me up to speed, then," Jesus bluffs.

"You must've heard of Jesus the Nazarene, no?" Cleopas comes back, looking for the lights to come on. "Totally God's courier[4]."

The other one has a go, explaining, "He was a major power player – words and actions – a phenomenal Coach, a supernatural healer. He got the thumbs up from God and all the people! What happened, right? The Big God Reps and the Powers That Be pronounced the Death Penalty on this Jesus Davidson and the Romans executed him, as only they can."

21-24

Cleopas adds in the back story, "See, we hoped he was The Liberator, the one to buy back the Nation of Israel from the Roman Occupying Forces. And it's two full days since all this went down."

Jesus still isn't letting on, so the other squad member pushes on, saying, "And then this morning our women fried our brains for us – they went to the tomb cave at sun up but couldn't find his body!"

Cleopas continues, "They burst through the doors and babbled on about seeing angel visions and angel voices telling them he was back alive! So some of the guys went down there, and the women weren't hallucinating – they got it spot on – the tomb was empty alright. But they didn't see Jesus anywhere."

25-26

Jesus finally lets on he knows something. "Just how dumb are you?! So slow on the uptake! How long does it take for you to trust what God's couriers said would happen? Wasn't all this always going to be part of the plot for The Liberator? Didn't he have to tough out the mess before dazzling heaven and earth?"

27-29

And so "the stranger" scrolls through The Good Book, highlighting all the bits with hints and clues of him, kicking off with Moses' Instruction Manual, lighting up all the Courier Files and going right through to the end. By this time they're in the outskirts of Emmaus Village and Jesus makes like he's still got miles ahead of him. But

[4] **God's Courier = Prophet.** Personal message delivery service direct from God. Think any package delivery corporation, but think "quick". Although, thinking about it, with their record, the depot for uncollected packages would've been pretty chocka by the end of the Old Testament.

they're not having it; they won't take no for an answer, saying "Kip down at our place! It's evening soon; the day's done."

So Jesus goes in to stay in their makeshift B&B.

30 – 32

Jesus is sitting at the meal table and he picks up the bread loaf, sends up some "thank yous", breaks the bread open and starts handing it round. It's the trigger! The spiritual cataracts clonk onto the stone floor – they realize who he is! But before they get to scream/cry/faint – vamoosh – he's out of there!

Cleopas asks his mate, "Did you get that burning sensation?"

"Yeah, somewhere round the heart?" his mate comes back.

"Yes! When he was unpacking The Good Book to us on the road, like I'd never read it before!"

Multiple sightings Luke 24:33-43

33 – 34

Cleopas and his mate bomb back to Jerusalem to tell the rest. They get there but the squad is already talking about Si, aka Pete, having seen Jesus. "It's true, it's all true! The Boss is back! Si got a sighting!"

35 – 36

"Us too!" Cleopas says, filling them in on the whole mobile coaching session with Jesus, and adding, "It only clicked when he did the bread-breaking thing!"

Voices are booming with excitement and then, from nowhere, Jesus turns up in person. He's telling them, "Whoa! Keep calm! Serenity to your souls!"

37 – 39

They freeze with fear and are wondering, *Is that a ghost? Apparition? Mirage?*

[Luke 24:37] So they still weren't doing what he says?! He says, "serenity", they freak! But then who wouldn't?

Jesus reads their thought bubbles and asks, "Why are you so freaked? Why are you juggling a dozen doubts? Need some evidence? Exhibit A – my war-torn hands; Exhibit B – my damaged feet. It's me! Touch me, take a good look. Ghosts don't have skin, muscle or bones! It's all here. It's me!"

40 – 43

He's standing there like an interactive museum piece, available for scrutiny. And they can't take any more in; they're exhilarated, stuffed to bursting with joy and Jesus says to them, "D'you have any food in?"

Overloaded, they dish up some broiled fish and he takes it and eats it with them watching his every mouthful.

The new job description Matthew 28:16 – 20

16 – 17

After this, all 11 of the Team are up a mountain in Galilee, the one Jesus directed them to. Jesus appears and most of them are off the charts with wonder, scouring their senses for better ways to worship.

But a few aren't sure – doubting whether they should join in.

[Matthew 28:17] How "real world" is this? After seeing Jesus raised from death's dungeon, some of the Team are still unsure! What's their problem? They're not doubting that he's back from death – he's physically in front of them. It's more that they're struggling to shift out of their comfort zone and worship him when before they'd always seen him as a mere mortal. So does Jesus kick these still-questioning ones down the mountain before commissioning the faithful few? Doesn't seem so; Jesus delivers the new job commission to everyone, the early adopters and the slow shifters.

[Matthew 28:18 – 20] How bitter are these lines for Satan to swallow? Back three years ago before Jesus goes public (flick back to it, go on!), Satan showed Jesus the view from a tower block and offered him all he could see. Seems a bit weak now, given that Jesus has the first and the last word in heaven and earth.

And how come it's global now? Back in Chapter 8 (see Matthew 10:5 – 7, page 153), Jesus sends them off with a big coaching session. "Don't go to the non-Jews. Don't even go to the Samaritans . Keep it 'in-house' for now. Focus on the lost kids of Israel. Your catchphrase: 'God's New World Order – just round the corner.'" Things have changed!

18-20

Jesus hits them with, "God's given me the absolute first and last word up in heaven and down here on earth. So, listen up. I'm commissioning you to do a job: Spread out, worldwide; help people commit 100 percent to my version of life. I want them baptized; I want them fully on board with God the Father, with me and with God the Holy Spirit. Inspire them with the instructions I gave you; coach them to keep living it out. Sure as you like, I'm with you 24/7 ... no, 24/7/52 ... right till the end of the era."

Last words Luke 24:44-49

44-45

Jesus works through The Good Book with them. "This is what I coached you in back while I was with you. Every mention, every hint of me in the Instruction Manuals, the Courier Files and the Song Lyrics has to be brought off the page and made real through me."

Then he clicks their brains onto "receive mode" so they can finally put together all the stuff in The Good Book and spot what was meant to be spotted.

46-49

He lays it out. "It's all here," he says. "The Liberator will go through pain and then two days later he'll come back from death! People will get to hear about turning round 180 degrees and facing their God. They'll know slates can be wiped clean through connection with my name. The news will spark off in Jerusalem and spread through every skin colour, every culture, every blood group on the planet. You're eyewitnesses of all this. But stay put in Jerusalem City till I send God's Holy Spirit to you, like my Dad promised. He'll fill you with the divine power you'll need for all this."

Going up Luke 24:50-53

50-51

Then Jesus escorts them back down southeast to Bethany Town (on the Olive Mountain). He lifts his hands up to the sky; he's coaching them, inspiring them, motivating them, doing them good. He's still in full flow when he starts hovering off the ground, gradually going up, crossing into heaven territory.

52

They're mind-blown, awestruck, dumbfounded, totally wowed by God and they let it rip by telling him. Eventually, still buzzing with worship, still struggling for ways to get close to how brilliant God is, they make their way back to Jerusalem as instructed, still bursting with celebration.

53

And they hardly leave the Religious HQ, spending loads of time finding new ways of talking up God.

[Luke 24:50 – 53] What kind of "Liberator" accepts the death sentence and leaves the Jews struggling under Roman Occupation? What kind of "Liberator" comes back from death and still leaves the Jews struggling under Roman Occupation? Why did Jesus exit through the ozone so soon after sorting death and all the mess? He seems to be acting like the pending Holy Spirit substitution is his big plan, his secret weapon, to bring in some Heaven on Earth . . . coming soon to a "Thanksgiving" Festival (aka Pentecost) near you?!

Now Jesus is where he said he'd be – sitting there on his throne next to the Awesome God. Now he's taken the worst; now the Religious HQ dividing curtain is torn; now he's beaten death; now he can start implementing the God's New World Order he talked about.

How? Is he really starting with just a team of twelve minus one, plus some loyal extras?

For the story of where the Jesus Liberation Movement (aka the church – the institution, not the building) goes from here, check out Acts in a proper Bible. World-changing stuff.

And...?

? What did they make of him?

"Petrified rock" – aka Pete Jonahson – about seven weeks later, with new oomph courtesy of God's Holy Spirit, wowing thousands of intrigued Jews:

" …Jesus held by death? Just not possible … God gave him a hand up and out of the grave – we saw him with our own eyes!… Then God gives Jesus full access, top priority, complete authority, total control, ultimate supremacy…"

Acts 2:24b,32–33a from *the word on the street*

? What have we made of him?

Do we really give Jesus complete authority?

Or do we just put his name to what we're planning to do anyway?

Why did he entrust the whole Jesus Liberation Movement to a bunch of AWOL losers with an iffy track record? Did he actually think they could handle it?

If Jesus has got total control, when's he going to use it?

When's he going to download a bit of Heaven on Earth? Or is that our job?

Where d'you find him these days?

How different is the church from the people who go there?

Is it possible to be in the "Team" and not go to church?

And why wasn't "going to church" included in *The (London) Times'* "One Hundred Things To Do This Easter" (2005)?

So is Jesus still making bodies, minds and spirits whole?

And why don't the genuine devotees get to tell their stories more?

Is Jesus the only good storyteller?

Is he The Liberator?

    Or is he only good "for those with a Religious gene,

    with a predisposed DNA for the hymn singing scene"?

    Is he only "good for the kids", "good for weddings"?

    Is he just "good for life's beginnings and endings"?

? What did they make of him?

Ex-Religious Leader Saul, aka Paul, Jesus' foreign rep, e-mailing from paul.benson@jailmail.rome.nt:

"Get an attitude, the same attitude Jesus The Liberator had: He was God right through to the marrow. But he didn't use his clout to put himself about heaven ... He said, 'I give it up' ... He allowed himself to be nailed up high and executed on a cross. So God brought him back, celebrated him, elevated him to the top spot..."

Philippians 2:5 – 6,8b,9 from *the word on the street*

? What have we made of him?

If we're supposed to be like Jesus, how much do we "give up"?

How do we use our clout?

Can people spot the Jesus impression?

Do we just pick and mix the bits we like? Do we only highlight the Jesus-lite?

Do we make Jesus in our own image?

Is this what "our own personal Jesus" should mean?

What's the general effect of his Movement being part of the Establishment now?

How ironic is that?!

Is that why there's so much Christophobia? Or is it more *Church*ophobia?

Does Jesus ever feel cramped working within an institution?

What's the difference between an institution and a Movement?

Between a building and a community? Religion and faith?

Has Satan given up the ghost or is he still sabotaging Heaven on Earth?

Is Jesus still head of the church?

Is he The Liberator?

    Or is he "a crutch", "a prop", "a soft touch", "a cosy club
               in which to enroll"?

    Just "the front man of the global guilt patrol"?

    Is he really "the cause of wars and military clashes"?

    Is he just "the opium of the masses"?

? What did they make of him?

Jonno, Pete's old fishing partner, 50-plus years later, sends out a circular as Big Noise in The Movement (from: jonno.zebson@ jlm-love-light.nt):

"I've seen the Real Thing. He was around from way back before history heard the starting gun. I was there! I heard him, clocked my eyes on him, hugged him. This is what I say about 'God's Voice': he showed up out of the blue (literally); some of us saw him and we'd swear in court that he's the genuine article ... he's limitless life from God the Father – we saw him!"

1 John 1:1 – 2 from *the word on the street*

? What have we made of him?

Is he really God's Voice or do we have other people doing more palatable impersonations?

If he's "limitless life", how come it's all been made to seem so dull?

How is it he wows some to kingdom come and leaves others stone cold?

Would we recognise him if he showed up out of the blue?

What would he make of what we've made of him?

How often do we trip out the word "Lord"?

Would we cut down if we knew what it meant?

Is he still countercultural when it comes to money, sex and power?

Is he still ranting against injustice and corruption in high places?

What does he liberate from?

Is he The Liberator?

Is he "mad", "bad" or just "sad",

or "to a secret family line – the dad"?

Is he "a fiction that may or may not have occurred"?

Is he just "a swear word"?

What do you make of him?

What have I made of him?

Your thoughts to: www.thewordonthestreet.co.uk/theliberator/ whoishe (unlike the other weblogs in this book, this one really does exist!).

Appendix (ie, you can probably live without this)

Absolutely = Amen

From the root "sure/steady". Used at the end of a prayer almost like an exclamation point, bold print or underlining. You could say, "I endorse those sentiments", but you'd sound pompous, or "Not half", but you'd sound common.

Awesome God = God Almighty

Term for God, meaning "all-sufficient", "unlimited". Technical term = "omnipotent", literally "all round potent".

Big God Reps = Chief priests

If "God Reps" (priests) were the "go between" for God and his people, then *chief* priests were the ones with real clout. This eminent group are the ones who've done their year's stint as Top God Rep (High Priest).

Big Ten Rules = Ten Commandments

Dictated by God to Moses on the top of the Sinai Mountain and the basis of Christo-Judaic law since then. Check out Exodus 20 for the breakdown.

Boss = Lord

Not in the sense of who pays your bills, more "the number one priority in your life". As Big Rule No. 3 says, "Handle my handle with care". (See Exodus 20 in a proper Bible.)

Celebrate = Praise

Often used in the context of words like "noise", "gestures" and "music" – sounds like a nightclub to me. Also means to throw a party to show gratitude.

Chat/discuss/thrash out with God = Prayer

A word for the ways in which the human spirit approaches God. If I knew any more about it would I be in this state?!

Coach = Rabbi/Teacher

From the Hebrew for "great". This came to be what you put in the title box of any official form, and probably got you what you were applying for since it was a highly respected pre-fix.

Councillors = Elders

The non-Religious element of the ruling of the people. Sort of civil servants.

Deep-as-you-like stories, riddles and images = Parables

From the Greek word to "put things side by side" (ie, parallel). An ancient craft where you say things different ways; where an earthly story can take on a heavenly meaning ... if you dig.

Doing the right thing = Righteousness

Possibly from the Arabic root "straightness", which none of us are without connection with Jesus.

Eviction = Exile

Posh word for "kicked out" from the Hebrew verb "to uncover" or "to remove" into captivity. "Home" was a big word back then too.

Flyby Festival = Passover

A major Jewish Religious festival, like our Easter/Christmas. It celebrates God liberating their ancestors from the sweatshops of Egypt. The name derives from when the angel of death passed over/flew by Jewish homes.

Giving some slack = Mercy

Traceable back to words like kindness/favour.

God Reps = Priests

The "go between" for God and his people – not to be mistaken for the "get-in-between". Years back, this guy named Aaron was the very first God Rep, and since then only his family line was eligible for the post.

God's Courier = Prophet

Personal message delivery service direct from God. Think any package delivery corporation, but think "quick". Although, thinking about it, with their record, the depot for uncollected packages would've been pretty chocka by the end of the Old Testament.

Good news story = Gospel

Like it says, good news. So what's the phrase "gospel truth" about then?

Heaven on Earth/God's New World Order = The kingdom of God

Like with monarchies, but with God in charge, so not like with monarchies. There's also a sense of "sort of already/but not yet" paradox. We get to download glimpses now, but the full package would cramp our hard drive's style.

Jesus Liberation Movement = The Church

Not the building – the institution. Like it or loathe it, it's God's chosen way of expressing/representing himself on planet Earth . . . don't ask me why.

Jewish Supreme Court = Sanhedrin

This powerful institution is an assortment of important Jewish men – the upper crust and the well respected. Lots of Religious Traditionalists (Sadducees), as well as the current and ex-Big God Reps (chief priests), the Religious Law Enforcers (teachers of the law), Councillors (elders of the people) and some top Religious Leaders (Pharisees). A rare case of rival "denominations" working together to keep things running smoothly.

Liberation = Salvation

Basic meaning is to "bring into a spacious place", implying a freedom from limitation.

Liberator = Christ/Messiah/Anointed One

Person set apart by God to sort whatever the Big Problem was for the Jews; the One Jews were on the edge of their seats waiting for. Obviously this heroic figure was about to kick the Romans up the toga and send their occupying army scarpering, no? Unless there's an even more sinister, oppressive superpower to be liberated from?

Local Religious HQ = Synagogue

Local meeting place for Religious Jews to worship their God. Central point of any Jewish community.

Made happy/laughing = Blessed

Mostly an Old Testament word, generally denotes a state of happiness. "To endue with power for success, prosperity, fecundity, longevity, abundance, etc." It's enough to make anyone happy.

Mess = Sin

Anything that gets in the way of us and God, generally "missing the goal", "rebellion against God", "twisting".

Military HQ = The Pretorium

The Roman Governor's official residence in Jerusalem. Complete with soldier barracks.

Outland Revenue = Roman Tax Department

Where the Empire collected its taxes from the minions. Hence Outland Revenue Officers weren't exactly popular.

Prospects = Hope

The Bible word "hope" doesn't mean "fingers crossed, it should happen"; it's way stronger. More like, "I know it's going to happen."

Purest Place = The Holy of Holies

The heart of the Religious HQ complex: the inner sanctum. Off-limits for all but the most devoted and then only once a year on a rota basis!

Religious HQ = Temple

Jerusalem's focal point of the Jewish Religion. Literally a house for God. Question is, how much does God get let out?

Religious Law Enforcers = Teachers of the Law/Scribes

Experts in Moses' law. Academics, who sadly, often became "academic" in the sense of "irrelevant".

Religious Leaders = Pharisees

A faction calling themselves literally "the separated ones" – "the exclusives" perhaps. Big into Rules, running a well-oiled propaganda machine which seemed to be fuelled by people's guilt.

Religious Traditionalists = Sadducees

These guys were only into Moses' first five books of the Instruction Manuals; anything later was to them liberal hoo-ha to be sniffed at. One of their big things was that all this rising from the dead malarkey was indulgent hogwash, brought in by liberal lightweights like Daniel, among others. Not natural partners for the Religious Leaders.

Rest Day = Sabbath

Rule No. 5 in Moses' Big Ten: "You'll keep my rest day special." By now this "special" had been defined down to the nth degree. There were plenty of things you shouldn't do.

Shalom = Peace/Serenity

Just one of the best words ever! Hebrew for peace and wholeness. Oh, and completeness. Throw in soundness and neighborliness, and you're nearly there. Just needs a bit of well-being and security and finish off by adding honest dealing and true justice. Not bad for a six-letter word (or, in Hebrew, a three-letter word plus optional assorted dots!).

Skull Hill = Golgotha (Aramaic)/Calvary (Latin)

Outside the Jerusalem City Limits, either to the west or northwest of the Religious HQ, depending on which archaeologist you ask for directions.

Straightened out and sorted = Saved

Less "sitting in church", more "being dragged from the freezing arctic ocean". Much more vivid.

Taking God at his word = Faith/Belief

Faith is more than just a Religious Club you belong to. Belief is more than just a vague whim. This big word is an active, gutsy, practical concept. Aka "trust".

Team = Disciples

Certainly the twelve "apostles" but probably also the women mentioned by Dr Luke (8:2,3). Maybe some other signed-up devotees too.

Team Twelve = The twelve apostles

Just the Difficult Dozen – as in the famous poster (not necessarily an exact likeness).

The Contract = The Law

The Jewish Torah, an order from a higher authority on expected standards of behaviour/lifestyle.

The Good Book = Old Testament

The bit of the Bible they had in first century Judah. Aka God's Instruction Manual.

The Man = Son of Man

Jesus' term for himself – lifted from Daniel 7, where it's a pretty blatant clue that this is no mere mortal: "the Son of Man . . . surfing in on the clouds . . . where the Ancient of Days . . . gives him . . . all the credit for running the show . . . and permanent position in the top spot." Nice name badge.

Top God Rep = High Priest

The main man, the head honcho responsible for all the people's spiritual health. His job description states he's the middleman between God and the people; a "go between" for all negotiations . . . in both directions. No pressure then?!

Turn back round to God = Repent

Even my 5-year-old son knows this. Him: "Sorry, papa." Me: "And what does sorry mean?" Him: "It means we don't do it again."

Victimisation/Religious intolerance = Persecution

In our PC world you can't be racist, sexist, ageist or any other "-ist" (and rightly so), but you can be Christian-ist, only it's not called that, it's called "freedom of speech".

Wipe the slate clean = Forgive

Carries the idea of "atonement", "to atone for", to make "at one" again . . . all that, and more.

Where to Find it in a Proper Bible

Now that you've read *The Liberator,* why not follow the life of Jesus in a proper Bible? The Bible features four unique accounts of Jesus' life (aka "gospels") from four different biographers – Matthew, Mark, Luke and John.

The Liberator was based mainly on Matthew, Mark and Luke's biographies (quote John: "hurrumph!"), because they're the most similar to each other. Use the list below to match up each section of *The Liberator* with its corresponding passage in a proper Bible. You can also check out a list of similar passages in the other biographies of Jesus.

And if you really want to compare the four gospels, consult *The NIV Harmony of the Gospels* by Robert L. Thomas and Stanley N. Gundry (HarperCollins, 1988).

PART ONE: WHO IS HE?

Chapter/Section	Passage	Similar Passage(s)
Prologue		
John's Voice	John 1:1 – 18	
1. And Finally...		
Exclusive?	Luke 1:1 – 4	
Expecting	Luke 1:5 – 25	
	Luke 1:26 – 38	
"Family Tree"	Matthew 1:1 – 17	Luke 3:23b – 38
Mums united	Luke 1:39 – 45	
Mary's big single	Luke 1:46 – 56	
John's delivery	Luke 1:57 – 66	
Zech's big release	Luke 1:67 – 80	
2. Christmas Presence		
Two teenagers in love	Matthew 1:18 – 25	
Delivery suite 38b	Luke 2:1 – 7	
Abandon sheep	Luke 2:8 – 20	
Old people's eyesight	Luke 2:21 – 38	
Eastern Astrologers	Matthew 2:1 – 12	

Chapter/Section	Passage	Similar Passage(s)
Not keen on competition!	Matthew 2:13 – 18	
How many Herods?	Matthew 2:19 – 23	Luke 2:39
Zitty?	Luke 2:40 – 52	

3. Do the Prep

Eighteen years later...	Mark 1:1	
Famous names	Luke 3:1 – 2	
Do a one-eighty	Matthew 3:1,2 Mark 1:2,3; Luke 3:5,6	Matthew 3:3b
Water proof	Mark 1:4 – 6	Matthew 3:4 – 6,11 – 12
Winning key friends?	Matthew 3:7 – 10	Luke 3:7 – 9
Interactive sermons	Luke 3:10 – 18	
Jesus takes a dive	Matthew 3:13 – 17	Mark 1:9 – 11; Luke 3:21 – 23a
Guess that's a "no" then	Matthew 4:1 – 11	Mark 1:12 – 13; Luke 4:1 – 13
Saying "no" to being a yes-man	Luke 3:19 – 20	Matthew 4:12; Mark 1:14a;

4. Liberator Launch

Whose line is it anyway?	Mark 1:14,15	Matthew 4:17; Luke 4:14a
The Liberator's job spec	Luke 4:14 – 30	
New tour base	Matthew 4:13 – 16	
Recruitment drive	Luke 5:1 – 11	Matthew 5:18 – 22; Mark 1:16 – 20
What does the enemy know?	Mark 1:21 – 28	Luke 4:31b – 37
Mobile miracle clinic	Mark 1:29 – 34	Matthew 8:14 – 16 Luke 4:38 – 41
Flashback	Matthew 8:17 Mark 1:35 – 38	Luke 4:42 – 44
The "God's New World Order" tour	Matthew 4:23 – 25	
(Dis)enfranchised	Mark 1:40 – 45	Matthew 8:2 – 4; Luke 5:12 – 16
Upping the stakes	Mark 2:1 – 12	Matthew 9:1 – 8; Luke 5:17 – 26
Eating with the wrong people?	Matthew 9:9 – 13	Mark 2:13 – 17; Luke 5:27 – 32
New and old	Luke 5:33 – 39	Matthew 9:14 – 17; Luke 2:18 – 22
Rest Day Rules?	Matthew 12:1 – 8	Mark 2:23 – 28; Luke 6:1 – 5

Chapter/Section	Passage	Similar Passage(s)
Plot thickening	Mark 3:1 – 6	Matthew 12:9 – 14; Luke 6:6 – 11
Broader fan base	Mark 3:7 – 12	
Not your typical celeb.	Matthew 12:15 – 21	
The unusual suspects	Mark 3:13 – 19	Luke 6:12 – 16

5. Team Training Session

Coaching on the level	Luke 6:17 – 20a	Matthew 5:1 – 2
Who's laughing?	Matthew 5:3 – 12	
Who's crying?	Luke 6:24 – 26	
Salt of the earth?	Matthew 5:13 – 16	
Dusted and done	Matthew 5:17 – 20	
Anger management	Matthew 5:21 – 26	
Wandering eye syndrome	Matthew 5:27 – 30	
Decree absolute	Matthew 5:31 – 32	
On my mother's life!	Matthew 5:33 – 37	
Have another go	Matthew 5:38 – 42	
Love, father style	Matthew 5:43 – 48	Luke 6:27 – 30,32 – 33
Fund your enemy's project	Luke 6:34 – 36	
Who's your audience	Matthew 6:1 – 4	
Template for talking to God	Matthew 6:5 – 15	
More than a diet?	Matthew 6:16 – 18	
Long-term investment strategy	Matthew 6:19 – 24	
Anti-stress programme	Matthew 6:25 – 34	
Don't play judge	Luke 6:37 – 42	Matthew 7:1 – 5
Keep on keeping on at God	Matthew 7:6 – 12	Luke 6:31
Don't follow the crowd	Matthew 7:13 – 14	
Charge up your Integrity Detector	Matthew 7:15 – 20	Luke 6:43 – 45
Saying v doing	Matthew 7:21 – 23	Luke 6:46
Rock solid crew	Matthew 7:24 — 8:1	Luke 6:47 – 49

Chapter/Section	Passage	Similar Passage(s)

6. Who's "The Man"?

Chapter/Section	Passage	Similar Passage(s)
Remote control healing	Luke 7:1–9; Matthew 8:11–13	Matthew 8:1–10
Funeral? What funeral?	Luke 7:11–17	
Is he "the One"?	Matthew 11:2–19	Luke 7:18–35
180 degrees – radius or temperature?	Matthew 11:20–24	
Access denied – retry or cancel?	Matthew 11:25–30	
How grateful?	Luke 7:36–50	
On the road again	Luke 8:1–3	
Crazy or evil?	Mark 3:20–22	
Enemy forces	Matthew 12:22–37	Mark 3:23–26; Luke 11:14–36
Bigger than Jonah and Solomon	Matthew 12:38–45	Mark 3:27–30
Family ties	Mark 3:31–35	Matthew 12:46–50; Luke 8:19–21

7. Just Stories

Chapter/Section	Passage	Similar Passage(s)
Good acoustics	Mark 4:1–2	Matthew 13:1–3a; Luke 8:4
Riddled with it	Matthew 13:4–23	Mark 4:3–20; Luke 8:5–18
Levels	Mark 4:21–25	
Sleep on it	Mark 4:26–29	
Enemy sabotage	Matthew 13:24–30	
It's the little things that count	Mark 4:30–32	Matthew 13:31–32; Luke 13:18–20
Influential	Matthew 13:33	
Just stories	Mark 4:33–34	Matthew 13:34
Always telling stories	Matthew 13:35	
Backstage debriefing	Matthew 13:36–43	
What's it worth?	Matthew 13:44–46	
Trawling techniques	Matthew 13:47–52	

8. Last Galilee Gigs

Chapter/Section	Passage	Similar Passage(s)
Who is this guy?	Luke 8:22–25	Matthew 8:18,23–27; Mark 4:35–41
Destructive tendencies	Luke 8:26–39	Matthew 8:28–34; Mark 5:1–20
Blood and death	Mark 5:21–43	Matthew 9:18–26; Luke 8:40–56
"See no evil, speak no evil"	Matthew 9:27–34	

Chapter/Section	Passage	Similar Passage(s)
Local reception	Mark 6:1–6	Matthew 13:54–58
Job vacancies	Matthew 9:35–38	Mark 6:6b
Working conditions	Matthew 10:1–42	Mark 6:7–11; Luke 9:1–5
Ambassadors	Mark 6:12–13	Matthew 11:1; Luke 9:6
Price of confrontation	Mark 6:14–29	Matthew 14:1–12; Luke 9:7–9

9. Super Natural

Spiritual retreat	Mark 6:30–31	Luke 9:10a
Jesus reads the headlines	Matthew 14:13–14	Mark 6:32–34a; Luke 9:10b–11; John 6:1–3
Thousands plus for a picnic	Mark 6:34b–44	Matthew 14:15–21; Luke 9:12–17; John 6:4–13
Extreme sports – water walking	Matthew 14:22–33	Mark 6:47–52; John 6:14–21
Magnet for the messed	Mark 6:53–56	
Religion!	Mark 7:1–23	John 7:1
Not just the Jews	Matthew 15:21–28	Mark 7:24–30
Talk, don't talk	Mark 7:31–37	Matthew 15:29–31
Supernatural supper – action replay	Mark 8:1–10	Matthew 15:32–38
"We want supernatural proof!"	Matthew 16:1–4	
Use your loaf	Mark 8:13–21	Matthew 16:5–12
Eye opening	Mark 8:22–26	

10. Team Catches On

More eyes opening	Matthew 16:13–20	Mark 8:27–30; Luke 9:18–21
Appointment with Death	Mark 8:31—9:1	Matthew 16:21–28; Luke 9:22–27
All "heavened-up"	Luke 9:28–36a	Matthew 17:1–8; Mark 9:2–8
Processing new info	Mark 9:9–13	Matthew 17:9–12; Luke 9:36b
So John B = Elijah!	Matthew 17:13	

PART TWO: DEAD MAN WALKING

11. Choosing Sides

Can't get the staff!	Mark 9:14–27; Matthew 17:19–20; Mark 9:29	Matthew 17:14–18; Luke 9:37–43a
Mountain v mustard seed	Matthew 17:19–20	

Chapter/Section	Passage	Similar Passage(s)
Spiritual retreat	Mark 9:30−32	Matthew 17:22−23; Luke 9:43b−45
Do royals pay tax?	Matthew 17:24−27	
Soft spot for kids	Mark 9:33−37	Matthew 18:1−2; Luke 9:46−48
The trust of a toddler	Matthew 18:3−5	
Competition?	Mark 9:38−41	Luke 9:49−50
Don't mess with the kids	Matthew 18:6−8	Mark 9:42−46
No added salt	Mark 9:47−50	
Looking out for the wanderer	Matthew 18:10−14	
Plural power	Matthew 18:15−20	
Bad debts	Matthew 18:21−35	

12. Southbound Highway

Chapter/Section	Passage	Similar Passage(s)
Jerusalem calling	Luke 9:51−56	John 7:10
Only the 100 percenters need apply	Luke 9:57−62	Matthew 8:19−22
Seventy-two times Jesus	Luke 10:1−16	
Kids outpoint the boffins	Luke 10:17−24	
Samaritan helpline for the Jews	Luke 10:25−37	
Workaholics anonymous	Luke 10:38−42	
Two-way conversation with God	Luke 11:1−13	
Religious Leaders for lunch	Luke 11:37−54	
More tips for the Team	Luke 12:1−12	
The rich idiot	Luke 12:13−21	
Stressing the point	Luke 12:22−34	
Batteries charged?	Luke 12:35−48	
Controversy	Luke 12:49−53	
Spiritual climate change?	Luke 12:54−59	
Fertilizer!	Luke 13:1−9	
Stand up for Jesus	Luke 13:10−17	

13. Change Community

Chapter/Section	Passage	Similar Passage(s)
Small door	Luke 13:22−30	
Sad old Jerusalem	Luke 13:31−35	

Chapter/Section	Passage	Similar Passage(s)
Old clues	Matthew 21:4−5	
Welcome party	Luke 19:36−38	
Confirm or deny	Luke 19:39−44; Matthew 21:10−11	
Kids! What do they know?	Matthew 21:14−17	
Figging curse words	Mark 11:12−14	Matthew 21:18−19a

PART THREE: (COM)PASSION WEEK

16. Confrontation

Chapter/Section	Passage	Similar Passage(s)
Vandals with a cause	Mark 11:15−19	Matthew 21:12−13; Luke 19:45−48
Mountain sculpting	Mark 11:20−25	Matthew 21:19b−22
Handling the hecklers	Matthew 21:23−27	Mark 11:27−33; Luke 20:1−8
Young people of today!	Matthew 21:28−32	
Workers' uncooperative	Matthew 21:33−46	Mark 12:1−12; Luke 20:9−19
Some reception!	Matthew 22:1−14	
Poll tax trick questions	Mark 12:13−17	Matthew 22:15−22; Luke 20:20−26
No confetti in heaven!	Mark 12:18−27; Matthew 22:33; Luke 20:39	Matthew 22:23−33; Luke 20:27−38,40
At last, someone gets it!	Mark 12:28−34	Matthew 22:34−40
Just a Davidson?	Matthew 22:41−45	Mark 12:35−36; Luke 20:41−44
Not my kind of people	Matthew 23:1−12	Mark 12:38−40; Luke 20:45−47
Bad news coming	Matthew 23:13−36	
Collection box techniques	Mark 12:41−44	Luke 21:1−4

17. Times Change

Chapter/Section	Passage	Similar Passage(s)
Alarm bells of disaster	Mark 13:1−23	Matthew 24:1−25; Luke 21:5−24
Enter The Man	Matthew 24:26−31 Mark 13:28−32	Mark 13:24−27; Luke 21:25−27
Top secret	Matthew 24:37−41; Luke 21:34−36; Mark 13:33−37	
Good management	Matthew 24:43−51	

Chapter/Section	Passage	Similar Passage(s)
Ten teenage girls and a wedding	Matthew 25:1 – 13	
Investment trust	Matthew 25:14 – 30	
Global court of justice	Matthew 25:31 – 46	

18. Mutiny

Ticking clock	Matthew 26:1 – 5	Mark 14:1 – 2; Luke 22:1 – 2
Burial prep	Mark 14:3 – 9	Matthew 26:6 – 13; John 12:2 – 8
Judas The Bounty Hunter	Luke 22:3 – 6	Matthew 26:14 – 16; Mark 14:10 – 11
Final Festival meal	Mark 14:12 – 16	Matthew 26:17 – 19; Luke 22:7 – 13
Bread breaking	Luke 22:14 – 16	Matthew 26:20; Mark 14:17
Status games	Luke 22:24 – 30	
Sold out	Mark 14:18 – 21; Matthew 26:25	Matthew 26:21 – 25; Luke 22:21 – 23; John 13:21 – 30
All words!	Mark 14:27 – 31; Luke 22:35 – 38	Matthew 26:31 – 35; Luke 22:31 – 34; John 13:37 – 38
Breaking bread	Matthew 26:26 – 30	Mark 14:22 – 26; Luke 22:17 – 20,39; John 18:1
Whose plan?	Mark 14:32 – 42	Matthew 26:36 – 46; Luke 22:39 – 46
Some treasurer!	Matthew 26:47 – 52a; Luke 22:51; Matthew 26:52b – 56	Mark 14:43 – 47; Luke 22:47 – 50; John 18:2 – 11; Mark 14:48 – 50; Luke 22:52 – 53; John 18:12
Eyewitness	Mark 14:51 – 52	

19. Trial Times

Tried Religiously	Mark 14:53 – 65	Matthew 26:57 – 68; Luke 22:54 – 55; John 18:15,24,26,27
Right on cue	Mark 14:66 – 72	Matthew 26:69 – 75; Luke 22:56 – 62; John 18:25
Death sentence	Matthew 27:1 – 2	Mark 15:1 – 5; Luke 22:66 – 71
Bloody money	Matthew 27:3 – 10	
Criminal delivery service	Luke 23:1 – 4	Matthew 27:11; John 18:28 – 38
Poor self-defence	Matthew 27:12 – 14	Mark 15:3 – 5
Pass the buck	Luke 23:5 – 12	
Amnesty for terrorists	Matthew 27:15 – 16 Mark 15:7b – 8	
Off the hook	Matthew 27:17 – 21	Mark 15:9 – 11; John 18:39 – 40
Nothing doing	Luke 23:13 – 16	

Chapter/Section	Passage	Similar Passage(s)
Public demand	Luke 23:20–22	Matthew 27:22–23; Mark 15:12–14; John 18:6–7
Blood on whose hands?	Matthew 27:24–26	Mark 15:15; Luke 23:23–24; John 18:15–16

20. Execution

Gratuitous violence	Matthew 27:27–30	Mark 15:16–19
Semi-dead already	Mark 15:20–21	Matthew 27:31,32; Luke 23:26; John 19:16b–17a
Public spectacle	Luke 23:27–32	Mark 15:22–23; John 19:17b
Drink the cup? Dry?	Matthew 27:33–34	
Roman execution	Luke 23:33b–34	Matthew 27:35,37–38; Mark 15:24; John 19:18–27
Jewish King?	Mark 15:25–27	
Verbal assassination	Matthew 27:39–44	
Beam me up to paradise	Luke 23:39–43	
Dying	Matthew 27:45–49	Mark 15:33–36; Luke 23:44
Dead	Matthew 27:50	Mark 15:37; John 19:30
Dead	Luke 23:46	
Out from behind the curtain	Matthew 27:51–54; Luke 23:48–49; Mark 15:40–41	Mark 15:38–39; Luke 23:45b,47; Matthew 27:55–56
He's buried	Mark 15:42–47; Luke 23:56	Matthew 27:57–61; Luke 23:50–55; John 19:38–42
Cover version	Matthew 27:62–66	

21. And Initially...

Unfinished work	Matthew 28:1–4	Mark 16:1
Ground shift	Mark 16:2–4	Luke 24:1–3; John 20:1
Ring any bells?	Luke 24:4–8; Mark 16:7	Matthew 28:5–8
First sight	Matthew 28:8–10	
The guys catch on ... nearly	Luke 24:9–12	John 20:2–10
The cover story	Matthew 28:11–15	
More sightings	Luke 24:13–32	
Multiple sightings	Luke 24:33–43	John 20:19–20
The new job description	Matthew 28:16–20	
Last words	Luke 24:44–49	
Going up	Luke 24:50–53	

FOR THOSE WHO'VE NEVER READ THE BIBLE AND FOR THOSE WHO'VE READ IT TOO MUCH.

the word on the street

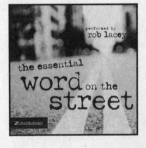

*"First off, nothing...but God.
No light, no time, no substance, no matter.
Second off, God says the word and WHAP!
Stuff everywhere!"* – Genesis 1:1

Experience more of Rob Lacey's "danger-ously real" retelling of Scripture in his award-winning* book *the word on the street*. This fresh paraphrase-come-running-commentary brings the text alive: Bible stories are retold as mini blockbust-ers; psalms as song lyrics; epistles as e-mails; Revelation as seen through a virtual reality headset.

Purist alert: This is not THE Bible (capital B) ... but it might just get you reaching for one.

*Book of the Year (2005), Christian Booksellers Convention Ltd. (UK). Borders' Best of 2004: Religion & Spirituality

Softcover 0-310-92268-2
Hardcover 0-310-92267-4

And listen to Rob as he performs Genesis to Revelation in 75 minutes on this musi-cal audio book. Finalist in the USA Audio Publishers Association "Audie Awards".

ISBN: 0-310-92139-2

Check out www.thewordonthestreet.co.uk.

Pick up a copy today at your favourite bookstore!

ZONDERVAN™

GRAND RAPIDS, MICHIGAN 49530 USA

WWW.ZONDERVAN.COM

Mealtime Habits of the Messiah

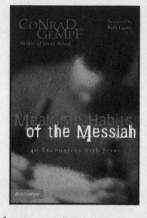

It's not exactly how one would expect God to occupy himself.

Lord of space and time, newly resurrected from the dead, and what is he doing? Sitting quietly by the lakeside, cooking up breakfast and waiting for the disciples to drop by.

The Gospels are full of odd quirks that most people never notice because the stories are so familiar. But Conrad Gempf notices. He uses his knowledge of Jesus' life and times to light up the meditations in this book.

The forty short encounters in this book focus on Jesus as a teacher, Jesus as a miracle worker, on Jesus' radical spirituality and on his death and resurrection. Seasoning its unique insights with humor, *Mealtime Habits of the Messiah* both satisfies the hungry soul and piques the reader's appetite for prayer.

> "Gempf's well-balanced approach ... will put fuel in the tanks of all our journeys toward wholeness and purpose."
> –Rob Lacey, from the foreword

> "Conrad's book is a delight. It's like its subject, Jesus: alive, fun, engaging, warm, and occasionally wonderfully dangerous."
> – Jeff Lucas

> "An inspiring and startling portrait of Jesus which will nourish your spirit and feed your soul."
> –Steve Chalke

Softcover 0-310-25717-4

Pick up a copy today at your favorite bookstore!

ZONDERVAN™

GRAND RAPIDS, MICHIGAN 49530 USA

WWW.ZONDERVAN.COM

JESUS ASKED.
What He Wanted
to Know

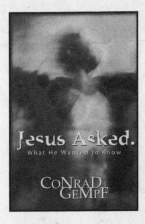

In the Gospels, when people asked Jesus a question, he often replied with one of his own: "Good teacher, what must I do to inherit eternal life?" "Why do you call me good?" Join Conrad Gempf as he invites readers to look at these questions and discover Jesus' motivation. What could the second person of the Trinity want to know that he doesn't already? Gempf concludes that Jesus wants to know where we stand.

He doesn't need to know more facts; he wants to know us.

Softcover 0-310-24773-X

Pick up a copy today at your favorite bookstore!

ZONDERVAN™

GRAND RAPIDS, MICHIGAN 49530 USA

WWW.ZONDERVAN.COM

Street Life

What have cables, billboards, lip gloss and latté got to do with Christian life?

Co-written by Rob Lacey and Nick Page

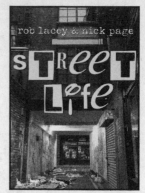

Street life is a funny, thought-provoking, God-revealing look at the real issues of 21st century lives. If it's on the street, it's in here – everything from chewing gum to mobile phones, traffic lights to trees, sex shops to scaffolding. All the things around us and all the ways in which we can use those sights to explore the kingdom of God.

Based on the bestselling approach of *the word on the street*, *street life* takes things one step further, generating discussion, engagement and resolve; offering wisdom from across the ages and ideas for action today; and, most of all, pointing readers back to the real thing – the Bible with a capital "B".

Ideal for individual Bible study, youth groups and house groups, street life is about going deeper than just reading the stories and actually creating a different lifestyle. It's about making the words count.

ISBN 0-310-25739-5

For more information on *the word on the street*,
check out www.thewordonthestreet.co.uk.

Available from your favorite bookstore!

ZONDERVAN™

GRAND RAPIDS, MICHIGAN 49530 USA

WWW.ZONDERVAN.COM